SOLOMON R. BAKER LIBRARY
BENTLEY COLLEGE

QA
76.64
.K65
1993

OBJECT-ORIENTED PROGRAMMING WITH TURBO PASCAL™ AND OBJECT PROFESSIONAL™

AF807951

Ken Knecht

P T R Prentice Hall, *Englewood Cliffs, New Jersey 07632*

Library of Congress Cataloging-in-Publication Data

Knecht, Ken
Object-oriented programming with Turbo Pascal and Object Professional / Ken Knecht.
p. cm.
Includes index.
ISBN 0-13-630310-2 :
1. Object-oriented programming (Computer science) 2. Pascal (Computer program language) 3. Turbo Pascal (Computer file) 4. Object professional. I. Title.
QA76.64.K65 1993
005.26′2--dc20 92-30877
CIP

Editorial/production supervision: bookworks
Cover design: Wanda Lubelska
Manufacturing buyer: Mary McCartney

Trademark List

Brief, Turbo Pascal, Turbo Pascal Professional, Turbo Vision, and Turbo Assembler are trademarks of Borland International.
TurboPower Software, Object Professional, B-Tree Filer, and Analyst are trademarks of TurboPower Software.
Compuserve Information Service is a trademark of Compuserve Inc.
Quarterdeck Office Systems, QEMM, and Vidram are trademarks of Quarterdeck Office Systems.
Invisible Network is a trademark of Invisible Software, Inc.
Qualitas, 386MAX, and BlueMAX are trademarks of Qualitas, Inc.
Microsoft is a trademark of Microsoft Corp.
Digital Research is a trademark of Digital Research, Inc.
Maynard Electronics is a trademark of Maynard Electronics, Inc.
WordPerfect is a trademark of WordPerfect Corp.

©1993 by P T R Prentice-Hall, Inc.
A Simon & Schuster Company
Englewood Cliffs, New Jersey 07632

All rights reserved. No part of this book may be reproduced, in any form or by any means, without permission in writing from the publisher.

The publisher offers discounts on this book when ordered in bulk quantities. For more information, write:
Corporate Sales Department
PTR Prentice-Hall
113 Sylvan Avenue
Englewood Cliffs, New Jersey 07632
Phone: 201-592-2863
Fax: 201-592-2249

Printed in the United States of America
10 9 8 7 6 5 4 3 2 1

ISBN 0-13-630310-2

Prentice-Hall International (UK) Limited, *London*
Prentice-Hall of Australia Pty. Limited, *Sydney*
Prentice-Hall Canada Inc., *Toronto*
Prentice-Hall Hispanoamericana, S.A., *Mexico*
Prentice-Hall of India Private Limited, *New Delhi*
Prentice-Hall of Japan, Inc., *Tokyo*
Simon & Schuster Asia Pte. Ltd., *Singapore*
Editora Prentice-Hall do Brasil, Ltda., *Rio de Janeiro*

Contents

Preface

Why?

This book was written to introduce the reader to the concepts of Object Oriented Programming, hereafter to be referred to as OOP. To that end, Turbo Pascal 6.0 was chosen as the base language.

It is difficult to write a state-of-the-art application without using windows, pick lists, dialog boxes, and other such items in the program's user interface. There is a very complete library of objects that supports windows, dialog boxes, and much more. This is published by

TurboPower Software
P.O. Box 49009
Colorado Springs, CO 80949-9009
(800) 333-4160

and is called Object Professional. This library is not event driven and therefore is easy to learn. As far as I can determine, Object Professional will do almost anything you can dream up. In the future I will refer to the Object Professional library as OPro. As you might have guessed, I have chosen to use OPro for the discussion and example applications in this book. An almost identical version of OPro is also available for C++. I said "almost," because a few of the Pascal OPro objects are not yet available (as this is written) in the first release of C++ version, but they will be added later.

TurboPower also supplies several other libraries for Turbo Pascal, including a very sophisticated single or multi-user database library called B-Tree Filer; a Pascal code analyzer, profiler, and editor called Analyst; a library much like Object Professional but not object oriented called Turbo Professional; a Pascal communications library; and more.

When you purchase OPro, you also receive many useful utility programs and examples as well as the complete source code for the library and utilities. Another advantage of OPro is that it contains a plethora of other useful objects, functions, and procedures such as string handling, long strings, large arrays, BCD arithmetic, TSR support, bit sets, using EMS, data entry, a complete editor, and much more. To be fair, I must also note that OPro must be purchased in addition to Turbo Pascal. Also, do not confuse Borland's Turbo Pascal Professional with TurboPower's Object Professional; they are totally different products from different software manufacturers.

Also, here's another feature of OPro that I believe is extremely important nowadays. The technical support is superb. It is provided by telephone and via CompuServe Information Service. A question on CompuServe is invariably answered in 24 hours or less (depending on the time you post the query and when and how often you check back for a response), frequently even on weekends.

The Readers

The book assumes the reader understands ordinary non-OOP programming in Turbo Pascal. I don't do anything very tricky, and the examples are very thoroughly annotated. However, it is assumed that the reader understands the basic concepts of constants, types, variables, records, arrays, functions, procedures, units, and random file handling and is familiar with the Turbo Pascal library.

A disk containing the source code for all the examples in this book is available. You must have OPro to compile that code. If you should compare that disk code with the same PAS files in this book, you will note that the code is much more thoroughly annotated in the book version. For a copy of the disk send \$25.00 to

Lawcom Co.
OOP Disk Offer
PO Box 10685
Yuma, AZ 85366-8685

Send check, money order, or credit card number (Visa or MasterCard), and disk size desired.

On the subject of program annotation, whenever a program unit function or procedure is used, or OPro object, method, function, or procedure is used, the unit in which it can be found is designated in bold. If only a constant or variable from a program or OPro unit is referenced, the unit is noted in nonbold. Pascal built-in procedures and functions are not noted at all.

Book Structure

At the beginning of the book, I use several chapters to discuss the fundamentals of OOP as implemented in Turbo Pascal.

Chapter 3 outlines the OPro library. It is not possible to supply a complete description of all the methods, as there are far too many. Instead, each of the units and the objects and methods they contain are introduced in general, not in detail. The OPro documentation is also examined, and the many program examples and utilities are also discussed.

In Chapter 4 a few short examples demonstrate the features of just a few of the OPro objects. The OPro documentation and disk files offer a tremendous number of examples, so I kept this portion of the book short.

The remainder of the book consists of two applications. Each of these was designed to demonstrate the use of some of the OPro objects while also providing the reader with a useful application. These are designed to be built upon. For example, neither includes on-line help. An example in Chapter 8 shows how this can easily be implemented. Not all of OPro's units were used; that would be impossible in a book of this size. Only those I thought would be the most useful or interesting to a programmer starting out with OOP and OPro appear.

Because the applications are discussed, I include a description of other options and parameters available for the object's methods other than those I used. I look upon the book as a reference tool. Rather than direct you back to the original description if these options are discussed again in another chapter, I repeat the options list. I personally do not enjoy searching for information in another portion of a book; I prefer to find all the information available near the point where it is referenced. I don't think there is enough repetition to annoy you—and besides, I do not visualize you reading the application chapters in detail. Rather, you will probably skim the material to see what is there, reading in detail when you need a detailed example of a unit or object's use.

The first example is a loan amortization table, which also keeps a record of the loan information and any payments that were not made or not made on time. The program supports late charges, compound interest, and many other features. One utility provided calculates a loan backwards; that is, given a loan of $L, a time of T, and a payoff amount of $P, what interest rate would have been required to earn the same amount if invested in a CD or another bank investment? Another utility accepts a loan amount, interest, and loan period and produces the payoff amount required. This example uses data entry screens, dialog boxes, several different pick lists, date calculations, the printer, and much more.

A short chapter follows discussing the program design trade-offs. Following that, program enhancements and possible modifications are discussed.

The second application is an example of a variable record length text database. The program can be used to enter text of any length, then later search for any word or words in the text to display it again. The program supports AND, OR, and nested parentheses in the search values. A small editor is built in, as is an unusual indexing system. Any record can be printed, modified, or deleted. This would be a useful tool for to-do items, dated reminders, phone and address lists, and much more. This example uses data entry screens, directory pick lists, the printer, BitSets, the memo editor, asciiz strings, dialog boxes, many string functions, and much more.

A short chapter follows discussing program design trade-offs and possible program modifications and enhancements.

The previous program is a stand-alone application, which reduces its value unless you are using a multitasking system. The next example converts this program to a swapping TSR, retaining only about 6K in memory. It will swap the interrupted program to EMS, or if not available, disk.

OPro Documentation

Please read the OPro documentation! All three volumes! Or at least skim through the documentation before you try to understand the three book applications in detail. Note how the material is organized. Be sure to look at the appendixes. Skim through the readme file. Decompress and print out the files Index.lzh and Index2.lzh, probably located on your Bonus disk. If your manuals do not include material on the OpDialog unit, print out the files OpDialog.doc and OpDrag.doc as additional required documentation. While you're at it, you might wish to print the Dialog1.pas, Dialog2.pas, Dialog3.pas, and Dialog4.pas as examples to refer to when reading OpDialog.doc. The documentation is rather dense, but if you read carefully you'll find the majority of your questions will be answered without resorting to TurboPower's technical support. You'll also probably serendipitously learn a great deal while looking for the answer to your question.

1

OOP Basics

In this chapter I'll discuss the basics of Object Oriented Programming (OOP). In later chapters I'll go into more detail about the same material and supply more examples.

What Are Objects and Why Would You Want to Orient Them?

OOP is a general-purpose approach to programming, just as structured programing is. Object Oriented Programming simply means using objects when designing your application. The objects should be designed as far as possible to mirror the pieces of the behavior you are trying to emulate in your application. Objects also make it easier for the object to evolve as required, with a minimum of changes. This is accomplished by adding to or modifying the object type's methods. (For the moment, just consider a method as a function or procedure that is part of the object and is used to create, manipulate, or destroy the object and its data.) If properly designed, the tested object will then be available for use in other applications. The object's methods should enforce the object's desired behavior.

Objects are something like records. However, records only define data. The object defines the data that makes up the object as well as the way the data is to be manipulated—its behavior. The methods would ordinarily know only about the object's data.

An object can also be compared to a Pascal unit. However, an object is more self-contained and normally concerns itself only with the object's data.

Of course, objects, records, and units can all appear in an application, together with interface functions and procedures to tie everything together. You can have arrays of objects too. But you cannot have a file of objects; instead investigate streams that provide the same thing.

Like structured programming, OOP was created to make an application easier to organize, understand, debug, and modify. In addition, it makes more of your code reusable, which can save a lot of your time and effort. Once an object has been debugged, you can use it in another application without worrying about introducing programming errors. For example, the object might be a line editor. In the future you can use that line editor object and its methods whenever you want to get a line of input from the user.

You can already see that an object should be as general-purpose as possible, so that it can be used in as many applications as possible. You would not want to restrict the line entry object to a certain number of characters or permit only digits to be entered into the line. Of course, it would be useful to set a minimum and maximum number of characters permitted in the line—perhaps 0 and 255—but you wouldn't want to specify that the entry must be 10 characters—no more, no less. The object should be smart enough to know how to extend its input area over several rows on the screen if necessary. (If you ever do need a restricted version of the line editor object, its methods can be modified. This technique will be described later on.)

As another example, let's say you want to create a new window object. You should not make it 20 columns wide by 12 rows high, centered in an 80 × 25 screen, with a double line border, and specific title text in the center of the first row. To do so would restrict the use of the object to very specific (and very few) other instances. It would be better to permit the window to have any dimensions, any border (or none), any position on the screen, and any title (or none) positioned anywhere in the window. You would also want to add code to the object's **initialization** method to be sure that the window would fit on the screen when it was created, otherwise producing an error message. You might prefer to add this error-checking code to the method that draws the window on the screen instead if you would rather not include this action in the initialization method. There are many other user-designated or optional possibilities, such as a choice of frame and interior color complete with default values, methods to save the window to a file or memory and restore it later, horizontal and/or vertical scroll bars, a way to clear the window interior, a way to draw the contents within a designated text area, mouse support, and more.

The idea is to make your object as reusable as possible while still retaining as much power and flexibility as you can. When Turbo Pascal links an object, methods are not linked into the final program unless they are called by the application functions and procedures or other methods (with one exception to be discussed later—see virtual methods). Therefore you do not need to be concerned that a large number of unused available methods will make the final application too large. Using the window example, if the user never wishes a window to have scroll bars, the method to create and interface scroll bars will never be called and therefore will not be linked into the final application's EXE file.

When the data and all the methods required to manipulate that data are contained in a single package, a descriptive term that can be used to refer to that condition is **encapsulization**. As you have seen, encapsulization is one of the features of objects.

Inheritance

As mentioned earlier, one of the prime rules in OOP is to keep the objects as generic, self-contained, and reusable as possible, so they can be used in as many situations in as many applications as possible or in many places in a given application. A few examples of objects that are usable in many situations and applications are windows, data entry screens, pick lists, editors, menus, help systems, and file browsers. Examples of objects that would be usable in many places in one application are the chess pieces for a chess application. Each piece would have methods for the ways in which it moves, appears, captures, and checks the opposing king, among other things. As you probably know, each chess piece moves and checks differently.

Returning to the window example, it would be better to break it down into two objects. One could be a frame object, the other a window object. The frame object could have methods for controlling the size and appearance of the frame, scroll bars, and frame color. The window object would then be a special kind of frame, built upon the frame object, which, while including the frame object's methods for controlling the size and type of frame, scroll bars, and frame color, would also include methods to control the interior color, titles, clearing and drawing window content, and storage and recovery of the window and its contents. Thus the window object would begin with the frame object and add additional methods. This technique is one of the big advantages of OOP, called **inheritance**. The window object would inherit all the methods from the frame object as well as add some new methods. Retaining the genealogical analogy, the frame is called the window's **ancestor**, the window is called the frame's **descendant**. Also, in this example, the frame object—the first ancestor—is sometimes called the **base object**. Also, descendants can be referred to as **derived types** of their ancestors.

Multiple Inheritance

Although some languages support multiple inheritance, such as C++, Turbo Pascal does not presently do so. *Multiple inheritance* means that the language permits you to derive a descendant object using the methods and data from more than one ancestor object. In Turbo Pascal, you must instead derive from a single object type. Then, if necessary, include other objects by making them part of the derived object's data. In such a case, it will make your programming life a lot easier if the combined objects do not have different methods with the same name.

Overriding Methods

It is also possible to inherit a method and then change it. This is called **overriding** a method. Inheritance and overriding are just a few of the features of objects that make them so powerful.

You can subtract a method from an object by overriding it with an abstract or empty method.

```
procedure MyMethod;
begin
  abstract;
end;
```

or

```
procedure MyMethod;
begin
end;
```

The first example is an abstract method, the second an empty method. If an abstract method is called, the Pascal "abstract" procedure causes the program to halt. This is to ensure that your application does not call a nonexistent method by mistake.

If you frequently find yourself having to subtract a large number of methods from some object, you should take the hint: The object is too complex. Simplify it and add those frequently unneeded methods only to the derived objects that do need them.

When you override a method, you can call the original method being overridden as part of the new method, if appropriate. This is a very common strategy. You can then add your own actions to the overridden method either before and/or after the call to the original method. This is a good strategy, especially if the original method was well tested when it was used in other situations.

As you can see, overriding methods is easy. Overriding data fields is more difficult. The usual solution is to use variant record types. The better solution is to choose your data types more carefully, or perhaps redesign the object.

Use of Suitable Base Objects

You must plan ahead when creating base objects and deriving descendant objects. It would not be correct to derive a frame object from a window object that included frame methods. By this I mean you have started with a base window object that includes methods for controlling the size and type of frame, scroll bars, frame color, interior color, titles, clearing and drawing window content, and storage and recovery of the window and its contents. After creating and testing this object, you discover that you need a frame object for another purpose, such as to place a frame around each of the fields in a data entry screen object. It would be improper to derive the new frame object from the window object, disregarding or subtracting the methods for scroll bars, interior color, titles, clearing and drawing window content, and storage and recovery of the window and its contents. Instead, you should have planned ahead and created the frame object as the base object, then derived the window object from it as described in a previous section.

Polymorphism

Let's look at another object, this time a bird. One of the bird object's methods would enable it to move. Some birds walk or run, a few swim, and others fly. Of those that fly, a bird might hover, glide, flutter, dart, dash, or use its wings in some other fashion. We could use a single movement method in an all-purpose bird object, with a case statement determining how any particular bird would move. For one thing, this would mean that the case statement would have to include all types of movement of any bird you *might* want to refer to, obviously a rather large, involved, complicated method. If you missed a type of bird, the method must be rewritten, a good thing to avoid in OOP. Instead, we build each different bird we wish to represent as a descendant of a generic bird object. Each descendant object would modify the general-purpose, empty, or **abstract** movement method found in the generic base bird object type and convert it to a run movement method for the descendant ostrich object, hover movement method for the hummingbird object, soar movement method for the buzzard object, and so on. This is known as **polymorphism**. Remember, an abstract method is one that *must* be replaced in any descendant object if the method is to be used; an empty method contains only

```
begin
end;
```

and a generic method could provide a generalized movement method for some common birds. It would be best to use an abstract movement method in the base bird object type.

Virtual Methods

Suppose in our generic bird object we had an all-purpose method for migrating. This method calls on the movement method to determine how the bird moves during migration. Thus there is only one migration method, part of the base generic bird object type. The migration method in turn calls the movement method. But which movement method? The generic version, the one for the hummingbird, or the one for the buzzard? Again, we could use a case statement in the migration method to choose the correct movement method. As noted earlier, this is not in the spirit of OOP and would be very complex. We could also write a special migration method for each descendant bird object. But if we assume the migration methods are all the same, except for calling a different movement method, it seems like a waste of memory (and effort) to store all those almost-identical migration methods in the final application. Instead, in this case we would use **virtual** methods. We end each method with the keyword *virtual.* Thus

```
procedure Buzzard.Movement; virtual;
```

Now we need write only one migration method and let each descendant bird object inherit it. We had to write the different movement methods anyway, so no extra memory or effort is required in this case. The only difference is the use of the keyword *virtual.* Using *virtual* does cost a little memory, as one small table is created in each object type's memory space, but not nearly as much memory as would be required through duplicating the migration method for each descendant object. The program will run very slightly slower, as the program requires the addition of code to determine which object's movement method to use at runtime (called **late binding**); ordinarily this decision is made by the compiler at compile time (called **early binding**, the normal Pascal behavior). Another disadvantage is that all virtual methods are linked into the application's final EXE file, whether called or not. However, these disadvantages are offset by the memory savings and the coding convenience if the situation warrants the use of virtual methods.

To use the hummingbird's movement method when calling the migration method instead of

```
Migration;
```

which would use the generic bird object's movement method, we'd instead say

```
Hummingbird.Migration;
```

which requires the generic migration method to use the hummingbird's movement method. A more complete example will be provided in the next chapter.

To return for a moment to the subject of overriding, an overridden method usually does not *have* to have the same argument list as the method it is replacing. However, an overridden virtual method *must* have exactly the same argument list—in the same order, with the same types and names.

Using Objects

When we use an object or descendant, the normal practice is not to directly use the defined object type, but instead to create an **instance** of the object. An instance is simply a copy of the object associated with a variable name. Thus, for example, if the object type was defined as Bird, the instance could be MyBird.

```
var
  MyBird : Bird;
```

Creating an instance of an object does not initialize that instance. The initialization, if required, must be accomplished through a call to the appropriate method. You'll see examples of object instances and initializing in the next chapter.

Descendants are derived from the base object type or its descendant types, not from instances of these objects. The instance is simply a copy of the object, not a descendant of the object, and the methods of the copied object (the instance) are not to be added to or modified. If modification is required, create a descendant and then use an instance of the descendant.

Objects in Objects

Objects can contain other objects—which can contain other objects, ad infinitum. For example, a data entry screen object might include a frame object so it could enclose entry fields in a frame if desired.

No Object Source?

Even if you do not have the source code, you can still derive objects from an object type through overriding, subtracting, or adding methods. If the library documentation for the object type from which you are deriving descendants denotes which methods are virtual, you enjoy additional possibilities. Note that calls to virtual methods do not require the *virtual* keyword, so the documentation would not necessarily indicate the virtual methods.

Public and Private Variables in Objects

As you know, you can have global data, procedures, and functions in a Pascal application. Variables declared within a procedure or function can be accessed only by that procedure or function; they are private. When you create a unit, you can make its variables, procedures, and functions global (public) or private by declaring them in the interface or implementation section of the unit, respectively. You can also make selected constants and variables available to the whole application (public) if it contains units. Simply create a new unit and include all the selected constants and variables in the interface portion. You need nothing in the implementation portion. (See LoanGlob and LookGlob in the description of the Loan and Look applications later in the book.) Then put that unit into every Uses list in the application. Its variables and constants will be available to the whole application. When you create an object type, you have much the same choices. You can define an object's data and methods as public or private. This means that the private methods and data are available only within the unit where the object is declared. Simply enter the word *private* after the public (which is the default) data and methods. Thus

```
type
  MyObject = Object
    Field1 : integer;
    Field2 : integer;
    procedure Method1;
  private
    Field3 : String;
    procedure Method2;
  end;
```

Field1, Field2, and Method1 are public, while Field3 and Method2 are private.

Constructors and Destructors

Any object can include methods called *constructors* and *destructors*. Constructors are used to initialize a newly instantiated object. Destructors are used to recover any memory allocated when instantiating the object and also any dynamic memory allocated and not released by the other methods. Thus

```
type
  MyObject = object
    constructor Init;
    destructor Done;
    procedure Method;
  end;
```

The names *Init* and *Done* are not required but are commonly used. The keywords *constructor* and *destructor* determine their identity, not their name. Thus

```
type
  MyObject = object
    constructor Startup;
    destructor Stopit;
    procedure Method;
  end;
```

In this case the former case the object could just as well have been defined as

```
type
  MyObject = object
    procedure Init;
    procedure Done;
    procedure Method;
  end;
```

since no virtual methods were used. Normally the constructor (and destructor, if needed) are used only with virtual methods. When virtual methods were introduced earlier in this chapter, I mentioned that the use of one or more virtual methods entailed the creation of a small table in the object type's memory area. This table, called the VMT (Virtual Method Table), contains some information about the object type and the addresses of all the object's virtual methods. Any object that contains or inherits virtual methods, constructors, or destructors has a VMT. There is only one VMT per object type, not one per instance. A pointer to the object type's VMT is automatically created in an object instance's memory area when the constructor of the instance is called. The VMT itself is part of the object type, not the instance(s). That's why the VMT pointer in each instance is necessary, so the instance knows where its object type's VMT can be found. The first word of the VMT itself contains the size of any instances of the object type. The constructor needs this information to know how much memory to allocate for an instance, and the destructor needs to know how much memory to release. The constructor places the negative value of the first word in the second word position in the VMT. When the compiler's range-checking option is on ($R+), a check is made to be sure the constructor has been called before any other methods. Range checking does this by making sure the VMT's first word is not zero and that the sum of the first two words is zero. Range checking does this every time a virtual method is called. The remainder of the VMT contains a list of 32-bit pointers, each containing the address of the entry point of one of the virtual methods.

If a static instance of an object type has no constructor and destructor, its memory usage cannot be specifically deallocated. It is handled just like any other static variable. However, if the object is dynamic—that is, you use New and a pointer to the object to allocate memory for the object instance—then you can deallocate the memory with Dispose. (See the next chapter for an example.)

If the object uses virtual methods, it *must* have a constructor. Moreover, the constructor *must* be called before any other of the object's methods. If it is not called, the pointer to the VMT will contain garbage and the program will very likely crash as soon as it is initialized, because the first word at the address where the VMT is thought to be located will be the wrong value, and therefore the instance will be created improperly. Even if it does not, the program will surely crash when the first virtual method is called, since the method is not located at the indicated address. However, if range checking is on, an error message will be generated instead of a program crash. Generally, constructors and destructors are used only when the object includes virtual methods. Note that a constructor cannot be declared virtual, though a destructor can. You can declare more than one constructor and/or destructor if you wish.

The first action of a constructor of a derived type is usually to call the constructor of its immediate ancestor to initialize the object's inherited fields. The next step is to initialize any fields the descendant introduced.

The destructor is used to recover any memory allocated by an instance of the object. The destructor must also recover (using Dispose) any memory the constructor or any of the methods allocate on the heap (using New). Done is usually (but not necessarily) the name used as a destructor to "uninstantiate" the object. However, Done must explicitly be used in the Dispose procedure. Thus

```
type
  MyObject = object
    p : ^integer;
    constructor Init;
    destructor Done;
  end;

constructor MyObject.Init
begin
  New(p);
  p^ := 100;
end;

destructor Done;
begin
  Dispose(p,Done);
end;
```

Note, you only need to use a destructor to release an object's memory if the object is dynamic (uses a pointer) and/or is an instance of an object type. (When you create a temporary object, you need to have a way to recover the memory.) Static objects do not need a destructor.

Both the constructor and the destructor can be empty methods; that is

```
MyObject = object
  constructor Init;
  destructor Done;
  procedure Methodl; virtual;
end;

constructor MyObject.Init;
begin
end;

destructor MyObject.Done;
begin
end;
```

The constructor will still create the VMT; the destructor will still release the memory reserved for the object instance.

2

OOP Basics, Examples

In this chapter I will illustrate most of the concepts described in Chapter 1 with very simple code examples. Note that these are not ideal or usable objects, but only examples that are as brief as possible while still illustrating the basic concept. Real objects would be much more complex. To see examples of real objects, look at some of the OPro objects—for example, those in the OpRoot, OpFrame, and OpEntry units.

Inheritance Example

As described in Chapter 1, inheritance means that a derived (descendant) object will include all methods and data declared in the base object. Here is an example:

```
program ex2_1;
{inheritance example}

uses
  crt; {for clrscr procedure}

type
  base = object               {base object}
    procedure Method1;        {method to be inherited}
  end;
```

```
  derived = object(base)  {descendant object}
    procedure Method2;    {added method}
  end;

procedure base.Method1; {method to be inherited}
begin
  writeln('This is method 1');
end;

procedure derived.Method2;
begin
  writeln('This is method 2');
end;

var
  TestDerived : Derived; {instance of descendant object}

begin
  clrscr;
  with TestDerived do begin
    Method1; {inherited}
    Method2; {added}
  end;
end.
```

When this little program is run, you will see two messages displayed:

This is method 1
This is method 2

This shows that method 1 was inherited by Derived, the descendant object. Method 2 was added to Derived. If you were to change

```
TestDerived : Derived; {instance of descendant object}
```

to

```
TestDerived : Base; {instance of base object}
```

then the compilation would fail because there is no Method2 procedure available to run.

Overriding Methods Example

If you'll remember, overriding methods means to modify an inherited method. Here is an example:

```
program ex2_2;
{override example}
```

```
uses
  crt; {for clrscr procedure}

type
  base = object          {base object}
    procedure Method1; {method to be inherited}
  end;

  derived = object(base) {descendant object}
    procedure Method1;    {override inherited method}
  end;

procedure base.Method1; {method to be inherited}
begin
  writeln('This is method 1 for base object');
end;

procedure derived.Method1; {override method}
begin
  writeln('This is method 1 for derived object');
end;

var
  TestDerived : Derived; {instance of descendant object}
  C : char;

begin
  clrscr;
  TestDerived.Method1; {run overridden method}
  writeln('');
  write('Press any key to continue ');
  readln(C);
end.
```

If you bother to enter and run this little example, you'll see

This is method 1 for derived object

showing that the base object's method was overridden. Had it not been overridden, the display would be

This is method 1 for base object

Polymorphism Example

Polymorphism is the concept of overriding all the descendant objects, giving each its own version of an overridden method. The overridden method can be empty or abstract. In this example, I made it abstract. Should the abstract method be inadvertently called, the program will display a message and halt. If you use an empty procedure such as

```
begin
end;
```

the program will continue without bringing the error to your attention. Of course, this assumes the base method should never be called.

```
program ex2_3;
{polymorphism example}

uses
  crt,      {for clrscr procedure}
  objects;  {turbo vision unit, for abstract procedure}

type
  base = object             {base object}
    procedure Movement;     {abstract method to be overridden}
  end;

  Hummingbird = object(base)
    procedure Movement;     {special method for this object}
  end;

  Buzzard = object(base)

    procedure Movement;     {special method for this object}
  end;

procedure base.Movement; {abstract method}
begin
  abstract;                 {from Turbo Vision Objects unit}
end;

procedure Hummingbird.Movement; {new method for this object}
begin
  writeln('Hummingbird - Hover - hover');
end;

procedure Buzzard.Movement; {new method for this object}
begin
  writeln('Buzzard - flap, flap - glide');
end;

var
  TestHummingbird: Hummingbird; {instance of objects}
  TestBuzzard: Buzzard;
  C : char;

begin
```

```
  clrscr;
  TestHummingbird.Movement; {overridden method}
  TestBuzzard.Movement;     {overridden method}
  writeln('');
  write('Press any key to continue ');
  readln(C);
end.
```

Virtual Methods Example

```
program ex2_4;
{virtual example}

uses
  crt,     {for clrscr procedure}
  objects; {turbo vision unit, for abstract procedure}

type
  base = object {base object}
    constructor init; {Initializer for base and derived
                       objects. Required because of virtual
                       method.}}
    procedure Movement; virtual; {this will be overridden}
    procedure Migration;         {this will not}
  end;

  Hummingbird = object(base)     {descendant object}
    procedure Movement; virtual; {must be virtual for base's
                                  Migration method to work}
  end;

  Buzzard = object(base)         {descendant object}
    procedure Movement; virtual; {must be virtual for base's
                                  Migration method to work}
  end;

constructor base.init;  {object constructor}
begin
end;

procedure base.Movement; {must be overridden}
begin
  abstract;
end;

procedure base.Migration; {not overridden}
begin
  Movement; {correct movement will be used because
             Movement method is virtual}
```

```
end;

procedure Hummingbird.Movement;
begin
  writeln('Hummingbird - Hover - hover');
end;

procedure Buzzard.Movement;
begin
  writeln('Buzzard - flap, flap - glide');
end;

var
  TestHummingbird: Hummingbird; {instances of objects}
  TestBuzzard: Buzzard;
  C : char;

begin
  clrscr;
  TestHummingbird.init; {set VMT pointer}
  TestBuzzard.Init;     {set VMT pointer}
  writeln('Hummingbirds migrate this way');
  TestHummingbird.Migration; {Hummingbird movement chosen
                              because of TestHummingBird
                              prefix to base object's
                              Migration method}
  writeln('Buzzards migrate this way');
  TestBuzzard.Migration;     {same as above}
  writeln('');
  write('Press any key to continue ');
  readln(C);
end.
```

Constructors and Destructors Example

This example shows how an object can be made dynamic. It also illustrates that the constructor uses memory.

```
program ex2_5;
{constructor/destructor example}

uses
  crt;

type
  base = object          {base object}
    Field1 : String;
    constructor init;
    destructor Done;
```

```
    procedure Methodl; virtual;
  end;

  DerivedPtr = ^Derived; {make it available as dynamic}
  derived = object(base) {descendant object}
    constructor init;    {override}
    destructor Done;     {override}
    procedure Method2;   {added method}
  end;

constructor Base.Init;
begin
end;

destructor Base.Done;
begin
end;

procedure Base.Methodl;
begin
  writeln('This is method l');
end;

constructor Derived.Init; {we could instead inherit this}
begin
  Base.Init;
end;

destructor Derived.Done; {we could instead inherit this}
begin
  Base.Done;
end;

procedure Derived.Method2;
begin
  writeln('This is method 2');
end;

var
  Ptr : DerivedPtr; {dynamic object}
  C : char;

begin
  clrscr;
  {before object put on heap}
  writeln('Maximum heap memory available = ',MemAvail);
  New(Ptr,Init); {store object on heap}
  with Ptr^ do begin
    Methodl;
    Method2;
```

```
    {while object on heap}
    writeln('Maximum heap memory available = ',MemAvail);
  end;
  Dispose(Ptr,Done); {recover heap memory}
  {after object removed from heap}
  writeln('Maximum heap memory available = ',MemAvail);
  writeln('');
  write('Press any key to continue ');
  readln(C);
end.
```

If you run this program, you'll see that the available memory is somewhat less (537,912 bytes, second message), while the object is on the heap compared with that available before and after (538,176 bytes). This is because the dynamic object has been placed on the heap. The constructor put the instance of the object there and created the VMT; the destructor disposed of the instance.

3

About Object Professional

As mentioned in the Introduction, I will be referring to TurboPower's Object Professional library as OPro.

The first thing to do is read the Introduction and Principles of Organization in volume one of the OPro documentation and at least skim the Overviews of all the objects in the documentation. Yes, there are three big books! Also look at the disks you received and print the readme file and any file with a DOC extension. You might also print out the Index2 file. Appendix A in this book contains an up-to-date version of the Index file, as of OPro version 1.10. If your OPro version is much later than mine and contains new objects or many new methods, you may wish to use the OPro Index file version instead of mine. Be sure to read Appendix G, "Compiling Large Programs," in volume three. As soon as you start constructing real applications you'll probably begin to run into out-of-memory problems, especially if you are trying to use the Turbo Pascal IDE. If you can't use the IDE because of memory problems, a stand-alone editor will be required. Ideally that editor should support swapping itself out of memory, compiling, and returning to the editor at the error point, if any. One such editor is TPE from TurboPower, available on CompuServe. It's free! Try out the Pophelp TSR and learn to find your way around in it if you prefer on-line help instead of using the printed documentation. If you're a bit old-fashioned, you may prefer printed materials.

When you want to start using an unfamiliar object, first read the Overview for that object very carefully, then skim through the method descriptions so you know what is available. Careful reading is important. The answer to just about every question can be found in the documentation, but the information is quite dense and sometimes difficult to absorb in a single reading. Look in the OPro directories and on the floppies for any PAS files that look like they might relate to the object. If you find any, print them. I advise you to check the floppies, too, because the OPro default install procedure does not uncompress and copy *all* the files to your hard disk. Personally, I initially learn much more from code examples than from documentation. But the examples should be simple; too much complexity is one problem when trying to learn Turbo Vision. I prefer to see the program broken down into units, with each unit easy to comprehend. Much of this book is Pascal code, for those who learn best as I do. I hope you agree with my decision.

Fortunately, TurboPower seems to agree with me, because they supply extensive example code, mostly easy to understand. Once I get an idea of how the example code works, the documentation makes much more sense to me. Next, do the same thing for any unfamiliar ancestors of the object you are concerned with, so you can use the inherited methods. In Appendix C in volume three of the OPro documentation, you'll find a listing of the object hierarchy so you can determine how the objects are related—who is whose descendant or ancestor. While you're there, you'll also find a handy list of unit dependencies in OPro Appendix B so you can get your program or unit's Uses list right (complete and in the correct order) the first time.

More About Memory and OPro

Here is how I go about setting up my computer for Pascal program development.

For small programs I use the convenient Turbo Pascal IDE. I set the options to link and compile to disk rather than memory. I turn off the debugging. As soon as I feel it is safe to do so, I turn off the range checking. This seems to avoid out-of-memory errors. If necessary, I use the Vidram program that comes with Quarterdeck Office Systems' QEMM memory manager. (There may be other sources for this kind of utility, but the only other one I am aware of comes with Invisible Network. The trouble is, to use it the network drivers have to be loaded. I generally use only the net for testing network-aware programs I have written.) If you are using a VGA monitor, the entire video buffer in the memory area above 640Kb is not required in text mode. Vidram is a TSR that makes about 96Kb of this buffer available to DOS programs. The Turbo Pascal IDE can use this memory and thus is less likely to run dry. I find that Vidram (from Version 5.13 of QEMM) has one side effect; sometimes the mouse behaves strangely. I'm told this can be cured by loading the mouse driver *after* Vidram is loaded. I'm not too fond of that idea because Vidram takes up memory when you use it, whether it is active or not. Loading the mouse after Vidram means it gets loaded every time I boot, whether I use it or not. The obvious solution is to use QEMM's Loadhi command to put Vidram in upper (high) memory (between 640Kb and 1000Kb). I haven't tried this because I haven't yet found it necessary. I load Turbo Pascal from a batch file that looks like this:

```
G:
CD \TP
Vidram on
Turbo
Vidram off
C:
CD \
```

Thus Vidram is used only when the IDE is running. This seems to eliminate most Vidram mouse side effects.

When large applications are being compiled, memory problems are more likely to occur. I begin by using a memory manager such as Quarterdeck's QEMM. Other possibilities include Quarterdeck's QRAM, Qualitas's 386Max or BlueMax, MicroSoft's DOS 5.0 or later, Digital Research's DOS 5.0 or later, or one of the many other memory managers. Then everything possible is loaded into upper memory. If all or part of a device driver or TSR has to load low, in base memory (0Kb to 640Kb), I am reluctant to use it. I use the Turbo Pascal command line compiler TPC with a stand-alone editor and Vidram. I generally use Brief, but any other would work. It is especially nice to use an editor that will swap itself out of memory when the compiler is called, then return to the editor when the compilation is completed. It is especially convenient if the editor reacts to any compiler syntax errors and puts the cursor on the offending line. TurboPower's Analyst editor and its free TPE editor do just that. Remember, TPE does not come with OPro, at least as of Version 1.10. Analyst must be purchased separately. Turbo Pascal Professional (no relation to Object Professional) includes an extended memory version of TPC called TPCX. If you have a reasonable amount of extended memory available, this should solve any out-of-memory problems, without having to use Vidram or worrying about conserving every possible byte of base (below 640Kb) memory. I've not found it necessary to use this compiler yet.

This book includes the source code for a simple little utility program called Configur. Configur is used to quickly replace your Autoexec.bat and Config.sys files and reboot. Thus you can have one pair for Pascal development, and different pairs for your other needs.

TurboPower Technical Support

I have found TurboPower's technical support to be outstanding. The only other one I have found that is as good as that of Maynard Electronics. I've also heard that WordPerfect's support is very good. (Of course I haven't tried them all, and I generally try to get support through Compuserve forums unless it's a dire emergency.) I'm sure you are aware that the tech support of many companies is slow, inept, unresponsive, doesn't return calls, keeps you on hold, costs a lot, doesn't care, has lines that are always busy, or doesn't answer the phone. TurboPower is different. Their phone support (toll charge to Colorado Springs, Colorado; no 800 line as of this writing) is good, but you do get busy signals sometimes. I prefer getting my support through the TurboPower CompuServe forum (currently section 6 of PCVENB). I have always found that a message placed one morning is generally answered by the next. If I checked into CompuServe more than once a day, I might get answers later the same day.

Over the years I've learned to find out about the quality of a company's tech support before I buy their product. Bad tech support can be extremely frustrating and stressful, at least for me. Of course, sometimes you have no choice and have to buy a specific company's product because it is unique or is head and shoulders above the others of the same type, regardless of the tech support.

Extending OPro

I've not yet found it necessary to derive my own objects from those in OPro. Every time I've needed an object or a method, it was already available. Thus my program examples in this book do not illustrate deriving OPro objects. However, if derivation were required, it should not be too difficult, considering you have the source code for all the units and excellent tech support.

What's in OPro?

Here is a list of all the OPro objects together with a brief description. Note that some of the units do not contain objects; they just consist of a number of useful procedures and functions, such as OpString, OpBCD, and OpCrt.

I'll take these in the order in which they appear in the OPro documentation. If I listed them alphabetically, the related objects would be separated. All appropriate objects contain Store and Load methods. This permits storing an initialized object to a stream and recovering it from the stream at a later time or times. All objects also contain initialization and Done methods. These methods will not be mentioned in the description.

Unit	Object	Description
OpCrt	None	This is an enhanced version of the Turbo Pascal CRT unit. Use it to adjust video attributes; limited screen content editing such as clearing, insertion, and deletion; sound; cursor appearance and location; fast screen writes; limited window support; save and restore the screen; and much more.
OpMouse	None	This unit contains most of the mouse functions and procedures. Use it to show and hide the mouse, set the mouse cursor's appearance, locate the mouse, move the mouse, determine how far the user

		moved the mouse and in which direction, monitor mouse buttons, install the mouse in a TSR, and more.
OpCmd	CommandProcessor	This object supplies an object with mouse support, defines a large number of command codes, permits adding new command definitions, turns specific command availability on and off, gets keystrokes from the keyboard buffer, gets commands from the user, recognizes command errors and returns the error number, and more.
OpCmd	CommandPacker	This object packs and unpacks the command tables. Packing reduces the memory requirements.
OpFrame	ScreenRect	Use this object to allocate a buffer area to contain the screen or portions thereof. Methods are supplied to save and restore all or portions of the screen; these are used by other objects that overwrite the screen.
OpFrame	Frame	Use this object to create frames with titles, scroll bars including mouse support, shadows, create one frame from another, recognize and return associated error codes, and the like.
OpWindow	RawWindow	The RawWindow object handles the tasks required by a normal text window. It can save and restore the area covered by the window, provide some mouse support, recognize and report errors, zoom and unzoom the window, move an unzoomed window, control the cursor within the window, initialize one window from another, display the window, write to it, clear it, and scroll the contents.
OpWindow	StackWindow	This window object, unlike RawWindow, can manage more than one active window at a time—eight—to be exact. The stack window stores a pointer to itself on the stack.
OpWindow	WindowStack	This object is mostly used by StackWindow to keep track of the window positions—that is, which window is on top of which. It also makes sure the mouse is in the active (top) window.
OpWindow	PackedWindow	Like the ScreenRect object, this object stores the window contents in a buffer and displays the contents when required. However, in this case, the window is compressed (packed) before saving it. This conserves memory.
OpWindow	VirtScreen	This object is used to create a screen in

		memory as if it were being displayed on the monitor. You can do anything to this screen you can do to a normal screen. When you are finished, the memory area containing the image can be copied to the video buffer and the new screen displayed almost instantly. The advantage is that a complex display can be created off screen, when the process of its creation might be visible had it been done in front of the user. Also, VirtScreen can create any size screen so long as the memory required does not exceed 64Kb. For example, the screen might have 200 rows. In this case, only the portions that can be displayed can be moved to the physical screen.
OpPick	PickList	The PickList object permits displaying a list of arbitrary strings, allowing the user to scroll through the list and make a selection. The format and content of the displayed strings is up to the user. More than one selection can be made. More than one column of strings can be offered for selection. The highlight can scroll horizontally (if more than one column appears) or vertically. Items can appear in different colors. Some items can be protected from being selected. The list can be sorted several different ways. The window can be automatically sized to fit the displayed list, up to a selected maximum width and height.
OpDir	DirList	The DirList object is much like PickList but is designed to work with file names. Since DirList is descended from PickList, most of PickList's methods are available. Wild cards, attributes, and other user-defined selection criteria generally available for file names are available.
OpDir	PathList	Use the PathList object when subdirectories are to be dealt with. Otherwise, it works much like DirList where applicable. A tree format display is available.
OpMenu	MenuItemNode	This object is generally called only by the OpMenu objects. Methods to search for, position, provide help, protect selections, and manipulate the item keys are available.
OpMenu	Menu	This is the main OpMenu object. It is used to create and use menus. You can control the menu's appearance and the available options. Methods to provide help and selection protection are also provided.

OpHelp	AbstractHelpWindow	This object is generally not used, as it does not have methods to handle the text within the help window. Instead, it is provided to supply functionality to its descendants, PagedHelpWindow and ScrollingHelpWindow, which do deal with the help text display. It displays an optional topic header, keeps track of and controls location and topic number in the help file, draws the help window, searches the help file, returns user commands, turns options on and off, supports a help index, and provides mouse support.
OpHelp	PagedHelpWindow	This descendant of AbstractHelpWindow moves page by page through the help file's selected help topic.
OpHelp	ScrollingHelpWindow	This descendant of AbstractHelpWindow moves line by line through the help file's selected help topic.
OpMemo	Memo	This is a very basic text editor. It will handle up to 65,521 bytes of text in a buffer, includes word wrap, and has mouse support. It lacks commands for block moves. There are many available options. Cursor movement, the size of the edit window, margins, and line length can be controlled. For a more powerful editor, see OpEditor.
OpMemo	MemoFile	This object is available when you want to edit text files with the Memo object. Methods are provided to retrieve and save the files.
OpMemo	None	There are two memo procedures available other than the methods of the two described objects contained in this unit. Use them to provide help and a status line.
OpEditor	TextEditor	This object supplies all the editing tools not provided by the OpMemo objects. It has every feature found in OpMemo and MemoFile, together with block text handling, search and replace, bookmarks, go to line number, printer selection, and much more.
OpBrowse	Browser	The Browser object is a much better choice than the OpMemo with MemoFile or OpEditor objects using the read-only option when just viewing file contents. It includes all of TextEditor's functionality in read-only mode plus conserving memory because of its size, being able to remove the eighth bit from all the characters, and optionally viewing the file in

		hex mode. Many other methods and options are available.
OpAbsFld	None	The variables, constants, procedures, and functions found in this unit are used by many descendant objects. It includes picture masks for data entry and the legal character sets for various field types.
OpField	TextField	This is another object whose methods are used mostly by its descendants. It consists mainly of the minimum object methods—Init, Draw, Load, and Store.
OpField	SelectField	This object contains a description of each item in its list of fields but does not concern itself with the contents of the fields. It is used by its descendants.
OpField	EntryField	EntryField is used to control the various types of fields, such as numeric, string, and Boolean. It includes entry validation.
OpFEdit	None	This unit supplies editors for the use of OpField.
OpSelect	AbstractSelector	This object supplies methods to its descendant Selector and OpEntry's EntryScreen object. It is used to add text fields to entry fields; control some of the field attributes such as making the field invisible, hidden, or protected; display entry field prompts; provide help; and more.
OpSelect	Selector	This object, a descendant of AbstractSelector, can be used like a pick list. However, the objects to choose from can be located anywhere on the screen, not in rows or columns. The object can also act much like a data entry screen. It has methods to add fields and provides a way to call a designated procedure when a field is entered or departed. This object is also used primarily by its descendants.
OpSelector	ScrollingSelector	The functionality of the Selector object is enhanced by permitting fields to be scattered over an area larger than the window.
OpEntry	EntryScreen	This object pulls together the methods derived from its ancestors TextField, EntryField, AbstractSelector, and others just described. Use it to set up a window or windows full of data entry fields and process them. Some additional methods for working with entry fields include entry conversion, range checking, determining whether a field's content was modified, turning EntryScreen options on and off, processing user commands,

		returning error messages, dealing with passwords, and much more.
OpEntry	ScrollingEntryScreen	EntryScreen fields can be zoomed and the entry area can extend over a larger area than the window covers if the methods found in this object are used.
OpEdit	LineEditor	This object provides a high-level interface to all of OpField's low-level fields, such as BCD, numeric, string, and Boolean. The object can also be used on its own, if desired. You can use it to receive and edit data provided by the user.
OpSEdit	SimpleLineEditor	Use this object when all of LineEditor's features are not required or when you want to conserve memory. Many of LineEditor's features are missing.
OpDate	None	This unit has a host of useful procedures and functions for manipulating a time or a date's appearance and format and performing time and date arithmetic. It will also convert strings to dates or time, and vice versa.
OpPrnLow	BasePrinter	This is an abstract object used to derive other printer objects.
OpPrnLow	DosPrinter	This object uses standard DOS function calls to send characters to a DOS file or character device, reset it, choose or discover the port or printer type, and receive error messages.
OpPrnLow	BiosPrinter	This object uses the BIOS interrupt $17 to send characters to, reset, or get status information from the printer. This object will also permit you to test for printer availability.
OpPrint	Printer	This is a powerful object that uses OpPrnLow's methods as well as adding many of its own. It has many options. It handles just about everything required to use a printer of any type, including a laser.
OpDevice	None	This unit takes care of supplying knowledge about specific popular printer hardware, such as Epson, IBM, Nec, and HP to other objects as required. You can add new printers to this library. The library data is used primarily by OpPrint to assist in configuring the printer objects.
OpForm	PrintField	OpForm is a unit that is used to produce printed forms in much the same way OpEntry supports data entry fields. The abstract PrintField object defines the data fields and methods for all the printed field types.

OpForm	PrintedForm	This object controls the placement of the text and data fields on all the pages. It includes turning the various form options on and off, setting margins, handling printer errors, and much more.
OpForm	Report	This is the ultimate descendant of OpForm and is used to design and process the form. It uses mostly inherited methods other than the basic Init, Done, Save, Load, and Process.
OpRoot	PointerStack	The PointerStack object manages a stack of pointers. These pointers can be typecast to permit the object to manage any 1-to-4-byte item of data. Generally, however, PointerStack is used to keep track of pointers to objects. Use the PointerStack to push, pop, and look at items on the stack. The stack dynamically resizes itself as necessary.
OpRoot	StaticQueue	This object is used to manage a circular queue of items of predetermined size. Items can be added as long as there is room in the queue. Use it for pointers or any data item, up to the total queue size of 64Kb. Queue items can be deleted, the queue cleared, and items read from anywhere in the queue.
OpRoot	SingleListNode	This is used by the linked-list objects to initialize a link node.
OpRoot	SingleList	The SingleList object manages a single-direction linked list. Use it to create a linked list, add items, delete items, and move through the list.
OpRoot	DoubleList	The DoubleList object manages a bidirectional linked list. Use it to create a linked list, add items, delete items, and move through the list in either direction.
OpRoot	BitSet	This object manages a group of bits. Determine if any bit is on or off, find the next on or off bit, turn a bit on or off, and more. Use it as an array of Boolean or for any purpose where you need only keep track of two states of an item. See the Look application for an example of usage. The maximum size is 65,534 bits.
OpRoot	LargeBitSet	Like BitSet this object manages a group of bits. However, the group can be as large as 8 million bits.
OpRoot	StringDict	Use this object to create and manage a string dictionary. Add, delete, and search for strings and clear the dictionary.
OpRoot	StringArray	Use this object to create and manage a

		string array. Add, delete, and search for strings and clear the array.
OpRoot	IdStream	OpRoot manages many types of streams. The IdStream object concerns the most primitive type of stream. The other more useful stream types to be described are derived from this object. IdStream reads from and writes to a stream and determines stream registration.
OpRoot	DosIdStream	Store the stream to and load it from a DOS file with this object's methods.
OpRoot	BufIdStream	This object stores streams in a buffer and manages reading and writing.
OpRoot	DirEntry	A library is a special form of a stream. It makes it possible to process stream items randomly rather than sequentially as in a regular stream. A DirEntry object manages each item in the library. DirEntry is used to turn library options on and off and find information about an entry item such as position, size, and name.
OpRoot	Library	The Library object manages all the library entry items. It stores, counts, deletes, searches for, retrieves, and renames the entries.
OpLarray	None	Turbo Pascal does not permit arrays to exceed 64Kb in size. The OpLarray unit permits creating and managing arrays larger than this limit. The large arrays can be one- or two-dimensional and can store any data type. Size is limited only by disk space and maximum DOS file size. You can create a large array, store or retrieve any array item, and more. You can store a large array to a stream.
OpString	None	This unit adds a host of new string-oriented procedures and functions to Turbo Pascal. Included are numeric data conversion to and from strings, hex, binary, and octal; various search algorithms; ability to parse and modify file and path names; string, array, and record comparison; trimming and padding; formatting data using pictures; converting alphabetic case; storing strings to and recovering strings from the heap; counting words; and performing word wrap.
OpAsciiz	None	Asciiz strings are a special OPro long string type, permitting strings up to 65,520 bytes in length. This unit provides you with the means to perform many of the operations available for regular strings on these special strings.
OpDos	None	Turbo Pascal requires that you write your

		own routine when you wish to make use of most of the DOS and BIOS calls. This unit makes many of these useful calls available as a procedure or function.
OpExec	None	Use this object to swap your program to expanded memory or disk, shell out to DOS or another program, and on return swap your program back into DOS memory and resume operation.
OpEnhKbd	None	Use this unit to easily make enhanced keyboards (12 function keys) available to your programs.
OpInt	None	This unit provides procedures and functions to help make ISR (Interrupt Service Routine) management much easier.
OpTsr	None	Use the procedures and functions in this unit to make writing TSR (Terminate and Stay Resident) programs easy. It supplies routines to install the TSR, uninstall the TSR, set and change the hot key if used, pop up or perform some operation every so many timer ticks, and deal with all the other special TSR requirements.
OpSwap1	None	See the preceding entry about TSRs. A swappable TSR requires only about 6Kb of memory when it is not popped up. When popped up, it can be any size that will fit into DOS memory. The program that is popped up over is swapped to expanded memory or disk. Except for this swapping ability, it is very much like OpTsr; however, swapping TSRs do not lend themselves to popping up or performing some function every so many timer ticks because it takes time to swap, especially to a slow disk.
Op8087	None	This unit is intended to be used by TSRs that utilize the 8087 (math coprocessor chip).
OpEMS	None	Use this unit to manage expanded memory and permit it to be used by your application.
OpMacro	None	Your application's user can record, save, retrieve, and delete keyboard macros by means of the procedures and functions found in this unit.
OpMacEd	None	This unit permits editing macros from within the application.
OpReplay	None	Replay the macros you recorded with OpMacro by means of this unit.
OpBCD	None	BCD (Binary Coded Decimal) is more accurate than floating point in most

		cases. Use these routines where every decimal place must be correct, such as in financial transactions. Almost all the floating point routines are here, including addition, subtraction, multiplication, division, absolute value, trigonometric functions, equality, squares, and square roots. Conversion of other numeric types and strings to BCD and back is also available.
OpClone	Cloner	This object permits you to write programs that are configured from stored information. An installation program is one way to provide or modify this information.
OpErrHan	None	The procedure in this unit permits your application to recover from a runtime error.
OpInLine	None	Many assorted inline procedures are supplied in this unit. Examples include pointer value modification, various CPU and register operations, data exchange without a temporary variable, MIN and MAX functions, and pointer arithmetic.
OpSort	None	Use this unit for fast sorts. You can sort up to 65,535 elements of data of any type. All elements to be sorted must fit in normal memory.

4

Using Objects

This chapter will provide a few simple examples of the use of OPro objects to help you get started. The remainder of the book will consist of useful example applications that will further demonstrate the use of OPro objects.

I will be concentrating on four different useful concepts here: menus, data entry screens, dialog boxes, and pick lists. Some of the examples are from the applications written for this book, and others were especially written for this chapter.

Payoff.pas and DialogBx.Pas

The LoanMsg unit is part of the Loan application. I am presenting a slightly altered version here, called DialogBx, as a very simple example of a dialog box. It uses the DialogBox object from OpDialog. The interfaced procedure called is ShowMsg. This unit provides a dialog box that displays the message supplied as the ShowMsg parameter. A single pushbutton is provided to indicate that the message has been read. The Payoff.pas program is used to demonstrate ShowMsg.

Unit names in bold in comments designate the unit that contains the method called. If the unit name is not in bold, it designates that the variable or constant is from that unit.

```
unit dialogbx;

INTERFACE

uses
  OpDialog,
  OpString,
  OpCrt,
  OpRoot,
  OpCmd,
  OpField,
  OpFrame,
  OpCtrl,
  OpMouse,
  OpWindow;

{display a message}
procedure ShowMsg(Message : String);


IMPLEMENTATION

{$I Colors.inc}

const
  hiOk = 1; {button ID}

var
  MBox        : DialogBox; {instance of DialogBox object}
  Status      : Word;      {initialization result}
  MouseInUse  : Boolean;   {mouse availability}
  Finished    : Boolean;   {flag to show dialog box is no longer needed}

function InitMsgBox(Message : String) : Word;
{Initialize dialog box}

const
  WinOptions = wBordered         {make sure there is room around window
                                  for a border}
              +wClear            {clear window when first displayed}
              +wUserContents;    {user will replace contents if required}
                                 {OpWindow}
var
  Len : Byte; {message length}

begin
  with MBox do begin
    {initialize dialog box}
    Len := Length(Message);
    if not InitCustom(40 - ((Len DIV 2) + 3), {X1}
                      8,                      {Y1}
                      40 + (Len DIV 2) + 3,   {X2}
```

```
                    15,                        {Y2}
                    Colors,                    {from Colors.inc}
                    WinOptions,                {see above const}
                    dColors) then begin        {from Colors.inc,}
                                               {OpDialog}
          InitMsgBox := InitStatus;            {why didn't it initialize}
          Exit;
        end;

      AddCenteredTextField(Message,3); {display message centered on line
                                        three of window, OpSelect}

      AddPushButton('&Ok',      {name of button}
                    05,         {relative Y,X of upper-left corner}
                    (Length(Message) + 6) - 7,
                    5,          {width of button}
                    hiOk,       {button identifier}
                    ccSelect,   {button return value}
                    True);      {default button?}
                                {OpDialog}

      InitMsgBox := RawError;   {function return value}
    end;
  end;


procedure ShowMsg(Message : String);
{display the message and wait for button press}

begin
  Status := InitMsgBox(Message); {initialize DialogBox}
  MouseInUse := True;            {set to false if no mouse is being
                                  used}

  if Status <> 0 then begin      {sorry about that}
    writeln('Error initializing MessageBox: '
           + Long2Str(Status)); {OpString}
    Halt;
  end;

  if MouseInUse then begin                        {LoanGlob}
    DialogCommands.cpOptionsOn(cpEnableMouse);    {dialog sees mouse,
                                                   Dialog Command
                                                   Processor}
    HideMouse;                                    {avoid mouse tracks,
                                                   OpMouse}
  end;

  {fill in a backdrop}
  TextAttr := $07;
```

```
    TextChar := '▒';
    ClrScr;

    Finished := False;

    MBox.Draw;              {OpDialog}
    repeat
      if MouseInUse then    {LoanGlob}
        ShowMouse;          {make mouse available, OpMouse}
      MBox.Process;         {display and get button press}
      if MouseInUse then    {LoanGlob}
        HideMouse;          {avoid mouse tracks, OpMouse}

      if MBox.GetLastCommand = ccSelect then {button was pressed,
                                              OpWindow, OpCmd}
          Finished := True;                  {we are done}
    until Finished;
    MBox.Erase; {erase message box, OpDialog}
    MBox.Done;  {recover memory used, OpDialog}
  end; {ShowMsg}

  end. {unit}
```

When we set WinOptions at the beginning of the unit, we have several options.

wBordered	Make space for window border
wClear	Clear window when it is first displayed
wSaveContents	Save the contents of the window when it is erased.
wUserContents	User will restore window contents
wSoundEffects	Use sound effects during explosions
wAltFrame	Use alternate frame type when not current
wSetMouse	Set mouse window, cursor on entry to window
wFullMouseWindow	Force to full mouse window on entry
wResizable	Can be resized and zoomed
wAllMouseEvents	Any combination of mouse buttons anywhere exits
wStoreContents	Store window contents in streams

You may wish to substitute one or more of these for my choices.

It is possible you have been puzzling over this portion of the code:

```
Len := Length(Message);
if not InitCustom(40 - ((Len DIV 2) + 3), {X1}
                  8,                      {Y1}
                  40 + (Len DIV 2) + 3,   {X2}
                  15,                     {Y2}
```

The Message variable contains the message to be displayed. It is passed as a parameter to the ShowMsg procedure. The 40 is the center of the screen. If screens wider than 80 characters are anticipated, perhaps this should be changed to ScreenWidth / 2. Subtracting Len DIV 2 + 3 from this value ensures that the window will be wide enough to contain the left half of the message plus a two- or three-character blank margin. The

```
40 + (Len DIV 2) + 3,    {X2}
```

does the same for the width of the right half of the window. Similar code is found at

```
AddPushButton('&Ok',      {name of button}
              05,         {relative Y,X of upper-left corner}
              (Length(Message) + 6) - 7,
              5,          {width of button}
```

where an attempt is made to place the pushbutton under the right half of the message.

The unit assumes that a mouse is available. If not, set the MouseInUse variable to False.

To show how this dialog box works, I have borrowed another unit from the Loan application. It contains a small data entry screen and will calculate a loan's worth and interest owed after a designated period of time. It was a unit called LoanPyof.pas but has been converted to a program called PayOff.pas. Here it is:

```
program Payoff;
{calculate payoff amount and interest}

uses DialogBx,
     OpCtrl,
     OpCmd,
     OpRoot,
     OpField,
     OpFrame,
     OpWindow,
     OpCrt,
     OpString,
     OpEntry,
     OpDate,
     OpMouse;

{calculate payoff amount given loan amount, interest, loan date, and
 payoff date. Interest is compounded annually}

{$I Colors.inc}

var
   Loan          : Real;        {amount of loan}
   PayDate       : Date;        {date of payoff}
```

```
  LoanDate        : Date;         {date of loan}
  TotalAmount     : Real;         {calculated amount to payoff}
  Interest        : Real;         {interest rate}
  S               : String;       {string temporary}
  InterestAmount  : Real;         {calculated amount of interest due}
  ESPayOff        : EntryScreen;  {instance of EntryScreen object}
  MouseInUse      : Boolean;      {is mouse available?}
  Finished        : Boolean;      {Entry screen processing is completed}

begin
  MouseInUse := True; {set to false if no mouse available}
  ClrScr;
  if not ESPayOff.InitCustom(20, 5, 60, 13,                {Window
                                                            coordinates}
                    Colors,                                 {Colors.inc}
                    DefWindowOptions or wBordered)          {Window options}
                    then begin                              {OpEntry}
    S := 'Failed to init payoff EntryScreen. Status = '
         + Long2Str(InitStatus);                            {OpString}
    ShowMsg(S);                                             {DialogBx}
    Halt;
  end;

  if MouseInUse then begin                             {LoanGlob}
    EntryCommands.cpOptionsOn(cpEnableMouse);          {mouse sees entry screen,
                                                        EntryScreen Command
                                                        Processor}
    HideMouse;                                         {avoid mouse tracks,
                                                        OpMouse}
  end;

  {add some window frills, OpFrame}
  ESPayOff.wFrame.AddShadow(shBR,              {shadow below and right of
                                                screen}
                           shOverWrite);       {opaque shadow}
  ESPayOff.wFrame.AddHeader(' Calculate Payoff Amount ', heTC);
  ESPayOff.wFrame.AddHeader(' Esc to abort, Ctrl-Enter to accept ',
                           heBC);

  {add fields}
  ESPayOff.esFieldOptionsOn(efClearFirstChar); {clear field if first
                                                character is ASCII,
                                                OpEntry}

  ESPayOff.esFieldOptionsOn(efRequired);       {following entries
                                                required, OpEntry}
  ESPayOff.AddRealField('Amount of loan:',   {prompt}
                    4,                       {V prompt position}
                    6,                       {H prompt position}
                    '999999.99',             {picture}
```

```
                     4,                         {data V position}
                     21,                        {data H position}
                     26,                        {help ID number}
                     0.01,                      {minimum valid entry}
                     999999.99,                 {maximum valid entry}
                     2,                         {number of decimal places}
                     Loan);                     {data variable}

ESPayOff.AddRealField('Interest in %:',         {prompt}
                     5,                         {V prompt position}
                     6,                         {H prompt position}
                     '99.999',                  {picture}
                     5,                         {data V position}
                     21,                        {data H position}
                     30,                        {ID number}
                     0.000,                     {minimum valid entry}
                     99.999,                    {maximum valid entry}
                     3,                         {number of decimal places}
                     Interest);                 {data variable}

ESPayoff.AddDateField('Loan date:',             {prompt}
                     6,                         {V prompt position}
                     6,                         {H prompt position}
                     'mm/dd/yyyy',              {picture}
                     6,                         {data V position}
                     21,                        {data H position}
                     27,                        {help ID number}
                     00,                        {minimum valid entry}
                     00,                        {maximum valid entry}
                     LoanDate);                 {data variable}

ESPayOff.AddDateField('Payoff date:',           {prompt}
                     7,                         {V prompt position}
                     6,                         {H prompt position}
                     'mm/dd/yyyy',              {picture}
                     7,                         {data V position}
                     21,                        {data H position}
                     31,                        {help ID number}
                     00,                        {minimum valid entry}
                     00,                        {maximum valid entry}
                     PayDate);                  {data variable}

ESPayOff.esFieldOptionsOff(efRequired);         {turn off required entries,
                                                OpEntry}

Finished := False; {not completed}
Loan     := 0.00;  {default values}
LoanDate := Today; {OpDate}
PayDate  := Today; {OpDate}
Interest := 0.000;
```

```
repeat
  if MouseInUse then  {LoanGlob}
    ShowMouse;        {make mouse available to entry screen, OpMouse}
  ESPayOff.Process;   {get entries, OpEntry}
  if MouseInUse then  {LoanGlob}
    HideMouse;        {avoid mouse tracks, OpMouse}
  case ESPayoff.GetLastCommand of {return from entry screen, OpWindow}
    ccError:                      {error occurred, OpCmd}
      begin
        S := 'Fatal error '+ Long2Str(ESPayoff.GetLastError);
                                                        {OpString}
        ShowMsg(S);               {DialogBx}
        Finished := True;         {abort operation}
      end;
    ccQuit :                      {escape, OpCmd}
      Finished := True;           {abort operation}
  end;

  if not Finished then begin      {Ctrl-Enter response}
    {calculate total amount due}
    TotalAmount := Exp(((PayDate - LoanDate) / 365) *
                   Ln(1 + (Interest / 100))) * Loan;  {OpDate}
    {calculate interest due}
    InterestAmount := TotalAmount - Loan;
    {display interest}
    ShowMsg('Interest is: ' +
            TrimLead(Real2Str(InterestAmount,9,2))); {DialogBx,
                                                      OpString}
    {display total amount due}
    ShowMsg('Payoff is: '
            + TrimLead(Real2Str(TotalAmount,9,2)));  {DialogBx,
                                                      OpString}

    Finished := True; {done}
  end;
until Finished;

ESPayOff.Erase; {erase entry screen, OpEntry}
ESPayOff.Done;  {recover entry screen's memory, OpEntry}
end.            {end of program}
```

In this section of code:

```
if not ESPayoff.InitCustom(20, 5, 60, 13,         {Window
                                                   coordinates}
                     Colors,                      {Colors.inc}
                     DefWindowOptions             {default options
                      or wBordered)               {leave room for
                                                   border}

                     then begin
```

The DefWindowOptions (default window options) mentioned consist of

wClear
wSaveContents
wResizable
wStoreContents

The complete list of possible options is

wBordered	Make space for window border
wClear	Clear window when it is first displayed
wSaveContents	Save the contents of the window when it is erased.
wUserContents	User will restore window contents
wSoundEffects	Use sound effects during explosions
wAltFrame	Use alternate frame type when not current
wSetMouse	Set mouse window, cursor on entry to window
wFullMouseWindow	Force to full mouse window on entry
wResizable	Can be resized and zoomed
wAllMouseEvents	Any combination of mouse buttons anywhere exits
wStoreContents	Store window contents in streams

In the line

```
ESPayoff.wFrame.AddShadow(shBR,         {shadow falls below and right}
                          shOverWrite); {opaque shadow}
```

the options are

shBR	shadow falls to bottom and right of frame
shBL	shadow falls to bottom and left of frame

and for the second argument

shOverWrite	opaque shadow
shSeeThru	transparent shadow

In the line

```
ESPayoff.wFrame.AddHeader(' Convert Interest Earned to Percent ',
                          heTC);
```

the options for the last parameter are

heTL	top left
heTC	top center

heTR	top right
heBL	bottom left
heBC	bottom center
heBR	bottom right

In the lines

```
ESPayoff.esFieldOptionsOn(efRequired);  {some input required}
ESPayoff.esFieldOptionsOff(efRequired); {cancel required}
```

popular options are

efProtected	not changeable
efHidden	not displayed, field cannot be moved to it
efInvisible	field is never drawn
efRequired	some entry required
efBeepOnError	invalid entry
efClearFirstChar	if first character entered during editing is character, clear the field

There are many, many more options. See the documentation on OpField for their names and descriptions. Note that these options can be used in methods other than esFieldOptionsOn and esFieldOptionsOff.

A very large number of field types are available that can be used in data entry screens, of which the following is only one example:

```
ESPayoff.AddRealField('Amount of loan:', {prompt}
                      4,                  {V prompt position}
                      6,                  {H prompt position}
                      '999999.99',        {picture}
                      4,                  {data V position}
                      21,                 {data H position}
                      26,                 {help ID number}
                      0.01,               {minimum valid entry}
                      999999.99,          {maximum valid entry}
                      2,                  {number of decimal places}
                      Loan);              {data variable}
```

The parameters of the various entry types are similar.

A full list of the Add fields consists of

AddArrayField	array of char
AddBcdField	binary coded decimal
AddBooleanField	Boolean response
AddByteField	byte
AddCharField	single character
AddChoiceField	for enumerated types, see HeaderInfo in LoanHead

AddCompField	comp precision
AddDateField	date—MM/DD/YY(YY)
AddDateStField	date string—ie: 16 Jan 1990
AddDblField	double precision
AddExtField	extended precision
AddIntField	integer
AddLongField	long integer
AddMultiLineField	edit string array
AddNestedField	brings up another entry screen when entered
AddNestedStringField	brings up another entry screen when entered
AddPickStringField	choose from pick list
AddRealField	real
AddSglField	single precision
AddShortField	short integer
AddStringField	string
AddTimeField	hours, minutes, seconds
AddUserField	user-defined field
AddWordField	word
AddYesNoField	yes/no choice—returns True/False

(uses simple character editor, no true pictures)

AddSimpleBcdField	binary coded decimal
AddSimpleBooleanField	Boolean
AddSimpleByteField	byte
AddSimpleCharField	character
AddSimpleCompField	comp
AddSimpleDblField	double precision
AddSimpleExtField	extended precision
AddSimpleIntField	integer
AddSimpleRealField	real
AddSimpleShortField	short integer
AddSimpleSngField	single precision
AddSimpleStringField)	string
AddSimpleWordField	word
AddSimpleYesNoField	yes or no—returns True or False

(uses number editor for numeric only fields)

AddNumericBcdField	binary coded decimal
AddNumericByteField	byte

AddNumericCompField	comp
AddNumericDblField	double precision
AddNumericExtField	extended precision
AddNumericIntField	integer
AddNumericLongField	long integer
AddNumericRealField	real
AddNumericShortField	short integer
AddNumericSngField	single precision
AddNumericWordField	word

See the documentation for OpEntry to get more details and parameter lists for each type.

Most fields have a picture parameter. The meaning of the picture characters is as follows:

X	Any character
!	Any character, force uppercase
L	Any character, force lowercase
x	Any character, first letter of each word upper-, others lowercase
a	Alphabetical characters only
A	Alphabetical characters only, force uppercase
l	Alphabetical characters only, force lowercase
9	Numbers and spaces only
#	Numbers, spaces, minus, period
E	Numbers, spaces, minus, period, e
K	0–9, A–F, force upper case (hex)
B	T, t, F, f (Boolean)
Y	Y, y, N, n

Date and time characters:

m	Month, zero-padded
M	Month, blank-padded
d	Day, zero-padded
D	Day, blank-padded
y	Year, zero-padded
n	Month name
N	Month name, force uppercase
w	Weekday
W	Weekday, force uppercase
/	Month, day, year separator
h	Hours, zero-padded

H	Hours, blank-padded
m	Minutes, zero-padded
M	Minutes, blank-padded
s	Seconds, zero-padded
S	Seconds, blank-padded
t	"p" or "a" in am/pm
e	"m" in am/pm
:	Minutes, hours, seconds separator

OSimple.pas

The next example contains a menu, a dialog box, and a pick list. This little program demonstrates how to set up a menu and dialog box, how to include a pick list in a dialog box as a child process, and how to use a "hook," which is available to immediately respond to a single mouse click or the press of the enter key on the pick list choice. The example following this one shows a delayed response.

```
{$V-}
{$I OPDEFINE.INC} {standard define list}

program OSimple;
{Menu, Dialog box, one button, and Pick list example}

uses
  Dos,
  OpRoot,
  OpDos,
  OpCrt,
{$IFDEF UseMouse}
  OpMouse,
{$ENDIF}
  OpCmd,
  OpField,
  OpCtrl,
  OpFrame,
  OpMenu,
  OpWindow,
  OpPick,
  OpSelect,
  OpDialog,
  OpString;

{$I COLORS.INC}  {designated color list}
```

```
const
  miGreetings    = 1;           {menu choice identifier}
  miShow         = 2;           {menu choice identifier}
  miQuit         = 3;           {menu choice identifier}
  hiWindow       = 0;           {dialog box choice identifier}
  hiCancel       = hiWindow+1;  {dialog box choice identifier}

  idWindow       = 0;           {not used}
  idCancel       = idWindow+1;  {not used}

var
  M                : Menu;           {object instance, OpMenu}
  DB               : DialogBox;      {object instance, OpDialog}
  PL               : PickList;       {object instance, OpPick}
  PLP              : PickListPtr;    {pick list pointer, OpPick}
  Status           : Word;           {init result in main program}
  Finished         : Boolean;        {process flag in main program}
  S                : String;         {temporary display string}

const
  RList : array[1..3] of string[14] = (   {list of three items}
    {01} 'Wonderful',                     {of no more than length 14}
    {02} 'So So',                         {for pick list}
    {03} 'Terrible');


function InitMenu : Word;
const
  {Frame constants}
  Frame1 = '╒╘╕╛══││';          {characters to form menu}
  Frame2 = '╤╘╧╛══││';          {characters to form submenu}
  WinOptions = wBordered        {leave room for border}
             +wClear            {clear window when first displayed}
             +wUserContents;    {user will replace contents if required}
var
  Result : String;   {store name choice}


begin
  with M do  {instance of Menu}
  begin
    if not InitCustom( 2,2,16,2,        {position - X1,Y1,X2,Y2}
                       Colors,          {from colors.inc}
                       WinOptions,      {menu display characteristics
                                         itemized above}
                       Horizontal) then {multiple choices displayed H}
    begin
      InitMenu := InitStatus; {function return if init failed}
      Exit;
    end;
```

```
    mnOptionsOn(mnAlphaMatch         {check for alphabetic matches}
                +mnSelectOnMatch     {implicit enter on alphabetic
                                      character match}
                +mnArrowSelect       {select submenus with arrow keys}
                +mnAllHotSpots);     {exit on any mouse menu hotspot
                                      (default is no hotspots)}
                                     {OpMenu}

    mnOPtionsOff(mnAllowPending      {submenu stays down after passing no
                                      submenu}
                 +mnPopOnSelect      {erase current submenu after
                                      selection}
                 +mnUseItemForTopic  {use current highlighted item for
                                      help topic}
                 +mnSelectOnClick);  {implicit enter on first mouse
                                      click}
                                     {OpMenu}

    wFrame.SetFrameType(Frame1);      {menu frame characters, OpFrame}

    AddItem('Greetings',     {menu choice, OpMenu}
            2,               {H position from frame edge}
            1,               {char position to use for character select}
            miGreetings);    {menu choice identifier}

    AddFramedSubMenu(3,4,9,5,    {submenu position - X1,Y1,X2,Y2}
                     Vertical,   {submenu item orientation}
                     Frame2);    {submenu frame characters}
                                 {OpMenu}

      AddItem('Show',        {submenu choice, OpMenu}
              1,             {first row}
              1,             {char position to use for character select}
              miShow);       {menu choice identifier}

      AddItem('Quit',        {submenu choice, OpMenu}
              2,             {second row}
              1,             {char position to use for character select}
              miQuit);       {menu choice identifier}
      ItemsDone;                     {no more submenu items, OpMenu}
    ItemsDone;                       {no more menu items, OpMenu}
    InitMenu := GetLastError;        {function return value}
  end;
end;

{$F+}  {use far memory}
procedure ResponseChoice(Item : Word;               {item number in pick
                                                     list, OpPick}
                         Mode : pkMode;             {Pick list mode,
                                                     OpPick}
```

```
                        var IType : pkItemType; {item type, OpPick}
                        var IString : string;   {item displayed in pick
                                                 list, OpPick}
                        PickPtr : PickListPtr); {make pick list methods
                                                 available, OpPick}
{Return a state string given an index}
begin
  if Mode = pkGetType then {just looking}
    Exit;
  IString := RList[Item];  {pick list choice to return}
end;
{$F-} {turn off far memory}


procedure Display(PLP : PickListPtr); far; {called by SetMoveProc,
                                            OpPick}
{process pick list commands}
begin
  {get rid of trailing spaces after pick list choice, add question
   mark, and pad right with spaces to cover previous displayed choice}
  S := Pad(TrimTrail(PL.GetLastChoiceString) + '?',10); {OpString,
                                                         OpPick}
  FastText(S,11,22); {string to display, absolute Y1, X1} {OpCrt}

  case PL.GetLastChoice of {item number of choice, OpPick}
    1 : FastText('That''s great!  ',13,22); {string to display, absolute
                                              Y1, X1, OpCrt}
    2 : FastText('Could be worse!',13,22);  {string to display, absolute
                                              Y1, X1, OpCrt}
    3 : FastText('Join the club! ',13,22);  {string to display, absolute
                                              Y1, X1, OpCrt}
  end;
end;


function InitPickList : Word; {Initialize pick list}
const
  WinOptions = wClear             {clear window when displayed}
             +wUserContents       {user will replace contents if
                                   required}
             +wNoCoversBuffer;    {does not retain copy of portion of
                                   window covered}
                                  {OpWindow}
begin
  with PL do
  begin
    if not InitCustom( 23, 8, 38, 13,      {absolute X1,Y1,X2,Y2}
                       Colors,             {from colors.inc}
                       WinOptions,         {display options}
```

```
                          14,                  {max width of choices}
                          3,                   {number of choices}
                          ResponseChoice,      {proc to use to get choice}
                          PickVertical,        {highlight moves vertically}
                          SingleChoice) then   {one choice, as opposed to
                                                multiple}
                                               {OpPick}
    begin
      InitPickList := InitStatus;  {init failure return value, OpPick}
      Exit;
    end;

    with dColors do
    begin
      SetTextAttr(ClusterColor,ClusterMono);  {text color from
                                                colors.inc, see OpCrt}
      SetPickAttr(pkNormal,       {item type, OpPick}
                  False,          {use colors when not selected}
                  ClusterColor,   {choice of colors from Colors.inc}
                  ClusterMono);
    end;

    SetPadSize(1, 1);  {Add one space to each end of choices, OpPick}

    SetMoveProc(Display);  {User hook, immediate reaction to any
                            pick list choice change, OpPick}

    InitPickList := RawError;   {function return value}
  end;
end;


function InitDialogBox : Word;  {Initialize dialog box}
const
  WinOptions = wBordered          {leave room for border around window}
               +wClear            {clear window when displayed}
               +wUserContents;    {user will replace contents if required}
                                  {OpWindow}
begin
  with DB do
  begin
    {initialize dialog box, OpDialog}
    if not InitCustom( 20, 5, 60, 15,  {absolute X1,Y1,X2,Y2}
                       Colors,         {from colors.inc}
                       WinOptions,     {display options}
                       dColors) then   {dialog box colors from
                                        colors.inc}
      begin
        InitDialogBox := InitStatus;   {init failed}
        Exit;
```

```
      end;

    with wFrame, Colors do
    begin
      {$IFDEF UseShadows}
        AddShadow(shBR, shSeeThru); {shadow Bottom Right, see thru
                                     shadow, OpFrame}
      {$ENDIF}
    end;

    AddCenteredTextField('Hi there!',1); {dialog box title, relative row
                                          1, OpSelect}

    {idWindow:} {add a child window to hold pick list, OpDialog}
    AddWindowControl('How are you today?', {pick list title}
                     02,4,      {Prompt relative Y,X}
                     3,3,       {window upper-left relative Y,X}
                     hiWindow,  {child window identifier}
                     ccNone,    {help}
                     PL);       {object to place in child window}

    {idCancel:}
    AddPushButton('Cancel',  {button text}
                  9,30,      {relative Y,X of upper-left corner}
                  8,         {button text width}
                  hiCancel,  {button identifier}
                  ccQuit,    {button return value}
                  False);    {default button?}
                             {OpDialog}

    InitDialogBox := RawError; {function return value}
  end;
end;


{main}
begin
  Status := InitMenu;   {initialize Menu}
  if Status <> 0 then   {error numbers in appendix D}
  begin
    WriteLn('Error initializing Menu: ', Status);
    Halt(1);
  end;

  Status := InitPickList; {initialize PickList}
  if Status <> 0 then     {error numbers in appendix D}
  begin
    WriteLn('Error initializing PickList: ', Status);
    Halt(1);
  end;
```

```
Status := InitDialogBox; {initialize DialogBox}
if Status <> 0 then      {error numbers in appendix D}
begin
  WriteLn('Error initializing DialogBox: ', Status);
  Halt(1);
end;

if MouseInstalled then {OpMouse}
  with Colors do
  begin
    {activate mouse cursor, OpMouse}
    SoftMouseCursor($0000, {mouse has own software cursor}
                (ColorMono(MouseColor, MouseMono) shl 8)+
                          Byte(MouseChar));
    {enable mouse support}
    DialogCommands.cpOptionsOn(cpEnableMouse); {dialog box sees mouse}
    MenuCommands.cpOptionsOn(cpEnableMouse);   {menu sees mouse}
    PickCommands.cpOptionsOn(cpEnableMouse);   {pick list sees mouse}
                                               {CommandProcessor}
  end;

PLP := @PL; {pointer to pick list object for display procedure}

{fill in a backdrop}
TextAttr := $07; {background attribute}
TextChar := '▒'; {background design}
ClrScr;

repeat
  ShowMouse;                          {OpMouse}
  M.Draw;                             {draw menu, OpMenu}
  M.Process;                          {process menu commands, OpMenu}
  if M.GetlastCommand = ccSelect then {Greetings choice selected,
                                       OpWindow, OpCmd}
    if M.MenuChoice = miShow then     {show submenu choice selected,
                                       OpMenu}
    begin
      M.Erase;                        {erase menu, OpMenu}
      DB.Draw;                        {display dialog box, OpDialog}
      ShowMouse;                      {OpMouse}
      Finished := False;              {done?}
      repeat
        DB.Process;                     {get any dialog box commands,
                                         OpDialog}
        if (DB.GetLastCommand = ccQuit) {button pushed, OpWindow,
                                         OpCmd}
          or (DB.GetLastCommand = ccError) then {OpWindow, OpCmd
          {process dialog box commands}
          begin
            Finished := True; {done with dialog box}
```

```
                DB.Erase;          {erase dialog box, OpDialog}
              end;
          until Finished;          {keep looping until button pushed or
                                    escape key pressed}
        end;
    until M.MenuChoice = miQuit; {Quit submenu choice made}
    DB.Done; {remove dialog box from memory, OpDialog}
    M.Erase; {erase menu, OpMenu}
    M.Done;  {remove menu from memory, OpMenu}

    ClrScr;
  end.
```

The window options are the same as those for a dialog box and are listed earlier in the chapter.

In the code

```
mnOptionsOn(mnAlphaMatch           {}
            +mnSelectOnMatch
            +mnArrowSelect
            +mnAllHotSpots);
```

and

```
mnOPtionsOff(mnAllowPending
             +mnPopOnSelect
             +mnUseItemForTopic
             +mnSelectOnClick);
```

the list of available options is

mnAllHotSpots	exit on any menu mouse hotspot (default is no hotspots)
mnAllowPending	submenu stays down after passing no submenu
mnAlphaMatch	check for alphabetic matches
mnArrowSelect	select submenus with arrow keys
mnMainHighlight	highlight alpha search characters on high-level menu
mnMainSelect	display top-level menu bar
mnMouseSupport	used by MakeMenu (Turbo Power utility)
mnPopOnSelect	erase current submenu after selection
mnSelectOnClick	implicit Enter on first mouse click
mnSelectOnMatch	implicit Enter on alphabetic character match
mnUseItemForTopic	use current highlighted item for help topic

The procedure

```
{$F+}  {use far memory}
procedure ResponseChoice(Item : Word;           {item number in pick
                                                 list, OpPick}
```

```
                         Mode : pkMode;          {Pick list mode,
                                                  OpPick}
                         var IType : pkItemType; {item type, OpPick}
                         var IString : string;   {item displayed in pick
                                                  list, OpPick}
                         PickPtr : PickListPtr); {make pick list methods
                                                  available, OpPick}
{Return a state string given an index}
begin
  if Mode = pkGetType then {just looking}
    Exit;
  IString := RList[Item];  {pick list choice to return}
end;
{$F-} {turn off far memory}
```

is required by the PickList object's initialization code. It is used by the program to tell the picklist how to display each item in the list. It also handles such things as protected fields, shape of the picklist, how many items can be selected, and other options to be discussed shortly.

First we'll discuss the Mode argument. Setting this argument to pkMode permits the PickList object to set the Mode to one of the following values as required:

pkDisplay	the string will be used for display and should include control characters for flexwrite (OpCrt) formatting used by the PickList object
pkSearch	the string will be used for searching and should not include padding or control characters
pkGetType	just check to see if string is normal or protected

The next sample program (OSimple2.pas) gives an example of adding a protected item.

Setting the IType argument to pkItemType lets the PickList object set IType to one of the following values:

pkNormal	video attributes defined for this type in Colors.Inc.
pkAlternate	video attributes defined for this type in Colors.Inc.
pkProtected	item can't be highlighted or selected
pkPrivate	reserved

IString is usually set to "string," but you could use a function to return different values depending on the item number and other circumstances. However, this function should be short and efficient as it is called very frequently.

The next two lines are added to save processing time.

```
if Mode = pkGetType then {just looking}
  Exit;
```

Finally, the last line determines what items will be displayed in the pick list and how they will be formatted.

```
IString := RList[Item];   {pick list choice to return}
```

Here's a more interesting example from the LoanPick.pas unit:

```
{string content to display}
  IString := ' ' + DateToDateString('mm/dd/yyyy',PayList[Item].PayDate)
             + ' ' + Real2Str(PayList[Item].Amount,9,2) + ' ';
```

The InitPickList function initializes the picklist and displays the choices. It contains the line

```
SetMoveProc(Display); {User hook, immediate reaction to any
                       choice change, OpPick}
```

which displays an appropriate response whenever a choice is made. The procedure it calls is

```
procedure Display(PLP : PickListPtr); far; {called by SetMoveProc}
{process pick list commands}
begin
  {get rid of trailing spaces after pick list choice, add question
   mark, and pad right with spaces to cover previous displayed choice}
  S := Pad(TrimTrail(PL.GetLastChoiceString) + '?',10); {OpString,
                                                         OpPick}
  FastText(S,11,22); {string to display, absolute Y1, X1} {OpCrt}

  case PL.GetLastChoice of {item number of choice, OpPick}
    1 : FastText('That''s great!  ',13,22); {string to display, absolute
                                             Y1, X1, OpCrt}
    2 : FastText('Could be worse!',13,22);  {string to display, absolute
                                             Y1, X1, OpCrt}
    3 : FastText('Join the club! ',13,22);  {string to display, absolute
                                             Y1, X1, OpCrt}
  end;
end;
```

The PLP variable was set with the line

```
PLP := @PL; {pointer to pick list object for display procedure}
```

which can be found in the main program code.

In InitPickList the first line sets the window options. The contents of DefWindowOptions and the other possible options were described after the DialogBx unit earlier in this chapter.

Next, the window to contain the pick list is initialized. Most of the arguments are explained by the annotation. The "ResponseChoice" argument determines the function to use to designate what goes into the pick list and how to display it. This is the function described earlier. Next we see the "PickVertical" argument. The possible options here are

PickVertical — If more than one column is used (determine with the column width setting), starting with the leftmost column, the highlight moves vertically down each column, to the end of the column even if not currently in the window (the window contents scroll up as necessary), to the top of the next column, and so forth.

PickHorizontal — If more than one column is used (determine with the column width setting), beginning with the top row, the highlight moves horizontally across each row, moving downward.

PickSnaking — If more than one column is used (determine with the column width setting), the highlight moves, starting with the left column, vertically down each column, to the end of the column visible in the window, then to the top of the next column, and so on.

The next argument, SingleChoice, has one other option, MultipleChoice. Obviously, this permits more than one selection from the pick list.

Another possible option is to set up a search method with, for example,

```
PL.SetSearchMode(PickCharSearch);   {OpPick}
```

I did not choose to do so in this example. The options available for this procedure are

PickStringSearch — This search method permits the user to enter a series of characters. As each is matched in the list, the highlight moves to that item. Thus entering "A" would match item "AAA." Entering "B" would move the highlight to item "ABA." As each character is entered and matched, it is added to an internal string with a length determined by the constant pkMaxSearchLen with a default value of 15. A nonmatching character will clear the internal string and not move the highlight. To choose the highlighted item, press the Enter key.

PickAltStringSearch — This works like the previous option, except that if a nonmatching character is entered, the internal string is cleared, set to the new character, and an attempt is made to match the new character. If not successful the highlight doesn't move and the internal string is cleared. To choose the highlighted item, press the Enter key.

PickCharSearch — An attempt is made to match only the first character of each item. If the same character is entered, a match further down the list of items is

	attempted. To choose the highlighted item, press the Enter key.
PickCharExit	An attempt is made to match the character entered with the first character of the list of items. If a match is found, that item is selected and the pick list is exited.
PickAnyCharExit	No attempt to match an item is made. Entry of any character exits the pick list. GetLastCommand will return ccChar, containing the character entered.

Protected items are never matched. The search is not case sensitive.

```
with dColors do
begin
  SetTextAttr(ClusterColor,ClusterMono); {text color from
                                          colors.inc, see OpColor}
```

is from OpColor. The choices are taken from the Colors.inc file.

```
     SetPickAttr(pkNormal,      {item type}
                 False,         {use colors when not selected}
                 ClusterColor,  {choice colors from colors.inc}
                 ClusterMono);
   end;
```

is an OpPick method to set the color attributes of the pick choices. The possible item types were listed earlier. If the second parameter is set to True, the designated attributes apply when the highlight bar is positioned over the item; otherwise this does not occur.

The dialog box options except for the AddWindowControl method were discussed earlier.

```
{idWindow:} {add a child window - to hold pick list, OpDialog}
AddWindowControl('How are you today?', {pick list title}
                 2,4,        {Prompt relative Y,X}
                 3,3,        {window upper-left relative Y,X}
                 hiWindow,   {child window identifier, a constant set
                              at beginning of the module}
                 ccNone,     {help}
                 PL);        {object to place in child window}
```

is used to place the pick list in the dialog box as a child window. The annotation makes the parameters clear.

In the main program code, first all three objects are initialized.

```
Status := InitMenu;    {initialize Menu}
if Status <> 0 then    {error numbers in appendix D}
begin
  WriteLn('Error initializing Menu: ', Status);
```

```
    Halt(1);
  end;


  Status := InitPickList; {initialize PickList}
  if Status <> 0 then     {error numbers in appendix D}
  begin
    WriteLn('Error initializing PickList: ', Status);
    Halt(1);
  end;


  Status := InitDialogBox; {initialize DialogBox}
  if Status <> 0 then      {error numbers in appendix D}
  begin
    WriteLn('Error initializing DialogBox: ', Status);
    Halt(1);
  end;
```

Next the mouse is made available and the user is permitted to make a choice from the picklist via the Process method. Once a choice is made, the mouse is hidden again to avoid leaving tracks on the screen.

The pick list is erased. The number of the item that was highlighted when the Enter key was pressed is stored in the global PayChoice variable. Finally, the instance of the PickList object is removed from memory.

Next the mouse is made available to the PickList, DialogBox, and Menu objects with

```
if MouseInstalled then {OpMouse}
 with Colors do
 begin
   {activate mouse cursor, OpMouse}
   SoftMouseCursor($0000, {mouse has own software cursor}
                  (ColorMono(MouseColor, MouseMono) shl 8)+
                            Byte(MouseChar));
   {enable mouse support}
   DialogCommands.cpOptionsOn(cpEnableMouse); {dialog box sees mouse}
   MenuCommands.cpOptionsOn(cpEnableMouse);   {menu sees mouse}
   PickCommands.cpOptionsOn(cpEnableMouse);   {pick list sees mouse}
                                              {CommandProcessor}
 end;
```

Finally the menu is processed. The ShowMouse procedure displays the mouse cursor. M.Process gets the menu choice. If "Greetings" is selected, we go to the dialog box. Because the pick list is a child window, it is available too. Any choice made in the pick list actuates the Display procedure via the SetMoveProc method, as discussed earlier.

Finally, when the "Cancel" dialog box button is pressed, we return to the menu. When "Quit" choice is selected from the menu, the program ends.

OSimple2.pas

The second example also contains a menu, dialog box, and pick list. This little program demonstrates how to set up a menu and dialog box, how to include a pick list in a dialog box as a child process, and how to respond to a double mouse click or the press of the enter key on the pick list choice. Note that the Choose button has to be pressed to permit a pick list choice.

OSimple2.pas Details

Here is a somewhat different version of the preceding example. It demonstrates how to set up a pick list in a dialog box and change the focus between the dialog box and the pick list by means of the dialog box pushbuttons. As you'll remember, in the previous version, the pick list and dialog box both were always ready for use. To make a choice from the pick list in this version, first press the Choose button, then make the pick list choice. If you wish to make another choice, you have to push the button again.

Since these two examples are so much alike, I will discuss only the few differences.

```
{$V-}
{$I OPDEFINE.INC} {standard define list}

program OSimple2;
  {Menu, Dialog box, and Pick list example,
   two button version of greetings}
uses
  Dos,
  OpRoot,
  OpDos,
  OpCrt,
{$IFDEF UseMouse}
  OpMouse,
{$ENDIF}
  OpCmd,
  OpField,
  OpCtrl,
  OpFrame,
  OpMenu,
  OpWindow,
  OpPick,
  OpSelect,
  OpDialog,
  OpString;

{$I COLORS.INC}  {designated color list}

  miGreetings    = 1;          {menu choice identifier}
```

```
    miShow          = 2;           {menu choice identifier}
    miQuit          = 3;           {menu choice identifier}
    hiWindow        = 0;           {dialog box choice identifier}
    hiChoose        = hiWindow+1;  {dialog box choice identifier}
    hiCancel        = hiChoose+1;  {dialog box choice identifier}

    idWindow        = 0;           {not used}
    idChoose        = idWindow+1;  {not used}
    idCancel        = idChoose+1;  {not used}

  var
    M                   : Menu;           {menu object instance}
    DB                  : DialogBox;      {dialog box object instance}
    PL                  : PickList;       {pick list object instance}
    Status              : Word;           {init result in main program}
    Finished            : Boolean;        {process flag in main program}
    S                   : String;         {temporary display string}

  const
    RList : array[1..4] of string[14] = (  {list of four items}
      {01} 'Wonderful',                    {of length 14}
      {02} 'So So    ',                    {for pick list}
      {03} 'Terrible ',
      {04} 'Yuk!     ');

  function InitMenu : Word;
  const
    {Frame constants}
    Frame1 = '╒╕╘╛══││';         {characters to form menu}
    Frame2 = '╤╘╧╛══││';         {characters to form submenu}
    WinOptions = wBordered         {leave room for border}
                 +wClear           {clear window when first displayed
                 +wUserContents;   {user will replace window contents if
                                    required
  var
    Result : String;   {store name choice}

  begin
    with M do   {instance of Menu}
    begin
      if not InitCustom( 2,2,16,2,    {position - X1,Y1,X2,Y2}
                         Colors,      {from colors.inc}
                         WinOptions,  {menu display characteristics
                                       itemized above}
                         Horizontal) then {multiple choices displayed H}
      begin
        InitMenu := InitStatus;   {function return if init failed}
        Exit;
      end;
      mnOptionsOn(mnAlphaMatch         {check for alphabetic matches}
```

```
              +mnSelectOnMatch     {implicit enter on alphabetic
                                    character match}
              +mnArrowSelect       {select submenus with arrow keys}
              +mnAllHotSpots);     {exit on any mouse menu hotspot
                                    (default is no hotspots)}
                                   {OpMenu}

    mnOptionsOff(mnAllowPending    {submenu stays down after passing no
                                    submenu}
               +mnPopOnSelect      {erase current submenu after
                                    selection}
               +mnUseItemForTopic  {use current highlighted item for
                                    help topic}
               +mnSelectOnClick);  {implicit enter on first mouse
                                    click}
                                   {OpMenu}

    wFrame.SetFrameType(Frame1);    {menu frame characters, OpFrame}

    AddItem('Greetings',   {menu choice}
            2,             {H position from frame edge}
            1,             {char position to use for character select}
            miGreetings);  {menu choice identifier}
                           {OpMenu}

    AddFramedSubMenu(3,4,9,5,  {submenu position - X1,Y1,X2,Y2}
                   Vertical,   {submenu item orientation}
                   Frame2);    {submenu frame characters}
                               {OpMenu}

      AddItem('Show',     {submenu choice}
              1,          {first row}
              1,          {char position to use for character select}
              miShow);    {menu choice identifier}
                          {OpMenu}


      AddItem('Quit',     {submenu choice}
              2,          {second row}
              1,          {char position to use for character select}
              miQuit);    {menu choice identifier}
      ItemsDone;                 {no more submenu items, OpMenu}
    ItemsDone;                   {no more menu items, OpMenu}
    InitMenu := GetLastError;  {function return value, OpCmd}
  end;
end;

{$F+}  {use far memory}
procedure ResponseChoice(Item : Word;            {item number in pick
                                                  list, OpPick}
```

```
                          Mode : pkMode;            {Pick list mode,
                                                     OpPick}
                          var IType : pkItemType;  {item type, OpPick}
                          var IString : string;    {item displayed in pick
                                                     list, OpPick}
                          PickPtr : PickListPtr);  {make pick list methods
                                                     available, OpPick}
{Return a state string given an index}
begin
  if Item = 3 then          {third pick list choice}
     IType := pkProtected; {can't be chosen, displayed in ProItemColor}

  if Mode = pkGetType then {just looking}
    Exit;
  IString := RList[Item];   {pick list choice to return}
end;
{$F-} {turn off far memory}


function InitPickList : Word; {Initialize pick list}
const
  WinOptions = wClear               {clear window when displayed}
             +wUserContents         {user will replace window contents if
                                      required}
             +wNoCoversBuffer;      {does not retain a copy of portion of
                                      screen covered}
begin
  with PL do
  begin
    if not InitCustom( 23, 8, 38, 13,      {absolute X1,Y1,X2,Y2}
                       Colors,              {from colors.inc}
                       WinOptions,          {display options}
                       14,                  {max width of choices}
                       4,                   {number of choices}
                       ResponseChoice,      {proc to use to get choice}
                       PickVertical,        {page 4-194}
                       SingleChoice) then {one choice, as opposed to
                                            multiple}
                                           {OpPick}
    begin
      InitPickList := InitStatus; {init failure return value}
      Exit;
    end;

    with dColors do
    begin
      SetTextAttr(ClusterColor,ClusterMono); {text color from
                                               colors.inc, see OpCrt}
      SetPickAttr(pkNormal,      {item type, OpPick}
```

```
                  False,        {use colors when not selected}
                  ClusterColor, {choice colors from colors.inc}
                  ClusterMono);
    end;

    SetPadSize(1, 1); {Add one space to each end of choices, OpPick}

    InitPickList := RawError;  {function return value}
  end;
end;


function InitDialogBox : Word; {Initialize dialog box}
const
  WinOptions = wBordered          {leave room for border}
             +wClear              {clear window when displayed}
             +wUserContents;      {user will replace window contents if
                                   required}
                                  {OpWindow}
begin
  with DB do
  begin
    {instantiate dialog box, OpDialog}
    if not InitCustom( 20, 5, 60, 15, {absolute X1,Y1,X2,Y2}
                       Colors,        {from colors.inc}
                       WinOptions,    {display options}
                       dColors) then  {dialog box colors from
                                       colors.inc}
    begin
      InitDialogBox := InitStatus;  {init failed}
      Exit;
    end;

    with wFrame, Colors do begin  {OpFrame}
      {$IFDEF UseShadows}
        AddShadow(shBR, shSeeThru); {shadow Bottom Right, see thru
                                     shadow, OpFrame}
      {$ENDIF}

    end;

    AddCenteredTextField('Hi there!',1); {dialog box title, relative row
                                          1, OpSelect}

  {idWindow:} {add a child window - to hold pick list, OpDialog}
    AddWindowControl('How are you today?', {pick list title}
                     02,4,      {Prompt relative Y,X}
                     3,3,       {window upper-left relative Y,X}
                     hiWindow,  {child window identifier}
                     ccNone,    {help}
```

```
                        PL);        {object to place in child window}

    {idChoose}
      AddPushButton('Choose',   {button text}
                     3,30,      {relative Y,X of upper-left corner}
                     8,         {button text width}
                     hiChoose,  {button identifier}
                     ccSelect,  {button return value}
                     True);     {default button?}
                                {OpDialog}

    {idCancel:}
      AddPushButton('Cancel',   {button text}
                     9,30,      {relative Y,X of upper-left corner}
                     8,         {button text width}
                     hiCancel,  {button identifier}
                     ccQuit,    {button return value}
                     False);    {default button?}
                                {OpDialog}

      InitDialogBox := RawError; {function return value}

    end;
  end;


  {main}
  begin
    Status := InitMenu;   {initialize Menu}
    if Status <> 0 then   {error numbers in appendix D}
    begin
      WriteLn('Error initializing Menu: ', Status);
      Halt(1);
    end;

    Status := InitPickList;   {initialize PickList}
    if Status <> 0 then       {error numbers in appendix D}
    begin
      WriteLn('Error initializing PickList: ', Status);
      Halt(1);
    end;

    Status := InitDialogBox; {initialize DialogBox}
    if Status <> 0 then      {error numbers in appendix D}
    begin
      WriteLn('Error initializing DialogBox: ', Status);
      Halt(1);
    end;

    if MouseInstalled then
```

```
  with Colors do begin
    {activate mouse cursor, OpMouse}
    SoftMouseCursor($0000, {mouse has own software cursor}
                (ColorMono(MouseColor, MouseMono) shl 8)+
                         Byte(MouseChar));
    {enable mouse support}
    DialogCommands.cpOptionsOn(cpEnableMouse); {dialog box sees mouse}
    MenuCommands.cpOptionsOn(cpEnableMouse);   {menu sees mouse}
    PickCommands.cpOptionsOn(cpEnableMouse);   {pick list sees mouse}
                                               {CommandProcessor}
  end;

{fill in a backdrop}
TextAttr := $07; {background attribute}
TextChar := '▒'; {background design}
ClrScr;

finished := False; {when true dialog box is no longer needed}

repeat
  ShowMouse; {OpMouse}
  M.Draw;    {draw menu, OpMenu}
  M.Process; {process menu commands, OpMenu}
  if M.GetlastCommand = ccSelect then {Greetings choice selected
                                       OpWindow, OpCmd}
    if M.MenuChoice = miShow then     {show submenu choice selected,
                                       OpMenu}
    begin
      M.Erase;             {erase menu, OpMenu}
      DB.Draw;             {display dialog box, OpDialog}
      ShowMouse;
      Finished := False; {done?}
      repeat
        DB.Process;        {get any dialog box commands, OpDialog}
        case DB.GetLastCommand of
          ccSelect : {choose button pushed, OpCmd}
          begin
            {process pick list commands}
            {click and press return or click twice}
            PL.Process; {get any pick list commands, OpPick}
            if PL.GetLastCommand = ccSelect then {choice made}
                                                 OpWindow, OpCmd}


            begin
              {get rid of trailing spaces after pick list choice, add
               question mark, and pad right with spaces to cover
               previous displayed choice}
             S := Pad(TrimTrail(PL.GetLastChoiceString) + '?',10);
                                                   {OpString, OpPick}
             FastText(S,12,22); {string to display, absolute Y1, X1,
```

```
                                        OpCrt}

                case PL.GetLastChoice of {item number of choice, OpPick}
                  1 : FastText('That''s great!  ',14,22); {string to
                                                           display,
                                                           absolute Y1,
                                                           X1, OpCrt}
                  2 : FastText('Could be worse!',14,22);  {string to
                                                           display,
                                                           absolute Y1,
                                                           X1, OpCrt}
                  3 : FastText('Join the club! ',14,22);  {string to
                                                           display,
                                                           absolute Y1,
                                                           X1, OpCrt}
                  4 : FastText('Must be Monday ',14,22);  {string to
                                                           display,
                                                           absolute Y1,
                                                           X1, OpCrt}
                end;
              end;
            end;

            ccQuit : {OpCmd}
            {process dialog box command}
              begin
                Finished := True; {done with dialog box}
                DB.Erase;         {erase dialog box, OpDialog}
              end;
          end;
        until Finished; {keep looping until button pushed or escape key
                         pressed}
      end;
    until M.MenuChoice = miQuit; {Quit submenu choice made, OpMenu, OpCmd}
    DB.Done;                     {remove dialog box from memory, OpDialog}
    M.Erase;                     {erase menu, OpMenu}
    M.Done;                      {remove menu from memory, OpMenu}

    ClrScr;
  end.
```

This example of ResponseChoice has a protected item to show how it's done. Use a line like the following from the example to protect an item from being chosen or to set an item to an alternate color with pkAlternate.

```
if Item = 3 then          {third pick list choice}
   IType := pkProtected;  {can't be chosen, displayed in ProItemColor}
```

The line must come before the following "if Mode . . ." line or it won't work. Of course, this could also be determined by a surrounding Case, possibly with included If statements to set different items to protected or alternate determined by the value of some variable.

The Display procedure is absent. The response display is found in the main part of the unit instead.

The call to SetMoveProc is not used because the pick list processing and displayed response is to be handled differently.

A second pushbutton, "Choose," has been added to choose the pick list.

In the main loop, the program waits for a menu choice. If it is "Quit," the program ends. If it is "Greetings," the menu is erased from the screen—not from memory. The dialog box (and pick list) is drawn. The mouse cursor is displayed next. Then the program loops until a pushbutton is pressed.

If it is the "Cancel" button, the dialog box is erased and the program returns to the menu. Should the user press the "Choose" button, the focus goes to the pick list by calling PL.Process. Then the pick list code takes over until a choice is made. When that occurs, the item picked is displayed below the pick list window. One of the four responses is selected depending on the pick list selection and displayed. The focus then moves back to the dialog box to wait for a button to be pressed again. Thus, the way this is written, the "Choose" button must be pressed to select from the pick list. Only one choice can be made. To choose again, you must press the "Choose" button again. Of course, you can change this around however you wish to get the effect you want.

5

The Loan Application, General

This chapter and the next two describe the first large application in this book. The application includes a menu, dialog boxes, a file pick list, several data pick lists, several data entry screens, use of the printer object, and other objects.

The objects used and discussed in this chapter are

- Menu and ancestors (OpMenu)
- DialogBox and ancestors (OpDialog)
- EntryScreen and ancestors (OpEntry)
- Various methods from objects in OpCrt, OpDate, OpString, OpMouse, OpInLine, and others.

The program is a useful one, used to print an amortization table or payment schedule. The user can enter payments that were not made on time or were for a different amount than that agreed upon. Here is a description of the program and its various menu choices. This material is much like that which would be provided to the end user. It will be followed by the annotated source for each module, together with some discussion of the code.

General Operational Description

This program is designed to produce amortization tables for loans. It has a few other associated features as well.

The loan payments can be weekly, semimonthly (twice a month), monthly, or yearly. A late charge can be added to the balance due, if desired. If a late charge is provided, you must select the number of days after the due date that must pass before the charge becomes effective—the grace period. Weekly payments are due on the same day of the week as the first payment-due date indicated. If monthly, the payments are due on the first payment-due day of every month. You should not use days after the 28th for the first monthly payment date because of February. If yearly, the payments are due every year on the first payment-due date. Obviously, avoid assigning February 29th. If you choose a semimonthly payment frequency, you must indicate the payment dates—the first any date between the 1st and 14th, the second from the 15th through the 28th. One of these must coincide with the date the first payment is due.

Loans of up to $999,999.99 can be entered. Payments and late charges of the same amount can be indicated as well. You can designate whether interest is to be charged from the date of the loan or from the first payment due date. If these two dates are the same, this information is moot.

When you indicate the amount of the payment as you first enter the loan information, be sure it will cover the interest charged between payment-due dates. If it will not, the printed table will never end, and eventually the number of digits allowed for the interest due and the balance will not be large enough ($999,999.99).

The program assumes that a payment of the correct amount was made on every due date unless you use the "Add Non-Standard Payments" from the Maintenance menu. You can use this to indicate a payment was made on a date other than the due date, or a payment of an amount other than that agreed upon, even $0. You must know the correct due date to use this feature.

Use "Print Table" from the Print menu to print the table. The Quit menu choice is used to leave the program.

Before you can add nonstandard payments or print a table, you must choose the correct debtor or create a new one. Use "Debtor" from the Choose menu for the first, or "Header" from the Create menu for the latter.

Two other useful features have been added to the program. One, "Interest Calculation," will calculate the equivalent compound interest rate if supplied with the loan or investment amount, the current balance or worth, and the date of each. A second feature tells you the payoff value of a loan made to be paid back as one installment on a date unknown at that time. Enter the loan amount, date of loan, interest rate in percent, and the payoff date when it becomes available. The program will tell you the amount of interest charged and the payoff amount, including the interest.

Program Operation by Menu Choice

Before we begin this section, note that to accept and use the information supplied to a data entry screen, press the Control Key. Then press the Enter key without releasing the Control key. In the future, this will be referred to as Ctrl-Enter. The Escape key can be used at any time to exit a data entry window. Any information entered since the last Ctrl-Enter will be discarded.

To select a menu from the menu bar click on the desired menu name with the mouse or use the Left- or Right-arrow to move to the desired menu, and press the Enter key. The menu choices available will be displayed in a submenu under the menu bar. To select from this submenu, click on it with the mouse or use the up- or down-arrow keys to move to the desired choice. You can also make a selection by entering the first letter of your choice and pressing the Enter key. The case does not need to match that displayed.

When in a data entry screen, you move from an entry to that under it by pressing the enter key. If your entry is not in the correct range, you cannot move to another entry field. If you try to leave the entire data entry screen with Ctrl-Enter without supplying some required data, the computer will beep and will not let you leave. The field where the required data is to be entered is selected for you. (The Escape key will always let you leave any time, but any information entered is discarded.) Examples of required information when filling in the debtor and loan information (Header) are the filename, debtor name, loan amount, and payment amount. Examples of information not required are the address and phone numbers of the debtor. In all the other data entry screens, all the entries are required. You can also move to another entry field by clicking on it with the mouse.

There is one entry field that gets its data in another way. This is the Payment Frequency field in the Debtor data entry screen. In this case you use the + and - keys to change the data in that field.

At times we will use the term "default value." This means the value supplied in the field before you make any entries. An example is all fields requiring a date default to the date the computer has stored as representing the current date. (In computers that do not set the date automatically, be sure to use the DOS Date command to enter the correct date. The current date is usually requested when you turn on the computer.)

Create Menu

You have three choices here. The first, "Header," permits you to add a new loan. You must supply the following information, so have it prepared:

- Filename: This is a group of up to eight letters. No spaces or other punctuation is allowed, only letters. The best choice is an abbreviation (if the name is too long) of the debtor's name. The name you choose must be unique; that is, no other file in the directory containing the Loan program can have that name. For example, you enter the filename as "Jones." The computer will create a file to hold this debtor's loan information. This file will be called JONES.HDR. No other files in that directory are permitted to have this name, so you must use a different name for different loans for lenders with identical names. Perhaps a second Jones loan could have the file name "Jones1." This information is required.
- Name: This entry permits up to 30 characters, including any spaces. If you have more than one loan out to this person or business, you may wish to

make the names used for each different in some manner so the name will tell you which loan you are working with. When you make menu selections that can alter the content of your debtor information or payment file, you will be shown this name and requested to verify that you wish to proceed. The first letter of every word you enter in this and the following three fields will automatically be capitalized, and the remaining letters will automatically be lowercase. You can override the lowercase with the Shift or Caps Lock key. This entry is required.

- Address line 1: Use this 30-character field to enter the debtor's address, such as street and number or post office box. This field is not required.
- Address line 2: This 30-character field is available if you need more room for the address. This field is not required either.
- City, State, Zip: Use this not-required 30-character field to enter the debtor's city, state, and ZIP code or foreign equivalent.
- Home phone: Enter the debtor's home telephone number in this field. Room to enter an area code is provided. This entry is not required.
- Business phone: Enter the debtor's business telephone number in this not-required field.
- Amount of loan: The loan amount goes here. The field will accept any amount between $0.01 and $999,999.99. Do not enter dollar signs or commas. The default is 0.00. This entry is required.
- Interest: Enter the interest rate in percent here. The acceptable values range from 0 to 99.999. The default is 0.000. This entry is required, but since the default 0.000 value is acceptable, you are not required to enter anything here.
- Amount of payment: The payment amount goes here. The field will accept any amount between $0.01 and $999,999.99. Do not enter dollar signs or commas. The default is 0.00. This entry is required. Be sure the payment is larger than the interest charged between payments. Thus, if you had a $1,000.00 loan at 12%, the monthly payment must be greater than $10.00. If you set it to $10.00 or less, no principle reduction will occur and the amortization table will run forever. This entry is required.
- Date of loan: The date the money was provided to the debtor should be entered here, in the format MM/DD/YYYY. The default is the current date. The program will check for a valid date. Thus, you cannot enter dates such as 02/30/1991 or 11/31/1991. This date will be referred to by the program only if you choose to start calculating interest at this date rather than the first payment date.
- Date of first payment: The date when the first payment is expected should be entered here in the format MM/DD/YYYY. This date can be the same as the loan date (previous field). The default is the current date. The program will check for a valid date. Thus, you cannot enter dates such as 02/30/1991 or 11/31/1991. Interest charges will begin on this date if you choose to start calculating interest on this date rather than the loan date.

If the payments are monthly, they are due on this day of the month every month. If the payments are weekly, they are due on this day of the week every week. If yearly payments are agreed upon, the payments are due in this month and on this day every year. If semimonthly payments are required, one of the designated payment days must match this day of the month. Avoid dates after the 28th of the month if the payment frequency is monthly (because of February) or February 29th if the frequency is yearly.

- Interest to first payment: Reply with "Y" if you wish to charge interest for the period between the loan date and first payment date. If the interest should start accumulating on the first payment date, then reply with an "N."
- Late charge: The late charge amount goes here. The field will accept any amount between $0.00 and $999,999.99. Do not enter dollar signs or commas. The default is 0.00. This is the amount that is added to the debt if the payment is made more than an indicated number of days after the due date. If you and the debtor agree that a payment can be skipped, enter the $0.00 with the Maintenance menu's "Add nonstandard payments" submenu choice, with the payment date as the due date. No late charge will then be made since the payment's date was within the specified period. To cause the late charge to be added, provide a payment date after the grace period.

  If the late charge is greater than $0.00, you are asked for the number of days that can elapse after the payment is due before the late charge is applied. In this material I will refer to this period as the grace period.
- Payment frequency: This field is different from the others. Instead of typing in your entry, you press the + or - keys until your choice appears. They are weekly, semimonthly (twice a month), monthly, and yearly. If you select semimonthly, you will see two new fields appear, asking for the two days of the month the payments are due. The first must be from the 1st through the 14th; the second from the 15th through the 28th. One of these should match the day of the first payment date field. The defaults are 0. Both fields are required.

When all the fields have been filled in to your satisfaction, press Ctrl-Enter to save the data. If a required field was left blank, the computer will beep and your cursor will be returned to the field that had no entry, or to the topmost if there was more than one.

The second Choose submenu choice is called "Interest Calculation." Interest Calculation will calculate the equivalent compound interest rate if supplied with the loan or investment amount, the current balance or worth, and the date of each. Here are the fields. All are required.

- Original amount: Enter the loan or investment amount here. The entry can range from $0.01 to $999,999.99. Do not enter dollar signs or commas. The default is 0.00.

- Date of above: Enter the date the money was loaned or invested. The default is the current date.
- Current amount: Enter the current value of the loan or investment amount here. The entry can range from $0.01 to $999,999.99. Do not enter dollar signs or commas. The default is 0.00.
- Date of above: Enter the date the value entered in the above field was correct. The default is the current date. This date must be after the first date entered.

After entering all the fields to your satisfaction, press Ctrl-Enter. A window will appear displaying the equivalent compound interest. That is, the money would have increased by the difference in the two amounts entered if it had been put in the bank at the displayed rate of compound interest. Press the Enter key to remove the window and resume the program.

If you change your mind, press the Escape key at any time to be returned to the menu.

The third and final choice in this submenu is "PayOff calculation." It tells you the payoff value of a loan made to be paid back in one installment on some date unknown at the time of the loan. Enter the loan amount, date of loan, interest rate in percent, and the payoff date when known. The program will display the amount of interest charged and the payoff amount, including the interest. The interest is compounded yearly. Press the Enter key to remove each window and resume the program.

Choose Menu

There is only one choice under Choose. That is "Debtor." You use it to choose the debtor, loan, and nonstandard payment (if any) information you wish to work with. You must use Header in the previous submenu or this choice before you can use any of the choices from the Maintenance and Print menus.

When you make this choice, you will see a window appear with a list of the filenames you had previously created. The topmost will be highlighted. Select the choice by moving the highlight with the mouse or Up- and Down-arrow keys. When your choice is highlighted, press the Enter key. That's all there is to it.

Maintenance Menu

This menu choice's submenu has six choices.

The first choice is "View debtor." The debtor is the one that you just created with Header or used Choose to select. If you have done neither since you started the program, you must use one or the other before you can view a debtor. A screen is presented just like the one you used to create the debtor with the Header submenu choice. You can look at all the field values you set, but you cannot add, change, or remove any of them. Press the Escape key when finished.

The second choice is "Edit debtor information." The debtor is the one that you just created with "Header" or used the Choose menu to select. If you have done neither since you started the program, you must use one or the other before you can modify a debtor. This is much like the previous choice but permits you to add, change, or remove any of the fields. Recall the cautions about required fields; they hold true here as well. Use Ctrl-Enter when finished if you want to retain the changes you made, or press the Escape key to abandon your modifications. You cannot change the filename. The date of first payment and payment frequency cannot be changed if any nonstandard payments have been entered. If the frequency or first payment date were changed, the previously entered nonstandard payment due dates would probably become invalid and therefore would not affect the amortization table as desired.

The third choice is "Add nonstandard payments." Use this choice to notify the program that a payment was paid on a date other than the due date (usually after the date, early payments of the proper amount are generally not entered but can save the debtor a bit of interest charges) or the payment is not of the agreed-upon amount or has been skipped. If a payment was made on the due date and was the proper amount, the program will assume that it was made that way; you could enter it here, but the entry would not affect the values in the generated amortization table.

First you'll see a window telling you the debtor's name and that you are about to enter one or more nonstandard payments. To continue, press the Enter key, click on the OK button with your mouse, or press the O key (for the OK button). If you discover you have chosen the wrong debtor or don't want to add a payment, press the C key (for the Cancel button) or click on the Cancel button with your mouse.

When you enter the first nonstandard payment, a file is created with the same name as your debtor file but with an extension of ".PAY." Here are the four entry fields:

- Payment date: Enter the actual payment date in the first field. The default is the current date.
- Due date: In the second field enter the date on which this payment should have been made. Be sure this is correct; the program will check to be sure it is a date on which a payment is due. The default is the current date.
- Amount: The third field is for the amount of the payment. The entry can range from $0.00 to $999,999.99. Do not enter dollar signs or commas. The default is 0.00.
- Another: If you wish to make further payment entries for this debtor, set this last field to Y, otherwise N. The default is N.

When the fields have been entered to your satisfaction, press the Ctrl-Enter key. If you change your mind, use the Escape key to discard the payment data you entered in this screen since the last time you used Ctrl-Enter to save a payment.

The fourth choice is "Change nonstandard payments." Use it to change a nonstandard payment entered earlier with the preceding submenu choice. After you verify the debtor name and the operation that will be performed, as mentioned earlier, you will see a screen list showing the payment date and amount for all previously entered nonstandard payments. The topmost will be highlighted. Select the choice by moving the highlight with the mouse or Up- and Down-arrow keys. When your choice is highlighted, press the Enter key. You will next see a screen much like that used to enter nonstandard payments. However, in this entry screen the "Another" field is absent. As usual, press Ctrl-Enter to save your changes or use the Escape key to abandon them.

The fifth choice is "Delete payment." This works like "Change nonstandard payments" in that you will see a screen list showing the payment date and amount for all previously entered nonstandard payments; however, you won't see the entry screen with the dates and amounts. Once you choose the payment to delete from the list displayed on the screen, it is erased from the nonstandard payment list. It cannot be recovered; you must enter the payment again instead.

The final choice in this submenu is "Remove debtor." First you will see a window containing the debtor name and the fact that debtor will be removed. If you press the Enter key, the Debtor loan and payment information will all be erased—forever! They cannot be recovered by the program. Be careful. Click on the Cancel Button or press the C key if you change your mind.

Print Menu

The single submenu selection, "Print Table," is used to print the amortization table for the currently selected debtor. No entries are required. Be sure the printer is on-line and ready to print.

Quit Menu

This last menu choice has one submenu selection, "End program." Use this to leave the program and return to DOS. You do not need to close any files before quitting.

Program Detail

In this section we will go through the code. As you will see, it is heavily annotated so not much description will be required. I will try to suggest options you might wish to try as well as describe the choices that are available other than those I used. When methods or procedures are referred to in a program line, the annotation indicates that object or unit in bold text. If a constant or variable in a unit only is referred to the unit or object will be indicated, but not in bold.

Loan.Pas

Here is the main program module. It uses the Menu object from the OpMenu unit. After linking and compiling, it is slightly over 200K in size. Note my discussion of compiling OPro in Chapter 3. You cannot compile the main module from the Turbo Pascal IDE (Interactive Development Environment); there will not be enough memory available. Also, as discussed earlier, be sure to use the IDE options to compile and link to disk. Also, if possible, set range checking and the debugger off. Even with these settings, you may run out of memory when you attempt to compile most of the units. As I did, you will have to use the command line compiler, TPC, or the extended memory compiler, TPCX. TPCX comes Turbo Professional; Turbo Professional also includes the Turbo Assembler and some other useful tools. To compile the main program modules using TPC, depending on the amount of base (0–640K) memory available, I sometimes had to use Quarterdeck Office System's Vidram, which can make up to 96Kb of your video buffer available if you are using VGA and not using graphics. I used a small batch file containing

```
vidram on
tpc loan.pas
vidram off
```

Leaving Vidram on sometimes caused me mouse cursor movement problems.

```
{Copyright 1991 by Kenneth B. Knecht}
{$V-}
{$R+}

program Loan;
{prints amortization table for a loan. accepts and stores late and
 wrong-amount payments. Can add late charges to debt}

uses
  LoanGlob,
  LoanPyof,
  Dos,
  OpRoot,
  OpDos,
  OpCrt,
  OpMouse,
  OpCmd,
  OpField,
  OpCtrl,
  OpFrame,
  OpMenu,
  OpWindow,
  OpSelect,
  OpString,
  LoanPay,
  LoanHead,
  LoanDir,
  LoanPick,
  LoanMsg,
```

```
    LoanTble,
    LoanRev,
    LoanVrfy;


  var
    S       : String;   {Message string}
    f       : String;   {temporary string}
    IoFlag  : Word;     {store IoResult return}


  function InitMenu : Word;
  {create application menu and initialize}


  const
    {Frame constants}
    Frame1 = '╒╘╕╛══││';            {characters to form menu}
    Frame2 = '╤╘╧╛══││';            {characters to form submenu}
    WinOptions = wBordered          {leave room for border}
                 +wClear            {clear window when displayed}
                 +wUserContents;    {user will refresh contents if required}
  var
    Result : String;   {store name choice}


  begin
    with M do begin {instance of OpMenu}
      if not InitCustom( 2,2,43,2,    {position - X1,Y1,X2,Y2}
                         Colors,      {from colors.inc}
                         WinOptions,  {menu display characteristics
                                       itemized above}
                         Horizontal)  {multiple choices displayed H}
                         then begin
        InitMenu := InitStatus; {function return if init failed}
        Exit;
      end;


      mnOptionsOn(mnAlphaMatch          {check for alpha matches}
                  +mnSelectOnMatch      {implicit Enter on alpha match}
                  +mnArrowSelect        {select submenus with arrows}
                  +mnAllHotSpots);      {exit with ccMouseSel code on any
                                         mouse hotspot. default is no
                                         hotspots}


      mnOptionsOff(mnAllowPending       {submenu stays down after passing
                                         no submenu}
                   +mnPopOnSelect       {erase submenu after selection}
                   +mnUseItemForTopic   {use menu choices as help topics}
                   +mnSelectOnClick);   {implicit Enter on first mouse
                                         click}

      wFrame.SetFrameType(Frame1);      {menu frame characters, OpFrame}
```

```
AddItem('Create',       {menu choice}
        2,              {H position from frame edge}
        1,              {char position to use for character select}
        miCreate);      {menu choice identifier}

AddFramedSubMenu(3,4,25,6, {submenu position - X1,Y1,X2,Y2}
                 Vertical, {submenu item orientation}
                 Frame2);  {submenu frame characters}

  AddItem('Header',       {submenu choice}
          1,              {first row}
          1,              {char position to use for character select}
          miHeader);      {menu choice identifier}

  AddItem('Interest calculation', {submenu choice}
          2,                      {second row}
          1,                      {char position to use for
                                   character select}
          miReverse);             {menu choice identifier}

  AddItem('PayOff calculation',   {submenu choice}
          3,                      {third row}
          1,                      {char position to use for
                                   character select}
          miPayOff);              {menu choice identifier}

  ItemsDone;   {no more submenu items}

AddItem('Choose',       {menu choice}
        10,             {H position from frame edge}
        1,              {char position to use for character select}
        miChoose);      {menu choice identifier}

AddFramedSubMenu(11,4,20,4, {submenu position - X1,Y1,X2,Y2}
                 Vertical,  {submenu item orientation}
                 Frame2);   {submenu frame characters}

  AddItem('Debtor',     {submenu choice}
          1,            {first row}
          1,            {char position to use for character select}
          miDebtor);    {menu choice identifier}

  ItemsDone;   {no more submenu items}

AddItem('Maintenance',      {menu choice}
        18,                 {H position from frame edge}
        1,                  {char position to use for character
                             select}
        miMaintain);        {menu choice identifier}
```

```
AddFramedSubMenu(19,4,50,9, {submenu position - X1,Y1,X2,Y2}
                 Vertical,  {submenu item orientation}
                 Frame2);   {submenu frame characters}

  AddItem('View debtor',  {submenu choice}
          1,              {first row}
          1,              {char position to use for character
                           select}
          miViewDebtor); {menu choice identifier}

  AddItem('Edit debtor information', {submenu choice}
          2,                         {second row}
          1,                         {char position to use for
                                      character select}
          miEditDebtor);             {menu choice identifier}

  AddItem('Add nonstandard payments', {submenu choice}
          3,                          {third row}
          1,                          {char position to use for
                                       character select}
          miAddPayment);              {menu choice identifier}

  AddItem('Change nonstandard payments', {submenu choice}
          4,                             {fourth row}
          1,                             {char position to use for
                                          character select}
          miEditPayment);                {menu choice identifier}

  AddItem('Delete payment',  {submenu choice}
          5,                 {fifth row}
          1,                 {char position to use for character
                              select}
          miDeletePayment); {menu choice identifier}

  AddItem('Remove Debtor',  {submenu choice}
          6,                {sixth row}
          1,                {char position to use for character
                             select}
          miRemoveDebtor); {menu choice identifier}

  ItemsDone;  {no more submenu items}

AddItem('Print',   {menu choice}
        31,        {H position from frame edge}
        1,         {char position to use for character select}
        miPrint); {menu choice identifier}

AddFramedSubMenu(30,4,44,4, {submenu position - X1,Y1,X2,Y2}
                 Vertical,  {submenu item orientation}
                 Frame2);   {submenu frame characters}
```

```
      AddItem('Print table',  {submenu choice}
              1,              {first row}
              1,              {char position to use for character
                                select}
              miPrintTable); {menu choice identifier}

      ItemsDone;  {no more submenu items}

    AddItem('Quit',     {menu choice}
            38,         {H position from frame edge}
            1,          {char position to use for character select}
            miQuit);    {menu choice identifier}

    AddFramedSubMenu(37,4,51,4, {submenu position - X1,Y1,X2,Y2}
                     Vertical,  {submenu item orientation}
                     Frame2);   {submenu frame characters}

      AddItem('End program',  {submenu choice}
              1,              {first row}
              1,              {char position to use for character
                               select}
              miEndProgram); {menu choice identifier}

      ItemsDone;             {no more submenu items}
    ItemsDone;               {no more menu items}
    InitMenu := GetLastError; {function return value}
  end;
end;


{main program loop}
begin
  if MouseInUse then                  {LoanGlob}
    MouseChar := #04;                 {diamond}
  CurFile := '';                      {no file selected}
  Status := InitMenu;                 {initialize Menu (in this module)}
  if Status <> 0 then begin           {error when initing menu}
    S := 'Error initializing Menu: '
         + Long2Str(Status);          {OpString}
    ShowMsg(S);                       {LoanMsg}
    Halt(1);
  end;

  if MouseInUse then begin  {LoanGlob}
    if MouseInstalled then  {OpMouse variable}
      with Colors do begin  {from Colors.inc (see LoanGlob)}
        {activate mouse cursor, make it a red diamond}
        SoftMouseCursor($0000, {mouse has own software cursor}
                    (ColorMono(MouseColor, MouseMono) shl 8)+
                           Byte(MouseChar));  {OpMouse procedure}
```

```
      {enable mouse menu support}
      MenuCommands.cpOptionsOn(cpEnableMouse); {menu sees mouse,
                                                OpMenu Command
                                                Processor}
      HideMouse;                               {avoid mouse tracks,
                                                OpMouse}
    end;
end;

{fill in a backdrop}
TextAttr := $07; {background attribute}
TextChar := '▒'; {background design}
ClrScr;

repeat
  M.Draw;            {draw menu, OpMenu}
  if MouseInUse then {LoanGlob}
    ShowMouse;       {make mouse available for menu selection,
                      OpMouse}
  M.Process;         {process menu commands, OpMenu}
  if MouseInUse then {LoanGlob}
    HideMouse;       {avoid mouse tracks, OpMouse}
  if M.GetlastCommand = ccSelect then  {a selection was made,
                                        OpWindow}
    case M.MenuChoice of      {OpMenu}
      miHeader : {create new header of debtor and loan info}
        begin
          CurFile     := '';  {cancel any previously selected debtor}
          MaxFile     := 0;   {no payments}
          EntryType   := 'N'; {new}
          M.Erase;            {erase menu from screen}
          HeaderInfo;         {get and store header information,
                               LoanHead unit}
        end;

      miReverse : {calculate % compound int from $loan, $int, and
                   dates}
        begin
          M.Erase; {erase menu from screen, OpMenu}
          Reverse; {call interest calculator, LoanRev unit}
        end;

      miPayOff : {calculate payoff from amount, %interest, and dates}
        begin
          M.Erase; {erase menu from screen, OpMenu}
          PayOff;  {call payoff amount calculator, LoanPyof unit}
        end;

      miDebtor : {choose a debtor to view, edit or process payments}
        begin
```

```
    CurFile := '';  {cancel any previously selected debtor}
    MaxFile := 0;   {no payments}
    M.Erase;        {erase menu from screen, OpMenu}
    MakeDirList;    {select debtor, get debtor and payment info,
                     LoanDir unit}
  end;


miViewDebtor : {view a debtor}
  begin
    M.Erase;                          {erase menu from screen,
                                       OpMenu}
    if CurFile <> '' then begin       {debtor currently selected}
      EntryType   := 'V';             {view debtor, no editing}
      HeaderInfo;                     {show debtor info,
                                       LoanHead unit}
    end
    else
      ShowMsg('No debtor chosen'); {LoanMsg unit}
  end;

miEditDebtor : {edit a debtor record}
  begin
    M.Erase;                          {erase menu from screen,
                                       OpMenu}
    if CurFile <> '' then begin       {debtor currently selected}
      VerifyType := 'E';              {we are going to edit}
      if Verify then begin            {user verified debtor and
                                       operation as correct,
                                       LoanVrfy unit}
        EntryType := 'E';             {edit debtor}
        HeaderInfo;                   {edit debtor info,
                                       LoanHead unit}
      end;
    end
    else
      ShowMsg('No debtor chosen'); {LoanMsg}
  end;

miAddPayment : {add a nonstandard payment}
  begin
    M.Erase;                          {erase menu from screen, OpMenu}
    if CurFile <> '' then begin       {debtor currently selected}
      VerifyType := 'A';              {we are going to add a payment}
      if Verify then begin            {user verified debtor and
                                       operation as correct,
                                       LoanVrfy unit}
        EntryType := 'N';             {new payment}
        PaymentInfo;                  {get and store payment info,
                                       LoanPay unit}
```

```
      end;
    end
    else
      ShowMsg('No debtor chosen'); {LoanMsg unit}
  end;

miEditPayment : {choose a payment and edit}
  begin
    M.Erase;                          {erase menu from screen,
                                       OpMenu}
    if CurFile <> '' then begin       {debtor currently
                                       selected, LoanGlob}
      PayChoice := 0;                 {no choice made,
                                       LoanGlob}
      if MaxFile <> 0 then begin      {at least one payment
                                       exists, LoanGlob}
        VerifyType := 'C';            {we are going to edit an
                                       existing payment,
                                       LoanGlob}
        if Verify then begin          {user verified debtor and
                                       operation as correct,
                                       LoanVrfy unit}
          ChoosePayment;              {select a payment to
                                       edit, LoanPick unit}
          if PayChoice <> 0 then begin {choice was made}
            EntryType := 'E';         {edit payment}
            PaymentInfo;              {edit payment info,
                                       LoanPay unit}
          end
          else
            ShowMsg('No payments choosen'); {LoanMsg unit}
        end;
      end
      else
        ShowMsg('No payments to choose');   {LoanMsg unit}
    end
    else
      ShowMsg('No debtor chosen');          {LoanMsg unit}
  end;

miDeletePayment : {delete a previously entered payment}
  begin
    M.Erase;                       {erase menu from screen,
                                    OpMenu}
    if CurFile <> '' then begin    {debtor currently selected,
                                    LoanGlob}
      if MaxFile <> 0 then begin   {at least one payment stored,
                                    LoanGlob}
        VerifyType := 'R';         {we are going to remove an
                                    existing payment, LoanGlob}
```

```
if Verify then begin      {user verified debtor and
                           operation as correct,
                           LoanVrfy unit}
  PayChoice := 0;          {no choice made, LoanGlob}
  ChoosePayment;           {select payment to remove,
                           LoanPick unit}
  if PayChoice <> 0 then begin              {a payment was
                                             selected,
                                             LoanGlob}
    for N := PayChoice to MaxFile - 1 do {all payments
                                             from chosen
                                             one to end
                                             of the array,
                                             LoanGlob}
      PayList[N] := PayList[N + 1];         {move payments
                                             down to fill
                                             gap caused
                                             by removing a
                                             payment from
                                             the array,
                                             LoanGlob}
    Dec(MaxFile);                           {one less
                                             payment
                                             in list,
                                             LoanGlob}
    {load new payment list into file}
    {$I-}
    f := TrimSpaces(CurFile) + '.PAY'; {file name,
                                        OpString unit}
    assign(PayFile,f);                 {assign file
                                        name to
                                        file variable,
                                        LoanGlob}
    rewrite(PayFile);                  {open file in
                                        write only mode,
                                        LoanGlob}
    IoFlag := IoResult;                {any I/O error?}
    if IoFlag <> 0 then begin          {yes}
      ShowMsg('Rewrite payment ' + f
              + ' error. IoResult is: '
              + Long2Str(IoFlag));     {LoanMsg unit,
                                        OpString unit}
      Halt;
    end;
    N := 1;                            {start with 1 in
                                        case list is
                                        empty
                                        (MaxFile = 0)}
    while N <= MaxFile do begin        {all payments in
                                        array}
```

```
              write(PayFile,PayList[N]);       {put Nth payment
                                                in file,
                                                LoanGlob}
              IoFlag := IoResult;              {any I/O error?}
              if IoFlag <> 0 then begin        {yes}
                ShowMsg('Write payment ' + f
                         + ' error. IoResult is: '
                         + Long2Str(IoFlag));  {LoanMsg unit,
                                                OpString unit}
                Halt;
              end;
              Inc(N);                          {next payment}
            end;

            close(PayFile);                    {save file
                                                buffers to
                                                disk}
            {$I+}
          end
          else
            ShowMsg('No payment chosen'); {LoanMsg unit}
        end;
      end
      else
        ShowMsg('No payments to delete'); {LoanMsg unit}
    end
    else
      ShowMsg('No debtor chosen');        {LoanMsg unit}
  end;

miRemoveDebtor : {delete files for chosen debtor}
  begin
    M.Erase;                              {erase menu from
                                           screen}
    if CurFile <> '' then begin           {debtor currently
                                           chosen, LoanGlob}
      VerifyType := 'D';                  {we are going to
                                           delete a debtor,
                                           LoanGlob}
      if Verify then begin                {user verified debtor
                                           and selected
                                           operation,
                                           LoanVrfy unit}
        {$I-}
        f := TrimSpaces(CurFile) + '.HDR'; {delete debtor info
                                           file, OpString unit}
        assign(HeadFile,f);               {assign file name to
                                           file variable,
                                           LoanGlob}
        erase(HeadFile);                  {delete debtor file,
                                           LoanGlob}
```

```
          IoFlag := IoResult;                   {any I/O errors?}
          if IoFlag <> 0 then begin             {yes}
            ShowMsg('Debtor file ' + f
                   + ' was not erased. IoResult is: '
                   + Long2Str(IoFlag));         {LoanMsg unit,
                                                 OpString unit}
            Halt;
          end;
          f := TrimSpaces(CurFile) + '.PAY';    {delete payment info
                                                 file, OpString unit}
          assign(PayFile,f);                    {assign file name to
                                                 file variable,
                                                 LookGlob}
          erase(PayFile);                       {delete payment file,
                                                 LookGlob}
          IoFlag := IoResult;                   {any I/O errors?}
          if IoFlag <> 0 then begin             {yes}
            if IoFlag <> 2 then begin           {don't show 'file not
                                                 found' error}
              ShowMsg('Payment file ' + f
                     + ' was not erased. IoResult is: '
                     + Long2Str(IoFlag));       {LoanMsg unit,
                                                 OpString unit}
              Halt;
            end;
          end;
          {$I+}
          CurFile := '';                        {no debtor currently
                                                 chosen}
          MaxFile := 0;                         {no payments,
                                                 LoanGlob}
        end;
      end
      else
        ShowMsg('No debtor chosen');            {LoanMsg unit}
    end;

  miPrintTable : {print amortization table}
    begin
      M.Erase;                  {erase menu from screen}
      if CurFile <> '' then     {debtor currently selected}
        PrintTable              {print the amortization table,
                                 LoanTble unit}
      else
        ShowMsg('No debtor chosen'); {LoanMsg unit}
    end;
  end;
until M.MenuChoice = miEndProgram; {Quit submenu choice made, OpMenu}
M.Erase; {erase menu, OpMenu}
```

```
    M.Done;  {remove menu from memory, OpMenu}

    ClrScr;
  end. {end of program}
```

Essentially, the main program initializes the menu. Then it loops through the menu, calling procedures in various units and performing operations as required, until the user selects the "End Program" choice. In the annotation I have tried to remember to note the unit where each called procedure, function, or variable resides.

In the line

```
WinOptions = wBordered       {leave room for border}
             +wClear         {clear window when displayed}
             +wUserContents; {user will refresh contents if required}
```

the complete list of possible options is

wBordered	Make space for window border
wClear	Clear window when it is first displayed
wSaveContents	Save the contents of the window when it is erased.
wUserContents	User will restore window contents
wSoundEffects	Use sound effects during explosions
wAltFrame	Use alternate frame type when not current
wSetMouse	Set mouse window, cursor on entry to window
wFullMouseWindow	Force to full mouse window on entry
wResizable	Can be resized and zoomed
wAllMouseEvents	Any combination of mouse buttons anywhere exits
wStoreContents	Store window contents in streams

The next procedure's last parameter

```
if not InitCustom( 2,2,43,2,    {position - X1,Y1,X2,Y2}
                   Colors,      {from colors.inc}
                   WinOptions,  {menu display characteristics
                                 itemized above}
                   Horizontal)  {multiple choices displayed H}
                   then begin
```

can be one of the following:

Horizontal	top menu bar choices displayed horizontally
Vertical	top menu bar choices displayed vertically

In the following lines

```
mnOptionsOn(mnAlphaMatch         {check for alpha matches}
            +mnSelectOnMatch     {implicit Enter on alpha match}
            +mnArrowSelect       {select submenus with arrows}
            +mnAllHotSpots);     {exit with ccMouseSel code on any
                                  mouse hotspot. default is no
                                  hotspots}

mnOptionsOff(mnAllowPending      {submenu stays down after passing
                                  no submenu}
             +mnPopOnSelect      {erase submenu after selection}
             +mnUseItemForTopic  {use menu choices as help topics}
             +mnSelectOnClick);  {implicit Enter on first mouse
                                  click}
```

The list of available options is

mnAllHotSpots	exit on any menu mouse hotspot (default is no hotspots)
mnAllowPending	submenu stays down after passing no submenu
mnAlphaMatch	check for alphabetic matches
mnArrowSelect	select submenus with arrow keys
mnMainHighlight	highlight alpha search characters on high level menu
mnMainSelect	display top level menu bar
mnMouseSupport	used by MakeMenu (Turbo Power utility)
mnPopOnSelect	erase current submenu after selection
mnSelectOnClick	implicit Enter on first mouse click
mnSelectOnMatch	implicit Enter on alphabetic character match
mnUseItemForTopic	use current highlighted item for help topic

LoanGlob.Pas

The next module is LoanGlob. This unit contains all the global constants, variables, types, defines, etc. It is called by all the modules, so it is appropriate to discuss it next.

```
unit LoanGlob;
{ Global variables and types for all units}

INTERFACE

{$I OPDEFINE.INC} {standard define list}

uses
  OpCrt,
  OpCtrl,
  OpDate,
```

```
    OpEntry,
    OpMenu;

  const
    {$IFDEF UseMouse}
       MouseInUse : Boolean = True;
    {$ELSE}
       MouseInUse : Boolean = False;
    {$ENDIF}

  {$I COLORS.INC}  {designated color list}

  {menu choice identifiers}
  const
    miCreate        = 1;                  {1}
    miChoose        = miCreate+1;         {2}
    miMaintain      = miChoose+1;         {3}
    miPrint         = miMaintain+1;       {4}
    miQuit          = miPrint+1;          {5}
    miHeader        = miQuit+1;           {6}
    miDebtor        = miHeader+1;         {7}
    miViewDebtor    = miDebtor+1;         {8}
    miEditDebtor    = miViewDebtor+1;     {9}
    miAddPayment    = miEditDebtor+1;     {10}
    miEditPayment   = miAddPayment+1;     {11}
    miDeletePayment = miEditPayment+1;    {12}
    miRemoveDebtor  = miDeletePayment+1;  {13}
    miPrintTable    = miRemoveDebtor+1;   {14}
    miEndProgram    = miPrintTable+1;     {15}
    miReverse       = miEndProgram+1;     {16}
    miPayOff        = miReverse+1;        {17}

    {entry screen help ids (not used)}
    idCurFile     = 1;                {1}
    idName        = idCurFile+1;      {2}
    idAddress1    = idName+1;         {3}
    idAddress2    = idAddress1+1;     {4}
    idCity        = idAddress2+1;     {5}
    idHomePhone   = idCity+1;         {6}
    idWorkPhone   = idHomePhone+1;    {7}
    idLoanAmount  = idWorkPhone+1;    {8}
    idInterest    = idLoanAmount+1;   {9}
    idPayAmount   = idInterest+1;     {10}
    idLoanDate    = idPayAmount+1;    {11}
    idFirstDue    = idLoanDate+1;     {12}
    idFrequency   = idFirstDue+1;     {13}
    idFirstDay    = idFrequency+1;    {14}
    idSecondDay   = idFirstDay+1;     {15}
    idPayIntFirst = idSecondDay+1;    {16}
    idPayDate     = idPayIntFirst+1;  {17}
```

```
  idDueDate     = idPayDate+1;      {18}
  idPAmount     = idDueDate+1;      {19}
  idMore        = idPAmount+1;      {20}
  idStarting    = idMore+1;         {21}
  idCurrent     = idStarting+1;     {22}
  idYears       = idCurrent+1;      {23}
  idLateCharge  = idYears+1;        {24}
  idLateDays    = idLateCharge+1;   {25}
  idOrgAmount   = idLateDays+1;     {26}
  idOrgDate     = idOrgAmount+1;    {27}
  idCurAmount   = idOrgDate+1;      {28}
  idCurAmtDate  = idCurAmount+1;    {29}
  idLoanInt     = idCurAmtDate+1;   {30}
  idLoanIntDate = idLoanInt+1;      {31}

type
  Freqtype = (Weekly,Semimonthly,Monthly,Yearly);

  Payrecord = record            {payment record}
                PayDate : Date; {date of payment}
                DueDate : Date; {date payment was due}
                Amount  : Real; {amount of payment}
              end;

  Debtor = record                             {specific loan info}
             Name        : String[30];
             Address1    : String[30];
             Address2    : String[30];
             City        : String[30];
             HomePhone   : String[12];
             WorkPhone   : String[12];
             LoanAmount  : Real;        {amount of loan}
             PayAmount   : Real;        {amount of scheduled payment}
             LoanDate    : Date;        {date of loan}
             LateCharge  : Real;        {late charge amount}
             LateDays    : Integer;     {how many days of grace before
                                         late charge}
             Frequency   : FreqType;    {payments weekly, monthly,
                                         semimonthly, or annual?}
             FirstDay    : Integer;     {if semimonthly first payment
                                         date (1 - 14)}
             SecondDay   : Integer;     {if semimonthly second payment
                                         date (15 - 28)}
             FirstDue    : Date;        {date first payment is due}
             Interest    : Real;        {interest rate in percent}
             PayIntFirst : Boolean;     {charge interest from date of
                                         loan or first payment?}
           end;
```

```
const
  {payment schedule}
  Frequency         : array[FreqType] of String[11] = ('Weekly     ',
                           'Semimonthly','Monthly    ','Yearly     ');
  MaxPaymentNumber = 200;  {maximum number of payments (to determine
                            payment array size)}

var
  CurFile       : String;           {current selected header file}
  ESPay         : EntryScreen;      {enter or edit payments, OpEntry}
  ESHeader      : EntryScreen;      {enter, view, or edit header, OpEntry}
  ESRev         : EntryScreen;      {enter data to calculate reverse
                                     interest, OpEntry}
  EntryType     : Char;             {view data (V), add new data (N), or
                                     edit (E)}
  Finished      : Boolean;          {process flag in main program}
  Header        : Debtor;           {loan info record}
  HeadFile      : File of Debtor;   {file variable}
  M             : Menu;             {object instance}
  MaxFile       : Integer;          {number of payment records}
  N             : Integer;          {miscellaneous counter}
  Pay           : PayRecord;        {payment record}
  PayChoice     : Integer;          {array position of chosen payment}
  PayFile       : File of PayRecord;
  PayList       : array [1..MaxPaymentNumber] of PayRecord;
  Status        : Word;             {init result in main program}
  VerifyType    : Char;             {what info to verify}

IMPLEMENTATION

end. {end of unit}
```

This module is required because programs and units cannot pass constant and variable declarations to one another except via procedure or function parameters. Using this unit and calling it from every other unit makes it possible to easily incorporate global constants and variables in an application. Note that this unit has no Implementation code, only the Interface portion.

There is little to discuss in the content of this module. Perhaps the code

```
const
  {$IFDEF UseMouse}
    MouseInUse : Boolean = True;
  {$ELSE}
    MouseInUse : Boolean = False;
  {$ENDIF}
```

is used to check and see if the use of a mouse was defined. If "UseMouse" is not defined in OpDefine.inc (called right after the INTERFACE statement) then "MouseInUse" will be set to false. All references to mouse actions in all the modules are invoked only if this variable is true. For example:

```
if MouseInUse then
  ShowMouse;
```

The version of OpDefine.inc that came with OPro had "UseMouse" defined. If you have changed your version of OpDefine.inc and wish to use the mouse in this application, you may wish to check this, or perhaps instead of

```
{$I OPDEFINE.INC}
```

you may wish to substitute your own define file. Here is how my file looks:

```
{*********************************************************}
{*                  OPDEFINE.INC 1.10                    *}
{*      Assorted conditional compilation directives      *}
{*     Copyright (c) TurboPower Software 1988, 1989.     *}
{*                 All rights reserved.                  *}
{*********************************************************}

{This compiler directive controls whether the Float type in OPSTRING is
defined as an Extended or a Real. It also controls the inclusion of
certain methods that apply only to 8087 numeric types.}

  {$N-}

{This directive forces all units to contain an initialization block,
even those that do not have any actual initialization code. Adding
these blocks helps to work around a bug in Turbo Debugger 1.5.}

  {$DEFINE InitAllUnits}

{This directive determines whether or not OPCRT is compiled in such a
way as to coexist peacefully with the standard Turbo Pascal CRT
unit.}

  {.$DEFINE UseCrt}

{This directive enables mouse support in several of the units, as
well as in some of the demo programs}

  {$DEFINE UseMouse}

{This directive enables scroll bar support in OPWINDOW and units that
depend on it}

  {$DEFINE UseScrollBars}

{This directive enables hot spot support in OPWINDOW and units that
depend on it}

  {$DEFINE UseHotSpots}
```

```
{This directive enables shadowing support in OPWINDOW}

  {$DEFINE UseShadows}

{This directive enables the AdjustWindow, ResizeWindow, MoveWindow,
and other methods in OPWINDOW}

  {$DEFINE UseAdjustableWindows}

{If FourByteDates is defined, dates in OPDATE are stored as longints,
giving a range of 01/01/1600-12/31/3999. If it isn't defined, dates
are stored as words giving a range of 01/01/1900-12/31/2078.}

  {$DEFINE FourByteDates}

{The following directive enables support for editing of dates in
OPEDIT and OPENTRY. It also enables certain options in OPDIR, OPEDIT,
OPENTRY, and OPFORM.}

  {$DEFINE UseDates}

{The following directive enables support for BCD reals in OPEDIT,
OPENTRY and OPFORM}

  {.$DEFINE UseBCD}

{The following directive enables support for pick list fields in
OPENTRY}

  {$DEFINE PickListFields}

{Deactivate the following define if the caller of OPSORT needs to
perform heap allocation or deallocation while the sort is in
progress, that is, within the user-defined procedures of the sort.
For large sorts with element size exceeding 4 bytes, FastDispose
makes a significant difference in the speed of heap deallocation when
the sort is finished.}

  {$DEFINE FastDispose}

{If the following directive is defined, OPTSR and OPSWAP try to
 thwart SideKick}

  {$DEFINE ThwartSideKick}

{If the following directive is defined, streams support is enabled in
all objects}

  {$DEFINE UseStreams}
```

```
{If the following directive is defined, XMS support is enabled in
OPSWAP and OPEXEC. IMPORTANT: In that case you must also define the
SupportXms constant in OPSWAP.ASM and OPEXEC.ASM and reassemble those
files. Failure to do so will cause an error when recompiling the
units.}

  {.$DEFINE SupportXms}                          {!!.02}

{If the following directive is defined, OPDRAG support will be
included in all units containing command windows.}

  {.$DEFINE UseDrag}                             {!!.03}

{The following define controls how various OPRO units react to the heap
changes of TP6. There is no need for you to modify it.}

  {$IFDEF Ver60}
  {$DEFINE Heap6}
  {$ENDIF}
```

The remarks are all by TurboPower Software. I have not yet found it necessary to alter the file.

The statement

```
{$I COLORS.INC}  {designated color list}
```

refers to the Color information included in many OPro documentation examples. I took the liberty of putting this information into an INC file so it could be included easily in my applications. The file looks like this:

```
const
  Colors : ColorSet = (
    TextColor       : $70; TextMono       : $70;
    CtrlColor       : $3A; CtrlMono       : $08;
    FrameColor      : $7F; FrameMono      : $70;
    HeaderColor     : $7F; HeaderMono     : $70;
    ShadowColor     : $08; ShadowMono     : $00;
    HighlightColor  : $4F; HighlightMono  : $70;
    PromptColor     : $70; PromptMono     : $70;
    SelPromptColor  : $7F; SelPromptMono  : $70;
    ProPromptColor  : $70; ProPromptMono  : $07;
    FieldColor      : $1E; FieldMono      : $07;
    SelFieldColor   : $1F; SelFieldMono   : $0F;
    ProFieldColor   : $70; ProFieldMono   : $07;
    ScrollBarColor  : $17; ScrollBarMono  : $07;
    SliderColor     : $17; SliderMono     : $0F;
    HotSpotColor    : $17; HotSpotMono    : $0F;
    BlockColor      : $1E; BlockMono      : $0F;
    MarkerColor     : $1F; MarkerMono     : $70;
    DelimColor      : $7E; DelimMono      : $0F;
    SelDelimColor   : $11; SelDelimMono   : $0F;
```

```
    ProDelimColor    : $7E; ProDelimMono     : $0F;
    SelItemColor     : $2F; SelItemMono      : $70;
    ProItemColor     : $37; ProItemMono      : $07;
    HighItemColor    : $7F; HighItemMono     : $0F;
    AltItemColor     : $3F; AltItemMono      : $0F;
    AltSelItemColor  : $2F; AltSelItemMono   : $70;
    FlexAHelpColor   : $7F; FlexAHelpMono    : $0F;
    FlexBHelpColor   : $7F; FlexBHelpMono    : $0F;
    FlexCHelpColor   : $7B; FlexCHelpMono    : $70;
    UnselXrefColor   : $7E; UnselXrefMono    : $09;
    SelXrefColor     : $9F; SelXrefMono      : $70;
    MouseColor       : $4F; MouseMono        : $70);
  dColors : DialogColorSet = (
    HiPromptColor    : $7E; HiPromptMono     : $0F;
    ButtonColor      : $20; ButtonMono       : $07;
    DefButtonColor   : $2B; DefButtonMono    : $07;
    HiButtonColor    : $2E; HiButtonMono     : $0F;
    SelButtonColor   : $2F; SelButtonMono    : $0F;
    ProButtonColor   : $70; ProButtonMono    : $70;
    BtnShadowColor   : $70; BtnShadowMono    : $70;
    ClusterColor     : $30; ClusterMono      : $07;
    ProClusterColor  : $70; ProClusterMono   : $07;
    HiClusterColor   : $3E; HiClusterMono    : $0F;
    SelClusterColor  : $3F; SelClusterMono   : $07);
  {$IFDEF UseMouse}
  MouseChar       : Char = #04;
  {$ENDIF}
```

I have not yet found it necessary to alter this file. You might wish to change some of the assignments in this file, or replace the whole file with one of your own. These colors are used in all methods that define colors.

The line

```
MaxPaymentNumber = 200;  {maximum number of payments (to determine
                          payment array size)}
```

limits nonstandard payments for an individual loan. If you anticipate a larger number of payments, increase this payment record array size designator or use a different method of storing the payment records, perhaps a linked list on the heap. I believe an array is by far the most convenient solution.

LoanMsg.Pas

The LoanMsg unit is called from almost all the other units. It used the DialogBox object from OpDialog. The interfaced procedure called is ShowMsg. This unit provides a dialog box, which displays the message supplied as the ShowMsg() parameter. A single pushbutton is provided to indicate that the message has been read.

```
unit loanmsg;

INTERFACE

uses
  LoanGlob,
  OpDialog,
  OpString,
  OpCrt,
  OpRoot,
  OpCmd,
  OpField,
  OpFrame,
  OpCtrl,
  OpMouse,
  OpWindow;

{display a message}
procedure ShowMsg(Message : String);


IMPLEMENTATION


const
  hiOk = 1; {button ID}

var
  MBox            : DialogBox; {instance of DialogBox object}

function InitMsgBox(Message : String) : Word;
{Initialize dialog box}

const
  WinOptions = wBordered        {make sure there is room around window
                                 for a border}
             +wClear            {clear window when first displayed}
             +wUserContents;    {user will replace contents if required}
                                {OpWindow}
var
  Len : Byte; {message length}

begin
  with MBox do begin
    {instantiate dialog box}
    Len := Length(Message);
    if not InitCustom(40 - ((Len DIV 2) + 3),  {X1}
                      8,                       {Y1}
                      40 + (Len DIV 2) + 3,    {X2}
                      15,                      {Y2}
                      Colors,                  {from Colors.inc}
                      WinOptions,              {see above const}
```

```
                    dColors) then begin      {from Colors.inc,}
                                             {OpDialog}
      InitMsgBox := InitStatus;              {why didn't it initialize}
      Exit;
    end;

    AddCenteredTextField(Message,3); {display message centered on line
                                      three of window, OpSelect}

    AddPushButton('&Ok',       {name of button}
                  05,          {relative Y,X of upper-left corner}
                  (Length(Message) + 6) - 7,
                  5,           {width of button}
                  hiOk,        {button identifier}
                  ccSelect,    {button return value}
                  True);       {default button?}
                               {OpDialog}

    InitMsgBox := RawError;    {function return value}
  end;
end;


procedure ShowMsg(Message : String);
{display the message and wait for button press}

begin
  Status := InitMsgBox(Message); {initialize DialogBox}

  if Status <> 0 then begin       {sorry about that}
    writeln('Error initializing MessageBox: '
            + Long2Str(Status)); {OpString}
    Halt;
  end;

  if MouseInUse then begin                        {LoanGlob}
    DialogCommands.cpOptionsOn(cpEnableMouse);    {dialog sees mouse,
                                                   Dialog Command
                                                Processor}
    HideMouse;                                    {avoid mouse tracks,
                                                   OpMouse}
  end;

  {fill in a backdrop}
  TextAttr := $07;
  TextChar := '▒';
  ClrScr;

  Finished := False;
```

```
    MBox.Draw;              {OpDialog}
    repeat
      if MouseInUse then    {LoanGlob}
        ShowMouse;          {make mouse available, OpMouse}
      MBox.Process;         {display and get button press}
      if MouseInUse then    {LoanGlob}
        HideMouse;          {avoid mouse tracks, OpMouse}

      if MBox.GetLastCommand = ccSelect then {button was pressed,
                                              OpWindow, OpCmd}
          Finished := True;                  {we are done}
    until Finished;
    MBox.Erase; {erase message box, OpDialog}
    MBox.Done;  {recover memory used, OpDialog}
  end; {ShowMsg}

  end. {unit}
```

When we set WinOptions at the beginning of the unit, we have several options:

wBordered	Make space for window border
wClear	Clear window when it is first displayed
wSaveContents	Save the contents of the window when it is erased.
wUserContents	User will restore window contents
wSoundEffects	Use sound effects during explosions
wAltFrame	Use alternate frame type when not current
wSetMouse	Set mouse window, cursor on entry to window
wFullMouseWindow	Force to full mouse window on entry
wResizable	Can be resized and zoomed
wAllMouseEvents	Any combination of mouse buttons anywhere exits
wStoreContents	Store window contents in streams

You may wish to substitute one or more of these for my choices.

It is possible you have been puzzling over this portion of the code:

```
Len := Length(Message);
if not InitCustom(40 - ((Len DIV 2) + 3), {X1}
                  8,                      {Y1}
                  40 + (Len DIV 2) + 3,   {X2}
                  15,                     {Y2}
```

The Message variable contains the message to be displayed. It is passed as a parameter to the ShowMsg procedure. The 40 is the center of the screen. If screens wider than 80 characters are anticipated, perhaps this should be changed to ScreenWidth / 2. Subtracting Len DIV 2 + 3 from this value ensures that the window will be wide enough to contain the left half of the message plus a two- or three-character blank margin. The

```
40 + (Len DIV 2) + 3,     {X2}
```

does the same for the width of the right half of the window. Similar code is found at

```
AddPushButton('&Ok',          {name of button}
              05,             {relative Y,X of upper-left corner}
              (Length(Message) + 6) - 7,
              5,              {width of button}
```

where an attempt is made to place the pushbutton under the right half of the message.

This is a very useful procedure and can be used in many applications. I have found it convenient when debugging to display the values of variables and to designate having reached some point in the code. Since it pops up and waits for permission to proceed, you can't miss it, as you can a WriteLn() or FastWrite(). If you have not already written something like this, you may wish to change the unit's name and borrow my version.

LoanVrfy.Pas

This unit is called from several other units. The DialogBox object from unit OpDialog is used. It is much like LoanMsg, except that two buttons are provided and the message is displayed by a function (Verify) rather than a procedure. The function return value tells the caller which button was pressed. In this application I use it to make sure the user knows what debtor information is being modified and how it is being modified. Most examples of use can be found in the Loan.Pas main code. The two buttons are labeled "Ok," which returns True when pressed, and "Cancel," which returns False.

Here is the code:

```
unit loanvrfy;

INTERFACE

uses
  LoanGlob,
  OpCrt,
  OpRoot,
  OpCmd,
  OpFrame,
  OpCtrl,
  OpWindow,
  OpDialog,
  OpString,
```

```
  OpInline,  {for MaxLong()}
  OpMouse,
  LoanMsg;

{display message and get Yes/No response}
function Verify : Boolean;

IMPLEMENTATION

const
  hiOk     = 1; {OK button ID}
  hiCancel = 2; {Cancel button ID}

var
  MBox     : DialogBox; {instance of DialogBox object}


function InitVerifyBox : Word;
{Initialize dialog box}

const
  WinOptions = wBordered        {make sure there is room around window
                                 for a border}
             +wClear            {clear window when first displayed}
             +wUserContents;    {user will replace contents if required}

var
  S   : String;  {string temporary}
  Len : Integer; {length of message}

begin
  with MBox do begin
    {instantiate dialog box}
    Len := Length(Header.Name) DIV 2;             {half of message
                                                    length}
    if not InitCustom(40 - (MaxLong(Len,12) + 3), {X1, OpInLIne}
                      7,                          {Y1}
                      40 + MaxLong(Len,12) + 3,   {X2, OpInLine}
                      17,                         {Y2}
                      Colors,                     {from Colors.inc}
                      WinOptions,                 {see const above}
                      dColors) then begin         {from Colors.inc}
      InitVerifyBox := InitStatus;                {error number}
      Exit;
    end;

    AddCenteredTextField('Debtor Verification',1); {centered header,
                                                     line 1, OpSelect}
    AddCenteredTextField('Current debtor is',3);   {centered, line 3}
    AddCenteredTextField(Header.Name,4);           {debtor name,
                                                     centered, line 4}
```

```
    case VerifyType of
      'R' : S := 'Delete payment';                    {what's going to
                                                       happen?}
      'E' : S := 'Edit debtor information';
      'P' : S := 'Choose payment';
      'A' : S := 'Add payment';
      'C' : S := 'Edit payment';
      'D' : S := 'Delete debtor';
    end;
    AddCenteredTextField(S,6);                        {display it,
                                                       OpSelect}

    AddPushButton('&Ok',       {button title}
                  08,          {relative Y,X of upper-left corner}
                  (Length(Header.Name) + 6) - 2,
                  8,           {width of button}
                  hiOk,        {button identifier}
                  ccSelect,    {button return value}
                  True);       {default button?}
                               {OpDialog}

    AddPushButton('&Cancel', {button title}
                  10,          {relative Y,X of upper-left corner}
                  (Length(Header.Name) + 6) - 2,
                  8,           {width of button}
                  hiCancel,    {button identifier}
                  ccQuit,      {button return value}
                  False);      {default button?}
                               {OpDialog}

    InitVerifyBox := RawError; {function return value}
  end;
end;


function Verify : Boolean;
{display dialog}

begin
  Status := InitVerifyBox; {initialize DialogBox}
  if Status <> 0 then      {error occurred}
  begin
    ShowMsg('Error initializing Verify dialog: '
            + Long2Str(Status)); {LoanMsg,OpString}
    Halt;
  end;

  if MouseInUse then begin                         {LoanGlob}
    {enable mouse dialog support}
```

```
      DialogCommands.cpOptionsOn(cpEnableMouse);    {dialog sees mouse,
                                                     Dialog Command
                                                     Processor}
      HideMouse;                                    {avoid mouse tracks
                                                      OpMouse}
    end;

    {fill in a backdrop}
    TextAttr := $07;
    TextChar := '▒';
    ClrScr;

    Finished := False;

    MBox.Draw;                      {display dialog, OpDialog}
    repeat
      if MouseInUse then            {LoanGlob}
        ShowMouse;                  {make mouse available, OpMouse}
      MBox.Process;                 {process commands, OpDialog}
      if MouseInUse then            {LoanGlob}
        HideMouse;                  {avoid mouse tracks, OpMouse}
      case MBox.GetLastCommand of   {OpDialog}
        ccSelect :                  {OK button was pressed, OpCmd}
          begin
            Verify := True;         {function return}
            Finished := True;       {done}
          end;
        ccQuit :                    {Cancel button pressed, OpCmd}
          begin
            Verify := False;        {function return}
            Finished := True;       {done}
          end;
      end;
    until Finished;
    MBox.Erase; {erase dialog from screen, OpDialog}
    MBox.Done;  {erase dialog from memory, OpDialog}

    ClrScr;
  end; {procedure}

  end. {unit}
```

The message displayed is determined by the contents of the VerifyType variable, which is normally set immediately before invoking the Verify function. Here is an example from the Loan.pas main code:

```
      miEditDebtor : {edit a debtor record}
        begin
          M.Erase;                       {erase menu from screen,
                                        OpMenu}
```

```
    if CurFile <> '' then begin  {debtor currently selected,
                                  Loan}
      VerifyType := 'E';         {we are going to edit,
                                  LoanGlob}
      if Verify then begin       {user verified debtor and
                                  operation as correct,
                                  LoanVrfy unit}
        EntryType := 'E';        {edit debtor, LoanGlob}
        HeaderInfo;              {edit debtor info,
                                  LoanHead unit}
      end;
    end
    else
      ShowMsg('No debtor chosen'); {LoanMsg unit}
  end;
```

In the Verify function the value of VerifyType is translated to a message to be displayed. This is the section of code to modify, to change, or to add any verification messages.

```
case VerifyType of
  'R' : S := 'Delete payment';               {what's going to
                                              happen?}
  'E' : S := 'Edit debtor information';
  'P' : S := 'Choose payment';
  'A' : S := 'Add payment';
  'C' : S := 'Edit payment';
  'D' : S := 'Delete debtor';
end;
AddCenteredTextField(S,6);                   {display it,
                                              OpSelect}
```

The Boolean value returned by the Verify function is determined by the following section of code:

```
case MBox.GetLastCommand of {OpWindow}
  ccSelect :                {OK button was pressed, OpCmd}
    begin
      Verify := True;       {function return}
      Finished := True;     {done}
    end;
  ccQuit :                  {Cancel button pressed, OpCmd}
    begin
      Verify := False;      {function return}
      Finished := True;     {done}
    end;
end;
```

In the following code fragment:

```
Len := Length(Header.Name) DIV 2;            {half of message
                                              length}
```

```
if not InitCustom(40 - (MaxLong(Len,12) + 3), {X1, OpInLine}
                  7,                           {Y1}
                  40 + MaxLong(Len,12) + 3,    {X2, OpInLine}
                  17,                          {Y2}
```

the MaxLong function selects the largest of the two arguments. This enables us to have a window with a minimum width of 30 columns. Otherwise, the push-buttons and other displayed material do not fit in it comfortably.

LoanRev.Pas

Before we get to the main modules of the Loan application, let's discuss the two ancillary features of the program, found under the Create menu heading. This unit uses the EntryScreen object from OpEntry. The first converts loan or investment information to equivalent compound interest. That is, given an original amount of $A and a current value of $B over the same period of time, had I put the money in the bank, at what interest rate would it have had to be invested for an equal return? The compound rate returned is yearly. Here's the code:

```
unit LoanRev;

INTERFACE

uses LoanGlob,
     LoanMsg,
     OpCmd,
     OpRoot,
     OpField,
     OpFrame,
     OpWindow,
     OpCrt,
     OpString,
     OpEntry,
     OpDate,
     OpMouse;

{calculate equivalent compound interest given amount of loan,
 payoff amount, and time}
procedure Reverse;


IMPLEMENTATION


procedure Reverse;
{calculate equivalent compound interest given amount of loan,
 payoff amount, and time}
```

```
var
   Current  : Real;    {current value of loan or investment}
   Starting : Real;    {starting value of loan or investment}
   Date1    : Date;    {date of loan or investment}
   Date2    : Date;    {date of current value of loan or investment}
   Interest : Real;    {calculated interest}
   S        : String;  {string temporary}

begin
  ClrScr;
  if not ESRev.InitCustom(20, 5, 60, 13,              {Window
                                                        coordinates}
                          Colors,                     {Colors.inc}
                          DefWindowOptions            {default options
                           or wBordered)              {leave room for
                                                        border}
                          then begin
    S := 'Failed to init reverse interest EntryScreen. Status = '
         + Long2Str(InitStatus); (OpString}
    ShowMsg(S);  {display initialization error message, LoanMsg}
    Halt;
  end;

  if MouseInUse then begin                      {LoanGlob}
    EntryCommands.cpOptionsOn(cpEnableMouse);   {entry screen sees mouse,
                                                 EntryScreen Command
                                                 Processor}
    HideMouse;                                  {avoid mouse tracks,
                                                 OpMouse}
  end;

  {add some window frills from OpFrame ancestor of OpEntry}
  ESRev.wFrame.AddShadow(shBR,          {shadow falls below and right}
                         shOverWrite);  {opaque shadow}
  ESRev.wFrame.AddHeader(' Convert Interest Earned to Percent ', heTC);
                                                      {top center}
  ESRev.wFrame.AddHeader(' Esc to abort, Ctrl-Enter to accept ', heBC);
                                                      {bottom center}
  {add fields}
  ESRev.esFieldOptionsOn(efClearFirstChar); {clear string if first
                                             character is ASCII,
                                             OpEntry}

  ESRev.esFieldOptionsOn(efRequired);       {some input required,
                                             OpEntry}
  ESRev.AddRealField('Original amount:',    {prompt}
                     4,                     {V prompt position}
                     6,                     {H prompt position}
                     '999999.99',           {picture}
                     4,                     {data V position}
```

```
                    21,                        {data H position}
                    26,                        {help ID number}
                    0.01,                      {minimum valid entry}
                    999999.99,                 {maximum valid entry}
                    2,                         {number of decimal places}
                    Starting);                 {data variable}

ESRev.AddDateField('Date of above:',           {prompt}
                    5,                         {V prompt position}
                    6,                         {H prompt position}
                    'mm/dd/yyyy',              {picture}
                    5,                         {data V position}
                    21,                        {data H position}
                    27,                        {help ID number}
                    00,                        {minimum valid entry}
                    00,                        {maximum valid entry}
                    Date1);                    {data variable}

ESRev.AddRealField('Current amount:',          {prompt}
                    6,                         {V prompt position}
                    6,                         {H prompt position}
                    '999999.99',               {picture}
                    6,                         {data V position}
                    21,                        {data H position}
                    28,                        {ID number}
                    0.01,                      {minimum valid entry}
                    999999.99,                 {maximum valid entry}
                    2,                         {number of decimal places}
                    Current);                  {data variable}

ESRev.AddDateField('Date of above:',           {prompt}
                    7,                         {V prompt position}
                    6,                         {H prompt position}
                    'mm/dd/yyyy',              {picture}
                    7,                         {data V position}
                    21,                        {data H position}
                    29,                        {help ID number}
                    00,                        {minimum valid entry}
                    00,                        {maximum valid entry}
                    Date2);                    {data variable}

ESRev.esFieldOptionsOff(efRequired);           {turn off required option,
                                               OpEntry}

Finished := False;  {completed?}
Starting := 0.00;   {default values}
Current  := 0.00;
Date1    := Today;
Date2    := Today;
Interest := 0.00;
```

```
  repeat
    if MouseInUse then {LoanGlob}
      ShowMouse;         {make mouse available in entry screen, OpMouse}
    ESRev.Process;       {enter data, OpEntry}
    if MouseInUse then {LoanGlob}
      HideMouse;         {avoid mouse tracks, OpMouse}
    case ESRev.GetLastCommand of {Entry screen return value, OpWindow}
      ccError:                   {error occurred, OpCmd}
        begin
          S := 'Fatal error '+ Long2Str(ESRev.GetLastError); {OpString}
          ShowMsg(S);                                        {LoanMsg}
          Finished := True;      {abort process}
        end;
      ccQuit : {escape}          {abandon process, OpCmd}
        Finished := True;        {abort process}
    end;

    if not Finished then begin
      {calculate equivalent interest}
      {exp and ln are used because TP has no power operator or function}
      Interest := 100 * (Exp((1 / ((Date2 - Date1) / 365))
                          * Ln(Current / Starting)) - 1); {OpDate}
      {display result}
      S := 'Interest is: ' + TrimLead(Real2Str(Interest,7,3)) {OpString}
            + '%';
      ShowMsg(S);  {LoanMsg}

      Finished := True; {done}
    end;
  until Finished;

  ESRev.Erase;  {erase entry screen, OpEntry}
  ESRev.Done;   {recover object's memory, OpEntry}
end;            {end of procedure}

end.            {end of unit}
```

In this section of code:

```
if not ESRev.InitCustom(20, 5, 60, 13,          {Window
                                                 coordinates}
                     Colors,                    {Colors.inc}
                     DefWindowOptions           {default options
                      or wBordered)             {leave room for
                                                 border}
                     then begin
```

the DefWindowOptions mentioned are

wClear
wSaveContents
wResizable
wStoreContents

Remember, the complete list of possible options is

wBordered	Make space for window border
wClear	Clear window when it is first displayed
wSaveContents	Save the contents of the window when it is erased.
wUserContents	User will restore window contents
wSoundEffects	Use sound effects during explosions
wAltFrame	Use alternate frame type when not current
wSetMouse	Set mouse window, cursor on entry to window
wFullMouseWindow	Force to full mouse window on entry
wResizable	Can be resized and zoomed
wAllMouseEvents	Any combination of mouse buttons anywhere exits
wStoreContents	Store window contents in streams

In the line

```
ESRev.wFrame.AddShadow(shBR,          {shadow falls below and right}
                       shOverWrite);  {opaque shadow}
```

the options are

shBR	shadow falls to bottom and right of frame
shBL	shadow falls to bottom and left of frame

and for the second argument

shOverWrite	opaque shadow
shSeeThru	transparent shadow

In the line

```
ESRev.wFrame.AddHeader(' Convert Interest Earned to Percent ', heTC);
```

the options for the last parameter are

heTL	top left
heTC	top center
heTR	top right
heBL	bottom left
heBC	bottom center
heBR	bottom right

In the lines

```
ESRev.esFieldOptionsOn(efRequired);      {some input required}
ESRev.esFieldOptionsOff(efRequired);     {cancel required}
```

popular options are

efProtected	not changeable
efHidden	not displayed, field cannot be moved to it
efInvisible	field is never drawn
efRequired	some entry required
efBeepOnError	invalid entry
efClearFirstChar	if first character entered during editing is character clear the field

There are many, many more options. See the documentation on OpField for their names and descriptions. Note that these options can be used in methods other than esFieldOptionsOn() and esFieldOptionsOff().

A very large number of field types are available that can be used in data entry screens of which the following is only one example:

```
ESRev.AddRealField('Original amount:',   {prompt}
                   4,                     {V prompt position}
                   6,                     {H prompt position}
                   '999999.99',           {picture}
                   4,                     {data V position}
                   21,                    {data H position}
                   26,                    {help ID number}
                   0.01,                  {minimum valid entry}
                   999999.99,             {maximum valid entry}
                   2,                     {number of decimal places}
                   Starting);             {data variable}
```

The parameters of the various entry types are similar.
A full list of the Add fields consists of

AddArrayField	array of char
AddBcdField	binary coded decimal
AddBooleanField	Boolean response
AddByteField	byte
AddCharField	single character
AddChoiceField	for enumerated types, see HeaderInfo in LoanHead
AddCompField	comp precision
AddDateField	date—MM/DD/YY(YY)

AddDateStField	date string—ie: 16 Jan 1990
AddDblField	double precision
AddExtField	extended precision
AddIntField	integer
AddLongField	long integer
AddMultiLineField	edit string array
AddNestedField	brings up another entry screen when entered
AddNestedStringField	brings up another entry screen when entered
AddPickStringField	choose from pick list
AddRealField	real
AddSglField	single precision
AddShortField	short integer
AddStringField	string
AddTimeField	hours, minutes, seconds
AddUserField	user-defined field
AddWordField	word
AddYesNoField	yes/no choice—returns True/False

(uses simple character editor, no true pictures)

AddSimpleBcdField	binary coded decimal
AddSimpleBooleanField	Boolean
AddSimpleByteField	byte
AddSimpleCharField	character
AddSimpleCompField	comp
AddSimpleDblField	double precision
AddSimpleExtField	extended precision
AddSimpleIntField	integer
AddSimpleRealField	real
AddSimpleShortField	short integer
AddSimpleSngField	single precision
AddSimpleStringField)	string
AddSimpleWordField	word
AddSimpleYesNoField	yes or no—returns True or False

(uses number editor for numeric only fields)

AddNumericBcdField	binary coded decimal
AddNumericByteField	byte
AddNumericCompField	comp
AddNumericDblField	double precision

AddNumericExtField	extended precision
AddNumericIntField	integer
AddNumericLongField	long integer
AddNumericRealField	real
AddNumericShortField	short integer
AddNumericSngField	single precision
AddNumericWordField	word

See the documentation for OpEntry to get more details and parameter lists for each type.

Most fields have a picture parameter. The meaning of the picture characters is as follows:

X	Any character
!	Any character, force uppercase
L	Any character, force lowercase
x	Any character, first letter of each word upper-, others lowercase
a	Alphabetical characters only
A	Alphabetical characters only, force uppercase
l	Alphabetical characters only, force lowercase
9	Numbers and spaces only
#	Numbers, spaces, minus, period
E	Numbers, spaces, minus, period, e
K	0—9, A—F, force uppercase (hex)
B	T, t, F, f (Boolean)
Y	Y, y, N, n

Date and time characters:

m	Month, zero-padded
M	Month, blank-padded
d	Day, zero-padded
D	Day, blank-padded
y	Year, zero-padded
n	Month name
N	Month name, force uppercase
w	Weekday
W	Weekday, force uppercase
/	Month, day, year separator
h	Hours, zero-padded
H	Hours, blank-padded
m	Minutes, zero-padded

M	Minutes, blank-padded
s	Seconds, zero-padded
S	Seconds, blank-padded
t	'p' or 'a' in am/pm
e	'm' in am/pm
:	Minutes, hours, seconds separator

LoanPyof.Pas

This feature is used to calculate the payoff amount of a loan when the amount of the loan, date of loan, interest rate, and date of payoff are known. It uses the EntryScreen object from the OpEntry unit. The interest is compounded annually. Here is the code:

```
UNIT LoanPyof;
{calculate payoff amount and interest}

INTERFACE

uses LoanGlob,
     LoanMsg,
     OpCmd,
     OpRoot,
     OpField,
     OpFrame,
     OpWindow,
     OpCrt,
     OpString,
     OpEntry,
     OpDate,
     OpMouse;

{calculate payoff amount given loan amount, interest, loan date, and
 payoff date. Interest is compounded annually}
procedure Payoff;


IMPLEMENTATION


procedure Payoff;
{calculate payoff amount given loan amount, interest, loan date, and
 payoff date. Interest is compounded annually}

var
   Loan          : Real;       {amount of loan}
   PayDate       : Date;       {date of payoff}
   LoanDate      : Date;       {date of loan}
```

```
    TotalAmount    : Real;        {calculated amount to payoff}
    Interest       : Real;        {interest rate}
    S              : String;      {string temporary}
    InterestAmount : Real;        {calculated amount of interest due}
    ESPayOff       : EntryScreen; {instance of EntryScreen object}

begin
  ClrScr;
  if not ESPayOff.InitCustom(20, 5, 60, 13,           {Window
                                                       coordinates}
                    Colors,                            {Colors.inc}
                    DefWindowOptions or wBordered)     {Window options}
                    then begin                         {OpEntry}
    S := 'Failed to init payoff EntryScreen. Status = '
         + Long2Str(InitStatus);                       {OpString}
    ShowMsg(S);                                        {LoanMsg}
    Halt;
  end;

  if MouseInUse then begin                      {LoanGlob}
    EntryCommands.cpOptionsOn(cpEnableMouse);   {mouse sees entry screen,
                                                 EntryScreen Command
                                                 Processor}
    HideMouse;                                  {avoid mouse tracks,
                                                 OpMouse}
  end;

  {add some window frills, OpFrame}
  ESPayOff.wFrame.AddShadow(shBR,          {shadow below and right of
                                            screen}
                          shOverWrite);    {opaque shadow}
  ESPayOff.wFrame.AddHeader(' Calculate Payoff Amount ', heTC);
  ESPayOff.wFrame.AddHeader(' Esc to abort, Ctrl-Enter to accept ',
                          heBC);

  {add fields}
  ESPayOff.esFieldOptionsOn(efClearFirstChar); {clear field if first
                                                character is ASCII,
                                                OpEntry}

  ESPayOff.esFieldOptionsOn(efRequired);       {following entries
                                                required, OpEntry}
  ESPayOff.AddRealField('Amount of loan:', {prompt}
                    4,                     {V prompt position}
                    6,                     {H prompt position}
                    '999999.99',           {picture}
                    4,                     {data V position}
                    21,                    {data H position}
                    26,                    {help ID number}
                    0.01,                  {minimum valid entry}
```

```
                    999999.99,             {maximum valid entry}
                    2,                     {number of decimal places}
                    Loan);                 {data variable}

ESPayOff.AddRealField('Interest in %:',    {prompt}
                    5,                     {V prompt position}
                    6,                     {H prompt position}
                    '99.999',              {picture}
                    5,                     {data V position}
                    21,                    {data H position}
                    30,                    {ID number}
                    0.000,                 {minimum valid entry}
                    99.999,                {maximum valid entry}
                    3,                     {number of decimal places}
                    Interest);             {data variable}

ESPayoff.AddDateField('Loan date:',        {prompt}
                    6,                     {V prompt position}
                    6,                     {H prompt position}
                    'mm/dd/yyyy',          {picture}
                    6,                     {data V position}
                    21,                    {data H position}
                    27,                    {help ID number}
                    00,                    {minimum valid entry}
                    00,                    {maximum valid entry}
                    LoanDate);             {data variable}

ESPayOff.AddDateField('Payoff date:',      {prompt}
                    7,                     {V prompt position}
                    6,                     {H prompt position}
                    'mm/dd/yyyy',          {picture}
                    7,                     {data V position}
                    21,                    {data H position}
                    31,                    {help ID number}
                    00,                    {minimum valid entry}
                    00,                    {maximum valid entry}
                    PayDate);              {data variable}

ESPayOff.esFieldOptionsOff(efRequired);    {turn off required entries,
                                            OpEntry}

Finished := False;  {not completed}
Loan     := 0.00;   {default values}
LoanDate := Today;
PayDate  := Today;
Interest := 0.000;

repeat
  if MouseInUse then   {LoanGlob}
    ShowMouse;         {make mouse available to entry screen, OpMouse}
```

```
    ESPayOff.Process;    {get entries, OpEntry}
    if MouseInUse then   {LoanGlob}
      HideMouse;         {avoid mouse tracks, OpMouse}
    case ESPayoff.GetLastCommand of {return from entry screen, OpWindow}
      ccError:                      {error occurred, OpCmd}
        begin
          S := 'Fatal error '+ Long2Str(ESPayoff.GetLastError);
                                                        {OpString}
          ShowMsg(S);               {LoanMsg}
          Finished := True;         {abort operation}
        end;
      ccQuit :                      {escape, OpCmd}
        Finished := True;           {abort operation}
    end;

    if not Finished then begin      {Ctrl-Enter response}
      {calculate total amount due}
      TotalAmount := Exp(((PayDate - LoanDate) / 365) *
                     Ln(1 + (Interest / 100))) * Loan;  {OpDate}
      {calculate interest due}
      InterestAmount := TotalAmount - Loan;
      {display interest}
      ShowMsg('Interest is: ' +
              TrimLead(Real2Str(InterestAmount,9,2))); {LoanMsg,
                                                        OpString}
      {display total amount due}
      ShowMsg('Payoff is: '
              + TrimLead(Real2Str(TotalAmount,9,2)));  {LoanMsg,
                                                        OpString}

      Finished := True; {done}
    end;
  until Finished;

  ESPayOff.Erase; {erase entry screen, OpEntry}
  ESPayOff.Done;  {recover entry screen's memory, OpEntry}
end;              {end of procedure}

end.              {end of unit}
```

This unit is almost the same as the previous module, LoanRev. The only differences are the entry screen fields (interest in percent instead of current amount) and the fact that two windows are displayed: one displaying the interest accumulated, the other the total amount due.

All the various options available to the methods have been discussed earlier.

6

The Loan Application, Debtor Files

This chapter continues describing the loan application modules. To keep the chapters a reasonable size, this chapter contains only modules that have to do with the debtor records.

The objects used and discussed in this chapter are

EntryScreen and ancestors (OpEntry)
DirList and ancestors (OpDir)
Various methods in objects from OpDate, OpString, OpSort, OpCrt, OpMouse, and others.

LoanHead.pas

This unit is used to create, edit, and view the loan and debtor information. The character stored in EntryType determines which action it will take. Several interesting features of the EntryScreen object are used.

```
UNIT LoanHead;

INTERFACE

uses LoanGlob,
     OpDos,
     OpRoot,
     OpEntry,
```

```
      OpCrt,
      OpFrame,
      OpWindow,
      OpDate,
      OpString,
      OpField,
      OpMouse,
      OpCmd,
      LoanMsg;

{get, look at, or revise debtor and loan information}
procedure HeaderInfo;


IMPLEMENTATION


var
  HLateCharge  : Real;     {penalty amount added to debt if a payment
                            was a designated number of days late}
  HLateDays    : Integer;  {days after which to levy late charge}
  HFrequency   : FreqType; {how often payments due}
  HFirstDay    : Integer;  {in semimonthly payments, day of first
                            payment}
  HSecondDay   : Integer;  {in semimonthly payments, day of second
                            payment}
  SemiFlag     : Boolean;  {payment frequency semimonthly?}


{$F+}
procedure IncChoice(var Value; ID : Word; Factor : Integer; var St :
String);
{display payment frequency choices in sequence by pressing +
or - key}

var
   HFrequency : FreqType Absolute Value; {actual value, not position in
                                          list of possible values}
                                         {see declaration in LoanGlob
                                          unit}

begin
  case Factor of                   {+ or - key pressed?}
    01 :                           {+ key}
      if HFrequency = Yearly then {currently at high end of list?}
        HFrequency := Weekly       {loop back to low end}
      else
        Inc(HFrequency);           {next item in list}
    -1 :                           {- key}
      if HFrequency = Weekly then {currently at low end of list?}
```

```
        HFrequency := Yearly      {loop around to high end}
      else
        Dec(HFrequency);          {previous item in list}
  end;
  St := Frequency[HFrequency];    {return value}
end;
{$F-}


{$F+}
procedure ErrorHandler(UnitCode : Byte; var ErrCode : Word;
                       Msg : String);
{show error cause in window}

var
  S : String; {string temp}

begin
  S := 'Error: ' + Long2Str(ErrCode);  {OpString}
  ShowMsg(S);                          {LoanMsg}
end;
{$F-}


{$F+}
procedure PostEdit(ESP : EntryScreenPtr);
{called after each field entry is completed}
{hide or show semimonthly due days and days before late charge when
 appropriate}

begin
  if EntryType <> 'V' then begin          {not in view mode, Loan}

    if (ESP^.GetCurrentId = 13)           {OpSelect}
        and (ESP^.CurrentFieldModified) then begin {late charge value
                                                    field changed?,
                                                    OpEntry}
      if HLateCharge <> 0.00 then begin   {late charge set?}
        ESheader.ChangeHidden(14,False);  {unhide late days field,
                                           OpSelect}
        ESheader.ChangeRequired(14,True); {make late days entry
                                           required, OpEntry}
      end
      else begin
        HLateDays := 0;                    {set late days to default}
        ESheader.ChangeHidden(14,True);    {hide late days field,
                                            OpSelect}
        ESheader.ChangeRequired(14,False); {late days field not
                                            required, OpEntry}
      end;
```

```
    end;


    if (ESP^.GetCurrentId = 15)                    {OpSelect}
        and (ESP^.CurrentFieldModified) then begin {payment frequency
                                                    field changed?,
                                                    OpEntry}
      if HFrequency = Semimonthly then begin {if so, changed to
                                              semimonthly?}
        ESheader.ChangeHidden(16,False);     {unhide first due day
                                              field, OpSelect}
        ESheader.ChangeHidden(17,False);     {unhide second due day
                                              field, OpSelect}
        ESheader.ChangeRequired(16,True);    {require first due day
                                              field, OpEntry}
        ESheader.ChangeRequired(17,True);    {require second due day
                                              field, OpEntry}
      end
      else begin
        HFirstDay := 0;                      {default first day}
        HSecondDay := 0;                     {default second day}
        ESheader.ChangeHidden(16,True);      {hide first due day field,
                                              OpSelect}
        ESheader.ChangeHidden(17,True);      {hide second due day field,
                                              OpSelect}
        ESheader.ChangeRequired(16,False);   {first due day field not
                                              required, OpEntry}
        ESheader.ChangeRequired(17,False);   {second due day field not
                                              required, OpEntry}
      end;
    end;

    ESP^.ResetScreen; {OpSelect}
  end;
end;
{$F-}


procedure HeaderInfo;
{get, look at, or revise debtor and loan information}

var
  HName        : String;  {debtor name}
  HAddress1    : String;  {debtor address, first line}
  HAddress2    : String;  {debtor address, second line}
  HCity        : String;  {debtor city, state, and zip}
  HHomePhone   : String;  {debtor home phone}
  HWorkPhone   : String;  {debtor work phone}
  HLoanAmount  : Real;    {amount of loan}
  HPayAmount   : Real;    {amount of payments}
```

```
  HLoanDate     : Date;     {date of loan}
  HFirstDue     : Date;     {date of first payment}
  HInterest     : Real;     {interest rate in percent}
  HPayIntFirst  : Boolean;  {start interest at loan date or first payment
                             date}
  S             : String;   {string temporary}
  IoFlag        : Word;     {result of I/O operation}
  f             : String;   {file name}
  Ok            : Char;     {entry screen completed ok?}

begin
  ClrScr;
  Ok := ' ';
  SemiFlag := False;        {payment frequency not set to semimonthly}
  if not ESHeader.InitCustom(5, 2, 75, 22, {Window coordinates}
                     Colors,               {Colors.inc}
                     DefWindowOptions      {default window options}
                       or wBordered)       {leave room for border}
                     then begin
    S := 'Failed to init header EntryScreen. Status = '
         + Long2Str(InitStatus);           {OpString}
    ShowMsg(S);                            {LoanMsg}
    Halt;
  end;

  ESHeader.SetErrorProc(ErrorHandler); {show error in window, OpWindow}
  ESHeader.SetPostEditProc(PostEdit);  {point to post error procedure,
                                        OpEntry}

  if MouseInUse then begin                   {LoanGlob}
    EntryCommands.cpOptionsOn(cpEnableMouse); {mouse available,
                                               EntryScreen Command
                                               Processor}
    HideMouse;                               {avoid mouse tracks,
                                              OpMouse}
  end;

  {add some window frills with OpFrame methods}
  ESHeader.wFrame.AddShadow(shBR,        {shadow bottom and right of
                                          screen}
                     shOverWrite); {opaque shadow}
  ESHeader.wFrame.AddHeader(' Debtor Screen ', heTC); {top centered}
  if EntryType <> 'V' then {new debtor or editing, not just viewing}
    ESHeader.wFrame.AddHeader(' Esc to abort, Ctrl-Enter to accept ',
                      heBC);          {bottom centered}

  {add fields}
  ESHeader.esFieldOptionsOn(efClearFirstChar); {clear field on entry if
                                                first character is
                                                ASCII, OpEntry}
```

```
if EntryType = 'N' then begin                          {new loan, Loan}
  ESheader.esFieldOptionsOn(efRequired);               {following field
                                                        required,
                                                        OpEntry}
  ESHeader.AddStringField('Filename (no extension):', {prompt}
                          3,                           {prompt V
                                                        position}
                          2,                           {prompt H
                                                        position}
                          'XXXXXXXX',                  {picture}
                          3,                           {data V
                                                        position}
                          35,                          {data H
                                                        position}
                          8,                           {data width}
                          1,                           {help ID number}
                          CurFile);                    {data variable}
  ESheader.esFieldOptionsOff(efRequired);              {turn off
                                                        required so
                                                        following
                                                        fields not
                                                        required,
                                                        OpEntry}
end
else begin
  ESheader.esFieldOptionsOn(efProtected);   {following field protected
                                             from alteration, OpEntry}
  ESHeader.AddStringField('Filename:',      {prompt}
                          3,                {prompt V position}
                          2,                {prompt H position}
                          'XXXXXXXX',       {picture}
                          3,                {data V position}
                          35,               {data H position}
                          8,                {data width}
                          1,                {help ID number}
                          CurFile);         {data variable}
  ESheader.esFieldOptionsOff(efProtected); {turn off protected,
                                             OpEntry}
end;


if EntryType = 'V' then                    {if viewing record, Loan}
  ESheader.esFieldOptionsOn(efProtected)   {protect all fields,
                                            OpEntry}
else
  ESheader.esFieldOptionsOn(efRequired);   {if not viewing record
                                            this field is required,
                                            OpEntry}
ESHeader.AddStringField('Name:',           {prompt}
                        4,                 {prompt V position}
                        2,                 {prompt H position}
```

```
                         CharStr('x',30),  {picture}
                         4,                {data V position}
                         35,               {data H position}
                         30,               {data width}
                         2,                {help ID number}
                         HName);           {data variable}
if EntryType <> 'V' then                   {if not viewing record}
  ESheader.esFieldOptionsOff(efRequired);  {done with required,
                                            OpEntry}

ESHeader.AddStringField('Address line 1:',  {prompt}
                         5,                 {prompt V position}
                         2,                 {prompt H position}
                         CharStr('x',30),   {picture}
                         5,                 {data V position}
                         35,                {data H position}
                         30,                {data width}
                         3,                 {help ID number}
                         HAddress1);        {data variable}

ESHeader.AddStringField('Address line 2:',  {prompt}
                          6,                {prompt V position}
                          2,                {prompt H position}
                          CharStr('x',30),  {picture}
                          6,                {data V position}
                          35,               {data H position}
                          30,               {data width}
                          4,                {help ID number}
                          HAddress2);       {data variable}

ESHeader.AddStringField('City, State, ZIP:',  {prompt}
                         7,                   {prompt V position}
                         2,                   {prompt H position}
                         CharStr('x',30),     {picture}
                         7,                   {data V position}
                         35,                  {data H position}
                         30,                  {data width}
                         5,                   {help ID number}
                         HCity);              {data variable}

ESHeader.AddStringField('Home phone:',        {prompt}
                         8,                   {prompt V position}
                         2,                   {prompt H position}
                         '999/999-9999',      {picture}
                         8,                   {data V position}
                         35,                  {data H position}
                         12,                  {data width}
                         6,                   {help ID number}
                         HHomePhone);         {data variable}
```

```
ESHeader.AddStringField('Work phone:',  {prompt}
                        9,              {prompt V position}
                        2,              {prompt H position}
                        '999/999-9999', {picture}
                        9,              {data V position}
                        35,             {data H position}
                        12,             {data width}
                        7,              {help ID number}
                        HWorkPhone);    {data variable}

if EntryType = 'V' then                  {if viewing record, Loan}
  ESheader.esFieldOptionsOn(efProtected) {retain field protection,
                                          OpEntry}
else
  ESheader.esFieldOptionsOn(efRequired); {if not viewing record the
                                          following fields are
                                          required}

ESHeader.AddRealField('Amount of loan:', {prompt}
                      11,                {prompt V position}
                      2,                 {prompt H position}
                      '999999.99',       {picture}
                      11,                {data V position}
                      35,                {data H position}
                      8,                 {help ID number}
                      0.01,              {minimum valid entry}
                      999999.99,         {maximum valid entry}
                      2,                 {number of decimal places}
                      HLoanAmount);      {data variable}

ESHeader.AddRealField('Interest (in %):', {prompt}
                      12,                 {prompt V position}
                      2,                  {prompt H position}
                      '99.999',           {picture}
                      12,                 {data V position}
                      35,                 {data H position}
                      9,                  {help ID number}
                      0.000,              {minimum valid entry}
                      99.999,             {maximum valid entry}
                      3,                  {number of decimal places}
                      HInterest);         {data variable}

ESHeader.AddRealField('Amount of payment:', {prompt}
                      13,                   {prompt V position}
                      2,                    {prompt H position}
                      '999999.99',          {picture}
                      13,                   {data V position}
                      35,                   {data H position}
                      10,                   {help ID number}
                      0.01,                 {minimum valid entry}
```

```
                     999999.99,            {maximum valid entry}
                     2,                    {number of decimal places}
                     HPayAmount);          {data variable}

ESHeader.AddDateField('Date of loan:', {prompt}
                     14,               {prompt V position}
                     2,                {prompt H position}
                     'mm/dd/yyyy',     {picture}
                     14,               {data V position}
                     35,               {data H position}
                     11,               {help ID number}
                     00,               {earliest valid date}
                     00,               {latest valid date}
                     HLoanDate);       {data variable}

{protect payment due dates already entered in LoanPay}
{if editing record and at least one nonstandard payment entered}
if (EntryType = 'E') and (MaxFile > 0) then {Loan, LoanGlob}
   ESheader.esFieldOptionsOn(efProtected); {protect next field,
                                            OpEntry}
ESHeader.AddDateField('Date of first payment:', {prompt}
                     15,                        {prompt V position}
                     2,                         {prompt H position}
                     'mm/dd/yyyy',              {picture}
                     15,                        {data V position}
                     35,                        {data H position}
                     12,                        {help ID number}
                     00,                        {earliest valid date}
                     00,                        {latest valid date}
                     HFirstDue);                {data variable}
{if editing record and at least one nonstandard payment entered}
if (EntryType = 'E') and (MaxFile > 0) then {Loan, LoanGlob}
  ESheader.esFieldOptionsOff(efProtected); {done with protection,
                                            OpEntry}

if EntryType <> 'V' then                  {if not viewing record,
                                           Loan}
  ESheader.esFieldOptionsOff(efRequired); {done with required,
                                           OpEntry}

ESHeader.AddYesNoField('Interest to first payment? (Y/N)', {prompt}
                       16,                                 {prompt V
                                                            position}
                       2,                                  {prompt H
                                                            position}
                       '',                                 {picture}
                       16,                                 {data V
                                                            position}
                       35,                                 {data H
                                                            position}
```

```
                         16,                              {help ID
                                                           number}
                         HPayIntFirst);                   {data
                                                           variable}

ESHeader.AddRealField('Late Charge:',  {prompt}
                      17,              {prompt V position}
                      2,               {prompt H position}
                      '999999.99',     {picture}
                      17,              {data V position}
                      15,              {data H position}
                      24,              {help ID number}
                      0.00,            {minimum valid entry}
                      999999.99,       {maximum valid entry}
                      2,               {number of decimal places}
                      HLateCharge);    {data variable}

if EntryType = 'V' then begin               {if not viewing record,
                                             Loan}
  if HLateCharge <> 0 then                  {if non-0 late charge}
    ESheader.esFieldOptionsOn(efProtected) {don't change following
                                             field, OpEntry}
  else                                      {if 0 late charge}
    ESheader.esFieldOptionsOn(efHidden);    {hide next field, OpEntry}
end
else                                        {if new header or editing}
    ESheader.esFieldOptionsOn(efHidden);    {hide next field (see
                                             PostEdit procedure here),
                                             OpEntry}

ESHeader.AddIntField('Late days for charge:', {prompt}
                      17,                     {prompt V position}
                      25,                     {prompt H position}
                      '99',                   {picture}
                      17,                     {data V position}
                      47,                     {data H position}
                      25,                     {help ID number}
                      0,                      {minimum valid entry}
                      28,                     {maximum valid entry}
                      HLateDays);             {data variable}

if EntryType = 'V' then begin                 {if viewing record,
                                               Loan}
  if HLateCharge <> 0.00 then                 {and late charge non-0}
    ESheader.esFieldOptionsOff(efProtected)   {done with protection,
                                               OpEntry}
  else                                        {late charge 0}
    ESheader.esFieldOptionsOff(efHidden);     {done with hidden,
                                               OpEntry}
end
```

```
else                                          {if new debtor or
                                               editing}
  ESheader.esFieldOptionsOff(efHidden);       {done with hidden,
                                               OpEntry}

{protect payment due dates already entered in LoanPay}
{if viewing record or (editing record and at least one nonstandard
 payment entered), Loan, LoanGlob}
if (EntryType = 'V') or ((EntryType <> 'N') and (MaxFile > 0)) then
   ESheader.esFieldOptionsOn(efProtected); {protect next field,
                                            OpEntry}
ESHeader.AddChoiceField('Payment frequency (use + or -):', {prompt}
                         18,                               {prompt V
                                                            position}
                         2,                                {prompt H
                                                            position}
                         'XXXXXXXXXXX',                    {picture}
                         18,                               {data V
                                                            position}
                         35,                               {data H
                                                            position}
                         13,                               {help ID
                                                            number}
                         01,                               {data size}
                         IncChoice,                        {selection
                                                            procedure}
                         HFrequency);                      {data
                                                            variable}
{if viewing record or (editing record and at least one nonstandard
 payment entered), Loan, LoanGlob}
if (EntryType = 'V') or ((EntryType <> 'N') and (MaxFile > 0)) then
  ESheader.esFieldOptionsOff(efProtected); {done with protection,
                                            OpEntry}

if EntryType = 'V' then begin               {if viewing record, Loan}
  if HFrequency = Semimonthly then          {semimonthly?}
    ESheader.esFieldOptionsOn(efProtected) {protect next two fields,
                                            OpEntry}
  else
    ESheader.esFieldOptionsOn(efHidden);    {hide next two fields
                                             (nothing to see), OpEntry}
end
else
    ESheader.esFieldOptionsOn(efHidden); {protect next two fields (see
                                          PostEdit procedure here),
                                          OpEntry}

ESHeader.AddIntField('First payment day (1 - 14):', {prompt}
                      19,                           {prompt V
                                                     position}
```

```
                      2,                              {prompt H
                                                       position}
                      '99',                           {picture}
                      19,                             {data V position}
                      30,                             {data H position}
                      14,                             {help ID number}
                      1,                              {minimum valid
                                                       entry}
                      14,                             {maximum valid
                                                       entry}
                      HFirstDay);                     {data variable}

ESHeader.AddIntField('Second (15 - 28):',             {prompt}
                      19,                             {prompt V
                                                       position}
                      33,                             {prompt H
                                                       position}
                      '99',                           {picture}
                      19,                             {data V position}
                      51,                             {data H position}
                      15,                             {help ID number}
                      15,                             {minimum valid
                                                       entry}
                      28,                             {maximum valid
                                                       entry}
                      HSecondDay);                    {data variable}
if EntryType = 'V' then begin                 {if viewing record, Loan}
  if HFrequency = Semimonthly then            {semimonthly?}
    ESheader.esFieldOptionsOff(efProtected)   {turn off protection,
                                               OpEntry}
  else
    ESheader.esFieldOptionsOff(efHidden);     {turn off hidden, OpEntry}
end
else                                          {new debtor or editing}
  ESheader.esFieldOptionsOff(efHidden);       {turn off hidden, OpEntry}

if EntryType = 'V' then                               {viewing record?,
                                                       Loan}
  ESHeader.AddCharField('Press Escape to continue',   {prompt}
                        21,                           {prompt V
                                                       position}
                        22,                           {prompt H
                                                       position}
                        'X',                          {picture}
                        21,                           {data V position}
                        47,                           {data H position}
                        0,                            {help ID number}
                        #27,                          {low value}
                        #27,                          {high value}
                        Ok);                          {data variable}
```

```
EsHeader.SetErrorProc(DefaultErrorProc); {beep on error, OpWindow}

Finished := False;             {done?}
if EntryType = 'N' then begin {new debtor, Loan}
  HName        := '';          {defaults for new record}
  HAddress1    := '';
  HAddress2    := '';
  HCity        := '';
  HHomePhone   := '';
  HWorkPhone   := '';
  HLoanAmount  := 0.00;
  HPayAmount   := 0.00;
  HLoanDate    := Today;
  HLateCharge  := 0.00;
  HLateDays    := 0;
  HFrequency   := Monthly;
  HFirstDay    := 0;
  HSecondDay   := 0;
  HFirstDue    := Today;
  HInterest    := 0.00;
  HPayIntFirst := False;
end
else begin                            {editing or viewing}
  HName        := Header.Name;        {show stored record values}
  HAddress1    := Header.Address1;
  HAddress2    := Header.Address2;
  HCity        := Header.City;
  HHomePhone   := Header.HomePhone;
  HWorkPhone   := Header.WorkPhone;
  HLoanAmount  := Header.LoanAmount;
  HPayAmount   := Header.PayAmount;
  HLoanDate    := Header.LoanDate;
  HLateCharge  := Header.LateCharge;
  HLateDays    := Header.LateDays;
  HFrequency   := Header.Frequency;
  HFirstDay    := Header.FirstDay;
  HSecondDay   := Header.SecondDay;
  HFirstDue    := Header.FirstDue;
  HInterest    := Header.Interest;
  HPayIntFirst := Header.PayIntFirst;
end;


repeat
  if MouseInUse then {LoanGlob}
    ShowMouse;       {mouse available, OpMouse}
  ESHeader.Process;  {get, view, or edit record info, OpEntry}
  if MouseInUse then {LoanGlob}
    HideMouse;       {avoid mouse tracks, OpMouse}
  case ESHeader.GetLastCommand of  {OpEntry, OpCmd}
```

```
  ccError :                         {OpCmd}
    begin
      S := 'Fatal error '
            + Long2Str(ESHeader.GetLastError); {OpString}
      ShowMsg(S);          {LoanMsg}
      Finished := True; {abandon operation}
    end;

  ccQuit :               {Escape key, OpCmd}
    Finished := True; {abandon operation}
end;

if EntryType = 'V' then {if viewing record we are done, Loan}
  Finished := True;      {Abandon operation}

if not Finished then begin          {Control-Enter}
  if EntryType <> 'V' then begin     {if not viewing, put field data
                                      in record, Loan}
    Header.Name         := HName;
    Header.Address1     := HAddress1;
    Header.Address2     := HAddress2;
    Header.City         := HCity;
    Header.HomePhone    := HHomePhone;
    Header.WorkPhone    := HWorkPhone;
    Header.LoanAmount   := HLoanAmount;
    Header.PayAmount    := HPayAmount;
    Header.LoanDate     := HLoanDate;
    Header.Frequency    := HFrequency;
    Header.LateCharge   := HLateCharge;

    if Header.Frequency = Semimonthly then begin
      Header.FirstDay   := HFirstDay;
      Header.SecondDay  := HSecondDay;
    end
    else begin
      Header.FirstDay   := 0;
      Header.SecondDay  := 0;
    end;

    if Header.LateCharge <> 0.00 then
      Header.LateDays   := HLateDays
    else
      Header.LateDays   := 0;

    Header.FirstDue     := HFirstDue;
    Header.Interest     := HInterest;
    Header.PayIntFirst  := HPayIntFirst;

    {save header record}
    f := TrimSpaces(CurFile) + '.HDR'; {name of file to hold record,
                                        OpString}
```

```
        if not ExistFile(f) then begin      {OpDos}
          assign(HeadFile,f);                 {assign file name to file
                                               variable, LoanGlob}
          {$I-}
          rewrite(HeadFile);                  {open file in write only
                                               mode, LoanGlob}
          IoFlag := IoResult;                 {get possible error}
          if IoFlag <> 0 then begin           {I/O error}
            ShowMsg('Rewrite debtor ' + f + ' error. IoResult is: '
                     + Long2Str(IoFlag));     {OpString, LoanMsg}
            Halt;
          end;
          write(HeadFile,Header);             {store record in file}
          IoFlag := IoResult;                 {get possible error}
          if IoFlag <> 0 then begin           {I/O error}
            ShowMsg('Write debtor ' + f + ' error. IoResult is: '
                     + Long2Str(IoFlag));     {OpString, LoanMsg}
            Halt;
          end;

          close(HeadFile);                    {save file buffers to disk}
          {$I+}
          Finished := True;                   {done}
        end
        else
          ShowMsg('File already exists. Choose another file name.');
                                                                  {LoanMsg}
      end;
    end;
  until Finished;
  ESHeader.Erase; {erase entry screen from screen, OpEntry}
  ESHeader.Done;  {erase entry screen from memory, OpEntry}
end; {end of procedure}

end. {end of unit}
```

I will be using the term "header" for the record that is created from this entry screen. It means the debtor and loan information. Now for a quick review of what is accomplished in this unit.

Add Mode

The HeaderInfo procedure is called. The global variable EntryType has been set to "N" (New debtor) in Loan.pas. The screen is cleared and the header entry screen is initialized.

```
ESHeader.SetErrorProc(ErrorHandler); {show error in window, OpWindow}
```

An error handler is supplied that displays the error in a window rather than just beeping.

```
{$F+}
procedure ErrorHandler(UnitCode : Byte; var ErrCode : Word;
                       Msg : String);
{show error cause in window}

var
  S : String; {string temp}

begin
  S := 'Error: ' + Long2Str(ErrCode);          {OpString}
  ShowMsg(S);                                   {LoanMsg}
end;
{$F-}
```

This error window is mostly for the programmer's benefit, as it will show any bad coordinates or other EntryScreen object errors. The user should never see this window. The error procedure is later switched back to the default beep before the user makes any entries. Next the mouse is made available.

```
if MouseInUse then begin                       {LoanGlob}
  EntryCommands.cpOptionsOn(cpEnableMouse);   {mouse available,
                                                EntryScreen Command
                                                Processor}
  HideMouse;                                   {avoid mouse tracks,
                                                OpMouse}
end;
```

When the Payment Frequency field is set to Semimonthly, we need to get two extra fields of information: the two payment dates. If the Payment Frequency is set to Weekly, Monthly, or Yearly, these fields are not needed. If the Late Charge field is set to 0.00, we need not find out what the grace period (contents of Late Days field) is to be before the charge is to take effect. These fields are hidden when not needed, and made required if they are appropriate. This is accomplished with a PostEdit procedure. The PostEdit procedure is called when the user attempts to leave the field. First we have to tell the EntryScreen object what procedure to use:

```
ESHeader.SetPostEditProc(PostEdit);  {point to post error procedure,
                                      OpEntry}
```

Here is the procedure:

```
{$F+}
procedure PostEdit(ESP : EntryScreenPtr);
{called after each field entry is completed}
{hide or show semimonthly due days and days before late charge when
 appropriate}

begin
  if EntryType <> 'V' then begin          {not in view mode, Loan}
```

```
    if (ESP^.GetCurrentId = 13)                        {OpSelect}
        and (ESP^.CurrentFieldModified) then begin {late charge value
                                                     field changed?,
                                                     OpEntry}
      if HLateCharge <> 0.00 then begin   {late charge set?}
        ESheader.ChangeHidden(14,False);  {unhide late days field,
                                           OpSelect}
        ESheader.ChangeRequired(14,True); {make late days entry
                                           required, OpEntry}
      end
      else begin
        HLateDays := 0;                    {set late days to default}
        ESheader.ChangeHidden(14,True);    {hide late days field,
                                            OpSelect}
        ESheader.ChangeRequired(14,False); {late days field not
                                            required, OpEntry}
      end;
    end;


    if (ESP^.GetCurrentId = 15)
        and (ESP^.CurrentFieldModified) then begin  {payment frequency
                                                      field changed?}
      if HFrequency = Semimonthly then begin {if so, changed to
                                              semimonthly?}
        ESheader.ChangeHidden(16,False);      {unhide first due day
                                               field, OpSelect}
        ESheader.ChangeHidden(17,False);      {unhide second due day
                                               field, OpSelect}
        ESheader.ChangeRequired(16,True);     {require first due day
                                               field, OpEntry}
        ESheader.ChangeRequired(17,True);     {require second due day
                                               field, OpEntry}
      end
      else begin
        HFirstDay := 0;                       {default first day}
        HSecondDay := 0;                      {default second day}
        ESheader.ChangeHidden(16,True);       {hide first due day field,
                                               OpSelect}
        ESheader.ChangeHidden(17,True);       {hide second due day field,
                                               OpSelect}
        ESheader.ChangeRequired(16,False);    {first due day field not
                                               required, OpEntry}
        ESheader.ChangeRequired(17,False);    {second due day field not
                                               required, OpEntry}
      end;
    end;

    ESP^.ResetScreen; {OpSelect}
  end;
```

```
end;
{$F-}
```

As you can see, although the PostEdit procedure is called upon leaving each field, it does something only when fields 13 and 15 have been altered. The numbers 13 and 15 are arrived at by counting the fields, starting with 0, beginning at the top of the field list. In this case the file name field is 0, the name field 1, and so on. The ChangeHidden procedure requires the field number (as just described) followed by True if it is to be hidden; otherwise it is False. The ChangeRequired procedure works the same way.

There are several other similar ChangeSomething procedures. An asterisk in the following list designates that the method was inherited by EntryScreen from the Abstract Selector object in OpSelect; otherwise it is an EntryScreen method.

ChangeConversion	Change conversion procedure of designated field (number base for example)
ChangeFieldAttr*	Change color of designated unselected fields
ChangeHidden*	Hide or unhide a designated field
ChangeInvisibility*	Make a designated field visible or invisible
ChangePromptAttr*	Change color of designated field's prompt when unselected
ChangeProtectedFieldAttr*	Change color of designated field when protected
ChangeProtectedPromptAttr*	Change color of designated field's prompt when protected
ChangeProtection*	Protect or unprotect a designated field
ChangeRange	Change valid entry range of designated field
ChangeRequired	Require or not require a designated field
ChangeSelectedFieldAttr*	Change color of designated field when selected
ChangeSelectedPromptAttr*	Change color of designated field's prompt when protected
ChangeValidation	Change the validation routine for a designated field

Next we come to the entry fields. Entry fields were described in the previous chapter. In the Add mode we wish to be able to make an entry in every applicable field. We start out with the two semimonthly date fields hidden, as well as the Late Days field, as described above. Required fields (some entry required) are preceded with

```
ESheader.esFieldOptionsOn(efRequired);
```

All the following fields are required until the procedure

```
ESheader.esFieldOptionsOff(efRequired);
```

is reached. We can protect a field (that is, the entry can't be changed) by using the parameter efProtected. Hidden fields can be controlled with efHidden.

The "X" picture means accept any character. The "x" mask means automatically capitalize the first character of every word: the remaining characters are lowercase. This can be overridden with the Shift or Caps Lock key. See the previous chapter for a list of all the picture characters.

The payment Frequency field is unusual in that instead of typing in an entry, the plus and minus keys are used to cycle through the possible entries. This is simpler than verifying an entry from a list when only a few choices are possible. The data variable must be set up like this:

```
type
  Freqtype = (Weekly,Semimonthly,Monthly,Yearly);
```

This data is in the LoanGlob unit. In this (HeaderInfo) unit we see

```
var
  HFrequency   : FreqType; {how often payments due}
```

We must also supply a procedure to cycle through the choices.

```
{$F+}
procedure IncChoice(var Value; ID : Word; Factor : Integer; var St :
String);
{display payment frequency choices in sequence by pressing + or - key}

var
   HFrequency : FreqType Absolute Value; {actual value, not position in
                                          list of possible values}
                                         {see declaration in LoanGlob
                                          unit}

begin
  case Factor of                  {+ or - key pressed?}
    01 :                          {+ key}
      if HFrequency = Yearly then {currently at high end of list?}
        HFrequency := Weekly      {loop back to low end}
      else
        Inc(HFrequency);          {next item in list}
    -1 :                          {- key}
      if HFrequency = Weekly then {currently at low end of list?}
        HFrequency := Yearly      {loop around to high end}
      else
        Dec(HFrequency);          {previous item in list}
  end;
```

```
  St := Frequency[HFrequency];     {return value}
end;
{$F-}
```

The name of the procedure is designated as the ninth parameter in the Payment Frequency field description. Here's what the field description looks like:

```
ESHeader.AddChoiceField('Payment frequency (use + or -):', {prompt}
                          18,                               {prompt V
                                                             position}
                          2,                                {prompt H
                                                             position}
                          'XXXXXXXXXXX',                    {picture}
                          18,                               {data V
                                                             position}
                          35,                               {data H
                                                             position}
                          13,                               {help ID
                                                             number}
                          01,                               {data size}
                          IncChoice,                        {selection
                                                             procedure}
                          HFrequency);                      {data
                                                             variable}
```

The last field,

```
if EntryType = 'V' then                          {viewing record?,
                                                  Loan}
  ESHeader.AddCharField('Press Escape to continue', {prompt}
                         21,                        {prompt V
                                                     position}
                         22,                        {prompt H
                                                     position}
                         'X',                       {picture}
                         21,                        {data V position}
                         47,                        {data H position}
                         0,                         {help ID number}
                         #27,                       {low value}
                         #27,                       {high value}
                         Ok);                       {data variable}
```

is only used to escape the screen when the View mode is in use.

The various if statements around the fields control whether a field is required, hidden, or protected. A list of these options can be found after the LoanRev.pas discussion in the previous chapter. All fields are protected in view mode. The sometimes-hidden, sometimes-required Semimonthly Payment Frequency due date (HFirstDay and HSecondDay) and the Late Days (HLateDays) fields were discussed earlier. The various picture characters were also covered in the previous chapter.

Now that the fields are all defined, the next step is to give all the field variables their default value. In the Add mode, the fields are set to blank in the case of strings, $0.00 for money fields, and that day's date for date fields. The payment frequency defaults to monthly.

The mouse is then made visible and the user is ready to process the screen. The program watches for the Escape key to abandon the entries or Ctrl-Enter to accept the data. If Ctrl-Enter is used and there are any required fields left blank, the program will not permit leaving. The first such field is then highlighted for an entry.

Once all the fields are entered or the Escape key is pressed, the mouse is hidden to avoid mouse tracks. If Escape is used, the module ends and the user is returned to the menu. Next all the field variables are transferred to the Header record. The entered file name is checked to be sure a file of that name does not already exist. If it does, the user is notified. If the file does not exist in the default directory, the new record is saved with the extension ".HDR."

Edit Mode

The "E" (Edit) mode is much like the Add mode, except the File name field is protected. Also, if any nonstandard payments have already been entered, the user is not permitted to change the first payment date. Thus

```
{protect payment due dates already entered in LoanPay}
{if editing record and at least one nonstandard payment entered}
if (EntryType = 'E') and (MaxFile > 0) then {Loan, LoanGlob}
   ESheader.esFieldOptionsOn(efProtected); {protect next field,
                                            OpEntry}
ESHeader.AddDateField('Date of first payment:', {prompt}
                      15,                       {prompt V position}
                      2,                        {prompt H position}
                      'mm/dd/yyyy',             {picture}
                      15,                       {data V position}
                      35,                       {data H position}
                      12,                       {help ID number}
                      00,                       {earliest valid date}
                      00,                       {latest valid date}
                      HFirstDue);               {data variable}
{if editing record and at least one nonstandard payment entered}
if (EntryType = 'E') and (MaxFile > 0) then {Loan, LoanGlob}
  ESheader.esFieldOptionsOff(efProtected); {done with protection,
                                            OpEntry}
```

The first payment date determines the day of the week for weekly payments, the day of the month for monthly payments, or the date for yearly payments. When nonstandard payments are entered, a valid due date must be entered, so the routine that prints the amortization table can tell which standard payment is to be replaced. If the date were changed, all these nonstandard payment-due dates would probably become invalid.

The payment frequency cannot be altered for the same reason; the payments already entered would probably end up with invalid due dates and therefore would never be incorporated into the amortization table.

```
{protect payment due dates already entered in LoanPay}
{if viewing record or (editing record and at least one nonstandard
 payment entered), Loan, LoanGlob}
if (EntryType = 'V') or ((EntryType <> 'N') and (MaxFile > 0)) then
   ESheader.esFieldOptionsOn(efProtected); {protect next field,
                                            OpEntry}
ESHeader.AddChoiceField('Payment frequency (use + or -):', {prompt}
                        18,                                {prompt V
                                                            position}
                        2,                                 {prompt H
                                                            position}
                        'XXXXXXXXXXX',                     {picture}
                        18,                                {data V
                                                            position}
                        35,                                {data H
                                                            position}
                        13,                                {help ID
                                                            number}
                        01,                                {data size}
                        IncChoice,                         {selection
                                                            procedure}
                        HFrequency);                       {data
                                                            variable}
{if viewing record or (editing record and at least one nonstandard
 payment entered), Loan, LoanGlob}
if (EntryType = 'V') or ((EntryType <> 'N') and (MaxFile > 0)) then
  ESheader.esFieldOptionsOff(efProtected); {done with protection,
                                            OpEntry}
```

Finally, in Edit mode the fields default to the data stored in the header record instead of blanks and zeros.

View Mode

In this mode all the fields but one are protected. Thus no changes can be made inadvertently. The added field

```
if EntryType = 'V' then                            {viewing record?,
                                                    Loan}
  ESHeader.AddCharField('Press Escape to continue', {prompt}
                        21,                         {prompt V
                                                    position}
                        22,                         {prompt H
                                                    position}
                        'X',                        {picture}
                        21,                         {data V position}
```

```
                   47,                         {data H position}
                   0,                          {help ID number}
                   #27,                        {low value}
                   #27,                        {high value}
                   Ok);                        {data variable}
```

is used to enable the user to gracefully leave the entry screen when desired. The Escape key will close the entry screen and return the user to the main menu. The EntryScreen object seems to require at least one unprotected field.

LoanDir.pas

The LoanDir unit is used to select a debtor by displaying all the files in the default directory that have the extension ".HDR." Once a filename is chosen, the program loads the associated nonstandard payment records into the PayList array, if any exist.

```
unit LoanDir;
{list loan files, choose one, load data from chosen file}

INTERFACE


uses
  LoanGlob,
  Dos,
  OpString,
  OpCrt,
  OpRoot,
  OpCmd,
  OpFrame,
  OpWindow,
  OpSort,
  OpPick,
  OpMouse,
  OpDir,
  OpDate,
  LoanMsg;

{list loan files so one can be chosen}
procedure MakeDirList;


IMPLEMENTATION


var
  Dir : Dirlist; {instance of object}
```

```
{$F+}
procedure GetPayList;
{feed payments from array into sort structures}
var
  N     : Integer;    {pay record counter}
  Value : PayRecord; {contents of record}


begin
  for N := 1 TO MaxFile do begin   {visit all the records, LoanGlob}
    Value := PayList[N];           {record content}
    if not PutElement(Value) then  {no room in sort area, OpSort}
      Exit;
  end;
end;



function Less(var x,y) : Boolean;
{compare records}
var
  X1 : PayRecord absolute X; {LoanGlob}
  Y1 : PayRecord absolute Y; {LoanGlob}
begin
  Less := (X1.PayDate < Y1.PayDate); {compare which fields?, LoanGlob}
end;



Procedure WritePayList;
{feed payments from sort structure back into array}
var
  N : Integer;        {payment counter}
  Value : PayRecord; {record contents, LoanGlob}


begin
  N := 1;                              {start at first record}
  while GetElement(value) do begin     {while more sorted records, OpSort}
    PayList[N] := Value;               {put record in array, LoanGlob}
    Inc(N);                            {next record}
  end;
end;
{$F-}



procedure MakeDirList;
{list loan files so one can be chosen}


var
  IoFlag : word;        {I/O error flag}
  S         : String;   {string temporary}
  Status : SortStatus; {sort result, overrides global Status variable}
```

```
begin
  {initialize directory lister}
  if not Dir.InitCustom(30, 5, 50, 20,   {Window coordinates}
                        Colors,          {Colors.inc}
                        DefWindowOptions {default options}
                          or wBordered,  {leave room for border}
                        MaxAvail,        {set buffer for filenames at
                                          least 64K}
                        PickVertical,    {pick orientation}
                        SingleFile)      {only one choice allowed}
                        then begin
    ShowMsg('Failed to init DirList, Status = ' + Long2Str(InitStatus));
                                                   {LoanMsg, OpString}
    Halt;
  end;


  if MouseInUse then begin                   {LoanGlob}
    PickCommands.cpOptionsOn(cpEnableMouse); {make mouse available,
                                              command processor}
    HideMouse;                               {avoid mouse tracks,
                                              OpMouse}
  end;


  {Set desired DirList features}
  Dir.SetPosLimits(1, 1, ScreenWidth, ScreenHeight - 1); {maximum screen
                                                          size,
                                                          OpWindow}
  DIR.SetPadSize(1, 1);                    {one space each side of
                                            displayed item, OpPick}


  Dir.diOptionsOn(diOptimizeSize);         {set size to fit list, OpDir}
  Dir.AddMaskHeader(True,                  {show full path?}
                    1,                     {add 1 space to each end of
                                            path }
                    40,                    {maximum width}
                    heTC);                 {display top centered}
                                           {OpDir}
  Dir.SetSortOrder(SortName);              {sort procedure to use. choices
                                            are SortNone (default),
                                            SortDirName, SortSize, and
                                            SortTime. This choice sorts on
                                            filename. You can substitute
                                            your own procedure, OpDir}
  Dir.SetMask('*.HDR',                     {all files with HDR extension}
              0);                          {normal file, no attribute,
                                            OpDir}


  {Pick a file}
  Finished := False;
  repeat
```

```
if MouseInUse then   {LoanGlob}
  ShowMouse;         {mouse available, OpMouse}
Dir.Process;         {make file choice, OpEntry}
if MouseInUse then   {LoanGlob}
  HideMouse;         {avoid mouse tracks, OpMouse}

case Dir.GetLastCommand of                          {OpWindow}
  ccError :                                         {OpCmd}
    begin
      if Dir.GetLastError = 0 then                  {OpWindow}
        ShowMsg('No files to select from')          {LoanMsg}
      else
        ShowMsg('Error in file selection: '
                 + Long2Str(Dir.GetLastError));  {LoanMsg, OpString}
      Finished := True;                             {done}
    end;

  ccQuit :               {escape key, OpCmd}
    Finished := True;    {abandon operation}

  ccSelect :             {choice made, OpCmd}
    begin
      {display file chosen with full path}
      FastWrite(Pad('Selected: '+Dir.GetSelectedPath,  {OpCrt,OpDir}
                     ScreenWidth),                      {OpCrt}
                ScreenHeight, 1, TextAttr);             {OpCrt}
      Finished := True;                                 {done}
      CurFile := JustName(Dir.GetSelectedFile);         {trim path or
                                                         extension,
                                                         OpString,
                                                         LoanGlob}

      {load header record}
      assign(HeadFile,TrimSpaces(CurFile) + '.HDR');  {assign debtor
                                                       filename to
                                                       file variable
                                                       OpString,
                                                       LoanGlob}
      {$I-}
      reset(HeadFile);                                {open file for
                                                       read or write,
                                                       LoanGlob}}
      read(HeadFile,Header);                          {load chosen
                                                       debtor
                                                       information
                                                       into record}
      close(HeadFile);                                {done with
                                                       file,
                                                       LoanGlob}
```

```
        {load payment array and sort}
        assign(PayFile,TrimSpaces(CurFile) + '.PAY');  {assign payment
                                                        filename to
                                                        file variable,
                                                        OpString,
                                                        LoanGlob}
        reset(PayFile);                                {open file for
                                                        read or write,
                                                        OpString,
                                                        LoanGlob}

        IoFlag := IoResult;                            {any error?}
        if IoFlag = 0 then begin                       {no, file must
                                                        exist}
          MaxFile := 0;                                {no payments
                                                        loaded yet,
                                                        LoanGlob}
          while not eof(PayFile) do begin              {read file till
                                                        end, LoanGlob}
                                                       {file will not
                                                        be read if
                                                        empty}
            inc(MaxFile);                              {another
                                                        payment,
                                                        LoanGlob}
            read(PayFile,PayList[MaxFile]);            {read payment
                                                        info,
                                                        LoanGlob}
          end;
          close(PayFile);                              {done with
                                                        file,
                                                        LoanGlob}
        end;
        {$I+}

        {sort payments, if any}
        if MaxFile > 1 then begin                      {any payments
                                                        to sort?,
                                                        LoanGlob}
          Status := Sort(MaxFile,SizeOf(PayRecord),GetPayList,Less,
                         WritePayList);                {OpSort}
          if Status <> SortSuccess then begin
            S := 'Sort failed: Status = '
                 + Long2Str(Word(Status));             {OpString}
            ShowMsg(S);                                {LoanMsg}
            Halt;
          end;
        end;
      end;
    end;
```

```
    until Finished;
    Dir.Done; {erase directory lister from memory, OpDir}
  end; {end of procedure}

  end. {end of unit}
```

The first three items are used with the instance of the OpSort object.

```
{$F+}
procedure GetPayList;
{feed payments from array into sort structures}
var
  N     : Integer;    {pay record counter}
  Value : PayRecord;  {contents of record}

begin
  for N := 1 TO MaxFile do begin    {visit all the records, LoanGlob}
    Value := PayList[N];            {record content}
    if not PutElement(Value) then   {no room in sort area}
      Exit;
  end;
end;


function Less(var x,y) : Boolean;
{compare records}
var
  X1 : PayRecord absolute X; {LoanGlob}
  Y1 : PayRecord absolute Y; {LoanGlob}
begin
  Less := (X1.PayDate < Y1.PayDate); {compare which fields?, LoanGlob}
end;


Procedure WritePayList;
{feed payments from sort structure back into array}
var
  N : Integer;        {payment counter}
  Value : PayRecord;  {record contents, LoanGlob}

begin
  N := 1;                            {start at first record}
  while GetElement(value) do begin   {while more sorted records}
    PayList[N] := Value;             {put record in array, LoanGlob}
    Inc(N);                          {next record}
  end;
end;
{$F-}
```

The GetPayList procedure copies the payment records from the PayList array to the sorting buffer (Supplied by OpSort). The Less function is used to compare two Payment records to see which comes first. In this case we are sorting on the payment date. Finally, the WritePayList procedure copies the sorted list from the sort area back into the PayList array.

The MakeDirList procedure uses an instance of the DirList object to display the selected filenames. The line

```
Dir.SetMask('*.HDR',                 {all files with HDR extension}
            0);                      {normal file, no attribute}
                                     {OpDir}
```

determines which file names will be displayed. In this case, all the files with an extension of ".HDR" are listed.

The line

```
Dir.diOptionsOn(diOptimizeSize);     {set size to fit list, OpDir}
```

tells DirList to use a window just large enough to hold the list. Other possible options are

diDirsUpcase	raise directory names to uppercase
diFilesUpcase	raise file names to uppercase
diExitIfOne	autoselect in GetFileName if one matching file
diSetFirstFile	position select bar on first nondirectory
diOptimizeSize	optimize window size when directory is read
diUserNewHdr	set for user move routine when header is changed

The next line determines what is used as the heading in the window and its size. The first argument determines whether the drive and path are to be included in the heading. If you set it to False, then only the filename is displayed.

```
Dir.AddMaskHeader(True,               {show full path?}
                  1,                  {add 1 space to each end of
                                       path }
                  40,                 {maximum width}
                  heTC);              {display top centered}
```

The last argument in AddMaskHeader can be one of the following:

heTL	top left
heTC	top center
heTR	top right
heBL	bottom left
heBC	bottom center
heBR	bottom right

SetSortOrder determines the order of the filenames.

```
Dir.SetSortOrder(SortName);          {sort procedure to use. choices
                                      are SortNone (default),
                                      SortDirName, SortSize, and
                                      SortTime. This choice sorts on
                                      filename. You can substitute
                                      your own procedure, OpDir}
```

The SetSortOrder method's parameter can be one of the following:

SortNone	no sort, the default
SortName	sort files and directories in alphabetical order
SortDirName	subdirectories first, then files, alphabetically
SortSize	smallest file first, subsort on name
SortTime	earliest date first, subsort by earliest time, then subsort by name

You can, if you wish, include the procedure

```
{what to display and in what order?}  {OpDir}
Dir.SetNameSizeTimeFormat('<dir>', 'Mm/dd/yy', 'Hh:mmt');
```

which could also be one of the following similar procedures:

SetNameFormat	name and extension only
SetNameSizeFormat	name and size in bytes
SetNameSizeKFormat	name and size in Kb
SetNameTimeFormat	name, date, and time
SetNameSizeTimeFormat	name, size in bytes, date, and time
SetNameSizeKTimeFormat	name, size in Kb, date, and time
SetAllFormat	name, size in bytes, date, time, attribute
SetUserFormat	user supplied display format

The date and time pictures available are

mm/dd/yy	01/02/91
MM/dd/yy	1/02/91
DD/mm/yyyy	2/01/1991
dd-NNN-yyyy	02-JAN-1991

hh:mm:ss	15:02:31
hh:mm	15:02
hh:mm te	03:02 pm
Hh:mmt	3:02p

The mouse is then made available to use in selecting a filename. The object now waits for a choice to be made. Once the user selects a filename or presses the Escape key, the mouse is hidden again.

If the Escape key was used or if an error occurs, the operation is abandoned. However, if the error number was 0, then there were no files matching the mask. The user is apprised of that fact and returned to the main menu. If a selection was made (Enter key) the name of the file, including its full path, is written at the bottom of the screen. The global CurFile variable is set to the file name, without extension; the applicable extension is added as necessary. A value stored in this variable signals that a debtor has been chosen and permits most of the other operations to take place. See the Loan.pas menu selection code in the previous chapter. The Header record is loaded from the chosen file. Then the payment file is opened. If an error occurs, then there were no payments made and therefore no payment file (CurFile + ".PAY"). In that case, MaxFile is set to 0 to indicate that the PayList array is empty.

If no error occurred when opening the payment file, the payment records, if any, are transferred to the Paylist array and MaxFile is set to indicate the number of payments. Once in the array, the payments are sorted by payment date.

The next chapter will describe the payment handling and the production of the amortization table.

7

Loan Application, Payment Files

This chapter completes the description of the loan application modules. This chapter contains the modules that have to do with the payment files, including the amortization table printing.

The objects used and discussed in this chapter are

EntryScreen and ancestors (OpEntry)
PickList and ancestors (OpPick)
Printer and ancestors (OpPrnLow, OpPrint)
Various object methods from OpDate, OpString, OpSort, OpCrt, OpSort, OpMouse, and others.

LoanPay.pas

```
UNIT LoanPay;
{enter nonstandard loan payments}

INTERFACE

uses
     LoanGlob,
     LoanMsg,
     OpCmd,
     OpRoot,
```

```
    OpField,
    OpFrame,
    OpWindow,
    OpSort,
    OpCrt,
    OpString,
    OpEntry,
    OpMouse,
    OpDate;

{get nonstandard payment detail from user}
procedure PaymentInfo;


IMPLEMENTATION


{$F+}
function ValidateDate(EFP : EntryFieldPtr; var ErrCode : Word;
                      var ErrorSt : StringPtr) : Boolean;
{make sure due date entered when entering payments is a valid due date
 so nonstandard payment can be found when table is printed}

var
  D1,M1,Y1  : Integer; {day, month, and year, used in comparisons}
  D2,M2,Y2  : Integer; {day, month, and year, used in comparisons}
  CheckDate : Date;    {date to verify}
  ErrStr    : String;  {error string for error handler procedure}

begin
  ValidateDate := False; {default}
  {get value designated for validation by ChangeValidation procedure}
  CheckDate := DateStringToDate('mm/dd/yyyy',EFP^.efEditSt^); {OpDate}
  DatetoDMY(Header.FirstDue,D1,M1,Y1); {convert header due date to
                                        D,M, & Y, OpDate}
  DatetoDMY(CheckDate,D2,M2,Y2);       {convert entered due date to
                                        D,M, & Y, OpDate}
  case Header.Frequency of
    Monthly :
      begin
        if D1 <> D2 then begin {day of month doesn't match, error}
          ErrStr := 'Must be the same day as loan date: ('
                     + Long2Str(D1) + ')'; {OpString, this function
                                            argument}
          ErrorSt := @ErrStr;              {this function parameter}
          ErrCode := ecBadFormat;          {this function argument}
        end
        else
          ValidateDate := True;            {passed}
      end;
```

```
SemiMonthly : {twice a month on designated days}
  begin
    {due date same as either first or second designated day?}
    if (D2 = Header.FirstDay) or (D2 = Header.SecondDay) then
      ValidateDate := True
    else begin
      ErrStr := 'Must be the same day as due days chosen: ('
                + Long2Str(Header.FirstDay) + ', '
                + Long2Str(Header.SecondDay) + ')'; {OpString, this
                                                     function
                                                     argument}
      ErrorSt := @ErrStr;         {this function argument}
      ErrCode := ecBadFormat;     {this function argument}
    end;
  end;

Weekly :
  begin
    {same day of week as header due date?}
    if DayofWeek(Header.FirstDue) <> DayOfWeek(CheckDate) then begin
      ErrStr := 'Must be the same day as loan date: ('
                + DayString[DayOfWeek(Header.FirstDue)]
                + ')';                                  {OpDate,
                                                         this
                                                         function
                                                         argument}
      ErrorSt := @ErrStr;         {this function argument}
      ErrCode := ecBadFormat;     {this function argument}
    end
    else
      ValidateDate := True;
  end;

Yearly :
  begin
    {same month and day as header due date?}
    if (D1 <> D2) or (M1 <> M2) then begin
      ErrStr := 'Must be the same day and month as loan date: ('
                + Long2Str(D1) + ', ' + Long2Str(M1)
                + ')';                                {OpString,
                                                       this
                                                       function
                                                       argument}
      ErrorSt := @ErrStr;         {this function argument}
      ErrCode := ecBadFormat;     {this function argument}
    end
    else
      ValidateDate := True;  {function return}
  end;
end;
```

```
end;
{$F-}


{$F+}
procedure ErrorHandler(UnitCode : Byte; var ErrCode : Word; Msg :
String);
{for making sure entered due date is a valid one}

var
  S        : String;   {string temp}
  BufPtr   : Pointer;  {pointer to buffer used to store screen}
  SaveFlag : Boolean;  {was screen saved?}

begin
  SaveFlag := True;    {default}
  {try to save screen so more entries can be made, OpCrt}}
  if not SaveWindow(1,             {X1}
                    1,             {Y1}
                    ScreenWidth,   {X2, entire width, OpCrt}
                    ScreenHeight,  {Y2, whole screen, OpCrt}
                    True,          {procedure supplies buffer}
                    BufPtr)        {where is screen stored?}
                    then begin
    ShowMsg('Not enough memory to save screen'); {LoanMsg}
    SaveFlag := False;                           {nope}
  end;
  S := Msg;
  ShowMsg(S); {display error message passed to procedure, LoanMsg}
  if SaveFlag then
    {put the entry screen back again, OpCrt}
    RestoreWindow(1,             {X1}
                  1,             {Y1}
                  ScreenWidth,   {X2, entire width, OpCrt}
                  ScreenHeight,  {Y2, while screen, OpCrt}
                  True,          {deallocate buffer}
                  BufPtr);       {where screen is stored}
end;
{$F-}


{$F+}
procedure GetPayList;
{feed payments from array into sort structures}

var
  N     : Integer;    {pay record counter}
  Value : PayRecord;  {contents of record}

begin
```

```
  for N := 1 TO MaxFile do begin  {visit all the records, LoanGlob}
    Value := PayList[N];          {record content, LoanGlob}
    if not PutElement(Value) then {no room in sort area, OpSort}
      Exit;
  end;
end;


function Less(var x,y) : Boolean;
{compare records}
var
  X1 : PayRecord absolute X; {LoanGlob}
  Y1 : PayRecord absolute Y; {LoanGlob}
begin
  Less := (X1.PayDate < Y1.PayDate); {compare which fields?, LoanGlob}
end;


Procedure WritePayList;
{feed payments from sort structure back into array}

var
  N : Integer;        {payment counter}
  Value : PayRecord;  {record contents, LoanGlob}

begin
  N := 1;                               {start at first record}
  while GetElement(value) do begin      {while more sorted records, OpSort}
    PayList[N] := Value;                {put record in array, LoanGlob}
    Inc(N);                             {next record}
  end;
end;
{$F-}


procedure PaymentInfo;
{get nonstandard payment detail from user}

var
   Counter     : Integer;    {pay record counter used when storing in
                              file}
   f           : String;     {file name}
   IoFlag      : Word;       {IO error?}
   More        : Boolean;    {continue?}
   NewPayments : Boolean;    {any payments added to array? if so save
                              array}
   PAmount     : Real;       {payment amount}
   PDueDate    : Date;       {payment due date}
   PPayDate    : Date;       {payment date}
   S           : String;     {string temp}
```

```
    Status      : SortStatus; {for sort object, overrides global status
                               variable}

begin
  NewPayments := False; {no payments added to array yet}
  ClrScr;
  if not ESPay.InitCustom(20, 5, 60, 15, {Window coordinates}
                      Colors,            {Colors.inc}
                      DefWindowOptions   {default options}
                        or wBordered)    {save room for border}
                      then begin
    S := 'Failed to init payment EntryScreen. Status = '
          + Long2Str(InitStatus);        {OpString}
    ShowMsg(S);                          {LoanMsg}
    Halt;
  end;

  if MouseInUse then begin                          {LoanGlob}
    EntryCommands.cpOptionsOn(cpEnableMouse);  {mouse available to entry
                                                 screen, EntryScreen
                                                 Command Processor}
    HideMouse;                                  {avoid mouse droppings,
                                                 OpMouse}
  end;

  {add some window frills with OpFrame methods}
  ESPay.wFrame.AddShadow(shBR,           {shadow bottom and right of
                                          screen}
                        shOverWrite);    {opaque shadow}
  ESPay.wFrame.AddHeader(' Payment Screen ', heTC); {top centered}
  ESPay.wFrame.AddHeader(' Esc to abort, Ctrl-Enter to accept ',
                        heBC);           {bottom centered}

  EsPay.SetErrorProc(DefaultErrorProc); {beep on error, OpWindow}

  {add fields}
  ESPay.esFieldOptionsOn(efClearFirstChar); {clear on entry if first
                                              character is ASCII,
                                              OpEntry}

  ESPay.esFieldOptionsOn(efRequired);       {all fields entry required,
                                             OpEntry}
  ESPay.AddDateField('Payment Date:',       {prompt}
                    4,                      {V prompt position}
                    6,                      {H prompt position}
                    'mm/dd/yyyy',           {picture}
                    4,                      {data V position}
                    21,                     {data H position}
                    17,                     {help ID number}
                    Header.FirstDue,        {earliest valid date}
```

```
                   0,                        {latest valid date}
                   PPayDate);                {data variable}

ESPay.AddDateField('Due Date:',              {prompt}
                   5,                        {V prompt position}
                   6,                        {H prompt position}
                   'mm/dd/yyyy',             {picture}
                   5,                        {data V position}
                   21,                       {data H position}
                   18,                       {ID number}
                   0,                        {earliest valid date}
                   0,                        {latest valid date}
                   PDueDate);                {data variable}
EsPay.ChangeValidation(1, ValidateDate);     {set special validation for
                                              just this field, found in
                                              ValidateDate function.
                                              Normally validation is only
                                              by designated picture and
                                              range, OpEntry}

ESPay.AddRealField('Amount:',                {prompt}
                   7,                        {V prompt position}
                   6,                        {H prompt position}
                   '999999.99',              {picture}
                   7,                        {data V position}
                   21,                       {data H position}
                   19,                       {help ID number}
                   0.00,                     {minimum valid entry}
                   Header.LoanAmount,        {maximum valid entry}
                   2,                        {number of decimal places}
                   PAmount);                 {data variable}

if EntryType = 'N' then                      {new record, not editing,
                                              Loan}
  ESPay.AddYesNoField('Another? (Y/N):',     {prompt}
                      9,                     {V prompt position}
                      6,                     {H prompt position}
                      '',                    {picture}
                      9,                     {data V position}
                      21,                    {data H position}
                      20,                    {ID number}
                      More);                 {data variable}
ESPay.esFieldOptionsOff(efRequired);         {turn off require criteria,
                                              OpEntry}

More := False;                               {another payment?}

repeat
  Finished := False;                            {not done yet}
  if EntryType = 'N' then begin                 {new record, not editing,
                                                 Loan}
```

```
    PAmount  := 0.00;                         {defaults}
    PPayDate := Today;
    PDueDate := Today;
  end
  else begin                                  {editing record}
    PAmount  := PayList[PayChoice].Amount;    {use stored values of
                                               chosen record, LoanGlob}
    PPayDate := PayList[PayChoice].PayDate;
    PDueDate := PayList[PayChoice].DueDate;
    More := False;                            {only payment, unless user
                                               changes this value in
                                               last field of entry
                                               screen}
  end;

  repeat
    if MouseInUse then                  {LoanGlob}
      ShowMouse;                        {mouse available, OpMouse}
    ESPay.SetErrorProc(ErrorHandler);   {show error in window, OpWindow}
    ESPay.Process;                      {get entries, OpEntry}
    if MouseInUse then                  {LoanGlob}
      HideMouse;                        {avoid mouse tracks, OpMouse}

    case ESPay.GetLastCommand of        {OpWindow}
      ccError:                          {error executing object, OpCmd}
        begin
          S := 'Fatal error '
          + Long2Str(ESPay.GetLastError); {OpString}
          ShowMsg(S);                     {LoanMsg}
          Finished := True;               {abandon operation}
        end;

      ccQuit :             {escape key, OpCmd}
        Finished := True;  {abandon operation}
    end;

    if MaxFile = MaxPaymentNumber then begin                {LoanGlob}
      ShowMsg('No room in array to store any more payments');{LoanMsg}
      Finished := True;   {abandon operation}
    end;

    if not Finished then begin
      if EntryType = 'N' then begin   {new record, Loan}
        {store payment}
        Inc(MaxFile);                 {next array position, also number
                                       of records in array, LoanGlob}
        PayList[MaxFile].PayDate := PPayDate; {store data in record,
                                               LoanGlob}
        PayList[MaxFile].DueDate := PDueDate;
```

```
        PayList[MaxFile].Amount  := PAmount;
        NewPayments := True;                {save changed array}
      end
      else begin                             {edited record}
        PayList[PayChoice].PayDate := PPayDate; {store data in record,
                                                 LoanGlob}
        PayList[PayChoice].DueDate := PDueDate;
        PayList[PayChoice].Amount  := PAmount;
        NewPayments := True;                 {save changed array}
      end;

      Finished := True; {done}
    end;
  until Finished;
until not More; {no more payments (field in entry screen)}

if NewPayments then begin            {array was changed}
  {save all payment(s) to file}
  {$I-}
  f := TrimSpaces(CurFile) + '.PAY'; {use payment record file,
                                      OpString}
  assign(PayFile,f);                 {assign to file variable,
                                      LoanGlob}
  rewrite(PayFile);                  {write only, LoanGlob}

  IoFlag := IoResult;                {I/O error?}
  if IoFlag <> 0 then begin          {yes}
    ShowMsg('Rewrite payfile ' + f
         + ' error. IoResult is: '
         + Long2Str(IoFlag));        {OpString, LoanMsg}
    Halt;
  end;

  Counter := 0;                      {array position}
  while Counter < MaxFile do begin   {visit all array positions,
                                      LoanGlob}
    Inc(Counter);                    {next array position}
    write(PayFile,PayList[Counter]); {store record in file, LoanGlob}
    IoFlag := IoResult;              {I/O error?}
    if IoFlag <> 0 then begin        {yes}
      ShowMsg('Write payfile '
           + f + ' error. IoResult is: '
           + Long2Str(IoFlag));      {OpString, LoanMsg}
      Halt;
    end;
  end;
  close(PayFile);                    {save file buffers to disk}
  {$I+}

  {sort payments, if more than one}
```

```
    if MaxFile > 1 then begin          {there is at least one payment in
                                        array, LoanGlob}
      {sort the payment array from OpSort}
      Status := Sort(MaxFile,SizeOf(PayRecord),GetPayList,Less,
                     WritePayList);          {OpSort}
      if Status <> SortSuccess then begin {sort failed}
        S := 'Sort failed: Status = '
              + Long2Str(Word(Status));    {OpString}
        ShowMsg(S);                        {LoanMsg}
        Halt;
      end;
    end;
  end;

  ESPay.Erase; {erase entry screen from screen, OpEntry}
  ESPay.Done;  {erase entry screen from memory, OpEntry}
end; {end of procedure}

end. {end of unit}
```

Add Mode

Two possible modes are possible when calling PaymentInfo; they are Add ("N" for New) and Edit ("E").

The ValidateDate code

```
{$F+}
function ValidateDate(EFP : EntryFieldPtr; var ErrCode : Word;
                      var ErrorSt : StringPtr) : Boolean;
{make sure due date entered when entering payments is a valid due date
 so nonstandard payment can be found when table is printed}

var
  D1,M1,Y1   : Integer; {day, month, and year, used in comparisons}
  D2,M2,Y2   : Integer; {day, month, and year, used in comparisons}
  CheckDate  : Date;    {date to verify}
  ErrStr     : String;  {error string for error handler procedure}

begin
  ValidateDate := False; {default}
  {get value designated for validation by ChangeValidation procedure}
  CheckDate := DateStringToDate('mm/dd/yyyy',EFP^.efEditSt^); {OpDate}
  DatetoDMY(Header.FirstDue,D1,M1,Y1); {convert header due date to
                                        D,M, & Y, OpDate}
  DatetoDMY(CheckDate,D2,M2,Y2);       {convert entered due date to
                                        D,M, & Y, OpDate}
  case Header.Frequency of
    Monthly :
      begin
        if D1 <> D2 then begin {day of month doesn't match, error}
```

```
        ErrStr := 'Must be the same day as loan date: ('
                   + Long2Str(D1) + ')'; {OpString, this function
                                          argument}
        ErrorSt := @ErrStr;               {this function parameter}
        ErrCode := ecBadFormat;           {this function argument}
      end
      else
        ValidateDate := True;             {passed}
    end;
  SemiMonthly : {twice a month on designated days}
    begin
      {due date same as either first or second designated day?}
      if (D2 = Header.FirstDay) or (D2 = Header.SecondDay) then
        ValidateDate := True
      else begin
        ErrStr := 'Must be the same day as due days chosen: ('
                   + Long2Str(Header.FirstDay) + ', '
                   + Long2Str(Header.SecondDay) + ')'; {OpString, this
                                                         function
                                                         argument}
        ErrorSt := @ErrStr;          {this function argument}
        ErrCode := ecBadFormat;      {this function argument}
      end;
    end;
  Weekly :
    begin
      {same day of week as header due date?}
      if DayofWeek(Header.FirstDue) <> DayOfWeek(CheckDate) then begin
        ErrStr := 'Must be the same day as loan date: ('
                   + DayString[DayOfWeek(Header.FirstDue)]
                   + ')';                                  {OpDate,
                                                            this
                                                            function
                                                            argument}
        ErrorSt := @ErrStr;          {this function argument}
        ErrCode := ecBadFormat;      {this function argument}
      end
      else
        ValidateDate := True;
    end;
  Yearly :
    begin
      {same month and day as header due date?}
      if (D1 <> D2) or (M1 <> M2) then begin
        ErrStr := 'Must be the same day and month as loan date: ('
                   + Long2Str(D1) + ', ' + Long2Str(M1)
                   + ')';                                {OpString,
                                                          this
                                                          function
                                                          argument}
```

```
          ErrorSt := @ErrStr;         {this function argument}
          ErrCode := ecBadFormat;     {this function argument}
        end
        else
          ValidateDate := True;   {function return}
      end;
    end;
  end;
  {$F-}
```

is used to make sure that the date entered as the Payment Due date is correct. If this date is not correct, the amortization table code will not substitute this payment information for the default payment information. Of course, the program cannot know which payment the incorrect payment due date is intended to refer to, so the ValidateDate function can only return an error message defining the correct days (and sometimes month) which the ErrorHandler procedure then displays in a window.

This code is called only when one field is exited, that with the variable PDueDate. To make this obvious, the necessary code

```
EsPay.ChangeValidation(1, ValidateDate); {set special validation ...}
```

is placed right after the field to be validated.

There are several other ChangeSomething procedures that are similar. An asterisk in the following list designates that the method was inherited by EntryScreen from the Abstract Selector object in OpSelect; otherwise it is an EntryScreen method.

ChangeConversion	Change conversion procedure of designated field (number base for example)
ChangeFieldAttr*	Change color of designated unselected fields
ChangeHidden*	Hide or unhide a designated field
ChangeInvisibility*	Make a designated field visible or invisible
ChangePromptAttr*	Change color of designated field's prompt when unselected
ChangeProtectedFieldAttr*	Change color of designated field when protected
ChangeProtectedPromptAttr*	Change color of designated field's prompt when protected
ChangeProtection*	Protect or unprotect a designated field
ChangeRange	Change valid entry range of designated field

ChangeRequired	Require or not require a designated field
ChangeSelectedFieldAttr*	Change color of designated field when selected
ChangeSelectedPromptAttr*	Change color of designated field's prompt when protected
ChangeValidation	Change the validation routine for a designated field

The "1" argument in the ChangeValidation procedure shown earlier is the ID number of the field. As explained in the previous chapter, this is calculated by counting the entry fields, with the first, in this case PPayDate, as 0. The ValidateDate of course refers to the validation function to use.

When the validation fails, an error handler is called. The line

```
ESPay.SetErrorProc(ErrorHandler); {show error in window, OpWindow}
```

which designates the procedure

```
{$F+}
procedure ErrorHandler(UnitCode : Byte; var ErrCode : Word; Msg :
String);
{for making sure entered due date is a valid one}

var
  S        : String;  {string temp}
  BufPtr   : Pointer; {pointer to buffer used to store screen}
  SaveFlag : Boolean; {was screen saved?}

begin
  SaveFlag := True;    {default}
  {try to save screen so more entries can be made, OpCrt}}
  if not SaveWindow(1,             {X1}
                    1,             {Y1}
                    ScreenWidth,   {X2, entire width, OpCrt}
                    ScreenHeight,  {Y2, whole screen, OpCrt}
                    True,          {procedure supplies buffer}
                    BufPtr)        {where is screen stored?}
                    then begin
    ShowMsg('Not enough memory to save screen'); {LoanMsg}
    SaveFlag := False;                           {nope}
  end;
  S := Msg;
  ShowMsg(S); {display error message passed to procedure, LoanMsg}
  if SaveFlag then
    {put the entry screen back again, OpCrt}
    RestoreWindow(1,            {X1}
                  1,            {Y1}
                  ScreenWidth,  {X2, entire width, OpCrt}
                  ScreenHeight,{Y2, whole screen, OpCrt}
```

```
                        True,          {deallocate buffer}
                        BufPtr);       {where screen is stored}
  end;
  {$F-}
```

as the error handler. This line occurs just before the ESP.Process line, which permits the user to make the field entries and processes them. Earlier the line

```
EsPay.SetErrorProc(DefaultErrorProc); {beep on error, OpWindow}
```

designates that only a beep be used to indicate an error. This is for the programmer's benefit, to indicate programming errors, most likely bad coordinates in the field entry procedures.

The three items

```
{$F+}
procedure GetPayList;
{feed payments from array into sort structures}

var
  N     : Integer;    {pay record counter}
  Value : PayRecord;  {contents of record}

begin
  for N := 1 TO MaxFile do begin  {visit all the records, LoanGlob}
    Value := PayList[N];          {record content, LoanGlob}
    if not PutElement(Value) then {no room in sort area, OpSort}
      Exit;
  end;
end;


function Less(var x,y) : Boolean;
{compare records}
var
  X1 : PayRecord absolute X; {LoanGlob}
  Y1 : PayRecord absolute Y; {LoanGlob}
begin
  Less := (X1.PayDate < Y1.PayDate); {compare which fields?, LoanGlob}
end;


Procedure WritePayList;
{feed payments from sort structure back into array}

var
  N : Integer;        {payment counter}
  Value : PayRecord; {record contents, LoanGlob}

begin
  N := 1;                            {start at first record}
```

```
    while GetElement(value) do begin {while more sorted records, OpSort}
      PayList[N] := Value;           {put record in array, LoanGlob}
      Inc(N);                        {next record}
    end;
  end;
  {$F-}
```

are used with the instance of the OpSort object. The GetPayList procedure copies the payment records from the PayList array to the sorting buffer (Supplied by OpSort). The Less function is used to compare two Payment records to see which comes first. In this case we are sorting on the payment date. Finally, the WritePayList procedure copies the sorted list from the sort area back into the PayList array.

In the main part of the unit, the PaymentInfo procedure begins by initializing the window that will contain the entry screen.

The DefWindowOptions mentioned are

wClear
wSaveContents
wResizable
wStoreContents

The complete list of available options is

wBordered	Make space for window border
wClear	Clear window when it is first displayed
wSaveContents	Save the contents of the window when it is erased.
wUserContents	User will restore window contents
wSoundEffects	Use sound effects during explosions
wAltFrame	Use alternate frame type when not current
wSetMouse	Set mouse window, cursor on entry to window
wFullMouseWindow	Force to full mouse window on entry
wResizable	Can be resized and zoomed
wAllMouseEvents	Any combination of mouse buttons anywhere exits
wStoreContents	Store window contents in streams

Next the mouse is brought to life if possible.

```
if MouseInUse then begin                      {LoanGlob}
  EntryCommands.cpOptionsOn(cpEnableMouse);  {mouse available to entry
                                               screen}
  HideMouse;                                  {avoid mouse droppings,
                                               OpMouse}
end;
```

As noted, MouseInUse was defined in LoanGlob, if the use of the mouse was defined in OpDefine.Inc and a mouse was detected in the system. The next three lines define the window shadow and headings. In the line from OpFrame:

```
ESPay.wFrame.AddShadow(shBR,          {shadow bottom and right of
                                       screen}
                       shOverWrite);  {opaque shadow}
```

the options are

shBR	shadow falls to bottom and right of frame
shBL	shadow falls to bottom and left of frame

and for the second argument

shOverWrite	opaque shadow
shSeeThru	transparent shadow

In the lines from OpFrame:

```
ESPay.wFrame.AddHeader(' Payment Screen ', heTC); {top centered}
ESPay.wFrame.AddHeader(' Esc to abort, Ctrl-Enter to accept ',
                        heBC);        {bottom centered}
```

the options for the last parameters are

heTL	top left
heTC	top center
heTR	top right
heBL	bottom left
heBC	bottom center
heBR	bottom right

Now we define the four fields in the entry screen. We begin with

```
ESPay.esFieldOptionsOn(efClearFirstChar); {clear on entry if first
                                           character is ASCII,
                                           OpEntry}
```

followed by the line

```
ESPay.esFieldOptionsOn(efRequired);       {some input required,
                                           OpEntry}
```

and after the fields are defined,

```
ESPay.esFieldOptionsOff(efRequired);      {cancel required, OpEntry}
```

popular options are

efProtected	not changeable
efHidden	not displayed, field cannot be moved to it
efInvisible	field is never drawn
efRequired	some entry required
efBeepOnError	invalid entry
efClearFirstChar	if first character entered during editing is character clear the field

There are many more options. See the documentation on OpField for their names and descriptions. Note that these options can be used in methods other than esFieldOptionsOn() and esFieldOptionsOff().

Next the fields are defined. Here is a typical field definition:

```
ESPay.AddDateField('Payment Date:',      {prompt}
                    4,                   {V prompt position}
                    6,                   {H prompt position}
                    'mm/dd/yyyy',        {picture}
                    4,                   {data V position}
                    21,                  {data H position}
                    17,                  {help ID number}
                    Header.FirstDue,     {earliest valid date}
                    0,                   {latest valid date}
                    PPayDate);           {data variable}
```

The parameters of the various entry types are similar.

A full list of the Add fields consists of

AddArrayField	array of char
AddBcdField	binary coded decimal
AddBooleanField	Boolean response
AddByteField	byte
AddCharField	single character
AddChoiceField	for enumerated types, see HeaderInfo in LoanHead
AddCompField	comp precision
AddDateField	date—MM/DD/YY(YY)
AddDateStField	date string—i.e., 16 Jan 1990
AddDblField	double precision
AddExtField	extended precision
AddIntField	integer
AddLongField	long integer
AddMultiLineField	edit string array
AddNestedField	brings up another entry screen when entered
AddNestedStringField	brings up another entry screen when entered

AddPickStringField	choose from pick list
AddRealField	real
AddSglField	single precision
AddShortField	short integer
AddStringField	string
AddTimeField	hours, minutes, seconds
AddUserField	user-defined field
AddWordField	word
AddYesNoField	yes/no choice—returns True/False

(uses simple character editor, no true pictures)

AddSimpleBcdField	binary coded decimal
AddSimpleBooleanField	Boolean
AddSimpleByteField	byte
AddSimpleCharField	character
AddSimpleCompField	comp
AddSimpleDblField	double precision
AddSimpleExtField	extended precision
AddSimpleIntField	integer
AddSimpleRealField	real
AddSimpleShortField	short integer
AddSimpleSngField	single precision
AddSimpleStringField)	string
AddSimpleWordField	word
AddSimpleYesNoField	yes or no—returns True or False

(uses number editor for numeric only fields)

AddNumericBcdField	binary coded decimal
AddNumericByteField	byte
AddNumericCompField	comp
AddNumericDblField	double precision
AddNumericExtField	extended precision
AddNumericIntField	integer
AddNumericLongField	long integer
AddNumericRealField	real
AddNumericShortField	short integer
AddNumericSngField	single precision
AddNumericWordField	word

See the documentation for OpEntry to get more details and parameter lists for each type.

Most fields have a picture parameter. The meaning of the picture characters is as follows:

X	Any character
!	Any character, force uppercase
L	Any character, force lowercase
x	Any character, first letter of each word upper, others lowercase
a	Alphabetical characters only
A	Alphabetical characters only, force uppercase
l	Alphabetical characters only, force lowercase
9	Numbers and spaces only
#	Numbers, spaces, minus, period
E	Numbers, spaces, minus, period, e
K	0–9, A–F, force uppercase (hex)
B	T, t, F, f (Boolean)
Y	Y, y, N, n

Date and time characters:

m	Month, zero-padded
M	Month, blank-padded
d	Day, zero-padded
D	Day, blank-padded
y	Year, zero-padded
n	Month name
N	Month name, force uppercase
w	Weekday
W	Weekday, force uppercase
/	Month, day, year separator
h	Hours, zero-padded
H	Hours, blank-padded
m	Minutes, xero-padded
M	Minutes, blank-padded
s	Seconds, zero-padded
S	Seconds, blank-padded
t	"p" or "a" in am/pm
e	"m" in am/pm
:	Minutes, hours, seconds separator

The field's default values are now set. In this mode (Add) the values are set to today's date or 0.

After the fields are defined, the mouse is made visible, the error handler is switched to the one defined at the beginning of the unit, and we process the entry screen.

```
if MouseInUse then                      {LoanGlob}
  ShowMouse;                            {mouse available, OpMouse}
ESPay.SetErrorProc(ErrorHandler);       {show error in window, OpWindow}
ESPay.Process;                          {get entries, OpEntry}
if MouseInUse then                      {LoanGlob}
  HideMouse;                            {avoid mouse tracks, OpMouse}
```

Processing continues until an error occurs, or the Escape or Control-Enter key is pressed. If an error occurs, a message is displayed and the user is returned to the menu. If the Escape key is pressed the user is returned to the menu. The Control-Enter key causes the fields to be processed.

First the MaxPaymentNumber value set in LoanGlob is compared with MaxFile. If they match, the PayList array is full for this debtor, so the user is informed and is returned to the menu. The user has no control over this variable. It is up to the programmer to be sure it is large enough or to increase its value when this error occurs. The default supplies room for 200 nonstandard payments.

MaxFile is incremented to the next array position and the fields are stored in a record at that position in the PayList array.

The user-set value in the More field determines whether the entry screen appears again for another entry or not. The default is No.

If any payments were added to the PayList array they are now saved to the "PAY" file. There is nothing special here.

Finally the PayList array is sorted. This identical sorting process was explained in the previous chapter.

After removing the entry screen from the screen, the object is removed from memory and the user is returned to the main menu.

Edit Mode

The Edit mode is almost identical to the Add mode. The only difference is that the fields are set to the values contained in a previously selected payment record (see next unit). The array position is stored in the PayChoice variable. When the user completes the entry screen and presses the Control-Enter key, the fields are stored back into the array where they came from, rather than being appended to the end of the array.

LoanPick.pas

This unit is used to display all the nonstandard payment dates and amounts in a pick list. The user highlights the payment to edit or delete with the arrow keys or by clicking on it with a mouse. Pressing the Enter key then indicates that the highlighted item has been chosen. The unit's implementation procedure returns the position of the chosen value in the array. It is called by selecting "Change nonstandard payments" or "Delete payment" in the Maintenance menu.

Here is the unit's code.

```
unit LoanPick;

INTERFACE

uses LoanGlob,
     LoanMsg,
     OpCrt,
     OpPick,
     OpDate,
     OpString,
     OpCmd,
     OpRoot,
     OpFrame,
     OpMouse,
     Opwindow;

{display payments, choose the payment to delete or edit}
procedure ChoosePayment;


IMPLEMENTATION


{$F+}
procedure MakeList(Item : Word;                 {current list item number}
                   Mode : pkMode;               {pkMode can be pkDisplay,
                                                 pkSearch, or pkGetType,
                                                 changing as object is used
                                                 or set by programmer}
                   var IType : pkItemType;      {pkItemType can be pkNormal,
                                                 pkAlternate, pkProtected,
                                                 or pkPrivate, changing as
                                                 object requires or set by
                                                 programmer. pkNormal is
                                                 default}
                   var IString : String;        {content set in code below}
                   PickPtr : PickListPtr);      {pointer to pick list object,
                                                 set when picklist inits}
{Sets item string and item options (if any)}
begin
  if Mode = pkGetType then {only looking to see if specified item is
                            normal or protected, not searching}
    Exit;

  {string content to display}
  IString := ' ' + DateToDateString('mm/dd/yyyy',PayList[Item].PayDate)
```

```
              + ' ' + Real2Str(PayList[Item].Amount,9,2)
              + ' ';                                          {OpString}
end;
{$F-}


procedure ChoosePayment;
{display payments, choose the payment to delete or edit}

var
   PickWindowOptions : LongInt;  {window characteristics}
   PaymentList       : PickList; {instance of object}
   S                 : String;   {string temp}

begin
  {Make a PickList with custom OpWindow options}
  PickWindowOptions := DefWindowOptions {default window settings}
                       or wBordered;    {leave room for a border}
  if not PaymentList.InitCustom(29, 5, 51, 15, {Initial window
                                                coordinates}
                                Colors,        {Color set to use,
                                                from Colors.Inc}
                                PickWindowOptions, {Window options (see
                                                above)}
                                24,            {Column width per item}
                                MaxFile,       {Number of pick list
                                                items}
                                MakeList,      {Item string function}
                                PickVertical,  {Orientation procedure}
                                SingleChoice)  {Command handler, only
                                                one choice}
                                then begin
    S := 'Failed to Init PickList,  Status = '
         + Long2Str(InitStatus);                {OpString}
    ShowMsg(S);                                 {LoanMsg}
    Halt;
  end;

  if MouseInUse then begin                   {LoanGlob}
    PickCommands.cpOptionsOn(cpEnableMouse); {make mouse available to
                                              picklist}
    HideMouse;                               {avoid mouse tracks,
                                              OpMouse}
  end;

  {Set some PickList features, OpPick}
  PaymentList.SetSearchMode(PickCharSearch); {options are
                                              PickStringSearch,
                                              PickAltStringSearch,
                                              PickCharSearch,
```

```
                                                    PickCharExit,
                                                    PickAnyCharExit, or
                                                    PickNoSearch (the
                                                    default).
                                                    PickCharSearch means look
                                                    for an item with the same
                                                    first char as the char
                                                    entered. If found select
                                                    it}
  {OpFrame methods}
  with PaymentList.wFrame do begin
    AddShadow(shBR,                                {display shadow bottom and
                                                    left of frame}
              shOverWrite);                        {opaque shadow}
    AddHeader(' Date and Payment ', heTC);         {top centered}
  end;

  {Pick an item}
  if MouseInUse then   {LoanGlob}
    ShowMouse;         {mouse available, OpMouse}
  PaymentList.Process; {make choice, OpPick}
  if MouseInUse then   {LoanGlob}
    HideMouse;         {avoid mouse tracks, OpMouse}
  PaymentList.Erase;   {erase pick list, OpPick}
  if PaymentList.GetLastCommand = ccSelect then {choice made, OpWindow,
                                                 OpCmd}
    PayChoice := PaymentList.GetLastChoice;     {store number of item
                                                 selected, LoanGlob,
                                                 OpPick}
  PaymentList.Done;                             {recover object's
                                                 memory, OpPick}
end; {end of procedure}

end. {end of unit}
```

The first procedure

```
{$F+}
procedure MakeList(Item : Word;              {current list item number}
                   Mode : pkMode;            {pkMode can be pkDisplay,
                                              pkSearch, or pkGetType,
                                              changing as object is used
                                              or set by programmer}
                   var IType : pkItemType;   {pkItemType can be pkNormal,
                                              pkAlternate, pkProtected,
                                              or pkPrivate, changing as
                                              object requires or set by
                                              programmer. pkNormal is
                                              default}
                   var IString : String;     {content set in code below}
                   PickPtr : PickListPtr);   {pointer to pick list object,
                                              set when picklist inits}
```

```
{Sets item string and item options (if any)}
begin
  if Mode = pkGetType then {only looking to see if specified item is
                            normal or protected, not searching}
    Exit;

  {string content to display}
  IString := ' ' + DateToDateString('mm/dd/yyyy',PayList[Item].PayDate)
             + ' ' + Real2Str(PayList[Item].Amount,9,2)
             + ' ';                                          {OpString}
end;
{$F-}
```

is required by the PickList object's initialization code.

It is used by the program to tell the pick list how to display each item in the list. It also handles such things as protected fields, shape of the pick list, how many items can be selected, and other options to be discussed in a moment.

First we'll discuss the Mode argument. Setting this argument to pkMode permits the PIckList object to set the Mode to one of the following values as required.

pkDisplay	the string will be used for display and should include control characters for flexwrite (OpCrt) formatting used by the PickList object
pkSearch	the string will be used for searching and should not include padding and/or control characters
pkGetType	just check to see if string is normal or protected

An earlier sample program (OSimple2.pas) in Chapter 4 gave an example of adding a protected item. Also, see the following.

Setting the IType argument to pkItemType lets the PickList object set IType to one of the following values:

pkNormal	video attributes defined for this type in Colors.Inc.
pkAlternate	video attributes defined for this type in Colors.Inc.
pkProtected	item can't be highlighted or selected
pkPrivate	reserved

IString is usually set to "string," but you could use a function to return different values, depending on the item number and other circumstances. However, this function should be short and efficient, as it is called very frequently.

If one or more items are to be protected or set to alternate colors, a line like this should be interposed at this point. It must come before the following "if Mode . . ." line or it won't work.

```
if Item = 3 then             {third pick list choice}
IType := pkProtected;  {can't be chosen, displayed in ProItemColor}
```

Of course, this could also be determined by a surrounding Case, possibly with included If statements to set different items to protected or alternate determined by the value of some variable.

The next two lines are added to save processing time:

```
if Mode = pkGetType then {only looking to see if specified item is
                          normal or protected, not searching}
  Exit;
```

Finally, the last line determines what items will be displayed in the pick list and how they will be formatted.

```
{string content to display}
IString := ' ' + DateToDateString('mm/dd/yyyy',PayList[Item].PayDate)
         + ' ' + Real2Str(PayList[Item].Amount,9,2) + ' ';
```

The ChoosePayment procedure is the main procedure in this unit. It displays the payments and accepts the choice.

The first line sets the window options. The contents of DefWindowOptions and the other possible options were described after the LoanPay unit earlier in this chapter.

Next, the window to contain the pick list is initialized. Most of the arguments are explained by the annotation. "MakeFile" determines how many items will appear in the pick list. Since this variable tells how many items are in the PayList array, all the payments will be displayed. The "MakeList" argument determines the function to use to designate what goes into the pick list and how to display it. This was the function just described. Next we see the "PickVertical" argument. The possible options here are as follows:

PickVertical	If more than one column is used (determine with the column width setting), starting with the leftmost column, the highlight moves vertically down each column, to the end of the column even if not currently in the window (the window contents scroll up as necessary), to the top of the next column, and so forth.
PickHorizontal	If more than one column is used (determine with the column width setting), beginning with the top row, the highlight moves horizontally across each row, moving downward.
PickSnaking	If more than one column is used (determine with the column width setting) the highlight moves, starting with the left column, vertically down each column, to the end of the column visible in the window, then to the top of the next column, and so on.

The next argument, SingleChoice, has one other option, MultipleChoice. Obviously, this permits more than one selection from the pick list.

As usual, the mouse is made available to the PickList object with

```
PickCommands.cpOptionsOn(cpEnableMouse); {make mouse available to
                                          picklist}
HideMouse;                                {avoid mouse tracks,
                                          OpMouse}
```

The search method is set with

```
PaymentList.SetSearchMode(PickCharSearch);   {OpPick}
```

The options for this procedure are

PickStringSearch	This search method permits the user to enter a series of characters. As each is matched in the list, the highlight moves to that item. Thus entering "A" would match item "AAA." Entering "B" would move the highlight to item "ABA." As each character is entered and matched, it is added to an internal string with a length determined by the constant pkMaxSearchLen with a default value of 15. A nonmatching character will clear the internal string and not move the highlight. To choose the highlighted item, press the Enter key.
PickAltStringSearch	This works like the previous option, except that if a nonmatching character is entered, the internal string is cleared, set to the new character, and an attempt is made to match the new character. If it is not successful, the highlight doesn't move and the internal string is cleared. To choose the highlighted item, press the Enter key.
PickCharSearch	An attempt is made only to match the first character of each item. If the same character is entered, a match further down the list of items is attempted. To choose the highlighted item, press the Enter key.
PickCharExit	An attempt is made to match the character entered with the first character of the list of items. If a match is found, that item is selected and the pick list is exited.
PickAnyCharExit	No attempt to match an item is made. Entry of any character exits the pick list. GetLastCommand will return ccChar containing the character entered.

Protected items are never matched. The search is not case sensitive.

You've seen the following OpFrame lines described earlier in this chapter:

```
AddShadow(shBR,                          {display shadow bottom and
                                          left of frame}
```

```
            shOverWrite);                {opaque shadow}
    AddHeader(' Date and Payment ', heTC); {top centered}
```

Next the mouse is made available and the user is permitted to make a choice from the picklist via the Process method. Once a choice is made, the mouse is hidden again to avoid leaving tracks on the screen.

The pick list is erased. The number of the item that was highlighted when the Enter key was pressed is stored in the global PayChoice variable. Finally, the instance of the PickList object is removed from memory.

LoanTble.Pas

The LoanTble unit prints the amortization table. This unit first checks to be sure the printer is turned on and ready. It then prints a list of all the loan information, such as debtor name and address, amount of loan, etc.—all the information that was entered into the header record. The table column heads are then printed. These are

Date Balance Interest Installment New Balance

The date is the date of the payment. The balance is the amount due before the interest is added and the payment and late charge, if any, is subtracted. The interest is the amount of interest that accrued since the last payment date. The installment is the amount of the payment. The New Balance is the amount after subtracting the interest and late charge (if any) from the old balance and adding the installment paid. If a late charge was subtracted, this value is followed by an asterisk.

When the table is completed, the total of the payments, interest, and late charges is printed,

Here is the code:

```
unit LoanTble;

INTERFACE

uses LoanGlob,
     LoanMsg,
     OpCrt,
     OpDate,
     OpString,
     OpRoot,
     OpPrnLow,
     OpPrint;

{print the amortization table}
procedure PrintTable;
```

```
IMPLEMENTATION

const
  Space : Char = #32;

var
  P : Printer; {instance of Printer object}

procedure PrintColumnHeads(var Ln : Integer);
{print heads of columns just above table}

begin
  P.Position(Ln,                      {vertical position (line),}
             9,                       {horizontal position (column)}
             rtAbsolute);             {use absolute page position, OpPrint}
  P.PrintStr('Date');                 {print this string, OpPrint}
  P.Position(Ln,22,rtAbsolute);
  P.PrintStr('Balance');
  P.Position(Ln,33,rtAbsolute);
  P.PrintStr('Interest');
  P.Position(Ln,42,rtAbsolute);
  P.PrintStr('Installment');
  P.Position(Ln,54,rtAbsolute);
  P.PrintStr('New Balance');
  Ln := Ln + 2;                       {skip a line}
end;


procedure TableHeader(var Pg,Ln : Integer);
{print page number and date}

begin
  Inc(Pg);                                  {next page number}
  Ln := Ln + 2;                             {skip a line}
  P.Position(Ln,10,rtAbsolute);
  P.PrintStr('Page ' + Long2Str(Pg));       {page number}
  P.Position(Ln,65,rtAbsolute);
  P.PrintStr(TodayString('mm/dd/yyyy')); {today's date}
  Ln := Ln + 2;                             {skip a line}

  PrintColumnHeads(Ln);
end;


procedure PrintTable;
{print the table}

var
  Counter      : Integer; {loop counter for payments in file}
  Day          : Integer; {day value of date}
```

```
    DInterest    : Real;     {daily interest rate}
    DueDate      : Date;     {date payment is due}
    Found        : Boolean;  {found a payment for current due date?}
    InterestDate : Date;     {date to start interest calculation}
    InterestDue  : Real;     {amount of interest due since last payment}
    LateFee      : Real;     {amount of late fee}
    LateFlag     : Boolean;  {late fee payment required?}
    Lines        : Integer;  {vertical position on page}
    Loan         : Real;     {amount of principle left}
    Month        : Integer;  {month value of date}
    OldDueDate   : Date;     {previous payment due date}
    Page         : Integer;  {page of report}
    Payment      : Real;     {amount of payment made}
    PaymentDue   : Real;     {amount of payment due}
    S            : String;   {string temporary}
    SetDate      : Date;     {date payment was made}
    TotalInt     : Real;     {running total of amount of interest paid}
    TotalLate    : Real;     {running total of amount of late fees paid}
    TotalPay     : Real;     {running total of amount of payments made}
    Year         : Integer;  {year value of date}

  begin
    LateFlag  := False; {late fee deducted from payment?}
    LateFee   := 0.00;  {set late fee to 0.00 as default}
    TotalPay  := 0.00;  {start payment running total at 0.00}
    TotalLate := 0.00;  {start late fee running total at 0.00}
    TotalInt  := 0.00;  {start interest paid running total at 0.00}

    Clrscr;
    if not P.Init('PRN',Prn,0) then begin {instance of Printer object}
      ShowMsg('Failed to init printer. Status : '
               + Long2Str(InitStatus));    {OpString, LoanMsg}
      Halt;
    end;

    while not P.PrinterReady do begin  {Test printer to be sure it's
                                        ready, OpPrint}
      ShowMsg('Printer is not ready'); {LoanMsg}
    end;

    Lines := 2; {print page header here}
    Page := 1;  {current page number}

    {page header}
    P.Position(Lines,10,rtAbsolute);
    P.PrintStr('Page ' + Long2Str(Page)); {OpString}
    P.Position(Lines,65,rtAbsolute);
    P.PrintStr(TodayString('mm/dd/yyyy'));{today's date, OpDate}
    Lines := Lines + 2;                   {skip a line}
```

```
{debtor name}
P.Position(Lines,(80 - Length(Header.Name))
          DIV 2,rtAbsolute);          {center}
P.PrintStr(Header.Name);              {debtor name}
Inc(Lines);                           {move to next line}

{debtor address, first line}
P.Position(Lines,(80 - Length(Header.Address1))
          DIV 2,rtAbsolute);          {center}
P.PrintStr(Header.Address1);          {debtor address line 1}
Inc(Lines);                           {move to next line}

{only if address line two exists}
if TrimSpaces(Header.Address2) <> '' then begin  {OpString}
  P.Position(Lines,(80 - Length(Header.Address2))
          DIV 2,rtAbsolute);                     {center}
  P.PrintStr(Header.Address2);                   {address line two}
  Inc(Lines);                                    {move to next line}
end;

{debtor city, state, and zip}
P.Position(Lines,(80 - Length(Header.City))
                 DIV 2,rtAbsolute);              {center}
P.PrintStr(Header.City);                         {debtor city, state,
                                                  zip}
Inc(Lines);                                      {move to next line}
Inc(Lines);                                      {skip a line}

{home phone}
P.Position(Lines,10,rtAbsolute);
P.PrintStr('Home phone: ' + Header.HomePhone);   {debtor home phone}
Inc(Lines);                                      {move to next line}

{work phone}
P.Position(Lines,10,rtAbsolute);
P.PrintStr('Work phone: ' + Header.WorkPhone);   {debtor work phone}
Inc(Lines);                                      {move to next line}
Inc(Lines);                                      {skip a line}

{amount of loan}
P.Position(Lines,10,rtAbsolute);
P.PrintStr('Loan amount: $'                                {amount of
                                                            loan}
         + TrimLead(Real2Str(Header.LoanAmount,9,2)));     {OpString,
                                                            LoanGlob}
Inc(Lines);                                                {move to
                                                            next line}

{interest rate in percent}
P.Position(Lines,10,rtAbsolute);
```

```
P.PrintStr('Interest rate: '
           + TrimLead(Real2Str(Header.Interest,6,3))
           + '%');                                     {Interest rate
                                                        OpString,
                                                        LoanGlob}
Inc(Lines);                                            {move to next
                                                        line}

{amount of payment}
P.Position(Lines,10,rtAbsolute);
P.PrintStr('Payment amount: $'
           + TrimLead(Real2Str(Header.PayAmount,9,2))); {installment,
                                                          OpString,
                                                          LoanGlob}
Inc(Lines);                                              {move to next
                                                          line}

{date loan was made}
P.Position(Lines,10,rtAbsolute);
P.PrintStr('Loan date: '
           + DateToDateString('mm/dd/yyyy',   {loan date, OpDate}
           Header.LoanDate));                 {LoanGlob}
Inc(Lines);                                   {move to next line}

{date of first loan payment}
P.Position(Lines,10,rtAbsolute);
P.PrintStr('First payment due: '
           + DateToDateString('mm/dd/yyyy',
           Header.FirstDue));                 {first payment due,
                                               OpDate, LoanGlob}
Inc(Lines);                                   {move to next line}

{amount of late charge, 0.00 if none}
P.Position(Lines,10,rtAbsolute);
P.PrintStr('Late charge: '
           + TrimLead(Real2Str(Header.LateCharge,9,2))); {late
                                                           charge,
                                                           OpString,
                                                           LoanGlob}

{grace period before late charge, if any}
if Header.LateCharge <> 0.00 then begin      {any charge required?}
  P.Position(Lines,35,rtAbsolute);
  P.PrintStr('Days to late charge: '
             + Long2Str(Header.LateDays));   {grace days, OpString}
end;
Inc(Lines);                                  {move to next line}

{how often are payments due?}
P.Position(Lines,10,rtAbsolute);
```

```
P.PrintStr('Payment frequency: '
           + Frequency[Header.Frequency]);  {payment frequency,
                                             LoanGlob}
{payments twice a month?}
if Frequency[Header.Frequency] = 'Semimonthly' then begin {LoanGlob}
  {which days are they due}
  P.Position(Lines,42,rtAbsolute);
  P.PrintStr('First day: '
             + Long2Str(Header.FirstDay));  {first day due, OpString,
                                             LoanGlob}
  P.Position(Lines,56,rtAbsolute);
  P.PrintStr('Second day: '
             + Long2Str(Header.SecondDay)); {second day due,
                                             OpString, LoanGlob}
end;
Inc(Lines);                                 {move to next line}

{start interest from loan date or date of first payment}
P.Position(Lines,10,rtAbsolute);
if Header.PayIntFirst then
   P.PrintStr('Pay interest starting from date of loan')
else
   P.PrintStr('Pay interest starting from first payment date');
Lines := Lines + 2; {skip a line}

P.Position(Lines,10,rtAbsolute);
P.PrintStr('Loan amounts followed by an asterisk (*)');
Inc(Lines);         {move to next line}
P.Position(Lines,15,rtAbsolute);
P.PrintStr('indicate a late charge was deducted');
Lines := Lines + 2; {skip a line}

PrintColumnHeads(Lines); {print column headings}

Finished   := False;                        {not done}
DInterest  := (Header.Interest / 100) / 365; {daily interest,
                                             LoanGlob}
Loan       := Header.LoanAmount;            {amount of loan,
                                             LoanGlob}
PaymentDue := Header.PayAmount;             {amount of payment made,
                                             LoanGlob}
Payment    := PaymentDue;                   {amount of payment due}

{calculate interest from this date}
if Header.PayIntFirst then          {LoanGlob}
   InterestDate := Header.LoanDate  {start charging interest on date
                                     of loan, LoanGlob}
else
   InterestDate := Header.FirstDue; {start charging interest when
                                     first payment is due, LoanGlob}
```

```
DueDate   := Header.FirstDue; {date payment is due, LoanGlob}
SetDate   := Header.FirstDue; {date payment was made, LoanGlob}

{check to see if first payment was late of not of agreed-upon amount}
Counter := 1;    {nonstandard payment counter}
Found := False; {nonstandard payment not found}

{check for current due date in nonstandard payment array until found
 or all nonstandard payments have been checked}
while (Counter <= MaxFile) and not Found do begin
  if (PayList[Counter].DueDate = DueDate) then begin
    {found it, LoanGlob}
    SetDate := PayList[Counter].PayDate; {actual payment date,
                                          LoanGlob}
    Payment := PayList[Counter].Amount;  {actual payment amount,
                                          LoanGlob}
    Found := True;                       {nonstandard payment found}

    {add a late charge?}
    if Header.LateCharge <> 0.00 then begin
      {was it late enough?}
      if (DueDate + Header.LateDays) < SetDate then begin {OpDate,
                                                      LoanGlob}
        LateFee  := Header.LateCharge; {amount of late charge,
                                        LoanGlob}
        LateFlag := True;              {late charge due}
      end;
    end;
  end;
  Inc(Counter); {next payment to test}
end;

while not Finished do begin
  {print date payment was made in table}
  P.Position(Lines,9,rtAbsolute);
  P.PrintStr(DateToDateString('mm/dd/yyyy',SetDate)); {OpDate}

  {print amount of principle remaining in table}
  P.Position(Lines,21,rtAbsolute);
  P.PrintStr(Real2Str(Loan,9,2));  {OpString}

  {calculate interest from date of last payment}
  InterestDue := (SetDate - InterestDate) * DInterest * Loan; {OpDate}

  {add interest and late fee, if any, to total amount due}
  {late fee is set to 0.00 if not required}
  Loan := Loan + InterestDue + LateFee;

  {calculate next interest from this date}
  InterestDate := SetDate;
```

```
{print current period's interest in table}
P.Position(Lines,31,rtAbsolute);
P.PrintStr(Real2Str(InterestDue,9,2));  {OpString}

{add to running total of interest paid}
TotalInt := TotalInt + InterestDue;

{print amount of payment here}
P.Position(Lines,41,rtAbsolute);
P.PrintStr(Real2Str(Payment,9,2));      {OpString}
TotalPay := TotalPay + Payment;

{reduce principle}
Loan := Loan - Payment;

{are we done?}
if Loan <= 0.00 then
  Finished := True;

{add late fee indicator?}
P.Position(Lines,53,rtAbsolute);
P.PrintStr(Real2Str(Loan,9,2));      {OpString}
if LateFlag then begin
  LateFlag := False;                 {reset}
  P.Position(Lines,62,rtAbsolute);
  P.PrintStr('*');                   {indicator}
  TotalLate := TotalLate + LateFee; {update late fee running total}
end;

OldDueDate := DueDate; {use copy of last due date to find next due
                        date}

{calculate next due date}
case Header.Frequency of
  Weekly :
    DueDate := OldDueDate + 7;  {OpDate}

  SemiMonthly :  {two payments per month on designated dates}
  begin
    DateToDMY(OldDueDate,Day,Month,Year); {convert julian date to
                                           day, month, year, OpDate}
    if Day = Header.FirstDay then {first half of month?, LoanGlob}
       Day := Header.SecondDay    {use second payment date,
                                   LoanGlob}
    else
    begin
       Day := Header.FirstDay;    {use first payment date, LoanGlob}
       Inc(Month);
       if Month = 13 then         {out of months?}
       begin
```

```
        Month := 1;                {start a new year}
        Inc(Year);
      end;
    end;
    DueDate := DMYtoDate(Day,Month,Year); {convert day, month, and
                                           year to julian date,
                                           OpDate}
  end;

  Monthly :
  begin
    DateToDMY(OldDueDate,Day,Month,Year); {convert julian to day,
                                           month, year, OpDate}
    Inc(Month);                           {same date, next month}
    if Month = 13 then                    {out of months?}
    begin
      Month := 1;                         {start a new year}
      Inc(Year);
    end;
    DueDate := DMYtoDate(Day,Month,Year); {convert day, month, and
                                           year to julian date,
                                           OpDate}
  end;

  Yearly :
  begin
    DateToDMY(OldDueDate,Day,Month,Year); {convert julian date to
                                           day, month, year, OpDate}
    Inc(Year);                            {same month, same date,
                                           next year}
    DueDate := DMYtoDate(Day,Month,Year); {convert day, month, year
                                           to julian date, OpDate}
  end;
end;

{check for current due date in nonstandard payment array until
 found or all nonstandard payments have been checked}
Counter := 1;   {nonstandard payment counter}
Found := False; {nonstandard payment not found}

LateFee := 0.00; {reset}
{look through payment array for matching due date until no more
 payments or match is found or loan has been paid off and no more
 payments required}
while (Counter <= MaxFile) and not Found and not Finished do begin
  if (PayList[Counter].DueDate = DueDate) then begin {found a match}
    SetDate := PayList[Counter].PayDate;             {actual payment
                                                      date,
                                                      LoanGlob}
    Payment := PayList[Counter].Amount;              {actual payment
                                                      amount,
                                                      LoanGlob}
```

```
      Found := True;                                        {quit looking}

      if Header.LateCharge <> 0.00 then begin                {late fees
                                                              being
                                                              charged?,
                                                              LoanGlob}
        if (DueDate + Header.LateDays) < SetDate then begin {add to
                                                              this
                                                              payment?,
                                                              OpDate,
                                                              LoanGlob}
          LateFee  := Header.LateCharge; {yes, LoanGlob}
          LateFlag := True;              {add late fee to running
                                          total and print late fee
                                          indicator}
        end;
      end;
    end;
    Inc(Counter);  {next payment}
  end;

  {nonstandard payment not found and loan not paid off}
  if not Found and not Finished then begin
    SetDate := DueDate;                  {must have been paid on due
                                          date}
    InterestDue := (SetDate - InterestDate)
                   * DInterest * Loan;   {calculate interest from last
                                          payment, OpDate}
    if (Loan + InterestDue + LateFee) >= PaymentDue then
      Payment := PaymentDue                    {still principle left
                                                over, use default
                                                payment}
    else
      Payment := Loan + InterestDue + LateFee; {last payment}
  end;


  Inc(Lines);                                  {next line}
  if (Lines >= 55) and not Finished then begin {start new page?}
    P.FormFeed;                                {next page}
    Lines := 2;                                {start page at this
                                                line}
    TableHeader(Page,Lines);                   {print header (date &
                                                page)}
  end;
end; {if not finished loop back and print next table line}

{Summary under table on last page}
```

```
    Lines := Lines + 2; {skip two lines}
    P.Position(Lines,35,rtAbsolute);
    P.PrintStr('Total amount paid:    '
               + Real2Str(TotalPay,10,2));  {payment summary, OpString}
    Inc(Lines);

    P.Position(Lines,35,rtAbsolute);
    P.PrintStr('Total interest paid:  '
               + Real2Str(TotalInt,10,2));  {interest summary, OpString}
    Inc(Lines);

    P.Position(Lines,35,rtAbsolute);
    P.PrintStr('Total late fees paid: '
               + Real2Str(TotalLate,10,2)); {late fee summary, OpString}
    P.Formfeed; {eject page, OpPrinter}
    P.Done;     {recover instance of printer object's memory, OpPrinter}
  end; {end of procedure}
  end. {end of unit}
```

Note that I use one command to position an item to be printed

```
P.Position(Ln,                    {vertical position (line),}
           9,                     {horizontal position (column)}
           rtAbsolute);           {use absolute page position, OpPrint}
```

and another to print the item

```
P.PrintStr('Date');              {print this string, OpPrint}
```

The Printer object has a method that includes both, called PrintStrPos. You may prefer to use this instead of my choice.

After the debtor information and column heads are printed, the first payment is checked to see if it is nonstandard. If it is, the correct payment amount and date are substituted for the default.

```
DueDate   := Header.FirstDue; {date payment is due, LoanGlob}
SetDate   := Header.FirstDue; {date payment was made, LoanGlob}

{check to see if first payment was late of not of agreed-upon amount}
Counter := 1;    {nonstandard payment counter}
Found := False; {nonstandard payment not found}

{check for current due date in nonstandard payment array until found
 or all nonstandard payments have been checked}
while (Counter <= MaxFile) and not Found do begin {LoanGlob}
  if (PayList[Counter].DueDate = DueDate) then begin
    {found it}
    SetDate := PayList[Counter].PayDate; {actual payment date,
                                          LoanGlob}
    Payment := PayList[Counter].Amount;  {actual payment amount,
                                          LoanGlob}
```

```
      Found := True;                    {nonstandard payment found}

      {add a late charge?}
      if Header.LateCharge <> 0.00 then begin
        {was it late enough?}
        if (DueDate + Header.LateDays) < SetDate then begin {LoanGlob}
          LateFee  := Header.LateCharge; {amount of late charge,
                                          LoanGlob}
          LateFlag := True;              {late charge due}
        end;
      end;
    end;
    Inc(Counter); {next payment to test}
  end;
```

Next we print the first line of the table.

```
{print date payment was made in table}
P.Position(Lines,9,rtAbsolute);
P.PrintStr(DateToDateString('mm/dd/yyyy',SetDate)); {OpDate}

{print amount of principle remaining in table}
P.Position(Lines,21,rtAbsolute);
P.PrintStr(Real2Str(Loan,9,2)); {OpString}

{calculate interest from date of last payment}
InterestDue := (SetDate - InterestDate) * DInterest * Loan; {OpDate}

{add interest and late fee, if any, to total amount due}
{late fee is set to 0.00 if not required}
Loan := Loan + InterestDue + LateFee;

{calculate next interest from this date}
InterestDate := SetDate;

{print current period's interest in table}
P.Position(Lines,31,rtAbsolute);
P.PrintStr(Real2Str(InterestDue,9,2));  {OpString}

{add to running total of interest paid}
TotalInt := TotalInt + InterestDue;

{print amount of payment here}
P.Position(Lines,41,rtAbsolute);
P.PrintStr(Real2Str(Payment,9,2));      {OpString}
TotalPay := TotalPay + Payment;

{reduce principle}
Loan := Loan - Payment;

{are we done?}
```

```
if Loan <= 0.00 then
  Finished := True;

{add late fee indicator?}
P.Position(Lines,53,rtAbsolute);
P.PrintStr(Real2Str(Loan,9,2));     {OpString}
if LateFlag then begin
  LateFlag := False;                {reset}
  P.Position(Lines,62,rtAbsolute);
  P.PrintStr('*');                  {indicator}
  TotalLate := TotalLate + LateFee; {update late fee running total}
end;
```

As you can see, while this line is being printed we also calculate the interest,

```
{calculate interest from date of last payment}
InterestDue := (SetDate - InterestDate) * DInterest * Loan; {OpDate}
```

adjust the remaining debt total,

```
{reduce principle}
Loan := Loan - Payment;
```

see if we have completed the table,

```
{are we done?}
if Loan <= 0.00 then
  Finished := True;
```

and adjust the late fee total and print the late fee indicator if necessary.

```
if LateFlag then begin
  LateFlag := False;                {reset}
  P.Position(Lines,62,rtAbsolute);
  P.PrintStr('*');                  {indicator}
  TotalLate := TotalLate + LateFee; {update late fee running total}
end;
```

The next step is to calculate the next due date.

```
OldDueDate := DueDate; {use copy of last due date to find next due
                        date}

{calculate next due date}
case Header.Frequency of
  Weekly :
    DueDate := OldDueDate + 7; {OpDate}

  SemiMonthly :  {two payments per month on designated dates}
  begin
    DateToDMY(OldDueDate,Day,Month,Year); {convert julian date to
                                           day, month, year, OpDate}
```

```
    if Day = Header.FirstDay then {first half of month?, LoanGlob}
       Day := Header.SecondDay    {use second payment date,
                                   LoanGlob}
    else
    begin
       Day := Header.FirstDay;    {use first payment date, LoanGlob}
       Inc(Month);
       if Month = 13 then         {out of months?}
       begin
         Month := 1;              {start a new year}
         Inc(Year);
       end;
    end;
    DueDate := DMYtoDate(Day,Month,Year); {convert day, month, and
                                           year to julian date,
                                           OpDate}
  end;

  Monthly :
  begin
    DateToDMY(OldDueDate,Day,Month,Year); {convert julian to day,
                                           month, year, OpDate}
    Inc(Month);                           {same date, next month}
    if Month = 13 then                    {out of months?}
    begin
      Month := 1;                         {start a new year}
      Inc(Year);
    end;
    DueDate := DMYtoDate(Day,Month,Year); {convert day, month, and
                                           year to julian date,
                                           OpDate}
  end;

  Yearly :
  begin
    DateToDMY(OldDueDate,Day,Month,Year); {convert julian date to
                                           day, month, year, OpDate}
    Inc(Year);                            {same month, same date,
                                           next year}
    DueDate := DMYtoDate(Day,Month,Year); {convert day, month, year
                                           to julian date, OpDate}
  end;
end;
```

Then we see if the due date is in the nonstandard payment array.

```
{check for current due date in nonstandard payment array until
 found or all nonstandard payments have been checked}
Counter := 1;    {nonstandard payment counter}
Found := False; {nonstandard payment not found}
LateFee := 0.00; {reset}
```

```
{look through payment array for matching due date until no more
 payments or match is found or loan has been paid off and no more
 payments are required}
while (Counter <= MaxFile) and not Found and not Finished do begin
  if (PayList[Counter].DueDate = DueDate) then begin {found a match}
    SetDate := PayList[Counter].PayDate;             {actual payment
                                                      date,
                                                      LoanGlob}
    Payment := PayList[Counter].Amount;              {actual payment
                                                      amount,
                                                      LoanGlob}
    Found := True;                                   {quit looking}

    if Header.LateCharge <> 0.00 then begin               {late fees
                                                           being
                                                           charged?,
                                                           LoanGlob}
      if (DueDate + Header.LateDays) < SetDate then begin {add to
                                                           this
                                                           payment?,
                                                           OpDate,
                                                           LoanGlob}
        LateFee  := Header.LateCharge; {yes, LoanGlob}
        LateFlag := True;              {add late fee to running
                                        total and print late fee
                                        indicator}
      end;
    end;
  end;
  Inc(Counter);  {next payment}
end;
```

If no matching nonstandard due date was found, then the installment must have been made on time, so the default due date and payment amount are used.

```
{nonstandard payment not found and loan not paid off}
if not Found and not Finished then begin
  SetDate := DueDate;                     {must have been paid on due
                                           date}
  InterestDue := (SetDate - InterestDate)
                * DInterest * Loan;       {calculate interest from last
                                           payment, OpDate}
  if (Loan + InterestDue + LateFee) >= PaymentDue then
    Payment := PaymentDue                       {still principle left
                                                 over}
  else
    Payment := Loan + InterestDue + LateFee; {last payment}
end;
```

Check to see if the page is filled. If it is, start a new page and print the date, page number, and column headings.

```
    Inc(Lines);                                       {next line}
    if (Lines >= 55) and not Finished then begin      {start new page?}
      P.FormFeed;                                     {next page, OpPrint}
      Lines := 2;                                     {start page at this
                                                       line}
      TableHeader(Page,Lines);                        {print header (date &
                                                       page)}
    end;
  end;
```

If we are not finished, we loop back and print the next table line.

If we are finished, we print the table summary, erase the instance of the Printer object from memory, and return to the main menu.

```
    {Summary under table on last page}
    Lines := Lines + 2; {skip two lines}
    P.Position(Lines,35,rtAbsolute);
    P.PrintStr('Total amount paid:    '
              + Real2Str(TotalPay,10,2));  {payment summary, OpString}
    Inc(Lines);

    P.Position(Lines,35,rtAbsolute);
    P.PrintStr('Total interest paid:  '
              + Real2Str(TotalInt,10,2));  {interest summary, OpString}
    Inc(Lines);

    P.Position(Lines,35,rtAbsolute);
    P.PrintStr('Total late fees paid: '
              + Real2Str(TotalLate,10,2)); {late fee summary, OpString}
    P.Formfeed; {eject page, OpPrint}
    P.Done;     {recover instance of printer object's memory, OpPrint}
  end; {end of procedure}
  end. {end of unit}
```

This completes the loan program.

Compiling

If you don't set up a Make file, compile the files in the following order:

LoanGlob
LoanMsg
LoanVrfy
LoanHead
LoanTble
LoanPay
LoanPick

LoanPyof
LoanRev
LoanDir
Loan

8

More About the Loan Application

Adding Help

To supply help in the data entry portion of an application, you usually provide a list of constants, each representing a different number for each field in each entry screen, one for each entry field for which you want to supply the help. I supplied the list for you in LoanGlob and the numbers in all the fields in each data entry screen, even though I didn't implement any help. Here is the list:

```
{entry screen help ids}
idCurFile     = 1;                {1}
idName        = idCurFile+1;      {2}
idAddress1    = idName+1;         {3}
idAddress2    = idAddress1+1;     {4}
idCity        = idAddress2+1;     {5}
idHomePhone   = idCity+1;         {6}
idWorkPhone   = idHomePhone+1;    {7}
idLoanAmount  = idWorkPhone+1;    {8}
idInterest    = idLoanAmount+1;   {9}
idPayAmount   = idInterest+1;     {10}
idLoanDate    = idPayAmount+1;    {11}
idFirstDue    = idLoanDate+1;     {12}
idFrequency   = idFirstDue+1;     {13}
idFirstDay    = idFrequency+1;    {14}
idSecondDay   = idFirstDay+1;     {15}
idPayIntFirst = idSecondDay+1;    {16}
idPayDate     = idPayIntFirst+1;  {17}
```

```
idDueDate      = idPayDate+1;      {18}
idPAmount      = idDueDate+1;      {19}
idMore         = idPAmount+1;      {20}
idStarting     = idMore+1;         {21}
idCurrent      = idStarting+1;     {22}
idYears        = idCurrent+1;      {23}
idLateCharge   = idYears+1;        {24}
idLateDays     = idLateCharge+1;   {25}
idOrgAmount    = idLateDays+1      {26}
idOrgDate      = idOrgAmount+1     {27}
idCurAmount    = idOrgDate+1       {28}
idCurAmtDate   = idCurAmount+1     {29}
idLoanInt      = idCurAmtDate+1    {30}
idLoanIntDate  = idLoanInt+1       {31}
```

You can also provide help for the memo editor, browser, line editor, and others with the use of the SetHelpIndex method for the applicable object. Menus use the AddItemHelp or AddItemHelpPtr method to indicate a menu choice's help message. Most other objects also have a help method available.

Write the help text using any ASCII editor, segregating the help by topic. Then use the supplied utility MakeHelp to compile the ASCII text to binary. This significantly reduces its size. You can supply help as an abstract window where you supply the code to display the correct material from the binary help file, a paged help window, or a scrolling help window. Display the help text using one of the three help objects and its methods from the OpHelp unit.

You can have up to 10,000 help topics in one file. Topics can include references to other topics—up to 50 cross-references per topic. If the help data is not too large, it can be linked into the application EXE; otherwise it would reside in a separate file.

One simple way to use the help system is to call a help topic by referring to the help id number, retrieved as HelpIndex, in the data entry field. The procedure that makes this call is designated by, for example,

```
EntryCommands.SetHelpProc(GetHelpProc)
```

This procedure might look something like

```
{$F+}
procedure GetHelpProc(UnitCode : Byte; IdPtr : Pointer;
                      HelpIndex : Word);
begin
  if HelpIndex <> 0 then begin
    LoanHelpWindow.SetTopic(HelpIndex);
    LoanHelpWindow.Process;
    LoanHelpWindow.Erase;
  end;
end;
{$F-}
```

where LoanHelpWindow is the instance of the help object. I like the scrolling window. As with all OPro objects, there are a myriad of ways to implement it, as simple or as complex as you wish. I've noted before that in this book I generally have elected to keep things simple.

Here is an example supplying help only for the LoanRev unit's entry screen. If you wish, you can expand it for all the application's entry screens.

First the ASCII help file. Save it to LoanHelp.txt. Be sure to keep the lines under 200 characters or so. When I created the first one, I made each topic one long line. The result was that MakeHelp truncated the lines in the compiled files to a little over 200 characters in length. Experiment!

```
!SCROLLING
!TOPIC 26 Original Amount
!INDEX 26
This entry is the amount of the loan or investment.
 The minimum allowable amount is 0.01; the maximum 999999.99.
 Do not enter the dollar sign or commas. The default amount is 0.00.
!PAGE
!TOPIC 27 Loan Date
!INDEX 27
This entry requires the date of the loan in the entry field immediately
above this.
 The date should be entered in the form MM/DD/YYYY where MM is the
month.
 Use two digits, 0 if necessary. Thus February would be entered as 02.
 The DD stands for the day of the month.
 Again, use two digits with a leading 0 if necessary.
 The YYYY represents the year in four digits, 1992 as an example.
 The default date is that day's date.
!PAGE
!TOPIC 28 Current Value
!INDEX 28
 The current value of the loan or investment goes here.
 The minimum allowable amount is 0.01; the maximum 999999.99.
 Do not enter the dollar sign or commas. The default amount is 0.00.
!PAGE
!TOPIC 29 Date of Current Value
!INDEX 29
 The date when the current amount has the value entered above.
 The date should be entered in the form MM/DD/YYYY where MM is the
month.
 Use two digits, 0 if necessary. Thus February would be entered as 02.
 The DD stands for the day of the month.
```

Again, use two digits with a leading 0 if necessary.
The YYYY represents the year in four digits; 1992 is an example.
The default date is that day's date.
!PAGE

Use

```
MakeHelp LoanHelp.txt Loan.hlp
```

to compile the file. You must compile it or it won't work in your program.
The

!SCROLLING

tells MakeHelp that the file will be used with the scrolling help window. Note, you can still use this file with the paged help window if you change your mind later. The

!TOPIC

must be present.

!INDEX

need not be as help is implemented here, but you might change your mind later and decide to let the user choose from a list of topics. If so, you already have the index in the file at the cost of a little larger help file. The

!PAGE

causes a new page to begin in the help window. You could probably leave this out with no harm. There are several other command words available; check the OPro documentation.

The new LoanRev unit would look like this:

```
UNIT LoanRev;

INTERFACE

uses LoanGlob,
     LoanMsg,
     OpCmd,
     OpRoot,
     OpField,
     OpFrame,
     OpWindow,
     OpCrt,
     OpString,
     OpEntry,
```

```
     OpDate,
     OpMouse,
     OpPick,
     OpHelp;

{calculate equivalent compound interest given amount of loan, payoff amount, and time}
procedure Reverse;


IMPLEMENTATION


var
   H : AbstractHelpWindowPtr;

{$F+}
procedure GetHelpProc(UnitCode : Byte; IdPtr : Pointer;
                      HelpIndex : Word);
{press F1 in entry screen field to call}
begin
  if HelpIndex <> 0 then begin {help id designated?}
    H^.SetTopic(HelpIndex);    {get applicable topic}
    H^.Process;                {display window and topic}
    H^.Erase;                  {remove window upon pressing Escape}
  end;
end;
{$F-}

procedure Reverse;
{calculate equivalent compound interest given amount of loan,
 payoff amount, and time}

const
   HelpFile = 'LOAN.HLP'; {define help file to use}

var
   Current   : Real;    {current value of loan or investment}
   Starting  : Real;    {current value of loan or investment}
   Date1     : Date;    {date of loan or investment}
   Date2     : Date;    {date of current value of loan or investment}
   Interest  : Real;    {calculated interest}
   S         : String;  {string temporary}

begin
  ClrScr;
  if not ESRev.InitCustom(20, 5, 60, 13, {Window coordinates}
                       Colors,           {ColorSet}
                       DefWindowOptions
                        or wBordered)    {Window options}
                       then begin
```

```
  S := 'Failed to init reverse interest EntryScreen. Status =
      ' + Long2Str(InitStatus);        {OpString}
  ShowMsg(S);  {display initialization error message, LoanMsg}
  Halt;
end;

{initialize help window, OpHelp}
H := New(ScrollingHelpWindowPtr,
        InitDeluxe(2,2,41,10,          {X1, Y1, X2, Y2}
                   DefaultColorSet,    {from Colors.inc in LoanGlob}
                   DefWindowOptions    {default window options,
                                        OpWindow}
                    or WBordered,      {leave space for border}
                   HelpFile,           {file of help topics}
                   PickVertical,       {when picking from index}
                   hwStaticNameBuffer
                    + hwPickIndex));   {when picking from index}
if H = nil then begin                  {initialization failed}
  ShowMsg('Error initializing help window: '
          + Long2Str(InitStatus));     {LoanMsg, OpString}
  Halt;
end;

EntryCommands.SetHelpProc(GetHelpProc); {designate help window
                                         procedure, command processor}

if MouseInUse then begin                    {LoanGlob}
  EntryCommands.cpOptionsOn(cpEnableMouse); {entry screen sees mouse,
                                             command processor}
  HideMouse;                                {avoid mouse tracks,
                                             OpMouse}
end;

{add some window frills from OpWindow}
ESRev.wFrame.AddShadow(shBR,           {shadow falls below and right}
                       shOverWrite);   {opaque shadow}
ESRev.wFrame.AddHeader(' Convert Interest Earned to Percent ', heTC);
ESRev.wFrame.AddHeader(' Esc to abort, Ctrl-Enter to accept ', heBC);

{add fields}
ESRev.esFieldOptionsOn(efClearFirstChar); {clear string if first
                                           character is ASCII,
                                           OpEntry}

ESRev.esFieldOptionsOn(efRequired);      {some input required,
                                          OpEntry}
ESRev.AddRealField('Original amount:',   {prompt}
                   4,                    {V prompt position}
                   6,                    {H prompt position}
                   '999999.99',          {picture}
```

```
                  4,                      {data V position}
                  21,                     {data H position}
                  idOrgAmount,            {help ID number}
                  0.01,                   {minimum valid entry}
                  999999.99,              {maximum valid entry}
                  2,                      {number of decimal places}
                  Starting);              {data variable}

ESRev.AddDateField('Date of above:',      {prompt}
                  5,                      {V prompt position}
                  6,                      {H prompt position}
                  'mm/dd/yyyy',           {picture}
                  5,                      {data V position}
                  21,                     {data H position}
                  idOrgDate,              {help ID number}
                  00,                     {minimum valid entry}
                  00,                     {maximum valid entry}
                  Date1);                 {data variable}

ESRev.AddRealField('Current amount:',     {prompt}
                  6,                      {V prompt position}
                  6,                      {H prompt position}
                  '999999.99',            {picture}
                  6,                      {data V position}
                  21,                     {data H position}
                  idCurAmount,            {ID number}
                  0.01,                   {minimum valid entry}
                  999999.99,              {maximum valid entry}
                  2,                      {number of decimal places}
                  Current);               {data variable}

ESRev.AddDateField('Date of above:',      {prompt}
                  7,                      {V prompt position}
                  6,                      {H prompt position}
                  'mm/dd/yyyy',           {picture}
                  7,                      {data V position}
                  21,                     {data H position}
                  idCurAmtDate,           {help ID number}
                  00,                     {minimum valid entry}
                  00,                     {maximum valid entry}
                  Date2);                 {data variable}

ESRev.esFieldOptionsOff(efRequired);      {turn off required option,
                                           OpEntry}

Finished := False; {completed}
Starting := 0.00;  {default values}
Current  := 0.00;
Date1    := Today;
Date2    := Today;
```

```
  Interest := 0.00;
  repeat
    if MouseInUse then {LoanGlob}
      ShowMouse;         {make mouse available in entry screen, OpMouse}
    ESRev.Process;       {enter data}
    if MouseInUse then {LoanGlob}
      HideMouse;         {avoid mouse tracks, OpMouse}
    case ESRev.GetLastCommand of {Entry screen return value, OpWindow}
      ccError:                   {error occurred, OpCmd}
        begin
          S := 'Fatal error '+ Long2Str(ESPay.GetLastError); {OpString}
          ShowMsg(S);            {LoanMsg}
          Finished := True;      {abort process}
        end;
      ccQuit : {escape}          {abandon process, OpCmd}
        Finished := True;        {abort process}
    end;

    if not Finished then begin
      {calculate equivalent interest}
      {exp and ln are used because TP has no power operator or function}
      Interest := 100 * (Exp((1 / ((Date2 - Date1) / 365))
                          * Ln(Current / Starting)) - 1);
      {display result}
      S := 'Interest is: ' + TrimLead(Real2Str(Interest,7,3)) + '%';
                                                         {OpString}
      ShowMsg(S);                                        {LoanMsg}

      Finished := True;                                  {done}
    end;
  until Finished;

  ESRev.Erase;  {erase entry screen, OpEntry}
  ESRev.Done;   {recover object's memory, OpEntry}
end;            {end of procedure}

end.            {end of unit}
```

The changes in the unit consist of

```
var
  H : AbstractHelpWindowPtr;

{$F+}
procedure GetHelpProc(UnitCode : Byte; IdPtr : Pointer;
                      HelpIndex : Word);
{press F1 in entry screen field to call}
begin
  if HelpIndex <> 0 then begin {help id designated?}
    H^.SetTopic(HelpIndex); {get applicable topic}
    H^.Process;             {display window and topic}
```

```
    H^.Erase;                {remove window upon pressing Escape}
  end;
end;
{$F-}

...

const
   HelpFile = 'LOAN.HLP'; {define help file to use}

...

  {initialize help window, OpHelp}
  H := New(ScrollingHelpWindowPtr,
          InitDeluxe(2,2,41,10,          {X1, Y1, X2, Y2}
                     DefaultColorSet,    {from Colors.inc in LoanGlob}
                     DefWindowOptions    {default window options,
                                          OpWindow}
                      or WBordered,      {leave space for border}
                     HelpFile,           {file of help topics}
                     PickVertical,       {when picking from index}
                     hwStaticNameBuffer
                      + hwPickIndex));   {when picking from index}
  if H = nil then begin                  {initialization failed}
    ShowMsg('Error initializing help window: '
             + Long2Str(InitStatus));    {LoanMsg,     OpString}
    Halt;
  end;

  EntryCommands.SetHelpProc(GetHelpProc); {designate help window
                                           procedure, command processor}
```

I also converted the help id numbers in the entry field to the listed help constants. Here's an example:

```
  ESRev.AddRealField('Original amount:',      {prompt}
                     4,                       {V prompt position}
                     6,                       {H prompt position}
                     '999999.99',             {picture}
                     4,                       {data V position}
                     21,                      {data H position}
                     idOrgAmount,             {help ID number}
                     0.01,                    {minimum valid entry}
                     999999.99,               {maximum valid entry}
                     2,                       {number of decimal places}
                     Starting);               {data variable}
```

The help window is activated by pressing the F1 key while in the field you want help for. To close the help window, press the Escape key.

In the last arguments of the code

```
H := New(ScrollingHelpWindowPtr,
      InitDeluxe(2,2,41,10,          {X1, Y1, X2, Y2}
                DefaultColorSet,     {from Colors.inc in LoanGlob}
                DefWindowOptions     {default window options,
                                      OpWindow)
                 or WBordered,       {leave space for border}
                HelpFile,            {file of help topics}
                PickVertical,        {when picking from index}
                hwStaticNameBuffer
                 + hwPickIndex));    {when picking from index}
```

the parameters have the following meaning:

hwStaticNameBuffer	Preallocate and keep name buffers at all times
hwPickIndex	Enable ccIndex command

Other possibilities are

hwClearStackAtExit	Clear the current topic when exiting help
hwMousePage	Click on scroll bar to scroll by page
hwAdjustScroll	Adjust horizontal scroll limits automatically
hwBlockMark	Enable block marking

Adding scroll bars requires the use of the AddScrollBar procedure from OpWindow. You can also add various headers within the window, as demonstrated in the LoanMsg unit, for example.

LoanRev.pas and LoanPyof.pas

You might wish to expand these two units to include true interest and compounded interest other than compounded yearly (the default). Perhaps use a pick list to let the user choose the interest type desired; then a case statement to do one of the different calculations.

LoanTble.pas

It might be useful to alter this unit to permit saving the table to be printed to a disk file to be printed later as well as printing immediately.

Also look into the different versions of printer testing for readiness as detailed in the OPro manual. You might want to use a test other than the one I chose.

LoanGlob.pas

The ESPay, ESHeader, and ESRev variables are set to instances of the EntryScreen object globally. To possibly make the EXE file a bit smaller, you might wish to move these to the units (LoanPay, LoanHead, LoanRev) where they are used.

LoanVrfy.pas

You might wish to combine this unit with LoanMsg, as I did in the next program, Look. There would be one less TPC to compile and you might end up with a slightly smaller EXE file.

Loan.pas

You might want to make it more difficult to erase a loan header and payment file than I did when the "Remove Debtor" menu choice is made. I do put up a verify message, but it could be overlooked. Should you use a special verify message in red? Or possibly verify twice?

Halts

When object initializations fail, I fall through to the Halt procedure. Perhaps you might wish to decode the error message (probably an out-of-memory error), post a suitable message to the user, and return to the main menu instead.

Flushing

When I add, modify, or delete any header or payment record on disk, I flush the new information to disk by closing and reopening the applicable file(s). After the application was written and tested, I discovered the FlushDosBuffers function in OpDos. I noted no particular program delay using my original method so did not change the code. You might wish to do so.

Interest

As I understand it, a lawyer cannot charge compound interest on some things—for example, payments required by a court decision, such as child support. Perhaps this is true only in certain states. (By compound interest I mean interest charged on unpaid interest.) At any rate, it would not be too difficult to make interest that is not compounded an option in the LoanTble unit.

9

Look Application, General

This chapter begins the description of the Look program. Look is a variable-length record text database. A search routine is included that uses And and Or to search for specific record material. Parentheses are available in these search statements. This type of database would be useful for phone numbers, reminders to do something on a specific date, to-do lists, phone call notes, and just about any other random text that does not lend itself to storage in tables in a standard database.

The objects covered are

Menu and ancestors (OpMenu)

DialogBox and ancestors (OpDialog)

Various methods from OpCrt, OpString, OpInLine, OpMouse, and others.

This version is a stand-alone program. However, after this program is described the altered and added modules to make the program a swapping (~6K only in base memory) TSR will be listed and discussed. The change is very simple.

Program Description

Lookup is a freeform database. You can enter a string of any length up to 1,024 bytes. That input value can be increased to as much as 65,520 bytes. The InputLen constant in LookGlob sets this value. After entering some strings (records), the program will search for any group or groups of characters in all of the records entered. If found, that entire record is displayed. The program will display all records containing the search string(s) (one at a time). Case is ignored in searches. The editor used to create and modify records is that found in OpMemo and uses mostly standard WordStar commands. A list of these commands will be provided later in this chapter.

The possible number of characters entered in the file can be over 16 Mb, so that is not a limit. The program as supplied has the file size set to approximately 102 Kb. Obviously, the larger the file, the slower the search time. Larger blocks will decrease the search time but can waste disk space.

You determine the size of the file by setting the HeaderSize and the BlockSize constant values in LookGlob. The bytes available for data storage can be calculated by HeaderSize * 8 * (BlockSize = 8).

The BlockSize value should be set for the average size of the strings (records) entered + 8. If the record is shorter than the BlockSize, it will be right-padded with spaces. A record can extend over any number of blocks. Each block requires 8 bytes for linkage, so blocks that are too small can waste disk space. Blocks will be split within words if necessary. Blocks include the OpMemo added line feed ($0A) and carriage return ($0D) characters at the end of each displayed line and a Control-Z ending the record. The positioning of the line feed/carriage return pair is determined by the length of the lines when the record is created. This in turn is determined by the width of the window used by the editor, found in the ShowInfo procedure in the LookData unit. This size, together with that of HeaderSize and BlockSize, should not be changed once you start using a given data file. The supplied value of BlockSize is 128; 263 is the maximum.

The HeaderSize constant * 8 sets the number of blocks available. The program's supplied HeaderSize is 100. The maximum value is 8191.

Lookup can search a file created by Lookup only through using the same BlockSize and HeaderSize with which the file was created. Plan ahead or you will be forced to use a separate copy of Lookup for different data file versions. I find that the default values work quite well. It would not be at all difficult to store these values in a file and make InputLen, BlockSize, and HeaderSize variables instead of constants; however, so far I have not seen any need to, as I use only one data file for my information.

The HeaderSize, BlockSize, and InputLen constants are found in the unit LookGlob.

Uses

I envision the program as creating a scratch pad for phone numbers, appointments, notes, to-do items, and addresses. Once you start using it, you'll discover many other uses. It would make a great "little black book." Remember, I'll show you how to convert this into a much more useful TSR in a later chapter.

Menus

There are four selections in the main menu bar.

1. Choose: The choices in the submenu are "Select file," "Create file," and "Close file." The select choice displays a pick list containing all the files in the default directory with the ".DAT" (data) extension. Be sure the file is a Look format file before you select it; if the companion ".IND" (index) file is not present, you will get a stream error and the program will end. Create permits you to create a new Look file. Just supply the file name; the program will supply the ".DAT" and ".IND" extensions. The program checks to be sure duplicate files do not already exist. The Close choice closes the selected Look file. This is not really necessary, because selecting a new file, creating a file, and ending the program close any open file automatically.

2. Entry: The choices in the submenu are "Add record" and "Search for record." "Add record" displays a data entry window. You can enter up to InputLen characters (default 1024). The window is an editor, so you can easily make corrections to or rearrange the information as you enter it. The editor commands (WordStar compatible) will be listed later in this chapter. Paragraphs are automatically reformatted if you have the Word wrap option set on (the OpMemo default); if it is not on, you must use Control-B to reformat. To leave the window after entering the record text, use Control-Enter; to abandon the new record, press the Escape key. These two keys are used whenever the editor window appears and are listed at the bottom of the window. The Search choice first asks for a search string (see the Search section later in the chapter for examples). When you locate the desired record in the window, no changes are allowed. However, by pressing the F2 key, you can print the displayed record (without the surrounding window frame and the rest of the screen). This is the only place in the program where printing is available. Of course you can use Shift-Print Screen any time, but then you print the window frame and other material you aren't interested in.

3. Maintenance: The choices in the submenu are "Edit record," "Delete record," and "Remove current file." Use "Edit record" to modify a record. This choice works like Search but permits editing. No printing is available. First enter the search string. After locating and editing the record, a dialog box asks if you wish to replace the record with the modified one. Press the Ok button to replace, Cancel to abandon the changes. Be careful: Ok is the default button. To delete a record enter the search string. When the record you wish to delete is displayed, press the OK button in the dialog box requesting permission to delete, otherwise cancel. Be careful; Ok is the default. Remove file erases both the data and index files of the name selected from a pick list.

4. Quit: The only choice is "End Program."

Operation

The program also deletes records no longer required. Select "Delete record" from the Maintenance menu and search for the record to be deleted. As each matching record is found, it is displayed, and you are asked if you wish to delete it. Ok to delete is the default.

There is no built-in way to print the contents of the file. The only printing ability is to print a single record by using the F2 key when the desired record is displayed in Search mode. This method prints only the record text; it does not include the surrounding screen contents. When looking for obsolete records to delete, you can search using the letter *e* for the search string. This should show all the records.

You can have many Look data files. Be sure to open (Select file or Create file from the Choose menu) the file you want via the menu before you try to use it. A "Close file" choice is available but is not required. The data file and index are flushed to disk every time a record is added, changed, or deleted. Data files can have any valid DOS file name, up to eight characters in length. The program supplies an extension of ".DAT" for the data file and ".IND" for the companion index file. If you supply an extension when naming the file, it is ignored.

When you edit a record, the new version is saved to the disk before the original version is erased. Thus, during that time, you must have room in the file for both versions. The program checks first to be sure that enough room is available.

How Does It Work?

It works like the way a disk directory FAT works. Each bit of the index bytes represents a block in the file. If the bit is 0, that block is unused; if 1, then it contains valid data. Each consecutive index bit represents a block. The last block of a record contains the data right-padded with spaces to fill out the block. The first 8 bytes in the block contain two long integer values. The first is the position in the file of the preceding block of the current record, the second the file position of the following block of the record. If there is no preceding block, the position value is set to 0, the same for an absent following block. Thus the blocks are linked to each other. This means that a multiblock record need not reside in adjacent blocks.

When adding a record, a free block is searched for starting at the beginning of the index by looking for the first 0 bit. A block's worth of record is stored. Next, the next free block is located and filled, until the record is completely stored and linked. The program checks first to be sure there is enough room available in the file for all the blocks.

When searching, each used block is retrieved, beginning with the first block in the file. If the link indicates there is a preceding block, the retrieved block is abandoned and the next used block is retrieved. If it is the first block in the record, all of the record's blocks are concatenated into one long string. Next the record is checked for a match with the searched-for ASCIIZ string. If a match is discovered, the record is displayed. Finally, we move to the next index bit after the one that started the current record retrieval and try again. Case is ignored when searching.

The advantage of this system is that a record can be any length up to Input-

Len (default 1,024 bytes, expandable to 65,520 bytes). The worst-case disk space wasted is BlockSize = 9. Smaller blocks mean less padding and wasted disk space. If the block is too small, there will be too many disk reads, and the many 8-byte link values will waste disk space.

Obviously, a big disk cache will improve Lock's search speed a great deal.

It would appear that it might be faster to step through all the used blocks looking for a match in each individual block when searching, but then we'd have to avoid displaying the same record more than once. To display a record after a match, we'd have to step back through the blocks to find the first one, then forward again block by block to display the record. We'd also miss a multiword search when the words spanned two blocks or even a single word if split between blocks.

When a record is deleted, all its blocks are filled with spaces, the link values set to 0, and the associated index bits set to 0.

When a Lookup file is created, the index bits and link values are set to 0 and the entire data area is filled with spaces.

Searching

Enter the word or consecutive words to search for. The search is not case-sensitive. You can use the ampersand (&) for AND and the vertical bar (|) for OR. If you don't like my character choices, it would not be difficult to change them. They appear in only one unit (LookSrch). Any substitute must be a single character and should not be one that might appear as part of a search string, such as a letter, number, or punctuation.

To search for both the words "now" AND "all" in a record, use

now & all

To search for either "now" OR "all" use

now | all

To search for "now is the time" AND "all good men" OR "cow" use

now is the time & all good men | cow

in the search string. This is equivalent to

(now is the time & all good men) | cow

There is no limit on the number of parameters except the search string length (40 characters, which can easily be expanded up to 255 by modifying the LookSrch program, GetSearchString procedure). Parentheses are permitted and can be nested. The innermost parentheses are parsed and compared first, then outer parentheses, and so forth, then from left to right. Sometimes the parentheses are preferred. Let's assume that you have two records: one containing the word "three," the other the words "big" and "records." If you entered

three | big & records

you'd find only the record containing "big" and "records." To find both, you'd need to use

three | (big & records)

or

big & records | three

I think the parentheses require a little less thought and are thus preferable. Be sure you have matching pairs in the correct order. Any such error will result in the program's leaving the leftover or mismatched parentheses in the search string and a likely search failure.

Editor Commands

In the following table, the caret (^) represents the Control key.

Cursor Positioning	
Left arrow, ^S	The cursor is moved left one character.
Right arrow, ^D	The cursor is moved right one character.
^Left arrow, ^A	The cursor is moved left one word. If it is at the beginning of the line, it is moved to the end of the previous line.
^Right arrow, ^F	The cursor is moved right one word. If the cursor is at the end of the line it will be moved to the beginning of the next line.
Home, ^Q S	The cursor is positioned at the beginning of the line.
End, ^Q D	The cursor is moved to the end of the line.
Up arrow, ^E	The cursor is moved up one line.
Down arrow, ^X	The cursor is moved down one line.
^W	Scroll the display up one line.
^Z	Scroll the display down one line.
PgUp, ^R	Scroll the display up one page.
PgDn, ^C	Scroll the display down one page.
^Home, ^Q E	Position the cursor to the top of the screen.
^End, ^Q X	Move the cursor to the bottom of the window.
^PgUp, ^Q R	Move the cursor to the beginning of the record.
^PgDn, ^Q C	Position the cursor at the end of the record.

Insertion and Deletion	
Del, ^G	Delete the character at the cursor.
Backspace, ^H, ^Backspace	Delete the character immediately to the left of the cursor. If the cursor is at the beginning of the line, the current line will be concatenated with the previous line.
^Y	Delete the line containing the cursor.
^Q Y	Delete all the characters from the cursor position to the end of the line.
^T	Delete the word directly to the right of the cursor. If the cursor is at the end of the line, the following line is concatenated with the current line.
Enter, ^M	End a paragraph and start a new line.
^N	Insert a new line at the cursor position.
Tab, ^I	Move the cursor to the next tab stop. The default tab stops are set every eight characters (1, 9, 17, . . .). You can use the SetTabSize procedure to change this.

^P	Insert a control character. Thus ^P ^I would insert a ^I at the cursor position. The video attribute for control characters must be different than that for normal characters (see the SetCtrlAttr procedure in the OPro documentation) and the teMapCtrls option must be on (see the meOptionsOn procedure documentation).

Mode Toggles	
Ins, ^V	Toggle the Insert mode on and off. A fat cursor indicates that the Insert is on; a thin cursor indicates that the Overtype mode is on.
^O I	This key combination toggles the Auto-indent mode on and off. When on, pressing the Enter key will automatically indent the new line to match the indentation of the preceding line. This mode also affects the word wrapping as the new line will have the same indentation as the previous line.
^O W	Use this combination to toggle the word wrap mode on and off. The default is on.

Text Formatting	
^B	If the word wrap mode is off, reformat the paragraph containing the cursor.
^K G	If the word wrap mode is off, reformat the entire record.

Other	
^Q L	Restore the original contents of the current line. This is used to undo an edit within a line before moving the cursor from that line.
F1, click both mouse buttons	If help has been provided by the programmer, either of these will access it.
^Enter	Quit editing and retain text.
Escape	Quit editing and abandon text.
F2 (in Search mode only)	Print record.

Program code

The remainder of this chapter will discuss the look program's menu, verify dialog, message dialog, and global unit's code.

Look.Pas

The Look module is the main program. It contains the code to handle the menu and perform the operations and/or call the required procedures and functions from the designated units.

```
{$V-}
{$R+}

{Copyright 1991 by Ken Knecht}
program Look;
{Menu}

uses
  LookGlob,
  Dos,
  OpRoot,
  OpDos,
  OpCrt,
  OpMouse,
  OpCmd,
  OpField,
  OpCtrl,
  OpFrame,
  OpMenu,
  OpWindow,
  OpSelect,
  OpString,
  LookDir,
  LookFile,
  LookData,
  LookMsg;

var
  S             : String;   {Message string}
  f             : String;   {temporary string}
  IoFlag        : Word;     {store IoResult return}
  FileWasOpened : Boolean;  {if file was never opened don't do
                             IndexBits.done}


function InitMenu : Word;
const
  {Frame constants}
  Frame1 = '╒╘╕╛══││';          {characters to form menu}
  Frame2 = '╤╘╤╛══││';          {characters to form submenu}
  WinOptions = wBordered        {include space for border}
             +wClear            {clear window when first displayed}
             +wUserContents;    {user will restore contents}
var
  Result : String;              {store menu choice}

begin
  with M do begin                      {instance of OpMenu}
    if not InitCustom( 2,2,38,2,       {position - X1,Y1,X2,Y2}
                       Colors,         {from colors.inc}
                       WinOptions,     {menu display characteristics
                                        itemized above}
```

```
                 Horizontal) {multiple choices displayed H}
                 then begin
   InitMenu := InitStatus; {function return if init failed}
   Exit;
 end;
 mnOptionsOn(mnAlphaMatch          {check for alpha matches}
            +mnSelectOnMatch       {implicit <Enter> on alpha char
                                    match}
            +mnArrowSelect         {select submenus with arrows}
            +mnAllHotSpots);       {exit on any mouse hotspot in menu
                                    system. Default is no hotspots}
                                   {OpMenu}

 mnOPtionsOff(mnAllowPending       {if current submenu pulled down,
                                    right arrow will automatically
                                    cause other submenus to appear}
             +mnPopOnSelect        {erase current submenu after
                                    selection}
             +mnUseItemForTopic    {use current item for help topic}
             +mnSelectOnClick);
                                   {OpMenu}

 wFrame.SetFrameType(Frame1);      {menu frame characters, OpFrame}

 AddItem('Choose',         {menu choice}
         2,                {H position from frame edge}
         1,                {char position to use for character select}
         miChoose);        {menu choice identifier}

 AddFramedSubMenu(3,4,17,6, {submenu position - X1,Y1,X2,Y2}
                  Vertical, {submenu item orientation}
                  Frame2);  {submenu frame characters}

   AddItem('Select file', {submenu choice}
           1,             {first row}
           1,             {char position to use for character select}
           miSelect);     {menu choice identifier}

   AddItem('Create file', {submenu choice}
           2,             {second row}
           1,             {char position to use for character select}
           miCreate);     {menu choice identifier}

   AddItem('Close file',  {submenu choice}
           3,             {third row}
           1,             {char position to use for character select}
           miClose);      {menu choice identifier}

   ItemsDone;  {no more submenu items}
```

```
AddItem('Entry',        {menu choice}
        11,             {H position from frame edge}
        1,              {char position to use for character select}
        miEntry);       {menu choice identifier}

AddFramedSubMenu(12,4,32,5, {submenu position - X1,Y1,X2,Y2}
                Vertical,   {submenu item orientation}
                Frame2);    {submenu frame characters}

  AddItem('Add record', {submenu choice}
          1,            {first row}
          1,            {char position to use for character select}
          miAdd);       {menu choice identifier}

  AddItem('Search for record', {submenu choice}
          2,                   {second row}
          1,                   {char position for character select}
          miSearch);           {menu choice identifier}

  ItemsDone;  {no more submenu items}

AddItem('Maintenance',  {menu choice}
        19,             {H position from frame edge}
        1,              {char position to use for character select}
        miMaintain);    {menu choice identifier}

AddFramedSubMenu(20,4,42,6, {submenu position - X1,Y1,X2,Y2}
                Vertical,   {submenu item orientation}
                Frame2);    {submenu frame characters}

  AddItem('Edit record', {submenu choice}
          1,             {first row}
          1,             {char position to use for character select}
          miEdit);       {menu choice identifier}

  AddItem('Delete record', {submenu choice}
          2,               {second row}
          1,               {char position to use for character
                            select}
          miDelete);       {menu choice identifier}

  AddItem('Remove current file', {submenu choice}
          3,                     {third row}
          1,                     {char position for character
                                  select}
          miRemove);             {menu choice identifier}

  ItemsDone;  {no more submenu items}
```

```
    AddItem('Quit',     {menu choice}
            33,         {H position from frame edge}
            1,          {char position to use for character select}
            miQuit);    {menu choice identifier}

    AddFramedSubMenu(34,4,48,4, {submenu position - X1,Y1,X2,Y2}
                     Vertical,  {submenu item orientation}
                     Frame2);   {submenu frame characters}

      AddItem('End program',  {submenu choice}
              1,              {first row}
              1,              {char position to use for character
                               select}
              miEndProgram); {menu choice identifier}

      ItemsDone;              {no more submenu items}
    ItemsDone;                {no more menu items}
    InitMenu := GetLastError; {function return value}
  end;
end;


procedure ErrorMsg;
{display any global errors}
var
 S : String; {string temporary}
begin
  if GlobError <> 0 then begin  {LookGlob}
    case GlobError of           {LookGlob}
      NoRoom :                  {LookGlob}
        S := 'Unable to open file';
      FileFull :                {LookGlob}
        S := 'No room left in file';
      OutofMemory :             {LookGlob}
        S := 'Out of memory';
      InvalidData :             {LookGlob}
        S := 'Invalid entry';
      FileExists :              {LookGlob}
        S := 'File already exists, cannot overwrite';
      NoSeek :                  {LookGlob}
        S := 'Unable to position within file';
      NoRead :                  {LookGlob}
        S := 'Unable to read file';
      NoWrite :                 {LookGlob}
        S := 'Unable to write to file';
      NoFile :                  {LookGlob}
        S := 'No data files available';
    end;
    ShowMsg(S);                 {LookMsg}
    GlobError := 0;             {reset, LookGlob}
```

```
    end;
  end;


  {main}
  begin
    FileWasOpened := False;     {use this to determine whether to do
                                 IndexBits.Done}
    GlobError := 0;             {reset GlobError to none, LookGlob}
    if MouseInUse then          {LookGlob}
      MouseChar := #04;         {mouse cursor (diamond)}
    CurFile := '';              {no file selected yet, LookGlob}
    Status := InitMenu;         {initialize Menu, LookGlob}
    if Status <> 0 then begin {error numbers in documentation appendix D}
      ShowMsg('Error initializing Menu: '
               + Long2Str(Status));         {OpString, LookMsg}
      Halt;
    end;

    if MouseInUse then begin    {LookGlob}
      if MouseInstalled then    {OpMouse, could Define.Inc be wrong?}
        with Colors do begin
          {activate mouse cursor, make it a red diamond}
          SoftMouseCursor($0000, {mouse has own software cursor}
                         (ColorMono(MouseColor, MouseMono) shl 8) +
                          Byte(MouseChar)); {OpMouse}
          {enable mouse menu support}
          MenuCommands.cpOptionsOn(cpEnableMouse); {menu sees mouse,
                                                    menu command
                                                    processor}
          HideMouse;                               {avoid mouse tracks,
                                                    OpMouse}
        end;
    end;

    {fill in a backdrop}
    TextAttr := $07; {background attribute}
    TextChar := '▒'; {background design}
    ClrScr;

    repeat
      M.Draw;                                {draw menu, OpMenu}
      if MouseInUse then                     {LookGlob}
        ShowMouse;                           {make mouse visible, OpMouse}
      M.Process;                             {process menu commands, OpMenu}
      if MouseInUse then                     {LookGlob}
        HideMouse;                           {avoid mouse tracks, OpMouse}
      if M.GetlastCommand = ccSelect then {menu selection occurred,
                                              OpWindow, OpCmd}
        case M.MenuChoice of             {OpMenu}
```

```
miCreate :                     {create new file}
  begin
    if CurFile <> '' then      {file is opened?, LookGlob}
      close(BlockFile);        {close it, LookGlob}
    CurFile := '';             {no file opened indicator,
                                LookGlob}
    M.Erase;                   {erase menu, OpMenu}
    MakeFile;                  {LookFile}
    if GlobError = 0 then      {no error creating file, LookGlob}
      FileWasOpened := True    {IndexBits was initialized}
    else                       {error occurred}
      CurFile := '';           {no file open, LookGlob}
    ErrorMsg;                  {display global error, if any}
  end;

miSelect :                       {choose from existing files}
  begin
    if CurFile <> '' then        {file is open, LookGlob}
      close(BlockFile);          {close it, LookGlob}
    CurFile  := '';              {no file open, LookGlob}
    M.Erase;                     {erase menu, OpMenu}
    PickFile;                    {LookDir}
    if GlobError = 0 then        {LookGlob}
      FileWasOpened := True      {IndexBits was initialized}
    else                         {error occurred}
      CurFile := '';             {no file open, LookGlob}
    ErrorMsg;                    {display any global errors, this
                                  unit}
  end;

miClose :                        {choose from existing files}
  begin
    if CurFile <> '' then begin  {file is open, LookGlob}
      M.Erase;                   {erase menu, OpMenu}
      close(BlockFile);          {close open file, LookGlob}
      CurFile  := '';            {no file open, LookGlob}
    end
    else
      ShowMsg('No file chosen'); {LookMsg}
  end;

miAdd  :                         {add records}
  begin
    M.Erase;                     {erase menu, OpMenu}
    if CurFile <> '' then begin  {file open, LookGlob}
      EntryType   := 'A';        {tell RecordInfo what to do,
                                  LookGlob}
      RecordInfo;                {LookData}
      ErrorMsg;                  {display any global errors,
                                  this unit}
```

```
    end
    else
      ShowMsg('No file chosen'); {LookMsg}
  end;

miSearch :                          {search for a record}
  begin
    M.Erase;                        {erase menu, OpMenu}
    if CurFile <> '' then begin     {file open, LookGlob}
      EntryType := 'S';             {tell RecordInfo what to do,
                                     LookGlob}
      RecordInfo;                   {LookData}
      ErrorMsg;                     {display any error message,
                                     this unit}
    end
    else
      ShowMsg('No file chosen'); {LookMsg}
  end;

miEdit :                            {edit record}
  begin
    M.Erase;                        {erase menu, OpMenu}
    if CurFile <> '' then begin     {file open, LookGlob}
      EntryType := 'E';             {tell RecordInfo what to do,
                                     LookGlob}
      RecordInfo;                   {LookData unit}
      ErrorMsg;                     {display any error message, this
                                     unit}
    end
    else
      ShowMsg('No file chosen'); {LookMsg}
  end;

miDelete :                          {delete a previously entered
                                     record}
  begin
    M.Erase;                        {erase menu, OpMenu}
    if CurFile <> '' then begin     {file open, LookGlob}
      EntryType := 'D';             {tell RecordInfo what to do,
                                     LookGlob}
      RecordInfo;                   {LookData}
      ErrorMsg;                     {display any error message,
                                     this unit}
    end
    else
      ShowMsg('No file chosen'); {LookMsg}
  end;

miRemove :                          {delete file}
  begin
```

```
            M.Erase;                    {erase menu, Opmenu}
            if Verify('The chosen file will be deleted') then begin
                                        {LookMsg}
              if CurFile <> '' then     {if file open, LookGlob}
                close(BlockFile);       {close it, LookGlob}
              PickFile;                 {get name of file to erase,
                                         LookDir}
              erase (BlockFile);        {erase file, LookGlob}
              CurFile := '';            {no file open, LookGlob}
              ErrorMsg;                 {display any global error, this
                                         unit}
            end;
          end;

        end;
    until M.MenuChoice = miEndProgram; {Quit submenu choice made, OpMenu}
    M.Erase;                           {erase menu, OpMenu}
    M.Done;                            {remove menu from memory, OpMenu}
    if FileWasOpened then
      IndexBits.Done;                  {remove index buffer object,
                                        OpRoot}
    ClrScr;
  end.
```

Essentially, the main program initializes the menu. Then it loops through the menu, calling procedures in various units and performing operations as required, until the user selects the "End Program" choice. In the annotation, I have tried to remember to note the unit where each called procedure, function, or variable resides.

In the line

```
WinOptions = wBordered        {leave room for border}
             +wClear          {clear window when displayed}
             +wUserContents;  {user will refresh contents if required}
```

the complete list of possible options is

wBordered	Make space for window border
wClear	Clear window when it is first displayed
wSaveContents	Save the contents of the window when it is erased.
wUserContents	User will restore window contents
wSoundEffects	Use sound effects during explosions
wAltFrame	Use alternate frame type when not current
wSetMouse	Set mouse window, cursor on entry to window
wFullMouseWindow	Force to full mouse window on entry
wResizable	Can be resized and zoomed
wAllMouseEvents	Any combination of mouse buttons anywhere exits

wStoreContents	Store window contents in streams

The next procedure's last parameter

```
if not InitCustom( 2,2,43,2,    {position - X1,Y1,X2,Y2}
                   Colors,      {from colors.inc}
                   WinOptions,  {menu display characteristics
                                 itemized above}
                   Horizontal)  {multiple choices displayed H}
                   then begin
```

can be one of the following:

Horizontal	top menu bar choices displayed horizontally
Vertical	top menu bar choices displayed vertically

In the following lines

```
mnOptionsOn(mnAlphaMatch          {check for alpha matches}
            +mnSelectOnMatch      {implicit Enter on alpha match}
            +mnArrowSelect        {select submenus with arrows}
            +mnAllHotSpots);      {exit with ccMouseSel code on any
                                   mouse hotspot. Default is no
                                   hotspots}

mnOptionsOff(mnAllowPending       {submenu stays down after passing
                                   no submenu}
             +mnPopOnSelect       {erase submenu after selection}
             +mnUseItemForTopic   {use menu choices as help topics}
             +mnSelectOnClick);   {implicit Enter on first mouse
                                   click}
```

The list of available options is

mnAllHotSpots	exit on any menu mouse hotspot (default is no hotspots)
mnAllowPending	submenu stays down after passing no submenu
mnAlphaMatch	check for alphabetic matches
mnArrowSelect	select submenus with arrow keys
mnMainHighlight	highlight alpha search characters on high-level menu
mnMainSelect	display top-level menu bar
mnMouseSupport	used by MAKEMENU
mnPopOnSelect	erase current submenu after selection
mnSelectOnClick	implicit Enter on first mouse click
mnSelectOnMatch	implicit Enter on alphabetic character match
mnUseItemForTopic	use current highlighted item for help topic

LookGlob.Pas

This module contains the global variables used throughout the application.

```
unit LookGlob;
{ Global variables and types for all units}

INTERFACE

{$I OPDEFINE.INC} {standard define list}

uses
  OpCrt,
  OpRoot,
  OpCtrl,
  OpEntry,
  OpMenu,
  OpMouse,
  OpAsciiz,
  OpDir;

const
  {$IFDEF UseMouse}
    MouseInUse : Boolean = True;
  {$ELSE}
    MouseInUse : Boolean = False;
  {$ENDIF}

{$I COLORS.INC}  {designated color list}


const
  InputLen    = 1024; {max entry length 65520}
                      {If this is set larger than 1024 adjust MaxAsciiz
                       constant in OpAsciiz to reflect this larger
                       value}
  FileNameLen = 8;
  Space       = #32;
  HeaderSize  = 100; {max 8191}
                     {8 records per header, block bytes per record. A
                      file this large will be created. For example, the
                      defaults will create a file of 102,400 bytes. The
                      maximum is 17,233,864 bytes.}
  BlockSize   = 128; {max 263 (Pascal string max + 8). Set slightly
                      larger than size of average expected record if
                      possible. Includes 8 bytes of linkage. Must be
                      larger than 8}

  {error codes}
  NoRoom      = 1901;
```

```
    FileFull    = 1902;
    OutofMemory = 1903;
    InvalidData = 1904;
    FileExists  = 1906;
    NoSeek      = 1907;
    NoRead      = 1908;
    NoWrite     = 1909;
    NoFile      = 1910;

    {menu id values}
    miChoose     = 0;
    miCreate     = miChoose    + 1;
    miSelect     = miCreate    + 1;
    miClose      = miSelect    + 1;
    miEntry      = miClose     + 1;
    miAdd        = miEntry     + 1;
    miSearch     = miAdd       + 1;
    miMaintain   = miSearch    + 1;
    miEdit       = miMaintain  + 1;
    miDelete     = miEdit      + 1;
    miRemove     = miDelete    + 1;
    miQuit       = miRemove    + 1;
    miEndProgram = miQuit      + 1;

    idName       = 1;
    idSearchStr  = 2;

  type
    Block = record
      LinkFrom : LongInt;              {previous record number}
      LinkTo   : LongInt;              {next record number}
      Data     : String[BlockSize - 8];
    end;

  var
    CurFile    : String[FileNameLen]; {name of currently open file}
    EntryType  : Char;                {edit, delete, search, or add a
                                       record}
    M          : Menu;                {instance of menu object}
    Status     : Word;                {results of object initializations}
    GlobError  : Word;                {See error codes above}
    ESName     : EntryScreen;         {file name EntryScreen object
                                       instance, OpEntry}
    ESSearch   : EntryScreen;         {search criteria EntryScreen object
                                       instance, OpEntry}
    Finished   : Boolean;             {used in many places}
    BlockFile  : File of Block;       {type of data file}
    FileData   : Block;               {file data buffer} {instance of data
                                       record}
    IndexBits  : BitSet;              {index block to locate used and
```

```
                                          unused records, OpRoot, instance of
                                          BitSet object}
  IStream    : BufIdStream;              {for storing/restoring index to/from
                                          stream, OpRoot, instance of
                                          BufIdStream object}
  Buffer     : Asciiz;                   {memo buffer, OpAsciiz}

IMPLEMENTATION

end.
```

This module is required because programs and units cannot pass constant and variable declarations to one another except via procedure or function parameters. Using this unit and calling it from every other unit makes it possible to easily incorporate global constants and variables in an application. Note that this unit has no Implementation code, only the Interface portion.

There is little to discuss in the content of this module, except perhaps the following code

```
const
  {$IFDEF UseMouse}
     MouseInUse : Boolean = True;
  {$ELSE}
     MouseInUse : Boolean = False;
  {$ENDIF}
```

which is used to check and see if the use of a mouse was defined. If "UseMouse" is not defined in OpDefine.Inc (called right after the INTERFACE statement), then "MouseInUse" will be set to false. All references to mouse actions in all the modules are invoked only if this variable is true. For example:

```
if MouseInUse then
   ShowMouse;
```

The version of OpDefine.Inc that came with OPro had "UseMouse" defined. If you have changed your version of OpDefine.Inc and wish to use the mouse in this application, you may wish to check this. I will not provide the contents of OpDefine.Inc or Colors.Inc here, as they both can be found in Chapter 5.

LookMsg.pas

Unlike the loan program, I decided to put both the Message dialog and the Verify dialog in one unit instead of providing them separately. Here is the code:

```
unit lookmsg;

INTERFACE
```

```
uses
  LookGlob,
  OpDialog,
  OpString,
  OpCrt,
  OpRoot,
  OpCmd,
  OpField,
  OpFrame,
  OpCtrl,
  OpMouse,
  OpInLine,
  OpWindow;

procedure ShowMsg(Message : String);

function Verify(Message : String) : Boolean;


IMPLEMENTATION

const
  hiOk     = 1; {button id}
  hiCancel = 2; {button id}

var
  MBox : DialogBox; {message box is instance of DialogBox object}



function InitMsgBox(Message : String) : Word;
  {Initialize message dialog box}
const
  WinOptions = wBordered        {make space for window border}
             + wClear           {clear window when first displayed}
             + wUserContents;   {user will restore contents}
             {the initial 'w' means window object constants}

var
  Len       : Integer; {half of message length + 3 or 15, whichever
                        larger}
  HalfWidth : Integer; {half of width of message box}

begin
  with MBox do begin
    {instantiate dialog box}
    Len := Length(Message) DIV 2; {for box width calculation}
    HalfWidth := MaxLong(15,Len + 3); {OpInLine}
    if not InitCustom(40 - HalfWidth, {X1}
                      8,              {Y1}
```

```
                    40 + HalfWidth, {X2}
                    15,             {Y2}
                    Colors,         {from Colors.inc file (LookGlob)}
                    WinOptions,     {see constants above}
                    dColors)        {from Colors.inc file (LookGlob)}
                      then begin
         InitMsgBox := InitStatus; {function return value, probably out
                                    of memory}
         Exit;                     {fatal error so leave procedure}
       end;

     AddCenteredTextField(Message,3); {display Message centered in
                                        relative line 3, OpSelect}

     AddPushButton('&Ok',      {OpDialog}
                   05,         {relative Y,X of upper-left corner}
                   HalfWidth * 2 - 7,
                   5,          {width of button}
                   hiOk,       {button identifier, see unit constants}
                   ccSelect,   {button return value, OpCmd constant}
                   True);      {default button?}

     InitMsgBox := RawError; {function return value, OpWindow}
   end;
 end;


 procedure ShowMsg(Message : String);
 {display Message}

 begin
   {initialize DialogBox}
   Status := InitMsgBox(Message);  {initialize function return value}
   if Status <> 0 then begin       {error}
     writeln('Error initializing MessageBox: '
             + Long2Str(Status));  {OpString}
     Halt(1);                      {fatal error so quit}
   end;

   if MouseInUse then begin
     DialogCommands.cpOptionsOn(cpEnableMouse); {dialog sees mouse,
                                                  Dialog command
                                                  processor}
     HideMouse;                                 {avoid mouse tracks,
                                                  OpMouse}
   end;

   {fill in a backdrop}
   TextAttr := $07;
   TextChar := '▒';
```

```
  ClrScr;

  Finished := False;

  MBox.Draw; {display the dialog box and contents, OpDialog}
  repeat
    {process commands}
    if MouseInUse then     {LookGlob}
      ShowMouse;           {make mouse available for button press,
                            OpMouse}
    MBox.Process;          {watch for a button press, OpDialog}
    if MouseInUse then     {LookGlob}
      HideMouse;           {avoid mouse tracks, OpMouse}
    if MBox.GetLastCommand = ccSelect then {OpWindow, OpCmd}
        Finished := True;  {a button was pushed}
  until Finished;
  MBox.Erase;              {get rid of dialog box, OpDialog}
  MBox.Done;               {get back the memory the object was using,
                            OpDialog}}
end; {ShowMsg}



function InitVerifyBox(Message : String) : Word;
  {Initialize verify dialog box}
const
  WinOptions = wBordered         {make space for window border}
             + wClear            {clear window when first displayed}
             + wUserContents;    {user will restore contents}
             {the initial 'w' means window object constants}

var
  Len       : Integer; {half of message length + 3 or 15, whichever
                        larger}
  HalfWidth : Integer; {half of width of message box}

begin
  with MBox do begin             {DialogBox instance}
    {instantiate dialog box}
    Len := Length(Message) DIV 2; {for box width calculation}
    HalfWidth := MaxLong(15,Len + 3); {OpInLine}
    if not InitCustom(40 - HalfWidth, {X1}
                      7,              {Y1}
                      40 + HalfWidth, {X2}
                      15,             {Y2}
                      Colors,         {from Colors.inc file (LookGlob)}
                      WinOptions,     {see constants}
                      dColors)        {from Colors.inc file (LookGlob)}
                        then begin
      InitVerifyBox := InitStatus;    {fatal error, probably out of
                                       memory}
```

```
      Exit;                              {bail out of procedure}
    end;

   AddCenteredTextField(Message,3);  {display message in center of
                                      relative line 3, OpSelect}

   AddPushButton('&Ok',
                 06,       {relative Y,X of upper-left corner}
                 HalfWidth * 2 - 10,
                 8,        {width of button}
                 hiOk,     {button identifier, see constants}
                 ccSelect, {button return value, from OpCmd}
                 True);    {default button?}

   AddPushButton('&Cancel',
                 8,        {relative Y,X of upper-left corner}
                 HalfWidth * 2 - 10,
                 8,        {width of button}
                 hiCancel, {button identifier, see constants}
                 ccQuit,   {button return value, from OpCmd}
                 False);   {default button?}

   InitVerifyBox := RawError; {function return value, OpWindow}
  end;
end;



function Verify(Message : String) : Boolean;

begin
  {initialize verify DialogBox}
  Status := InitVerifyBox(Message); {result of initialization of dialog
                                     object}
  if Status <> 0 then begin         {error}
    ShowMsg('Error initializing Verify dialog: '
          + Long2Str(Status));      {OpString, LookMsg}
    Halt(1);                        {quit}
  end;

  if MouseInUse then begin                    {LookGlob}
    {enable mouse dialog support}
    DialogCommands.cpOptionsOn(cpEnableMouse); {dialog sees mouse,
                                                Dialog command
                                                processor}
    HideMouse;                                 {avoid mouse tracks,
                                                OpMouse}
  end;
```

```
  {fill in a backdrop}
  TextAttr := $07;
  TextChar := '▒';
  ClrScr;

  Finished := False;

  MBox.Draw; {display dialog box and contents, OpDialog}
  repeat
    {process commands}
    if MouseInUse then       {LookGlob}
      ShowMouse;             {make mouse available for pressing a button,
                              OpMouse}
    MBox.Process;            {watch for button press, OpDialog}
    if MouseInUse then       {LookGlob}
      HideMouse;             {avoid mouse tracks, OpMouse}
    case MBox.GetLastCommand of {OpWindow, OpCmd}
      ccSelect :             {Ok button was pressed, OpCmd}
        begin
          Verify := True;    {Ok means yes}
          Finished := True;  {let's go home}
        end;
      ccError :              {uh oh!, OpCmd}
        begin
          ShowMsg('Fatal error. Error: '
                   + Long2Str(MBox.GetLastCommand)); {OpString, LookMsg}
          halt;
        end;
      ccQuit :               {OpCmd}
        begin
          Verify := False;   {pressed Cancel button}
          Finished := True;  {one button to a customer}
        end;
    end;
  until Finished;
  MBox.Erase;                {erase dialog box, OpDialog}
  MBox.Done;                 {recover dialog box object's memory,
                              OpDialog}

  ClrScr;
end; {procedure}

end. {unit}
```

When we set WinOptions at the beginning of both units

```
const
  WinOptions = wBordered         {make space for window border}
             + wClear            {clear window when first displayed}
             + wUserContents;    {user will restore contents}
             {the initial 'w' means window object constants}
```

we have several options:

wBordered	Make space for window border
wClear	Clear window when it is first displayed
wSaveContents	Save the contents of the window when it is erased
wUserContents	User will restore window contents
wSoundEffects	Use sound effects during explosions
wAltFrame	Use alternate frame type when not current
wSetMouse	Set mouse window, cursor on entry to window
wFullMouseWindow	Force to full mouse window on entry
wResizable	Can be resized and zoomed
wAllMouseEvents	Any combination of mouse buttons anywhere exits
wStoreContents	Store window contents in streams

You may wish to substitute one or more of these for my choices.

Unlike the Verify function in the Loan program, the message is passed to the function as a parameter, rather than the contents of another variable designating which message from a list of messages is to be displayed.

The Boolean value returned by the Verify function is determined by the following section of code:

```
case MBox.GetLastCommand of {OpWindow}
  ccSelect :              {Ok button was pressed, OpCmd}
    begin
      Verify := True;     {Ok means yes}
      Finished := True;   {let's go home}
    end;
  ccError :               {uh oh!, OpCmd}
    begin
      ShowMsg('Fatal error. Error: '
              + Long2Str(MBox.GetLastCommand)); {OpString, LookMsg}
      halt;
    end;
  ccQuit :                {OpCmd}
    begin
      Verify := False;    {pressed Cancel button}
      Finished := True;   {one button to a customer}
    end;
end;
```

In the following code fragment from both ShowMsg and Verify:

```
Len := Length(Message) DIV 2; {for box width calculation}
HalfWidth := MaxLong(15,Len + 3); {OpInLine}
if not InitCustom(40 - HalfWidth, {X1}
                  7,              {Y1}
                  40 + HalfWidth, {X2}
```

the MaxLong function selects the largest of the two arguments. This enables us to have a window with a minimum width of 36 columns. Otherwise, the push-button(s) and other displayed material may not fit in it comfortably.

Code like the following is required wherever the use of the mouse is desired.

```
if MouseInUse then begin                     {LookGlob}
  {enable mouse dialog support}
  DialogCommands.cpOptionsOn(cpEnableMouse); {dialog sees mouse,
                                              Dialog command
                                              processor}
  HideMouse;                                 {avoid mouse tracks,
                                              OpMouse}
end;
```

The name of the command processor varies, but is always in some form of "SomethingCommands." There does not seem to be a list of these commands anywhere in the documentation. Just try the obvious choice, such as MenuCommands or PickCommands. If that gives you a syntax error when you compile, try the name of an object's immediate ancestor, such as PickCommands instead of DirCommands. You can also try looking up your choice in Index.lzh on your OPro bonus diskette. This contains a mostly complete list of all the functions and procedures in alphabetical order. I've found it to be very useful. By the way, you will also find an Index2.lzh file, which is an alphabetical list of all the constants, types, and variables in the OPro objects. In my version, both of these indexes did not include the OpDialog and OpCtrl references, probably because these two units were just added to OPro.

The next chapter will cover the creation and selection of data and index files.

10

Look Application, Data and Index Files

This chapter continues with the description of the Look application. Creating a new data and index file and selecting an existing file pair are discussed here.

The objects used and discussed in this chapter are

EntryScreen and ancestors (OpEntry)
BitSet and ancestors (OpRoot)
BufIdStream and ancestors (OpRoot)
DirList and ancestors (OpDir)

Various object methods from OpCrt, OpString, OpMouse, OpDos, and others.

LookFile.pas

This unit creates a new data and index file when supplied with a filename.

```
UNIT LookFile;
{create a new data file and index}

INTERFACE

uses LookGlob,
     LookIndx,
     LookMsg,
```

```
     OpDos,
     OpCmd,
     OpRoot,
     OpField,
     OpFrame,
     OpWindow,
     OpCrt,
     OpString,
     OpEntry,
     OpMouse;

procedure MakeFile;
{create a new data file and index}

IMPLEMENTATION

{$F+}
procedure ErrorHandler(UnitCode : Byte; var ErrCode : Word;
                       Msg : String);
var
  BufPtr   : Pointer; {store screen here}
  SaveFlag : Boolean; {was screen-store successful?}

begin
  SaveFlag := True;
  {store the screen if possible, OpCrt}
  if not SaveWindow(1,1,ScreenWidth,ScreenHeight,True,BufPtr) then begin
    ShowMsg('Not enough memory to save screen'); {LookMsg}
    SaveFlag := False;
  end;
  ShowMsg(Msg);      {show the message}           {LookMsg}
  {if storage was successful retrieve the screen}
  if SaveFlag then
    RestoreWindow(1,1,ScreenWidth,ScreenHeight,True,BufPtr); {OpCrt}
end;
{$F-}


procedure MakeFile;
var
  Name        : String;  {name of data file and index to create}
  LongCounter : LongInt; {used to count blocks in data file}
  IoFlag      : Word;    {I/O result}

begin
  GlobError := 0; {no errors - yet, LookGlob}
  ClrScr;
  if not ESName.InitCustom(25, 5, 55, 10, {Window coordinates}
                       Colors,            {Color set from Colors.inc,
                                            LookGlob}
```

```
                    DefWindowOptions
                      or wBordered)      {Window options}
                    then begin           {instance of EntryScreen,
                                          OpEntry}
  ShowMsg('Failed to init filename EntryScreen. Status = '
           + Long2Str(InitStatus));      {OpString, LookMsg}
  Halt;
end;

if MouseInUse then begin                     {LookGlob}
  EntryCommands.cpOptionsOn(cpEnableMouse); {entry screen uses mouse,
                                              OpEntry command
                                              processor}
  HideMouse;                                 {avoid mouse tracks,
                                              OpMouse}
end;

{fill in a backdrop}
TextAttr := $07; {background attribute}
TextChar := '▒'; {background design}
ClrScr;

{add some window frills from OpFrame}
ESName.wFrame.AddShadow(shBR,          {place shadow bottom and right}
                        shOverWrite); {opaque shadow}

{prompt messages in entry screen from OpFrame}
ESName.wFrame.AddHeader(' Filename Entry Screen ', heTC);
ESName.wFrame.AddHeader(' Esc to abort, Ctrl-Enter to accept ', heBC);

{set error handler to default procedure}
EsName.SetErrorProc(DefaultErrorProc); {beep on error, OpWindow}

{add fields}
ESName.esFieldOptionsOn(efClearFirstChar); {OpEntry}

ESName.AddStringField('Filename (no extension):', {prompt}
                      2,                          {prompt V position}
                      3,                          {prompt H position}
                      CharStr('X',8),             {picture}
                      4,                          {data V position}
                      11,                         {data H position}
                      8,                          {data width}
                      1,                          {help ID number}
                      Name);                      {data variable}
                                                  {OpEntry}
repeat
  Finished := False; {not yet}
  if MouseInUse then {LookGlob}
    ShowMouse;       {make mouse visible, OpMouse}
```

```
{switch to the user supplied error handler}
ESName.SetErrorProc(ErrorHandler); {show error in window, OpWindow}

Name := '';           {to contain file name}
ESName.Process;       {get the name, OpEntry}
if MouseInUse then    {LookGlob}
  HideMouse;          {avoid mouse droppings, OpMouse}
case ESName.GetLastCommand of {OpWindow}
  ccError:            {entry error occurred, OpCmd constant}
    begin
      ShowMsg('Error supplying file name '
               + Long2Str(ESName.GetLastError)); {OpString, LookMsg}
      Name := '';
    end;

  ccQuit : {Escape key} {OpCmd constant}
    begin
      Finished := True; {let's get out of here}
      Name := '';       {indicate no valid name entered}
    end;
end;

{name must be ok}
if not Finished then begin
  if Name = '' then begin
    ShowMsg('No file name entered');    {LookMsg}
    CurFile := '';                      {indicates no file selected}
  end
  else begin
    CurFile := JustName(Name);          {in case an extension was
                                         entered, OpString}
    if ExistFile(CurFile + '.DAT') then {duplicate name, don't use,
                                         OpDos}
      GlobError := FileExists;          {LookGlob}
    if ExistFile(CurFile + '.IND') then {duplicate name, don't use,
                                         OpDos}
      GlobError := FileExists;          {LookGlob}
    if GlobError = 0 then begin         {LookGlob}
      assign(BlockFile,CurFile + '.DAT'); {assign to file variable,
                                           LookGlob}
      {$I-}                               {turn off built-in I/O
                                           error reporting}
      rewrite(BlockFile);                 {open new file, LookGlob}

      IoFlag := IoResult;
      if IoFlag <> 0 then begin
        GlobError := NoRoom;              {couldn't open file,
                                           LookGlob}
        close(BlockFile);                 {LookGlob}
        {$I+}                             {turn on built-in I/O
```

```
                                              error reporting}
        end
        else begin
          FileData.Data := CharStr(' ',BlockSize - 8);  {empty block}
          FileData.LinkTo := 0;                          {no links}
          FileData.LinkFrom := 0;
          LongCounter := 1;                              {first block
                                                          stored}
          {stop writing empty blocks when desired number have been
           stored in file and no errors occur, LookGlob}
          while (LongCounter <= (HeaderSize * 8) - 1) and
                  (GlobError = 0) do begin
            write(BlockFile,FileData);  {store block, LookGlob}

            IoFlag := IoResult;
            if IoFlag <> 0 then
              GlobError := NoWrite;    {write error, LookGlob}
            Inc(LongCounter);          {next block}
          end;

          {flush new file to disk, built-in flush procedure only works
           with text files}
          if GlobError = 0 then begin {no errors, LookGlob}
            close(BlockFile);          {LookGlob}
            reset(BlockFile);          {LookGlob}
            IoFlag := IoResult;
            if IoFlag <> 0 then
              GlobError := NoRoom;     {LookGlob}
          end;

          {$I+} {turn on built-in I/O error reporting}
        end;
      end;
    end;
    Finished := True; {we're finished no matter what}
  end;
until Finished;

ESName.Erase;        {erase entry screen object, OpEntry}
ESName.Done;         {recover entry screen object's memory, OpEntry}
if GlobError > 0 then begin {error occurred, LookGlob}
  Close(BlockFile);         {something wrong with file, LookGlob}
  CurFile := '';            {indicate no current file, LookGlob}
end
else                        {no errors}
  if CurFile <> '' then     {data file was created, LookGlob}
    MakeIndexBits;          {create index file for data file,
                             LookIndx}}
end; {end of procedure}
end. {end of unit}
```

The ErrorHandler procedure is used to display an error message instead of the default beep on error. If possible, the screen is saved, the error displayed, and the screen restored. If there is not enough memory to save the screen, that fact is displayed before the error message.

```
{$F+}
procedure ErrorHandler(UnitCode : Byte; var ErrCode : Word;
                       Msg : String);
var
  BufPtr    : Pointer; {store screen here}
  SaveFlag : Boolean; {was screen-store successful?}

begin
  SaveFlag := True;
  {store the screen if possible, OpCrt}
  if not SaveWindow(1,1,ScreenWidth,ScreenHeight,True,BufPtr) then begin
    ShowMsg('Not enough memory to save screen'); {LookMsg}
    SaveFlag := False;
  end;
  ShowMsg(Msg);      {show the message}              {LookMsg}
  {if storage was successful retrieve the screen}
  if SaveFlag then
    RestoreWindow(1,1,ScreenWidth,ScreenHeight,True,BufPtr); {OpCrt}
end;
{$F-}
```

The SetErrorProc procedure is used to define the desired error handler procedure. Thus, in this unit,

```
{switch to the user supplied error handler}
ESName.SetErrorProc(ErrorHandler); {show error in window, OpWindow}
```

In the main part of the unit, the MakeFile procedure begins by initializing the window that will contain the entry screen.

The DefWindowOptions mentioned are

wClear
wSaveContents
wResizable
wStoreContents

The complete list of available options is

wBordered	Make space for window border
wClear	Clear window when it is first displayed
wSaveContents	Save the contents of the window when it is erased
wUserContents	User will restore window contents
wSoundEffects	Use sound effects during explosions

wAltFrame	Use alternate frame type when not current
wSetMouse	Set mouse window, cursor on entry to window
wFullMouseWindow	Force to full mouse window on entry
wResizable	Can be resized and zoomed
wAllMouseEvents	Any combination of mouse buttons anywhere exits
wStoreContents	Store window contents in streams

Next the mouse is made available:

```
if MouseInUse then begin                      {LookGlob}
  EntryCommands.cpOptionsOn(cpEnableMouse);   {entry screen uses mouse,
                                               OpEntry command
                                               processor}
  HideMouse;                                  {avoid mouse tracks,
                                               OpMouse}
end;
```

As noted, MouseInUse was defined in LoanGlob, if the use of the mouse was defined in OpDefine.Inc and a mouse was detected in the system. The next three lines define the window shadow and headings. In the line

```
  {add some window frills, OpFrame}
ESName.wFrame.AddShadow(shBR,          {place shadow bottom and right}
                        shOverWrite);  {opaque shadow}
```

the options are

shBR	shadow falls to bottom and right of frame
shBL	shadow falls to bottom and left of frame

and for the second argument

shOverWrite	opaque shadow
shSeeThru	transparent shadow

In the lines

```
{prompt messages in entry screen, OpFrame}
ESName.wFrame.AddHeader(' Filename Entry Screen ', heTC);
ESName.wFrame.AddHeader(' Esc to abort, Ctrl-Enter to accept ', heBC);
```

the options for the last parameter are

heTL	top left
heTC	top center
heTR	top right
heBL	bottom left

heBC	bottom center
heBR	bottom right

The error procedure is set to the default procedure, which emits a beep on an error.

```
{set error handler to default procedure}
EsName.SetErrorProc(DefaultErrorProc); {beep on error, OpWindow}
```

Thus you should eliminate any beep you hear when the field is being defined. Any error is probably an invalid coordinate. Now we define the single field in the entry screen. We begin with

```
ESName.esFieldOptionsOn(efClearFirstChar); {OpEntry}
```

Other popular options are

efProtected	not changeable
efHidden	not displayed, field cannot be moved to it
efInvisible	field is never drawn
efRequired	some entry required
efBeepOnError	invalid entry
efClearFirstChar	if first character entered during editing is character clear the field

There are many more options. See the documentation on OpField for their names and descriptions and the descriptions of other units of the Look and Loan programs for examples. These options can be used in methods other than esFieldOptionsOn().

Next the entry field is defined:

```
ESName.AddStringField('Filename (no extension):', {prompt}
                      2,                          {prompt V position}
                      3,                          {prompt H position}
                      CharStr('X',8),             {picture}
                      4,                          {data V position}
                      11,                         {data H position}
                      8,                          {data width}
                      1,                          {help ID number}
                      Name);                      {data variable}
                                                  {OpEntry}
```

The parameters of the various entry field types are similar.

A full list of the Add fields consists of

AddArrayField	array of char
AddBcdField	binary coded decimal
AddBooleanField	Boolean response

AddByteField	byte
AddCharField	single character
AddChoiceField	for enumerated types, see HeaderInfo in LoanHead
AddCompField	comp precision
AddDateField	date—MM/DD/YY(YY)
AddDateStField	date string—ie: 16 Jan 1990
AddDblField	double precision
AddExtField	extended precision
AddIntField	integer
AddLongField	long integer
AddMultiLineField	edit string array
AddNestedField	brings up another entry screen when entered
AddNestedStringField	brings up another entry screen when entered
AddPickStringField	choose from pick list
AddRealField	real
AddSglField	single precision
AddShortField	short integer
AddStringField	string
AddTimeField	hours, minutes, seconds
AddUserField	user-defined field
AddWordField	word
AddYesNoField	yes/no choice—returns True/False

(uses simple character editor, no true pictures)

AddSimpleBcdField	binary coded decimal
AddSimpleBooleanField	Boolean
AddSimpleByteField	byte
AddSimpleCharField	character
AddSimpleCompField	comp
AddSimpleDblField	double precision
AddSimpleExtField	extended precision
AddSimpleIntField	integer
AddSimpleRealField	real
AddSimpleShortField	short integer
AddSimpleSngField	single precision
AddSimpleStringField)	string
AddSimpleWordField	word
AddSimpleYesNoField	yes or no—returns True or False

(uses number editor for numeric-only fields)

AddNumericBcdField	binary coded decimal
AddNumericByteField	byte
AddNumericCompField	comp
AddNumericDblField	double precision
AddNumericExtField	extended precision
AddNumericIntField	integer
AddNumericLongField	long integer
AddNumericRealField	real
AddNumericShortField	short integer
AddNumericSngField	single precision
AddNumericWordField	word

See the OPro documentation for OpEntry to get more details and parameter lists for each type.

Most fields have a picture parameter. The meaning of the picture characters is as follows:

X	Any character
!	Any character, force uppercase
L	Any character, force lowercase
x	Any character, first letter of each word upper-, others lowercase
a	Alphabetical characters only
A	Alphabetical characters only, force uppercase
l	Alphabetical characters only, force lowercase
9	Numbers and spaces only
#	Numbers, spaces, minus, period
E	Numbers, spaces, minus, period, e
K	0–9, A–F, force uppercase (hex)
B	T, t, F, f (Boolean)
Y	Y, y, N, n

Date and time characters:

m	Month, zero-padded
M	Month, blank-padded
d	Day, zero-padded
D	Day, blank-padded
y	Year, zero-padded
n	Month name
N	Month name, force uppercase
w	Weekday

W	Weekday, force uppercase
/	Month, day, year separator
h	Hours, zero-padded
H	Hours, blank-padded
m	Minutes, zero-padded
M	Minutes, blank-padded
s	Seconds, zero-padded
S	Seconds, blank-padded
t	"p" or "a" in am/pm
e	"m" in am/pm
:	Minutes, hours, seconds separator

Next we enter a Repeat loop to process the user's entry. We begin by setting the error procedure to the one we described earlier. Then the mouse is made available. Next we process the entry screen, after which the mouse is hidden again. If an error occurred or the Escape key was pressed while making the entry, a message appears and the program returns to the main menu. Otherwise, the Control-Enter combination was used. After verifying that a string was entered, we check for the existence of the filenames. If either is found, we notify the user and return to the main menu without disturbing the existing files.

Next we open the new data file and set up one block of the default data. Thus:

```
FileData.Data := CharStr(' ',BlockSize - 8);   {empty block}
FileData.LinkTo := 0;                          {no links}
FileData.LinkFrom := 0;
```

This is accomplished by filling the block's data area with spaces and setting the link fields to 0. The next step is to write HeaderSize * 8 of these blocks to the data file.

```
LongCounter := 1;                                  {first block
                                                    stored}
      {stop writing empty blocks when desired number have been
       stored in file and no errors occur}
      while (LongCounter <= (HeaderSize * 8)) and
              (GlobError = 0) do begin  {LookGlob}
        write(BlockFile,FileData);  {store block, LookGlob}

        IoFlag := IoResult;
        if IoFlag <> 0 then
          GlobError := NoWrite;    {write error, LookGlob}
        Inc(LongCounter);          {next block}
end;
```

Then we flush the new file to disk by closing and reopening the file. I could have used FlushDosBuffers from the OpDos unit, but at the time I wrote the applications I hadn't noticed this function. You might wish to try it. The regular Flush function works only for text files.

Just before leaving this unit the index file is created:

```
if CurFile <> '' then      {data file was created}
  MakeIndexBits;           {create index file for data file,
                            LookIndx}}
```

This unit will be discussed next.

LookIndx.Pas

The LookIndx unit is used to create an index file, save it as a stream to the disk, and recover the stream from the disk. Here is the code:

```
Unit LookIndx;
{contains index procedures and functions}

INTERFACE

Uses
  LookGlob,
  LookMsg,
  OpString,
  OpRoot;

{create file index (IndexBits) from instance of BitSet object in OpRoot
 and store it to a stream (IdStream)}
procedure MakeIndexBits;

{load stored index object from stream file when loading new data
file}
procedure FetchIndexBits;

{store modified index to stream file}
procedure StoreIndexBits;

IMPLEMENTATION

procedure MakeIndexBits;
{create file index (IndexBits) from instance of BitSet object in OpRoot
 and store it to a stream (IdStream)}
begin
  if not IndexBits.Init(HeaderSize * 8) then begin {variable created in
                                                    LookGlob, bit for
                                                    each block,
                                                    OpRoot}
    ShowMsg('Failed to init bitset, status : '
           + Long2Str(InitStatus));               {OpString, LookMsg}
    halt;
  end;
```

```
  {set up stream, instance of BufIdStream object (OpRoot)}
  IStream.Init(CurFile + '.IND',SCreate,1024); {create stream, variable
                                                created in LookGlob,
                                                1024 buffer size,
                                                OpRoot}
  IndexBits.Store(IStream);                    {save new index to file
                                                as stream, OpRoot}
  Status := IStream.GetStatus;                 {did it save ok?, OpRoot}
  if Status <> 0 then begin                    {sorry about that}
    ShowMsg('Stream initialization error. Status : '
          + Long2Str(Status));                 {OpString, LookMsg}
    Halt;
  end;
  IStream.Done;                                {recover object's memory,
                                                OpRoot}
end;


procedure FetchIndexBits;
{load stored index object from BufIdStream (OpRoot) stream file when
 loading new data file}
begin
  IStream.Init(CurFile + '.IND',SOpen,1024); {identify stream, variable
                                              created in LookGlob, 1024
                                              buffer size, OpRoot}
  IndexBits.Load(IStream);                   {try to put index in
                                              memory, OpRoot}
  Status := IStream.GetStatus;               {did it work?, OpRoot}
  if Status <> 0 then begin                  {nope}
    ShowMsg('Stream load error. Status : '
          + Long2Str(Status));               {OpString, LookMsg}
    Halt;
  end;
  IStream.Done;                              {recover object's memory,
                                              OpRoot}
end;


procedure StoreIndexBits;
{store modified index to BufIdStream (OpRoot) stream file}
begin
  IStream.Init(CurFile + '.IND',SOpen,1024); {identify stream, variable
                                              created in LookGlob, 1024
                                              buffer size, OpRoot}
  IndexBits.Store(IStream);                  {try to put index on disk,
                                              OpRoot}
  Status := IStream.GetStatus;               {did it work?, OpRoot}
  if Status <> 0 then begin                  {nope}
    ShowMsg('Stream store error. Status : '
          + Long2Str(Status));               {OpString, LookMsg}
```

```
    Halt;
  end;
  IStream.Done;                        {recover object's memory,
                                        OpRoot}
end; {end of procedure}
end. {end of unit}
```

The BitSet object was chosen because it had all the functions and procedures to do everything necessary in the program. It can be used to create the bit set of the desired size, store it to a stream, recover it from the stream, check any bit to see if it is set, check any bit to see if it is clear (not set), set any bit, clear any bit, find the first set bit, and find the first clear bit. In this unit we only use methods to create the bit set, store it to a stream, and recover it from a stream. The other methods are used in LookData and LookSrch.

The BufIdStream object from OpRoot was chosen for the stream (IStream.Init). In this object, the stream is transferred to a buffer located on the heap. If the entire object cannot be stored, then portions of the stream are read into memory as required. In this case, the buffer was set to 1,024 bytes. The size of the stream data (bit set) is HeaderSize (100) bytes plus five bytes of overhead. If you do not ever anticipate using a larger header size, or if memory is tight, the buffer size could be made much smaller. By leaving it at 1,024 there is one less thing to remember to modify when increasing the header size.

LookDir.Pas

The LookDir unit contains the procedure (PickFile) to present the data (.DAT) file names for a choice when the "Select file" choice is made from the Choose menu.

```
unit LookDir;
{select a data file from the list presented}

INTERFACE

uses
  LookGlob,
  LookIndx,
  Dos,
  OpString,
  OpCrt,
  OpRoot,
  OpCmd,
  OpFrame,
  OpWindow,
  OpPick,
  OpDir,
  OpMouse,
  LookMsg;
```

```
{select a data file from the list presented}
procedure PickFile;

IMPLEMENTATION

procedure PickFile;
{select a data file from the list presented}
var
  Dir : DirList; {instance of DirList object, OpDir}
  IoFlag : Word; {result of I/O operations}

begin
  if not Dir.InitCustom(25, 5, 55, 20,     {Window coordinates}
                        Colors,             {Color set from Colors.inc}
                        DefWindowOptions
                         or wBordered,      {Window options}
                        MaxAvail,           {Heap space for files, set
                                             to at least 64K}
                        PickVertical,       {Pick orientation}
                        SingleFile)         {How many files can be
                                             selected?}
                                            {OpDir}
  then begin
    ShowMsg('Failed to Init DirList,  Status = '
            + Long2Str( InitStatus);        {OpString, LookMsg)
    Halt;
  end;

  if MouseInUse then begin                   {LookGlob}
    PickCommands.cpOptionsOn(cpEnableMouse); {directory list uses mouse,
                                              command processor}
    HideMouse;                               {avoid mouse droppings,
                                              OpMouse}
  end;

  {fill in a backdrop}
  TextAttr := $07; {background attribute}
  TextChar := '▒'; {background design}
  ClrScr;

  {Set desired DirList features}

  {window can be drawn and moved only within this rectangle}
  {supplied parameters permit entire screen to be used}
  {OpWindow}
  Dir.SetPosLimits(1,                {Minimum x}
                   1,                {minimum y}
                   ScreenWidth,      {current screen width, OpCrt}
                   ScreenHeight-1); {current screen depth, OpCrt}
```

```
{spaces added to returned item}
{from OpPick}
Dir.SetPadSize(1,  {left pad}
               1); {right pad}

{optimize window size to fit data}
Dir.diOptionsOn(diOptimizeSize);    {OpDir}

{limit files displayed to those matching this criteria}
Dir.SetMask('*.DAT', {any name with 'DAT' extension}
             0);     {file attribute byte - 0 means all normal files}
                     {OpDir}

{the mask is shown preceding this line}
Dir.AddMaskHeader(True,  {display full path}
                  1,     {number of spaces to add to both ends of
                          header before displaying it}
                  30,    {maximum length of path displayed}
                  heTC); {display header at top center in window}
                         {OpDir}

{sort on file name}
Dir.SetSortOrder(SortName);  {OpDir}

{what to display and in what order?}  {OpDir}
Dir.SetNameSizeTimeFormat('<dir>', 'Mm/dd/yy', 'Hh:mmt');

{Pick a file}
Finished := False;    {not done yet}
repeat
  if MouseInUse then  {LookGlob}
    ShowMouse;        {make mouse visible, OpMouse}
  Dir.Process;        {OpDir}
  if MouseInUse then  {LookGlob}
    HideMouse;        {to avoid mouse droppings, OpMouse}

  case Dir.GetLastCommand of  {OpWindow}
    ccSelect :  {a file was selected, OpCmd}
      begin
        {display chosen file at the bottom of the screen}
        FastWrite(Pad
                  ('Selected: '           {display full path}
                    + Dir.GetSelectedPath, {right-padded to fill,
                                           OpDir}
                    ScreenWidth),          {width of screen, OpCrt}
                  ScreenHeight, {at last line of screen, OpCrt}
                  1,            {beginning in column 1}
                  TextAttr);    {using current video attributes,
                                 OpCrt}
                  {OpCrt}
```

```
          CurFile := JustName(Dir.GetSelectedPath); {no extension or
                                                     path, OpString}
          assign(BlockFile,Curfile + '.DAT');       {assign to file
                                                     variable, LookGlob}
          {$I-}                          {turn off built-in I/O error
                                          reporting}
          reset(BlockFile);              {open file to read or write,
                                          LookGlob}
          IoFlag := IoResult;            {did it open ok?}
          if IoFlag <> 0 then begin      {no}
            GlobError := NoRoom;         {LookGlob}
            close(BlockFile);            {file didn't open correctly,
                                          LookGlob}
            CurFile := '';               {no file chosen, LookGlob}
          end
          else                           {file opened ok}
            FetchIndexBits;              {load index for opened file into
                                          memory, LookIndx}
          {$I+}                          {turn on built-in I/O validation}
          Finished := True;              {all done}
        end;

      ccError   :     {an error occurred when using Dir object instance,
                       OpCmd}
        begin
          Finished := True; {don't try again}
          CurFile := '';    {no file selected}
          if Dir.GetLastError = 0 then  {OpWindow}
            GlobError := NoFile {no files matched mask, LookGlob}
          else
            ShowMsg('Error in file selection: '
                  + Long2Str(Dir.GetLastError)); {OpString, LookMsg}
        end;

      ccQuit    :   {Escape key pressed, OpCmd}
        begin
          Finished := True;   {don't try again}
          ShowMsg('No file name selected');         {LookMsg}
          Curfile := '';      {no file selected}
        end;
    end;
  until Finished;
  Dir.Done;  {recover memory used by Dir object instance, OpDir}
end; {end of procedure}
end. {end of unit}
```

First the pick window is initialized.

```
if not Dir.InitCustom(25, 5, 55, 20,        {Window coordinates}
                      Colors,               {Color set from Colors.inc}
                      DefWindowOptions
```

```
 or wBordered,        {Window options}
MaxAvail,             {Heap space for files}
PickVertical,         {Pick orientation}
SingleFile)           {How many files can be
                       chosen?}
                      {OpDir}
```

The DefWindowOptions and other window options were discussed earlier in this chapter.

The MaxAvail option makes, at most, 64K available on the heap for the file list. Next we see the "PickVertical" argument. The possible options here are as follows:

PickVertical	if more than one column is used (determine with the column width setting), starting with the leftmost column, the highlight moves vertically down each column, to the end of the column even if not currently in the window (the window contents scroll up as necessary), to the top of the next column, and so forth.
PickHorizontal	if more than one column is used (determine with the column width setting), beginning with the top row, the highlight moves horizontally across each row, moving downward.
PickSnaking	if more than one column is used (determine with the column width setting) the highlight moves, starting with the left column, vertically down each column, to the end of the column visible in the window, then to the top of the next column, and so on.

The next argument, SingleFile, has one other option, MultipleFile. Obviously, this permits more than one selection from the file list.

As usual, the mouse is made available to the DirList object with

```
PickCommands.cpOptionsOn(cpEnableMouse); {make mouse available to
                                          picklist}
HideMouse;                               {avoid mouse tracks,
                                          OpMouse}
```

Note that PickCommands must be used (the ancestor), not DirCommands. The procedure

```
{optimize window size to fit data}
Dir.diOptionsOn(diOptimizeSize);     {OpDir}
```

has the options

diDirsUpcase	raise directory names to uppercase
diFilesUpcase	raise filenames to uppercase

diExitIfOne	autoselect and exit if only one matching file
diSetFirstFile	select first nondirectory
diOptimizeSize	set window size to match list of files read within range set in initialization
diUserNewHeader	indicates a user move routine when new directory is moved to (see AddMaskHeader and PickList .PreMove).

The last argument in AddMaskHeader can be one of the following:

heTL	top left
heTC	top center
heTR	top right
heBL	bottom left
heBC	bottom center
heBR	bottom right

The SetSortOrder method's parameter can be one of of the following:

SortNone	no sort, the default
SortName	sort files and directories in alphabetical order
SortDirName	subdirectories first, then files, alphabetically
SortSize	smallest file first, subsort on name
SortTime	earliest date first, subsort by earliest time, then subsort by name

The procedure

```
{what to display and in what order?}  {OpDir}
Dir.SetNameSizeTimeFormat('<dir>', 'Mm/dd/yy', 'Hh:mmt');
```

could also have been one of the following similar procedures:

SetNameFormat	name and extension only
SetNameSizeFormat	name and size in bytes
SetNameSizeKFormat	name and size in Kb
SetNameTimeFormat	name, date, and time
SetNameSizeTimeFormat	name, size in bytes, date, and time
SetNameSizeKTimeFormat	name, size in Kb, date, and time
SetAllFormat	name, size in bytes, date, time, attribute
SetUserFormat	user supplied display format

The date and time pictures available are

mm/dd/yy	01/02/91

MM/dd/yy	1/02/91
DD/mm/yyyy	2/01/1991
dd-NNN-yyyy	02-JAN-1991
hh:mm:ss	15:02:31
hh:mm	15:02
hh:mm te	03:02 pm
Hh:mmt	3:02p

The loop to get the file choice begins with a command to show the mouse, then the user highlights the file and presses the Enter key or abandons the operation by pressing the Escape key. The mouse is hidden again.

If an error occurred or the Escape key was pressed, a suitable message is displayed and the program returns to the main menu. Otherwise, the name of the chosen file with its path is displayed at the bottom of the screen. The filename has any extension removed and is stored in CurFile. The data file is opened for use. The index bit set is loaded from the stream file (Curfile + ".IND"). If the user carelessly chooses a nonlook program ".DAT" file, there will be no ".IND" file with a matching name, or if there is one it will certainly have the wrong format, and a stream error and program crash will result. This could be a problem with the TSR version of the program, where you don't want such crashes. Perhaps it might be best to check the ".IND" file somehow at this point before calling FetchIndexBits, perhaps by checking its existence and size. For example, with the default BlockSize and HeaderSize the ".IND" files seem to consistently be 105 bytes in length.

11

Look Application, Searching

This chapter continues the Look program. In it the procedures and functions used for searching for records that match the search criteria are discussed.

The objects used and discussed in this chapter are

EntryScreen and ancestors (OpEntry)

and methods from OpString, OpDate, OpRoot, OpAsciiz, and many others.

LookSrch.Pas

This unit gets the string to search for and locates the record(s) that match the search criteria.

```
UNIT LookSrch;
{search and comparison routines}

INTERFACE

uses LookGlob,
     LookMsg,
     OpDos,
     OpCmd,
     OpRoot,
     OpField,
```

```
     OpFrame,
     OpWindow,
     OpCrt,
     OpString,
     OpEntry,
     OpMouse,
     OpAsciiz;

{get the data to search for}
procedure GetSearchString(var SearchStr : String; var Abort : Boolean);

{load next record into record buffer}
procedure SearchBuf(var BufPos  : LongInt;  {keeps track of index
                                             position}
                    var Abort   : Boolean); {True if out of records}

{check record buffer for search data}
{return True if found, otherwise False}
function CompareBuf(SearchStr : String) : Boolean;

{process search strings within parenthesis}
procedure ProcessParens(var SearchStr : String);


IMPLEMENTATION


{$F+}
procedure ErrorHandler(UnitCode : Byte; var ErrCode : Word;
                       Msg : String);
var
  BufPtr       : Pointer; {location of buffer}
  SaveFlag     : Boolean; {was screen saved?}

begin
  {save screen so data entry screen will be restored after message
   is displayed}
  SaveFlag := True; {remember if screen successfully saved for restore}
  if not SaveWindow(1,1,ScreenWidth,ScreenHeight,True,BufPtr) then begin
                                                                 {OpCrt}
    ShowMsg('Not enough memory to save screen'); {LookMsg}
    SaveFlag := False;                           {nope, not saved}
  end;
  ShowMsg(Msg);     {show the message}            {LookMsg}
  if SaveFlag then {was screen saved ok?}
    RestoreWindow(1,1,ScreenWidth,ScreenHeight,True,BufPtr); {OpCrt}
end;
{$F-}
```

```
procedure GetSearchString(var SearchStr : String; {Search data entered}
                          var Abort : Boolean);   {True if Esc is used
                                                   leave data entry
                                                   screen}
{get the data to search for}
begin
  GlobError := 0; {no errors so far, LookGlob}
  ClrScr;
  if not ESSearch.InitCustom(18, 5, 62, 11,      {Window coordinates}
                             Colors,             {Color set, Colors.inc}
                             DefWindowOptions
                              or wBordered)      {Window options}
                                                 {OpEntry}
                             then begin
    ShowMsg('Failed to init search string EntryScreen. Status = '
         + Long2Str(InitStatus));               {OpString, LookMsg}
    Halt;
  end;

  {set up mouse}
  if MouseInUse then begin                     {LookGlob}
    EntryCommands.cpOptionsOn(cpEnableMouse); {make mouse visible,
                                               command processor}
    HideMouse;                                 {to avoid mouse droppings,
                                               OpMouse}
  end;

  {fill in a backdrop}
  TextAttr := $07; {background attribute}
  TextChar := '▒'; {background design}
  ClrScr;          {display background}

  {add some window frills from OpFrame}
  ESSearch.wFrame.AddShadow(shBR,          {display shadow bottom and
                                            right of window}
                            shOverWrite); {shadow is opaque}


  {window titles from OpFrame}
  ESSearch.wFrame.AddHeader(' Use & for and, | for or ', heTC);
  ESSearch.wFrame.AddHeader(' Esc to abort, Ctrl-Enter to accept ',
                            heBC);

  {designate user supplied error procedure}
  ESSearch.SetErrorProc(ErrorHandler); {show error in window, OpWindow}

  {add fields}
  ESSearch.esFieldOptionsOn(efClearFirstChar); {OpEntry}

  ESSearch.AddStringField('Search string:', {prompt}
```

```
                        2,                {prompt V position}
                        15,               {prompt H position}
                        CharStr('X',40),  {picture}
                        4,                {data V position}
                        2,                {data H position}
                        40,               {data width}
                        2,                {help ID number}
                        SearchStr);       {data variable}
  repeat
    Finished := False; {loop till this is set to True}
    Abort := False;    {cancel search string entry}
    if MouseInUse then {LookGlob}
      ShowMouse;       {to avoid mouse droppings, OpMouse}

    {switch to built-in error procedure to avoid displaying errors for
     such things as skipping a must-enter field}
    EsSearch.SetErrorProc(DefaultErrorProc); {beep on error, OpWindow}

    SearchStr := '';   {start with blank search string}
    ESSearch.Process;  {OpEntry}
    if MouseInUse then {LookGlob}
      HideMouse;       {avoid mouse droppings, OpMouse}

    case ESSearch.GetLastCommand of  {OpWindow}
      ccError :                      {OpCmd}
        begin
          ShowMsg('Error getting search string '
                  + Long2Str(ESName.GetLastError)); {OpString, LookMsg}
          Finished := True; {give up}
          Abort := True;    {likely no valid search string entered}
        end;

      ccQuit :              {Escape key, OpCmd}
        begin
          Finished := True; {no search string will be entered or ignore
                             the one that has been entered}
          Abort := True;    {disregard any search string entered}
        end;
    end;

    if SearchStr = '' then  {no string entered - same results as Escape}
      Abort := True;
    Finished := True;

  until Finished;
  ESSearch.Erase; {erase entry screen, OpEntry}
  ESSearch.Done;  {recover memory used by entry screen object, OpEntry}
end;
```

```
procedure GetToken(var OpStr : Char;        {And or Or symbol}
                   var SearchStr : String;  {data to search for}
                   var Token : String);     {data before, after, or
                                             between symbols}
{by symbols is meant the | for Or and & for And between search words or
 phrases}
var
  OpPos    : Integer; {symbol position}
  OpPos1   : Integer; {first symbol position if more than one is used}
  OpPos2   : Integer; {second symbol position if more than one is used}
  OpStr1   : Char;    {first symbol if more than one is used}
  OpStr2   : Char;    {second symbol if more than one is used}
  Found    : Boolean; {a symbol has been found}
  Position : Integer; {temporary symbol position value}
  Start    : Integer; {start position of current token in search string}

begin
  Found  := False; {no symbols found}
  OpStr1 := ' ';   {space}
  OpStr2 := ' ';   {space}
  OpPos1 := 255;   {highest possible value}
  OpPos2 := 255;
  Start  := 1;     {beginning of string}

  Position := pos('|',SearchStr); {look for first occurrence of Or
                                   in search string}
  if Position > 0 then begin      {found it}
    OpStr1 := '|';                {found what?}
    OpPos1 := Position;           {found it where?}
    Found := True;
  end;

  Position := pos('&',SearchStr); {look for first occurrence of And
                                   in search string}

  if Position > 0 then begin      {found it}
    OpStr2 := '&';                {found what?}
    OpPos2 := Position;           {found it where?}
    Found := True;
  end;

  if Found then begin              {found at least one symbol}
    if OpPos1 < OpPos2 then begin  {which symbol is first in search
                                    string?}
      OpPos := OpPos1;             {symbol at position 1 was first}
      OpStr := OpStr1;             {store symbol & position in variables
                                    used by subsequent code}
    end
    else begin
      OpPos := OpPos2;             {symbol at position 2 was first}
```

```
      OpStr := OpStr2;              {store symbol & position in variables
                                     used by subsequent code}

    end;

    Token := Copy(SearchStr,Start,OpPos - Start); {retrieve the data
                                                   preceding current
                                                   symbol}

    {delete data just retrieved, including symbol, from search string
     to make future searches simpler}
    Delete(SearchStr,Start,(OpPos - Start) + 1);
  end

  else begin                      {no symbol found}
    OpPos := Length(SearchStr);  {position set to end of search string}
    OpStr := ' ';                {no symbol found}
    Token := SearchStr;          {therefore use the entire search string}
    SearchStr := '';             {delete search string to indicate done}
  end;
  Token := StUpCase(Token);      {convert token to uppercase. All
                                  searches use uppercase so they won't
                                  be case-sensitive, OpString}

end;



function CompareBuf(SearchStr : String) : Boolean;
{symbols are And = '&', Or = '|'}
{search for token in record}
var
  CompBuf    : Asciiz;      {compare buffer}
  Token      : String;      {string to search for}
  Arg        : Integer;     {current token found (1 : True, 0 : False)}
  LastArg    : Integer;     {previous token found (1 : True, 0 : False)}
  OpStr      : Char;        {current symbol}
  OldOpStr   : Char;        {previous symbol}
  DoneFlag   : Boolean;     {no more CR LF pairs}
  Position   : Word;        {position of CR LF in Asciiz buffer}
  CrLfString : String[2];   {to hold CR LF for search}
  Space      : String[1];   {to hold space character to replace CR LF}

begin
  AscUpCase(Buffer,CompBuf);       {make record text uppercase for
                                    case-insensitive searching,
                                    OpAsciiz}

  {remove CR LFs from compare string, otherwise they could interfere
   with matching search string if imbedded in matching Asciiz area}
  CrLfString := chr(13) + chr(10);          {CR LF to delete}
```

```
Space := chr(32);                        {space to replace CR LF}
DoneFlag := False;                       {setup for loop}
while not DoneFlag do begin              {delete all CR LFs}
  Position := PosStr(CrLfString,CompBuf); {is CR LF in Asciiz?,
                                          OpAsciiz}
  if Position = NotFound then            {no more CR LFs, OpAsciiz}
    DoneFlag := True                     {finis}
  else begin
    DeleteAsc(CompBuf,Position,2);       {delete CR LF, OpAsciiz}
    InsertStr(Space,CompBuf,Position);   {replace CR LF with space,
                                          OpAsciiz}
  end;
end;

GetToken(OpStr,SearchStr,Token); {get the current token and symbol
                                  from current search string. As
                                  tokens are extracted the search
                                  string is shortened. Procedure in
                                  this unit}
Token := TrimSpaces(Token);      {get rid of any of token's leading or
                                  trailing spaces. This is very
                                  important as such spaces are usually
                                  included in the token, which could
                                  cause the search to fail, OpString}
{check to see if ~0~ or ~1~ is first item in Buffer}
if Token = '~1~' then
  LastArg := 1                             {set argument to 1 for
                                            True}
else begin
  if Token := '~0~' then
    LastArg := 0                           {set argument to 0 for
                                            False}
  else begin
    if PosStr(Token,CompBuf) = NotFound then {first token not found,
                                            OpAsciiz}
      LastArg := 0                         {set argument to 0 for
                                            False}
    else
      LastArg := 1;                        {set argument to 1 for
                                            True}
  end;
end;

if OpStr <> ' ' then begin              {no symbols found in search
                                         string}
  repeat
    OldOpStr := OpStr;                  {save current symbol}
    GetToken(OpStr,SearchStr,Token);    {get new token and symbol,
                                         procedure in this unit}
    Token := TrimSpaces(Token);         {get rid of surrounding
```

```
                                      spaces, OpString}
case OldOpStr of
  '|' :                               {Or}
    begin
      if TrimSpaces(Token) = '~1~' then   {compared result of
                                           search data in
                                           parentheses, found,
                                           OpString}
        Arg := 1
      else begin
        if TrimSpaces(Token) = '~0~' then {compared result of
                                           search data in
                                           parentheses, not found,
                                           OpString}

          Arg := 0
        else begin
          if PosStr(Token,CompBuf) = NotFound then {OpAsciiz}
            Arg := 0                      {set argument to 0 for
                                           False, not found}
          else
            Arg := 1;                     {set argument to 1 for
                                           True, found}
        end;
      end;
      LastArg := LastArg or Arg;      {OR current with previous
                                       cumulative results}
    end;

  '&' :
    begin
      if TrimSpaces(Token) = '~1~' then   {compared result of
                                           search data in
                                           parentheses, found,
                                           OpString}

        Arg := 1
      else begin
        it TrimSpaces(Token) = '~0~' then {compared result of
                                           search data in
                                           parentheses, not found,
                                           OpString}

          Arg := 0
        else begin
          if PosStr(Token,CompBuf) = NotFound then {OpAsciiz}
            Arg := 0                      {set argument to 0 for
                                           False, not found}
          else
            Arg := 1;                     {set argument to 1 for
```

```
                                              True, found}
             end;
            end;
            LastArg := LastArg and Arg;     {AND current with previous
                                             cumulative results}
          end;
      end;
    until OpStr = ' ';                      {search string completed}
  end;

  if LastArg = 1 then                       {search successful}
    CompareBuf := True                      {function return}
  else
    CompareBuf := False;                    {function return}
end;



procedure SearchBuf(var BufPos : LongInt;
                    var Abort  : Boolean);
{retrieve the next complete record and put in Buffer for search}
var
  Counter      : Integer; {number of blocks in the record}
  NextPosition : LongInt; {index position (and Pascal record number)}
  IoFlag       : Word;    {store error result of I/O}
  Temp         : String;  {temporary string}

begin
  Abort := False;                         {so far so good}
  {$I-}                                   {turn off built-in I/O
                                           error reporting}
  BufPos := IndexBits.NextSet(BufPos);    {find next index position
                                           designating a stored block,
                                           OpRoot (BitSet)}
  if BufPos = NoMoreBits then begin       {no more index bits set so
                                           no more blocks, OpRoot
                                           (BitSet)}
    ShowMsg('No records to search');      {LookMsg}
    Abort := True;                        {let's go home}
  end
  else begin                              {found a block}
    seek(BlockFile,BufPos);               {let's see if first block,
                                           LookGlob}
    IoFlag := IoResult;                   {make copy of I/O result}
    if IoFlag <> 0 then
      GlobError := NoSeek                 {error: can't seek to block,
                                           LookGlob}
    else begin
      read(BlockFile,FileData);           {read block from file,
                                           LookGlob}
```

```
IoFlag := IoResult;                         {make copy of I/O result}
if IoFlag <> 0 then                         {error}
  GlobError := NoRead                       {can't read block, LookGlob}
else begin
  if FileData.LinkFrom <> 0 then begin         {not first block}
    repeat
      BufPos := IndexBits.NextSet(BufPos);     {get next block
                                                position from index,
                                                OpRoot (BitSet)}
      if BufPos = NoMoreBits then begin        {no more blocks
                                                designated in index
                                                OpRoot (BitSet)}
        ShowMsg('No more records to search');{LookMsg}
        Abort := True;                         {nothing left to
                                                search}
      end
      else begin
        seek(BlockFile,BufPos);                {found another block,
                                                let's get it,
                                                LookGlob}
        IoFlag := IoResult;
        if IoFlag <> 0 then                    {problem}
          GlobError := NoSeek                  {seek error,
                                                LookGlob}
        else begin
          read(BlockFile,FileData);            {try to read block,
                                                LookGlob}
          IoFlag := IoResult;
          if IoFlag <> 0 then                  {error}
            GlobError := NoRead;               {can't read it,
                                                LookGlob}
        end;
      end;
    {until first block of record found, an error occurred
     (LookGlob), or ran out of blocks to search}
    until (FileData.LinkFrom = 0) or (GlobError > 0) or Abort;
  end;

  if not Abort and (GlobError = 0) then begin {we have a record,
                                                LookGlob}
    Counter := 0;                              {keep track of
                                                blocks stored in
                                                buffer for append
                                                operation (see
                                                InsertStr
                                                parameters)}
    DeleteAsc(Buffer,0,LenAsc(Buffer));        {clear buffer,
                                                OpAsciiz}
    repeat
      NextPosition := FileData.LinkTo;         {record number of
                                                next block}
```

```
            Temp := FileData.Data;                {put block in
                                                   string}
            {append block string to Asciiz string search buffer.
             Asciiz string is used because if Pascal string were used
             record could only be 255 characters long. Using Asciiz
             makes it very easy to insert, delete, and search}
            InsertStr(Temp,Buffer,Word(Counter * (BlockSize - 8)));
                                                  {LookGlob, OpAsciiz}
            Inc(Counter);                         {next block}
            if NextPosition <> 0 then begin       {there is another
                                                   block in this
                                                   record}
              seek(BlockFile,NextPosition);       {point to it,
                                                   LookGlob}
              IoFlag := IoResult;
              if IoFlag <> 0 then                 {error}
                GlobError := NoSeek               {seek error,
                                                   LookGlob}
              else begin
                read(BlockFile,FileData);         {read new block,
                                                   LookGlob}
                IoFlag := IoResult;
                if IoFlag <> 0 then               {error}
                  GlobError := NoRead             {read error,
                                                   LookGlob}
              end;
            end;
          {until all record's blocks retrieved or error occurred}
          until (NextPosition = 0) or (GlobError > 0); {LookGlob}
        end;
      end;
    end;
  end;
  {$I+} {turn built-in I/O error reporting back on}
  if GlobError > 0 then {LookGlob}
    Abort := True;      {found an error, abandon search operation}
end; {end of procedure}


procedure ProcessParens(var SearchStr : String);
{process search strings within parenthesis}
const
  Left  : Char = '(';
  Right : Char = ')';
var
  Abort          : Boolean; {no parentheses or they are mismatched}
  Comparison     : String;  {result of comparison - ~0~ False, ~1~
                             True}
```

```
  Counter         : Integer; {for stepping through search string}
  FirstLeftParen  : Integer; {position of first left parentheses in
                              search string - used to be sure
                              parentheses exist in string}
  FirstRightParen : Integer; {see above}
  LeftPos         : Integer; {position of rightmost left parentheses}
  RightPos        : Integer; {position of first right parentheses to
                              right of LeftPos}
  Size            : Integer; {size of search string}
  TempSearch      : String;  {to contain search data from within
                              parentheses}


begin
  Abort := False;
  repeat
    Size := length(SearchStr);                 {number of characters in
                                                search string}
    FirstLeftParen := Pos(Left,SearchStr);     {is there at least one left
                                                parentheses in search
                                                string?}
    FirstRightParen := Pos(Right,SearchStr);   {is there at least one
                                                right parentheses in
                                                search string?}

    if (FirstLeftParen = 0) or (FirstRightParen = 0) {one or no
                                                       parentheses
                                                       found}
        or (FirstRightParen < FirstLeftParen) then    {mismatched
                                                       parentheses}
      Abort := True                                   {can't process
                                                       search string}
    else begin
      Counter := Size;
      {look for rightmost left parentheses}
      while (SearchStr[Counter] <> Left) and (Counter > 0) do
        Dec(Counter);
      LeftPos := Counter; {position of rightmost left parentheses}
      {now look for first right parentheses following it}
      while (SearchStr[Counter] <> Right) and (Counter <= Size) do
        Inc(Counter);
      RightPos := Counter; {position of first right parentheses
                            following rightmost left parentheses}
      if (RightPos > Size) or (LeftPos > RightPos) then
        Abort := True  {no right paren found after left}
      else begin
        {isolate contents of parentheses pair we found}
        TempSearch := copy(SearchStr,LeftPos + 1,RightPos - (LeftPos
                           + 1));
```

```
        {found match in record?}
        if CompareBuf(TempSearch) then {function in this unit}
          Comparison := ' ~1~ '          {yes}
        else
          Comparison := ' ~0~ ';         {no}
        {I tried to use something that user would be unlikely to be
         included in the search string}

        {delete parentheses and contents from search string}
        delete(SearchStr,LeftPos,(RightPos - LeftPos) + 1);
        {replace with ~0~ or ~1~}
        insert(Comparison,SearchStr,LeftPos);
      end;
    end;
  until Abort; {repeat until we run out of parentheses pairs}
end; {end of procedure}

end. {end of unit}
```

ErrorHandler Procedure

The user-supplied error handler procedure consists of

```
{$F+}
procedure ErrorHandler(UnitCode : Byte; var ErrCode : Word;
                       Msg : String);
var
  BufPtr       : Pointer; {location of buffer}
  SaveFlag     : Boolean; {was screen saved?}

begin
  {save screen so data entry screen will be restored after message
   is displayed}
  SaveFlag := True; {remember if screen successfully saved for restore}
  if not SaveWindow(1,1,ScreenWidth,ScreenHeight,True,BufPtr) then begin
                                                                  {OpCrt}
    ShowMsg('Not enough memory to save screen'); {LookMsg}
    SaveFlag := False;                           {no, not saved}
  end;
  ShowMsg(Msg);      {show the message}          {LookMsg}
  if SaveFlag then {was screen saved ok?}
    RestoreWindow(1,1,ScreenWidth,ScreenHeight,True,BufPtr); {OpCrt}
end;
{$F-}
```

which saves the screen in a buffer if memory permits, so then when the error message window is erased, the underlying entry screen will be restored. The error message is displayed, and the screen, if saved, is restored. It replaces the normal beep on error default. The error handler is called by

```
{designate user supplied error procedure}
ESSearch.SetErrorProc(ErrorHandler); {show error in window, OpWindow}
```

in the GetSearchString procedure.

GetSearchString Procedure

The characters to search for in the file are entered via this procedure. It starts by initializing the instance of the EntryScreen object, ESSearch. The DefWindowOptions consist of

wClear
wSaveContents
wResizable
wStoreContents

The complete list of available options is

wBordered	Make space for window border
wClear	Clear window when it is first displayed
wSaveContents	Save the contents of the window when it is erased.
wUserContents	User will restore window contents
wSoundEffects	Use sound effects during explosions
wAltFrame	Use alternate frame type when not current
wSetMouse	Set mouse window, cursor on entry to window
wFullMouseWindow	Force to full mouse window on entry
wResizable	Can be resized and zoomed
wAllMouseEvents	Any combination of mouse buttons anywhere exits
wStoreContents	Store window contents in streams

Next the mouse is brought to life if possible.

```
{set up mouse}
if MouseInUse then begin
  EntryCommands.cpOptionsOn(cpEnableMouse); {make mouse visible,
                                             OpEntry}
  HideMouse;                                {to avoid mouse droppings,
                                             OpMouse}
end;
```

As noted, MouseInUse was defined in LoanGlob, if the use of the mouse was defined in OpDefine.Inc and a mouse was detected in the system. The next three lines define the window shadow and headings. In the lines

```
{add some window frills from OpFrame}
ESSearch.wFrame.AddShadow(shBR,          {display shadow bottom and
                                          right of window}
                           shOverWrite); {shadow is opaque}
```

the options are

shBR	shadow falls to bottom and right of frame
shBL	shadow falls to bottom and left of frame

and for the second argument

shOverWrite	opaque shadow
shSeeThru	transparent shadow

In the lines

```
{window titles from OpFrame}
ESSearch.wFrame.AddHeader(' Use & for and, | for or ', heTC);
ESSearch.wFrame.AddHeader(' Esc to abort, Ctrl-Enter to accept ',
                          heBC);
```

the options for the last parameter are

heTL	top left
heTC	top center
heTR	top right
heBL	bottom left
heBC	bottom center
heBR	bottom right

Now we define the entry screen's single field. We begin with

```
{add fields}
ESSearch.esFieldOptionsOn(efClearFirstChar); {OpEntry}
```

Other options are

efProtected	not changeable
efHidden	not displayed, field cannot be moved to it
efInvisible	field is never drawn
efRequired	some entry required
efBeepOnError	invalid entry
efClearFirstChar	if first character entered during editing is character, clear the field

There are many more options. See the documentation on OpField for their names and descriptions. Note that these options can be used in methods other than esFieldOptionsOn() and esFieldOptionsOff().

Now for the actual entry field:

```
ESSearch.AddStringField('Search string:', {prompt}
                        2,                {prompt V position}
                        15,               {prompt H position}
                        CharStr('X',40),  {picture}
                        4,                {data V position}
                        2,                {data H position}
                        40,               {data width}
                        2,                {help ID number}
                        SearchStr);       {data variable}
```

The parameters of the various entry types are similar. A full list of the Add fields consists of the following:

AddArrayField	array of char
AddBcdField	binary coded decimal
AddBooleanField	Boolean response
AddByteField	byte
AddCharField	single character
AddChoiceField	for enumerated types, see HeaderInfo in LoanHead
AddCompField	comp precision
AddDateField	date—MM/DD/YY(YY)
AddDateStField	date string—ie: 16 Jan 1990
AddDblField	double precision
AddExtField	extended precision
AddIntField	integer
AddLongField	long integer
AddMultiLineField	edit string array
AddNestedField	brings up another entry screen when entered
AddNestedStringField	brings up another entry screen when entered
AddPickStringField	choose from pick list
AddRealField	real
AddSglField	single precision
AddShortField	short integer
AddStringField	string
AddTimeField	hours, minutes, seconds
AddUserField	user-defined field
AddWordField	word
AddYesNoField	yes/no choice—returns True/False

(uses simple character editor, no true pictures)

AddSimpleBcdField	binary coded decimal
AddSimpleBooleanField	Boolean
AddSimpleByteField	byte
AddSimpleCharField	character
AddSimpleCompField	comp
AddSimpleDblField	double precision
AddSimpleExtField	extended precision
AddSimpleIntField	integer
AddSimpleRealField	real
AddSimpleShortField	short integer
AddSimpleSngField	single precision
AddSimpleStringField)	string
AddSimpleWordField	word
AddSimpleYesNoField	yes or no—returns True or False

(uses number editor for numeric only fields)

AddNumericBcdField	binary coded decimal
AddNumericByteField	byte
AddNumericCompField	comp
AddNumericDblField	double precision
AddNumericExtField	extended precision
AddNumericIntField	integer
AddNumericLongField	long integer
AddNumericRealField	real
AddNumericShortField	short integer
AddNumericSngField	single precision
AddNumericWordField	word

See the documentation for OpEntry to get more details and parameter lists for each type.

Most fields have a picture parameter. The meaning of the picture characters is as follows:

X	Any character
!	Any character, force uppercase
L	Any character, force lowercase
x	Any character, first letter of each word upper-, others lowercase
a	Alphabetical characters only
A	Alphabetical characters only, force uppercase

l	Alphabetical characters only, force lowercase
9	Numbers and spaces only
#	Numbers, spaces, minus, period
E	Numbers, spaces, minus, period, e
K	0–9, A–F, force uppercase (hex)
B	T, t, F, f (Boolean)
Y	Y, y, N, n

Date and time characters:

m	Month, zero-padded
M	Month, blank-padded
d	Day, zero-padded
D	Day, blank-padded
y	Year, zero-padded
n	Month name
N	Month name, force uppercase
w	Weekday
W	Weekday, force uppercase
/	Month, day, year separator
h	Hours, zero-padded
H	Hours, blank-padded
m	Minutes, zero-padded
M	Minutes, blank-padded
s	Seconds, zero-padded
S	Seconds, blank-padded
t	"p" or "a" in am/pm
e	"m" in am/pm
:	Minutes, hours, seconds separator

A repeat loop follows permitting the user to enter the search string. Note that the search string is limited to 40 characters. To change this, change the fourth and seventh parameters in the entry field description. You will probably have to modify the entry screen's width in the Initialization statement as well.

There are three ways to leave the entry screen. If the user presses the Escape key (ccQuit), the operation is abandoned and the main menu appears. An error (ccError) will have the same result, together with an error message window. The user's only other option is to press Control-Enter. This will accept the string and pass it back to the GetSearchString procedure's caller.

GetToken Procedure

Token, in this procedure, means the part of the search string between the ends of the search string and an And (&) or Or (|) operator, or between operators if there is more than one.

The search string is scanned from left to right. As each token is isolated, it is placed in a variable and the operator to its right, if any, is saved in another variable. If there is no operator, a space is stored instead. If there are no operators, the entire search string is stored as the token. The token and saved operator are then removed from the search string. Since the SearchString is passed to GetToken as a var argument, the caller must keep a backup copy of the search string in case it is needed again. By the way, the ProcessParens procedure is called before GetToken to eliminate any parentheses.

The token is converted to uppercase to avoid case sensitivity when searching. (The record text being compared has also been converted to uppercase by the CompareBuf function, discussed later in this unit.)

Finally, the truncated search string, token, and operator are passed back to the caller.

CompareBuf Function

This function does the comparison between the token and the current record.

First the asciiz string {global Buffer variable} containing the record is converted to uppercase (to eliminate case sensitivity) and stored in another asciiz string variable, CompBuf. Asciiz strings are used because the OpAsciiz unit has many useful methods available for them, such as searching for a string, deleting, inserting, and many others. A Pascal string would be too small, limiting records to 255 characters; asciiz strings can be as large as 65,520 characters (default 1024). Asciiz strings are terminated with an ASCII value of 0 (null terminated). There is no length byte at the beginning as there is in a Pascal string.

Next, all the carriage return (CR) line feed (LF) pairs inserted by the Memo object to indicate the end of each line in the edit window are removed and replaced by a space. This enables a search target that contain characters that span the end of one line and the beginning of the next to match correctly; the CR LF in the middle of the string would always cause the comparison to fail. The GetToken procedure is then called to get the first token and operator. The spaces, if any, surrounding the token are removed. If they were allowed to remain, the search could fail. The token, now converted to uppercase, is then searched for in CompBuf.

If the search was unsuccessful, the LastArg variable is set to 0, otherwise 1. (The ~1~ indicates a successful search for tokens that were within parentheses; ~0~ indicates the search was unsuccessful or the And condition within the parentheses was not met.) If tokens remain (OpStr not a space), the repeat loop is entered.

The loop merely repeats what has gone before. Get the token and see if it is within CompBuf and the And condition, (if "&" stored in OpStr,) is met. If the search was successful, then Arg is set to 1, otherwise 0. If OpStr contains a "&," then Arg is Anded with LastArg, with the results stored in LastArg, if "|" then Arg is Ored with LastArg, with the results stored in LastArg.

If, at the end of the function, LastArg is 1, the search was successful and all And conditions were met, so the function returns True, otherwise False.

SearchBuf Procedure

This procedure is used to find the next record and load it into the global asciiz string variable, Buffer. It begins by looking for the next bit set in the index. If the search is just beginning, BufPos (current bit position in BitSet) was set to -1 so the search for a set bit will begin at bit 0, otherwise the current value of BufPos is used.

If a set bit is found, BufPos it set to its position. The block is retrieved from the disk in the form of the three-field global record, FileData. If the LinkFrom field is not set to 0, then it is not the first block in the record, so the next set bit is searched for and another block is checked. This goes on until either there are no more set bits in the index, an I/O error occurs, or a block is found that is the first block of a record (LinkFrom field is 0). In that event, the global asciiz string variable Buffer is cleared and the first block is stored there. Next, if the LinkTo field is not set to 0 (which means that block is the last one in a record), the block pointed to by the first block is retrieved and appended to Buffer. This continues until a block with a LinkTo field of 0 is stored or an I/O error occurs. If an error occurred Abort is set to True and the calling procedure discards the partial record.

ProcessParens Procedure

This procedure is used to get rid of any parentheses in the search string. The tokens in the parentheses are searched for in CompBuf (via the CompareBuf function). If any tokens are found and And conditions are met, the parentheses pair and contents are replaced with a ~1~. If not, they are changed to a ~0~. This combination was used because I felt it was very unlikely to be used in a search string. The way CompareBuf handles these replacement tokens was discussed earlier.

First, the procedure checks the position of the first left and right parenthesis in the search string. If both are absent, there are no parentheses in the string. If only one is absent or the first left parenthesis follows the first right parenthesis, then the parentheses are mismatched (not paired) and the procedure returns to the caller.

The procedure scans the string from right to left, first inner parenthesis, then outer. It begins by finding the last left parenthesis, then the first right parenthesis following it. The contents of this pair, including any And or Or operators, is sent to CompareBuf as the search string. If CompareBuf returns True, a ~1~ is substituted for the parenthesis and contents, otherwise ~0~. This is repeated until the procedure runs into a mismatched pair or until it runs out of parentheses. The procedure then ends and returns the search string to the caller with (if all went well and they were paired correctly) no more parenthesis.

The next chapter will discuss the unit that calls these search procedures and functions.

12

Look Application, Record Maintenance

This chapter concludes the Look program. In it, adding, displaying, editing, deleting, and printing records are discussed.

The objects used and discussed in this chapter are

Memo and ancestors (OpMemo)
Printer (OpPrint and OpLow)
and methods from OpString, OpRoot, OpDate, OpAsciiz, and many others.

LookData.pas

This unit is a very important one. It handles all the record maintenance and interfaces with the Look (main menu) and LookSrch (record search) units.

```
Unit LookData;
{delete, add, print, search for, edit, and display data and guide the
 selection and order of these operations}

INTERFACE

Uses
  LookGlob,
  LookMsg,
  LookIndx,
```

```
  LookSrch,
  OpCrt,
  OpRoot,
  OpCmd,
  OpFrame,
  OpWindow,
  OpString,
  OpAsciiz,
  OpMouse,
  OpPrnLow,
  OpPrint,
  OpDate,
  OpMemo;

procedure RecordInfo;
{control selection and order of operations}

procedure ShowInfo(var Abort : Boolean);
{display and/or enter or edit a record}

IMPLEMENTATION


function FindRoom : Integer;
{be sure there is enough room in the file to store a record before
attempting to store it. Return number of blocks required, 0 if there
is not enough room}
var
  Size   : Word;     {size of record}
  N      : Integer; {for loop counter}
  Next   : LongInt; {current index position}
  Blocks : Integer; {number of blocks (Pascal records) required to
                     store data record}

begin
  Size := LenAsc(Buffer);                {size of record, OpAsciiz,
                                          LookGlob}
  Blocks := Size DIV (BlockSize - 8);    {number of whole blocks
                                          needed, LookGlob}
  if Size mod (BlockSize - 8) > 0 then   {partial block needed?,
                                          LookGlob}
    Inc(Blocks);                         {add another block}
  Next := IndexBits.FirstClear;          {first available block, OpRoot
                                          (BitSet)}
  if Next <> NoMoreBits then begin       {no more blocks, OpRoot
                                          (BitSet)}
    FindRoom := Blocks;                  {success so far, function
                                          returns number of blocks
                                          required}
    for N := 2 to Blocks do begin        {make sure all blocks needed
```

```
                                                  are available}
      Next := IndexBits.NextClear(Next);          {next block, OpRoot (BitSet)}
      if Next = NoMoreBits then begin             {no next block, OpRoot
                                                   (BitSet)}
        FindRoom := 0;                            {not enough blocks}
        GlobError := FileFull;                    {error code, LookGlob}
      end;
    end;
  end
  else begin                                      {couldn't find first block}
    FindRoom := 0;                                {no blocks}
    GlobError := FileFull;                        {error code, LookGlob}
  end;
end;


procedure DeleteRecord(NextPosition : LongInt);
{delete all blocks of a record given position in index of first block
 of record}
{note: index bit position and Pascal record number of associated data is
 the same value}
var
  IoFlag       : Word;     {I/O result}
  SavePosition : LongInt;  {index position of block just deleted}
  Blank        : String;   {block of spaces to replace deleted block}

begin
  Blank := CharStr(' ',BlockSize - 8); {block of spaces to replace
                                        deleted block, OpString,
                                        LookGlob}
  {$I-}                                {turn off built-in I/O error
                                        reporting}
  Repeat
    seek(BlockFile,NextPosition);      {point to desired block,
                                        LookGlob}
    SavePosition := NextPosition;      {retain value for later clearing
                                        of index bit}
    IoFlag := IoResult;                {see if seek worked}
    if IoFlag <> 0 then                {nope}
      GlobError := NoSeek              {seek error, LookGlob}
    else begin
      read(BlockFile,FileData);        {read block, LookGlob}
      IoFlag := IoResult;              {see if read worked}
      if IoFlag <> 0 then              {nope}
        GlobError := NoRead            {read error, LookGlob}
      else begin
        NextPosition := FileData.LinkTo; {link to next block}
        seek(BlockFile,SavePosition);    {move pointer back to current
                                          block, previous read moved
                                          pointer to next block,
                                          LookGlob}
```

```
        FileData.LinkTo := 0;            {set deleted block links to 0,
                                          LookGlob}
        FileData.LinkFrom := 0;
        FileData.Data := Blank;          {replace deleted block with
                                          blanks}
        write(BlockFile,FileData);       {write blank block, LookGlob}
        IoFlag := IoResult;              {did write work?}
        if IoFlag <> 0 then              {no}
          GlobError := NoWrite           {write error, LookGlob}
        else
          IndexBits.ClearBit(SavePosition); {set index to make block
                                             available, OpRoot (BitSet)}
      end;
    end;
  {until last block deleted or error occurs}
  until (NextPosition = 0) or (GlobError > 0); {LookGlob}

  {flush}
  {built-in flush only for text files}
  close(BlockFile);        {LookGlob}
  reset(BlockFile);        {LookGlob}
  IoFlag := IoResult;
  if IoFlag <> 0 then      {error}
    GlobError := NoRoom;   {reset error, LookGlob}

  {$I+}   {turn on built-in I/O error reporting}
  StoreIndexBits; {flush index from memory to stream, LookIndx}
end;



procedure PutRecord(NextPosition : LongInt;Blocks : Integer);
{divide a record (in buffer) into blocks and store them starting with
 first block at indicated position (NextPosition)}
{Blocks parameter indicates number of blocks required to store
record}
{note: index bit position and Pascal record number of associated data is
 the same value}
var
  IoFlag : Word;           {I/O results}
  Counter : Integer;       {block counter}
  Temp : Asciiz;           {temporary Asciiz string}
  SavePosition : LongInt;  {index bit position}

begin
  {$I-}                 {turn off built-in I/O error reporting}
  Counter := 1;         {first block being processed}
  SavePosition := 0;    {saved current block's index position}
```

```
repeat
  seek(BlockFile,NextPosition); {point to first block of record}
  IoFlag := IoResult;           {seek worked?}
  if IoFlag <> 0 then           {no}
    GlobError := NoSeek         {seek error, LookGlob}
  else begin                    {yes}
    FileData.LinkFrom := SavePosition; {previous block, 0 if none}
    if Counter < Blocks then           {any more blocks?}
      FileData.LinkTo := IndexBits.NextClear(NextPosition) {yes, link
                                                             to next
                                                             available
                                                             block,
                                                             OpRoot
                                                             (BitSet)}
    else
      FileData.LinkTo := 0;                                 {no, set
                                                             link to 0
                                                             to
                                                             indicate
                                                             no more
                                                             blocks,
                                                             LookGlob}

    if Counter = Blocks then                     {last block}
      CopyAsc(Buffer,                            {copy from where?,
                                                  OpAsciiz}
              (Counter - 1) * (BlockSize - 8),   {start at position}
              LenAsc(Buffer) - ((Counter - 1)    {how many bytes?,
                                                  OpAsciiz}
              * (BlockSize - 8)),                {just text, no white
                                                  space, LookGlob}
              Temp)                              {destination}
    else                                         {not last block}
      CopyAsc(Buffer,                            {copy from where?,
                                                  OpAsciiz, LookGlob}
              (Counter - 1) * (BlockSize - 8),   {start at position,
                                                  LookGlob}
              BlockSize - 8,                     {how many bytes?,
                                                  LookGlob}
              Temp);                             {destination}

    FileData.Data := Pad(Asc2Str(Temp),    {OpString, OpAsciiz}
                         BlockSize - 8);   {pad to fill block, LookGlob}
    write(BlockFile,FileData);             {store to disk, LookGlob}
    IoFlag := IoResult;                    {any error?}
    if IoFlag <> 0 then                    {yes}
      GlobError := NoWrite                 {write error, LookGlob}
    else                                   {no error}
      IndexBits.SetBit(NextPosition);      {mark block as used in index,
                                            OpRoot (BitSet)}
```

```
      SavePosition := NextPosition;         {now previous block position}
      NextPosition := FileData.LinkTo;      {now current block position,
                                             LookGlob}
      Inc(Counter);                         {next block}
    end;
  {until all blocks stored or error}
  until (NextPosition = 0) or (GlobError > 0); {LookGlob}

  {flush}
  {built-in flush only for text files}
  close(BlockFile);       {LookGlob}
  reset(BlockFile);       {LookGlob}
  IoFlag := IoResult;
  if IoFlag <> 0 then     {error}
    GlobError := NoRoom; {reset error, LookGlob}

  {$I+}              {turn on built-in I/O validation}
  StoreIndexBits;    {flush index from memory to stream, LookIndx}
end;



procedure PrintMemo;
{print the record currently being displayed as the result of a
search}
{see ShowInfo procedure in this unit}
var
  Lf : String;         {line feed character for finding end of line in
                        record}
  Lines : Integer;     {current line being printed}
  P : Printer;         {instance of Printer object}
  Page : Integer;      {number of current page being printed}
  Pos : Word;          {position of line feed or record end in Asciiz
                        string}
  PrintBuf : Asciiz;  {temporary Asciiz string containing record}
  S : String;          {Pascal string to print}
  Start : Word;        {start position in Asciiz string}
  Temp : Asciiz;       {intermediate Asciiz string holding string to
                        print}
  Z : String;          {Control-Z character for finding end of record}

begin
  Clrscr;
  if not P.Init('PRN',Prn,0) then begin        {OpPrint}
    S := 'Failed to init printer. Status : '
          + Long2Str(InitStatus);               {OpString}
    ShowMsg(S);                                 {LookMsg}
  end;
  while not P.PrinterReady do begin            {OpPrint}
    ShowMsg('Printer is not ready');            {LookMsg}
```

```
  end;

  Lines := 2;            {start printing at this line}
  Page := 1;             {first page number}
  Lf := #10;             {line feed}
  Z := #26;              {control Z}
  PrintBuf := Buffer;    {store record in temporary buffer as we will be
                          deleting it, line by line}
  Start := 0;            {starting position of current record - always 0}
  P.Position(Lines,10,rtAbsolute);          {OpPrint}
  P.PrintStr('Page: ' + Long2Str(Page));    {page number in header,
                                             OpPrint, OpString}
  P.Position(Lines,60,rtAbsolute);
  P.PrintStr(TodayString('mm/dd/yyyy'));    {today's date in header,
                                             OpDate}
  Lines := Lines + 2;                       {start printing record here}
  while LenAsc(PrintBuf) > 2 do begin       {While buffer contains more
                                             than closing ^Z and Asciiz
                                             null (0) keep printing,
                                             OpAsciiz}
    Pos := PosStr(Lf,PrintBuf);             {find end of first line in
                                             buffer, OpAsciiz}
    if Pos = NotFound then                  {no line feed, must be end of
                                             record, OpAsciiz}
      Pos := PosStr(Z,PrintBuf);            {find end of record in buffer}
    CopyAsc(PrintBuf,Start,(Pos - Start) + 1,Temp); {get line from
                                                     buffer, OpAsciiz}
    DeleteAsc(PrintBuf,Start,(Pos - Start) + 1);     {delete line we just
                                                     got from buffer,
                                                     OpAsciiz}
    S := TrimTrail(Asc2Str(Temp));          {convert to Pascal string and
                                             get rid of CR/LF, OpString,
                                             OpAsciiz}
    P.Position(Lines,10,rtAbsolute);        {print line here}
    P.PrintStr(S);                          {line to print}
    Inc(Lines);                             {next line position}
    if Lines >= 55 then begin               {end of page?}
      Inc(Page);                            {next page number}
      P.FormFeed;                           {next sheet of paper, OpPrint}
      Lines := 2;                           {print header here}
      P.Position(Lines,10,rtAbsolute);      {print header}
      P.PrintStr('Page: ' + Long2Str(Page)); {OpString}
      P.Position(Lines,60,rtAbsolute);
      P.PrintStr(TodayString('mm/dd/yyyy')); {OpDate}
      Lines := Lines + 2;                   {print first record line here}
    end;
  end;
  P.FormFeed; {eject last page, OpPrint}
  P.Done;     {recover memory used by Printer object instance, OpPrint}
end;
```

```
procedure ShowInfo(var Abort : Boolean);
{enter new record, display record, or edit record}
const
  BufSize = InputLen; {value set in LookGlob unit}

var
  Mem          : Memo; {instance of Memo object}
  ExitCommand : Word; {key used to leave memo editor}

begin
  Abort := False; {so far so good}

  if not Mem.InitCustom(10,                    {X1}
                        5,                     {Y1}
                        71,                    {X2}
                        18,                    {Y2}
                        Colors,                {from Colors.Inc}
                        DefWindowOptions       {default window options}
                        or WBordered,          {make room for border}
                        BufSize,               {memo edit buffer size}
                        @Buffer)               {where is memo edit buffer?}
                                               {OpMemo}
                        then begin
    ShowMsg('Failed to init memo. Status: '
            + Long2Str(InitStatus));           {OpString, LookMsg}
    Halt;
  end;

  {fill in a backdrop}
  TextAttr := $07; {background attribute}
  TextChar := '▒'; {background design}
  ClrScr;

  {read only if search or delete mode}
  if (EntryType = 'D') or (EntryType = 'S') then {Look}
    Mem.meOptionsOn(meReadOnly);                 {OpMemo}

  {use built-in status and error handlers}
  Mem.SetStatusProc(MemoStatus);                 {OpMemo}
  Mem.SetErrorProc(MemoError);                   {OpWindow}

  MemoCommands.AddCommand(ccUser0,1,$1C0A,$0000);   {^ Enter exit
                                                     command, OpCmd}
  if EntryType = 'S' then                           {search mode only,
                                                     Look}
    MemoCommands.AddCommand(ccUser1,1,$3C00,$0000); {F2 (for print
                                                     command), OpCmd}

  {memo edit screen prompt lines, OpFrame}
  if EntryType = 'S' then  {if search mode, Look}
```

```
  Mem.wFrame.AddHeader(' Esc aborts, Ctrl-Enter accepts, F2 prints ',
                        heBC)
else                    {if add, edit, or delete mode}
  Mem.wFrame.AddHeader(' Esc to abort, Ctrl-Enter to accept ',heBC);

if MouseInUse then begin                          {LookGlob}
  MemoCommands.cpOptionsOn(cpEnableMouse);  {use mouse to edit}
  HideMouse;                                {avoid mouse droppings,
                                             OpMouse}
end;

Finished := False;                  {not done yet}
repeat
  if MouseInUse then                {LookGlob}
    ShowMouse;                      {make mouse visible, OpMouse}
  Mem.Process;                      {do display and/or add or edit,
                                     OpMemo}
  if MouseInUse then                {LookGlob}
    HideMouse;                      {avoid mouse tracks, OpMouse}
  ExitCommand := Mem.GetLastCommand; {what key used to leave editor?
                                     OpWindow}
  case ExitCommand of
    ccUser0 :                       {^ Enter, OpCmd}
      begin
        Abort := False;             {all finished ok}
        Finished := True;           {done}
      end;

    ccUser1 :                       {F2, OpCmd}
      PrintMemo;                    {print record, not finished,
                                     procedure in this unit}

    ccQuit :                        {Escape key, OpCmd}
      begin
        Abort := True;              {abandon current operation}
        Finished := True;           {done}
      end;

    ccError :                       {OpCmd}
      begin                         {error using memo object}
        ShowMsg('Error during memo processing: '
                + Long2Str(Mem.GetLastError)); {LookMsg, OpString}
        Finished := True;           {done}
        Abort := True;              {abandon operation}
      end;
  end;

until Finished;

Mem.Erase; {erase memo window, OpMemo}
```

```
  Mem.Done;  {recover memory used by instance of memo object, OpMemo}
  ClrScr;
end;



procedure RecordInfo;
{control selection and order of operations}
var
  Abort        : Boolean;  {abandon operation}
  CtrlZPos     : Word;     {end of edit buffer marker}
  EditPosition : LongInt;  {position of first block of edited record}
  Found        : Boolean;  {record found that meets search criteria}
  FoundOnce    : Boolean;  {at least one record found in search}
  Last         : String;   {0 marker indicating end of Asciiz string}
  Position     : LongInt;  {current index position}
  Blocks       : Integer;  {number of blocks to store record}
  Z            : String;   {Control-Z, end of memo buffer}
  SaveSearch   : String;   {search info, ProcessParens (LookSrch)
                            modifies original}
  SearchStr    : String;   {original search criteria}

begin
  Last := #0;            {end of Asciiz string marker}
  Z := #26;              {Control Z}
  Abort := False;        {so far so good}
  FoundOnce := False;    {no records found yet}
  case EntryType of      {Look}
    'A' : {add}
      begin
        repeat
          InsertStr(Z,Buffer,0);     {put ^Z in first character position
                                      in buffer, OpAsciiz}
          ShowInfo(Abort);           {start memo editor and enter record,
                                      procedure in this unit}
          if not Abort then begin    {keep new record}
            CtrlZPos := PosStr(Z,Buffer); {find end of buffer, OpAsciiz}

            {if end of edit buffer found and user has entered a record
             then}
            if (CtrlZPos <> NotFound) and (LenAsc(Buffer) > 1){OpAsciiz}
                                                              then begin
              InsertStr(Last,Buffer,CtrlZPos + 1); {mark end of Asciiz
                                                    string with 0 right
                                                    after end of memo
                                                    buffer marker,
                                                    OpAsciiz, LookGlob}
              Blocks := FindRoom;                  {how many blocks to
                                                    store record?
                                                    function in
```

```
                                              this unit}
      if Blocks > 0 then begin                {room to store found}
        Position := IndexBits.FirstClear;     {Pascal record
                                              position of
                                              first block, OpRoot
                                              (BitSet)}
        PutRecord(Position,Blocks);           {store the record -
                                              see procedure in
                                              this unit}
      end
      else begin                              {no room}
        ShowMsg('Not enough room to store memo'); {LookMsg}
        Abort := True;                        {abandon operation}
      end;
    end
    else begin                                {end of buffer not
                                              found, program
                                              error}
      if CtrlZPos = NotFound then begin       {OpAsciiz}
        ShowMsg('Memo end not found');
        Abort := True;
      end
      else
        ShowMsg('No memo entered');           {no record entered,
                                              LookMsg}
    end;
  end;
 {until user abandons operation or chooses not to enter more
  records}
 until Abort or not Verify('Add another?'); {LookMsg}
end;
'E','S','D' : {edit, search, delete}
  begin
    GetSearchString(SearchStr,Abort); {get info to locate string to
                                      be searched for, deleted, or
                                      edited, LookSrch}
    SaveSearch := SearchStr;
    if not Abort then begin
      Position := -1;                 {next index position will be
                                      0}
      Found := False;                 {record not found yet}
      repeat
        SearchStr := SaveSearch;
        SearchBuf(Position,Abort);    {get a record to search,
                                      LookSrch}
        ProcessParens(SearchStr);     {process strings in
                                      parentheses, LookSrch}
        {if not abandoned and search successful}
        if not Abort and CompareBuf(SearchStr) then begin {LookSrch}
          EditPosition := Position;           {save position of
```

```
                                                      first block so
                                                      record can be
                                                      deleted later}

      CtrlZPos :=  PosStr(Z,Buffer);                 {find end of
                                                      buffer, OpAsciiz}
      if CtrlZPos <> NotFound then begin             {end of buffer
                                                      found, OpAsciiz}
        InsertStr(Last,Buffer,CtrlZPos + 1);         {put end-of-Asciiz
                                                      string marker
                                                      right after end of
                                                      edit buffer
                                                      marker}
        ShowInfo(Abort);              {display record and edit (if
                                       selected), procedure in this
                                       unit}
        if not Abort then begin       {not abandoned}
          Found := True;              {record accepted}
          FoundOnce := True;          {at least one record accepted}
        end;
      end
      else begin
        ShowMsg('Memo end not found'); {LookMsg}
        Abort := True;
      end;
    end;
  until Abort or Found;
  if not Abort then begin
    case EntryType of  {Look}
      'E' :            {edit mode}
        begin
          repeat
            {delete displayed record?}
            if Verify('Replace this record?') then begin
              CtrlZPos := PosStr(Z,Buffer);           {find end
                                                       of buffer,
                                                       OpAsciiz}
              if CtrlZPos <> NotFound then begin      {end of
                                                       buffer
                                                       found,
                                                       OpAsciiz}
                InsertStr(Last,Buffer,CtrlZPos + 1);  {put end-
                                                       of-Asciiz
                                                       string
                                                       marker
                                                       after
                                                       end-of-
                                                       buffer
                                                       marker,
                                                       OpAsciiz}
```

```
      Blocks := FindRoom;                     {how many
                                               blocks to
                                               store this
                                               record?
                                               function
                                               in this
                                               unit}

      if Blocks > 0 then begin                {room
                                               found}
        Position := IndexBits.FirstClear;     {first
                                               block
                                               available,
                                               OpRoot
                                               (BitSet)}
        PutRecord(Position,Blocks);           {store the
                                               record -
                                               procedure
                                               in this
                                               unit}
        DeleteRecord(EditPosition);           {delete old
                                               version
                                               of record,
                                               procedure
                                               in this
                                               unit}
      end;
    end
    else begin
      ShowMsg('Memo end not found');           {LookMsg}
      Abort := True;
    end;
  end;
  Found := False;                            {find a new
                                              record}
  if Verify('Search again?') then begin      {try again?,
                                              LookMsg}
    repeat                                   {yes}
      SearchStr := SaveSearch;
      SearchBuf(Position,Abort);             {load next
                                              record
                                              into buffer,
                                              LookSrch}

      ProcessParens(SearchStr);              {process
                                              strings in
                                              parentheses,
                                              LookSrch}
      {if record loaded and search string matches
       record, LookSrch}
```

```
              if not Abort and CompareBuf(SearchStr)
                                                        then begin
                EditPosition := Position;     {save position
                                               of first block}
                CtrlZPos := PosStr(Z,Buffer); {find end of
                                               buffer,
                                               OpAsciiz}
                if CtrlZPos <> NotFound then begin {found it,
                                                    OpAsciiz}
                  {put end-of-Asciiz string marker right after
                   end of edit buffer marker}
                  InsertStr(Last,Buffer,CtrlZPos + 1);
                                                    {OpAsciiz}
                  ShowInfo(Abort);    {display record,
                                       procedure in this unit}
                  if not Abort then
                    Found := True;    {record accepted for
                                       replacement}
                end
                else begin {no buffer end - program error}
                  ShowMsg('Memo end not found'); {LookMsg}
                  Abort := True;
                end;
              end;
            until Found or Abort;
          end
          else {don't search again}
            Abort := True;
        until Abort;
      end;
    'D' :  {delete mode}
      begin
        repeat
          if Verify('Delete this record?') then {delete
                                                 displayed
                                                 record?,
                                                 LookMsg}
            DeleteRecord(EditPosition);         {yes,
                                                 procedure in
                                                 this unit}
          Found := False;                       {find a new
                                                 record}
          if Verify('Search again?') then begin {try again?,
                                                 LookMsg}
            repeat                              {yes}
              SearchStr := SaveSearch;
              SearchBuf(Position,Abort);        {load next
                                                 record
                                                 into buffer,
                                                 LookSrch}
```

```
        ProcessParens(SearchStr);          {process
                                            strings in
                                            parentheses,
                                            LookSrch}
        {if record loaded and search string matches
         record, LookSrch}
        if not Abort and CompareBuf(SearchStr)
                                              then begin
          CtrlZPos := PosStr(Z,Buffer);       {find end
                                               of buffer,
                                               OpAsciiz}
          if CtrlZPos <> NotFound then begin {found it,
                                               OpAsciiz}
            {put end-of-Asciiz string marker right after
             end of edit buffer marker, OpAsciiz}
            InsertStr(Last,Buffer,CtrlZPos + 1);
            ShowInfo(Abort);   {display record,
                                procedure in this unit}
            if not Abort then
              Found := True;   {record accepted for
                                deletion}
          end
          else begin {no buffer end - program error}
            ShowMsg('Memo end not found'); {LookMsg}
            Abort := True;
          end;
        end;
      until Found or Abort;
    end
    else {don't search again}
      Abort := True;
  until Abort;
 end;
'S' :  {search only mode}
 begin
   {while not abandoned and another record to look for}
   while not Abort and Verify('Search again?') do begin
                                              {LookMsg}
     Found := False;  {not found yet}
     repeat
       SearchStr := SaveSearch;
       SearchBuf(Position,Abort); {load next record into
                                   buffer, LookSrch}
       ProcessParens(SearchStr);  {process strings in
                                   parentheses, LookSrch}
       {record loaded and search criteria matches}
       if not Abort and CompareBuf(SearchStr) then begin
         CtrlZPos := PosStr(Z,Buffer);      {find end of
                                             buffer,
                                             OpAsciiz}
```

```
                        if CtrlZPos <> NotFound then begin {end of
                                                             buffer
                                                             found,
                                                             OpAsciiz}
                          {put end-of-Asciiz string marker right after
                           end of edit buffer marker}
                          InsertStr(Last,Buffer,CtrlZPos + 1);{OpAsciiz}
                          ShowInfo(Abort); {display record found,
                                            procedure in this unit}
                          Found := True;   {record accepted}
                        end
                        else begin {no buffer end - program error}
                          ShowMsg('Memo end not found'); {LookMsg}
                          Abort := True;
                        end;
                      end;
                    until Abort or Found;
                  end;
                end;
            end; {case}
          end; {if}
        end;
      end;
    end;
    if (EntryType <> 'A') and not FoundOnce then {Look}
      ShowMsg('No records found');              {LookMsg}
  end; {procedure end}

  end. {unit end}
```

FindRoom Function

This function is used to be sure there is enough room in a data file before an attempt is made to save a record.

First, the size of the global asciiz variable Buffer, which contains the record, is determined. It is divided by the BlockSize (global constant) - 8 (for the two 4 byte link fields), and the result is stored in Size. If there is a remainder after the division, Size is incremented. This is the number of cleared bits that must be found in the index. As you'll remember, each index bit designates one block. The function then looks for the first clear bit. If found, the function loops to find the remaining bits. If enough clear bits are located, the function returns the number of bits (blocks) required, otherwise 0.

DeleteRecord Procedure

Upon being supplied with the file number (and bit position; they are the same) of a record's first block, this procedure deletes all the record's blocks from the file, replacing them with 0s in the link fields and spaces in the data field. The associated index bits are cleared. To understand this procedure, it is important to know that the record number (used by seek) and the index bit position are identical values. When completed, the data file DOS buffers and index stream are flushed to disk. This flushing occurs every time file data or index bits change to avoid possible loss because of power failure, computer malfunction, or operator error.

PutRecord procedure

This procedure stores the record it finds in the global Buffer variable, stored there by ShowInfo (this unit), the editor. Before this procedure is called, the calling procedure (RecordInfo in this unit) first determines if the data blocks required are available by calling FindRoom (in this unit, described earlier). Assured of enough room, RecordInfo calls this procedure, passing it the index bit position (file record number). The FileData record's link fields are set appropriately; that is, LinkFrom contains the file record number of the previous block, otherwise 0. LinkTo contains the file record number of the next available block or 0 if no more blocks are required. The routine knows how many blocks are needed because that value was passed to it by RecordInfo; thus it knows whether to put a file record number or 0 in a LinkTo field. The Data field contains the first BlockSize (global constant) - 8 (8 for the link fields) characters from Buffer. A variable Counter is used to step through Buffer, copying BlockSize - 8 characters into the Data field each time through a loop. The last block is right-padded with blanks if it does not fill the block. When the designated number of blocks have been stored in the file and the associated index bits set, the procedure ends. The index stream and data file DOS buffers are then flushed to disk.

PrintMemo Procedure

In Search mode, while a record is being displayed in the editor window, pressing the F2 key will call this procedure. It prints the record using an instance of the Printer object. First the object is initialized:

```
if not P.Init('PRN',Prn,0) then begin        {OpPrint}
  S := 'Failed to init printer. Status : '
        + Long2Str(InitStatus);               {OpString}
  ShowMsg(S);                                 {LookMsg}
end;
```

The printer is checked to be sure it is ready:

```
while not P.PrinterReady do begin            {OpPrint}
  ShowMsg('Printer is not ready');            {LookMsg}
end;
```

Note that several routines to check printer readiness are supplied by Turbo Power with OPro. You may wish to look at this material and perhaps choose another routine than the one I choose. Next a page header is printed.

```
Lines := 2;           {start printing at this line}
Page := 1;            {first page number}
Lf := #10;            {line feed}
Z := #26;             {control Z}
PrintBuf := Buffer;   {store record in temporary buffer as we will be
                       deleting it, line by line, LookGlob}
Start := 0;           {starting position of current record - always 0}
P.Position(Lines,10,rtAbsolute);          {OpPrint}
P.PrintStr('Page: ' + Long2Str(Page));    {page number in header,
                                           OpPrint, OpString}
P.Position(Lines,60,rtAbsolute);
P.PrintStr(TodayString('mm/dd/yyyy'));    {today's date in header,
                                           OpDate}
Lines := Lines + 2;                       {start printing record here}
```

The record is then printed. Lines are extracted from Buffer one at a time. The end of the line is signaled by a CR (carriage return) LF (line feed) pair. The asciiz string is converted to a regular Pascal string, and any trailing white space, which includes the CR LF pair, is removed and the line is sent to the printer. This goes on until a Control-Z at the end of a line signals that it is the last one in the buffer. The editor needs a Control-Z to signal the end of the text; it is handled automatically by the Memo object.

ShowInfo Procedure

This procedure contains the editor, used for displaying, entering, and modifying records.

The Memo editor object, Memo, is initialized.

```
if not Mem.InitCustom(10,                {X1}
                      5,                 {Y1}
                      71,                {X2}
                      18,                {Y2}
                      Colors,            {from Colors.Inc}
                      DefWindowOptions   {default window options}
                      or WBordered,      {make room for border}
                      BufSize,           {memo edit buffer size}
                      @Buffer)           {where is memo edit buffer?}
                                         {OpMemo}
```

The DefWindowOptions makes the following window options available:

wClear
wSaveContents
wResizable
wStoreContents

The complete list of available options is

wBordered	Make space for window border
wClear	Clear window when it is first displayed
wSaveContents	Save the contents of the window when it is erased.
wUserContents	User will restore window contents
wSoundEffects	Use sound effects during explosions
wAltFrame	Use alternate frame type when not current
wSetMouse	Set mouse window, cursor on entry to window
wFullMouseWindow	Force to full mouse window on entry
wResizable	Can be resized and zoomed
wAllMouseEvents	Any combination of mouse buttons anywhere exits
wStoreContents	Store window contents in streams

The BufSize argument was set at the beginning of the procedure, to InputLen, a global constant.

When in the delete or search mode, the user should not be able to modify the record. That is reserved for Edit mode. To enforce this,

```
{read only if search or delete mode}
if (EntryType = 'D') or (EntryType = 'S') then {Look}
  Mem.meOptionsOn(meReadOnly);                 {OpMemo}
```

Other available options are

meInsert	Start with insert mode on as opposed to typeover mode.
meIndent	When Enter is pressed, a new line is started with the same indentation as the previous line. Word wrap must be on.
meReadOnly	Read only, no editing when on.
meWordWrap	Words are not split at the ends of lines.
meDeleteJoins	Pressing Del at the end of a line concatenates the following line.
meModified	This internal flag is automatically set to on when the text has been modified since it was last saved.
meIndentIsPara	This option affects the behavior when Control-B (reformat paragraph) is pressed. If on, spaces at the beginning of a line indicate a new paragraph; otherwise one or more blank lines indicate a new paragraph.
meMousePage	Clicking on the up or down arrow of the scroll bar scrolls one page; if not on, clicking scrolls one line.
meAllowTrunc	If on, a warning is given if the text is too long to fit

	in the buffer (initialization buffer size argument) and only as much text as will fit is loaded, otherwise no attempt to load is made and a fatal error will be generated.
meMapCtrls	This option determines how control characters other than M, J, and Z (never shown) are displayed. If on, the letters are displayed as uppercase in the alternate color (initialization color parameter); otherwise they are displayed normally.
meMakeBackups	If on, when the file is saved, any existing file of the same name is given a BAK extension.
meStreamReLoad	If on, Store saves the name of the file in the editor in the stream. The Load command then reloads that file if it is available.
meReformatting	This internal flag is automatically set on while reformatting. It suppresses screen updates and error messages while on.
meNewFile	This internal flag is set on when a new file is loaded. After any status line has been changed to reflect the new name, it is turned off.
meDeallocate	Set this option on if you, rather than the constructor, allocates the editor buffer. Done will then deallocate the buffer for you.
meWrapAtLeft	If on, this option will join the current line to the end of the previous line if the left arrow is pressed in column 1; otherwise the left arrow is ignored in that situation.
meNoCtrlZ	If on, the Control-Z at the end of the buffer will not be written to disk; otherwise it will.

```
{use built-in status and error handlers}
Mem.SetStatusProc(MemoStatus);                    {OpMemo}
Mem.SetErrorProc(MemoError);                      {OpWindow}
```

You can substitute your own status routine, which will display whatever you wish just before MemoCommands. GetCommand is called to get the next editing command. The default status procedure indicates the editor cursor line and column positions, percentage of the buffer filled with text, whether insert, indent, word wrap are on or off, and whether the text has been modified since it was last saved. The line is displayed at the value of the StatusRow (OpMemo variable) value; the default is 2. You can see this work by entering Add or Edit mode and displaying a record.

The default error procedure beeps-on-error. See the LookSrch unit in the previous chapter for an example of a user-supplied error handler.

When meReadOnly option is on, the Control_Enter key, among others, is not recognized. However, ccUser0 through ccUser9 are always recognized. To be consistent throughout the application, I wished to use Control-Enter to accept the text and leave the editor. The Control-Enter pair must be mapped to one of the ccUser keys to do so.

```
MemoCommands.AddCommand(ccUser0,1,$1C0A,$0000);    {^ Enter exit
                                                    command, OpCmd}
```

I wanted the editor to recognize the F2 key with meReadOnly on and only in Search mode. Therefore

```
if EntryType = 'S' then                            {search mode only,
                                                    Look}
 MemoCommands.AddCommand(ccUser1,1,$3C00,$0000);   {F2 (for print
                                                    command), OpCmd}
```

This key is used to print the record.

The editor window prompt line is different in Search mode than it is in the other modes. This is because the F2 print key is available only in Search. Therefore

```
{memo edit screen prompt lines, OpFrame}
if EntryType = 'S' then  {if search mode, Look}
  Mem.wFrame.AddHeader(' Esc aborts, Ctrl-Enter accepts, F2 prints ',
                        heBC)
else                     {if add, edit, or delete mode}
  Mem.wFrame.AddHeader(' Esc to abort, Ctrl-Enter to accept ',heBC);
```

As usual we use

```
if MouseInUse then begin                      {LookGlob}
  MemoCommands.cpOptionsOn(cpEnableMouse);    {use mouse to edit}
  HideMouse;                                  {avoid mouse droppings,
                                               OpMouse}
end;
```

to make the mouse available.

Next a loop is set up to wait for the user to press the Escape, F2 (in Search mode only), or Control-Enter key or an error occurs.

The F2 key causes the PrintMemo procedure (described earlier in this chapter) to be called followed by a return to the editor window.

If we get either of the remaining two keys, we are done with the editor and return to the calling program, RecordInfo (procedure to be described later in this chapter). Otherwise an error message is displayed and the calling program is notified that the record in the editor is invalid by setting Abort to True.

RecordInfo Procedure

This procedure handles all the Add, Edit, Delete, and Search operations. In any of these modes, it is called by Look.

If in Add mode, the procedure first puts a Control-Z character at the beginning of Buffer, the global asciiz variable, and calls ShowInfo (procedure described earlier in this chapter). This is required by the memo editor object. When the editor returns and no error occurred (Abort is False), an attempt is made to locate the Control-Z character, which should be positioned at the end of the buffer. If it is not found, a program error occurred. A message is displayed and the user is returned to the main menu. If found and the user has entered some text, (LenAsc(Buffer) > 1), then a null (ASCII 0) is placed right after the Control-Z. (It should already be there, but inserting the null is faster then checking to be sure it is.) The null indicates the end of the text in an asciiz string. FindRoom (function described earlier in this chapter) is called to be sure there are enough free blocks in the file to store the record. If so, the record is stored by calling PutRecord (procedure described earlier in this chapter). If not, the user is notified.

So much for adding. All the other modes start the same way. The search unit procedures are used to find the record to view, edit, or delete. If a matching record is found, it is loaded into Buffer. As we did earlier, we make sure the null follows the Control-Z in Buffer. The memo editor is called next.

Upon leaving the editor, if the user did not press Escape or get an error (Abort = False), we set the flag FoundOnce to True. This flag, if False, indicates that the user later be told no records were found. If Abort is False, we continue searching for matching records.

From here on, the program behaves differently depending on the mode: Edit, search, or delete. First let's consider the Edit mode.

The procedure checks with the user via the Verify function to see if he or she wishes to replace the original copy of the record with the version currently in Buffer. Remember, in the edit mode the user was able to modify the record while it was being displayed by ShowInfo. If replacement is desired, again we make sure the null directly follows the Control-Z in the buffer. (If it does not, we end up saving any garbage between the ^Z and the null as part of the record, a waste of disk space.) Next, FindRoom is called to be sure enough blocks are available, then the record is saved. Finally, if all goes well to this point, the original record is deleted. Thus, for a few moments, both versions of the record are in the file.

Verify is then called to see if the user wants to search for another record with the same search criteria. If so, we repeat the whole business again: search, load into Buffer, display (and modify if desired), adjust null, etc.

The delete mode is a bit simpler. After locating a matching record, it is displayed. The user then gets a message asking if deletion is desired. If the Ok pushbutton is pressed, the record is deleted via DeleteRecord, described earlier in this chapter. Then Verify is called to see if the user wishes to search (and maybe delete) again with the same search criteria.

In search mode we first check to see if the user wishes to continue searching. If so, we follow the earlier search routine: If found adjust the null, load the record into Buffer, and display it. Upon returning from the Buffer, loop back, verify, and search again. This continues until the user presses the Cancel button in verify or no more records match.

Compiling Order

LookGlob.pas
LookMsg.pas
LookIndx.pas
LookSrch.pas
LookData.pas
All other files except Look.pas.
Look.pas

This completes the description of the Look program. In the next chapter I'll describe how to convert Look to a TSR.

13

Look As a TSR

To convert Look to a TSR, two modules have to be modified and two units added. The main program, Look.pas, is not used in this version.

These units use the object

Menu (OpMenu)

and methods from OpSwap, OpSwap1, OpMouse, OpDos, OpString, and others.

Lookup.pas

The main program module is called Lookup.pas, as opposed to the Look.pas of the stand-alone version.

```
{Copyright 1991 by Ken Knecht}
{Lookup.pas - resident portion of lookup tsr}

{$M 10240,0,655360} {if you changed the program you might need to adjust
                     these values, especially the stack size (first
                     value)}
{S-,R-}
program lookup;

uses
  LookMain, {swappable portion of swappable TSR manager}
  LookPath, {to store Tsr's drive and directory as global variables}
  OpDos,    {for DefaultDrive function}
```

```
    OpSwap;    {resident portion of swappable TSR manager, must be last
                unit}

  begin
    LookDrive := DefaultDrive;                      {where is program and its
                                                     data files?, OpDos.
                                                     global variable LookDrive
                                                     declared in LookPath unit}
    GetDir(ord(LookDrive) - 64,LookLocation);      {convert the drive letter
                                                     stored in LookDrive to a
                                                     number for the TP GetDir
                                                     function. Store the
                                                     application's path and
                                                     directory name in
                                                     the global variable
                                                     LookLocation declared in
                                                     the LookPath unit}
    InitializeLookup;                               {init TSR, LookMain}
  end.
```

This is the main program module and should be compiled last. The final EXE file ends up with this name unless you specify another.

LookPath.pas

To make the resident portion of the TSR as small as possible, I put these two global variables in a separate unit. If they were added to LookGlob, all the LookGlob variables would be stored in the resident TSR kernel.

```
unit LookPath;

INTERFACE

var
  LookLocation : String; {path and directory of application}
  LookDrive    : Char;   {drive letter of application}

IMPLEMENTATION

end.
```

When Lookup is popped up, it could be from any drive and directory. The data and index files are normally stored in the same directory as Lookup. When "Select file" from the Choose menu is chosen, the LookDir unit displays all the DAT files in the current directory. Thus the desired DAT file will not appear in the list if the Lookup application's directory is not the default directory. To ensure that it is, the default drive and directory are stored in LookDrive and LookLocation when Lookup is loaded. Now all Lookup needs to do to find its files when popped up is to refer to these two global variables and switch to the stored drive and directory. "Create file" works much the same way. Lookup stores a new file and index in the default directory. The names of that drive and directory must be known to Lookup so the new files can be stored to the correct directory, that of the application.

Two other ways to do this come immediately to mind. Store the drive and directory in an environment variable. The problem with that is having to rely on the user to set this variable correctly or else have the program create the variable. In that case, there might not be enough room available in the environment. After due reflection, I chose to use a separate unit.

There is no way for the user to change the hot key. Should you wish to do this, add the choice to the menu and call it from the MainPop procedure. You'll also have to store the user-supplied hot key; probably LookPath would be the best place to put it.

LookMain.pas

```
{LookMain.pas swappable portion of LookUp TSR}
{$S-,R+,V-,I-}

unit LookMain;


INTERFACE



Uses
  LookGlob,
  LookPath,
  Dos,
  OpRoot,
  OpDos,
  OpCrt,
  OpMouse,
  OpCmd,
  OpField,
  OpCtrl,
  OpFrame,
  OpMenu,
  OpWindow,
  OpSelect,
  OpString,
  OpInLine,
  LookDir,
  LookFile,
  LookData,
  LookMenu,
```

```
    LookMsg,
    OpSwap1;  {must be last}

  procedure InitializeLookUp;
  {initialize the TSR, check for install, init popups, and go resident}


  IMPLEMENTATION


  const
    HotKey     = $0829; {Alt-~}                     {press this key to pop up
                                                     TSR}
    TsrName    : String[9] = 'LOOKUP1.0';           {used by the InstallCheck,
                                                     InitOurPopups, and
                                                     TryToUnload procedures in
                                                     this unit}
    SwapFile1 : String[15] = 'C:\LOOKSWP1.$$$'; {swapped out application
                                                     goes here, unless enough
                                                     EMS is available}
    SwapFile2 : String[15] = 'C:\LOOKSWP2.$$$'; {ditto}

  var
    MSP     : MouseStatePtr; {mouse state pointer, OpMouse}
    MSPsize : Word;          {size of mouse buffer}



  procedure MainPop; far;
  {when the TSR is popped up by pressing the hot key, this is the code
   that is executed}

  var
    BufPtr          : Pointer; {place to save screen}
    Counter         : Word;
    f               : String;  {temporary string}
    FileWasOpened   : Boolean; {if file was never opened don't do
                                IndexBits.done}
    IoFlag          : Word;    {store IoResult return}
    OldDrive        : Char;    {swapped out program's default drive}
    OldPath         : String;  {swapped out program's default directory}
    S               : String;  {Message string}
    SaveFlag        : Boolean; {was screen saved when popping up?}
    SaveXY,SaveSL   : Word;    {saved cursor state before popping up}

  begin
    ReInitCrt;   {OpCrt}
    {don't pop up if in graphics mode}
    if not InTextMode then begin
       RingBell;   {OpCmd}
```

```
      Exit;
   end;

   {save the swapped out program's scree. It will be restored when we
    leave Lookup. The OPro TSR units do not do this for you}
   SaveFlag := True;
   if not SaveWindow(1,1,ScreenWidth,ScreenHeight,True,BufPtr) then begin
                                                                    (OpCrt}
     ShowMsg('Not enough memory to save screen'); {LookMsg}
     SaveFlag := False;
   end;
   GetCursorState(SaveXY,SaveSL); {save cursor, OpCrt}
   if MouseInstalled then begin   {OpMouse}
     {make mouse available in TSR}
     SaveMouseState(MSP,False);    {OpMouse}
     InitializeMouse;              {OpMouse}
     FullMouseWindow;              {OpMouse}
     EnableEventHandling;          {OpMouse}
   end;

   {$I-}
   {so we can return just before we exit MainPop}
   OldDrive := DefaultDrive;              {save current drive, OpDos}
   GetDir(ord(OldDrive) - 64,OldPath); {save current path, TP function}
   IoFlag := IoResult;                    {any IO problems?}
   if IoFlag <> 0 then begin
     ShowMsg('Can''t save current directory, error: '
             + Long2Str(IoFlag));                    {OpString, LookMsg}
     Halt;
   end;

   {so Lookup's data files will show up in file pick list}
   SelectDrive(LookDrive); {change to TSR's drive, OpDos}
   ChDir(LookLocation);    {change to TSR's path, TP procedure}
   IoFlag := IoResult;     {any problems?}
   if IoFlag <> 0 then begin  {change didn't work}
     ShowMsg('Can''t switch to Lookup''s directory, error: '
             + Long2Str(IoFlag));                           {OpString,
                                                             LookMsg}
     Halt;
   end;

   {$I+}

 {from here on, the code is much like that of Look.pas. The code to
  initialize the menu bar and submenus {InitMenu} is in the LookMenu
  unit}

  FileWasOpened := False;    {use this to determine whether to do
                                IndexBits.Done, LookIndx}
```

```
GlobError := 0;             {reset GlobError to none, LookGlob}
if MouseInUse then          {LookGlob}
  MouseChar := #04;         {mouse cursor (diamond)}
CurFile := '';              {no file selected yet, LookGlob}
Status := InitMenu;         {initialize Menu, LookMenu}
if Status <> 0 then begin {error numbers in documentation appendix D}
  ShowMsg('Error initializing Menu: ' + Long2Str(Status)); {OpString,
                                                           LookMsg}
  Halt;
end;

if MouseInUse then begin  {LookGlob}
  if MouseInstalled then  {OpMouse}
    with Colors do begin
      {activate mouse cursor, make it a red diamond}
      SoftMouseCursor($0000, {mouse has own software cursor}
                       (ColorMono(MouseColor, MouseMono) shl 8) +
                        Byte(MouseChar));
      {enable mouse menu support}
      MenuCommands.cpOptionsOn(cpEnableMouse); {menu sees mouse}
      HideMouse;                               {avoid mouse tracks,
                                                OpMouse}
    end;
end;

{fill in a backdrop}
TextAttr := $07; {background attribute}
TextChar := '▒'; {background design}
ClrScr;

repeat
  M.Draw;              {draw menu, OpMenu}
  if MouseInUse then {LookGlob}
    ShowMouse;         {make mouse visible, OpMouse}
  M.Process;           {process menu commands, OpMenu}
  if MouseInUse then {LookGlob}
    HideMouse;         {avoid mouse tracks, OpMouse}
  if M.GetlastCommand = ccSelect then {menu selection occurred,
                                        OpWindow, OpCmd}
    case M.MenuChoice of            {OpMenu}
      miCreate :                    {create new file, LookMenu}
        begin
          if CurFile <> '' then     {file is opened, LookGlob}
            close(BlockFile);       {close it, LookGlob}
          CurFile := '';            {no file opened indicator,
                                     LookGlob}
          M.Erase;                  {erase menu, OpMenu}
          MakeFile;                 {in unit LookFile}
          if GlobError = 0 then     {no error creating file, LookGlob}
            FileWasOpened := True   {IndexBits was initialized,
```

```
                                    LookGlob}
      else                         {error occurred}
        CurFile := '';             {no file opened, LookGlob}
      ErrorMsg;                    {display global error, if any,
                                    LookMenu}
    end;

  miSelect :                       {choose from existing files,
                                    LookMenu}
    begin
      if CurFile <> '' then        {file is open, LookGlob}
        close(BlockFile);          {close it, LookGlob}
      CurFile  := '';              {no file open, LookGlob}
      M.Erase;                     {erase menu, OpMenu}
      PickFile;                    {in LookDir unit}
      if GlobError = 0 then        {LookGlob}
        FileWasOpened := True      {IndexBits was initialized,
                                    LookGlob}
      else                         {error occurred}
        CurFile := '';             {no file opened, LookGlob}
      ErrorMsg;                    {display any global errors,
                                    LookMenu}
    end;

  miClose :                        {choose from existing files,
                                    LookMenu}
    begin
      if CurFile <> '' then begin {file is open, LookGlob}
        M.Erase;                   {erase menu, OpMenu}
        close(BlockFile);          {close open file, LookGlob}
        CurFile  := '';            {no file open, LookGlob}
      end
      else
        ShowMsg('No file chosen'); {LookMsg}
    end;

  miAdd  :                         {add records, LookMenu}
    begin
      M.Erase;                     {erase menu, OpMenu}
      if CurFile <> '' then begin {file open, LookGlob}
        EntryType   := 'A';        {tell RecordInfo what to do,
                                    LookGlob}
        RecordInfo;                {LookData}
        ErrorMsg;                  {display any global errors,
                                    LookMenu}
      end
      else
        ShowMsg('No file chosen'); {LookMsg}
    end;
```

```
miSearch :                      {search for a record, LookMenu}
  begin
    M.Erase;                    {erase menu, OpMenu}
    if CurFile <> '' then begin {file open, LookGlob}
      EntryType := 'S';         {tell RecordInfo what to do,
                                 LookGlob}
      RecordInfo;               {LookData}
      ErrorMsg;                 {display any error message,
                                 LookMenu}
    end
    else
      ShowMsg('No file chosen'); {LookMsg}
  end;

miEdit :                        {edit record, LookMenu}
  begin
    M.Erase;                    {erase menu, OpMenu}
    if CurFile <> '' then begin {file open, LookGlob}
      EntryType := 'E';         {tell RecordInfo what to do,
                                 LookGlob}
      RecordInfo;               {LookData}
      ErrorMsg;                 {display any error message,
                                 LookMenu}
    end
    else
      ShowMsg('No file chosen'); {LookMsg}
  end;

miDelete :                      {delete a previously entered
                                 record, LookMenu}
  begin
    M.Erase;                    {erase menu, OpMenu}
    if CurFile <> '' then begin {file open, LookGlob}
      EntryType := 'D';         {tell RecordInfo what to do,
                                 LookGlob}
      RecordInfo;               {LookData}
      ErrorMsg;                 {display any error message,
                                 LookMenu}
    end
    else
      ShowMsg('No file chosen'); {LookMsg}
  end;

miRemove :                      {delete file, LookMenu}
  begin
    M.Erase;                    {erase menu, OpMenu}
    if Verify('The chosen file will be deleted') then begin
                                                      {LookMsg}
      if CurFile <> '' then     {if file open, LookGlob}
        close(BlockFile);       {close it, LookGlob}
```

```
            PickFile;                  {get name of file to erase,
                                        LookDir}

            erase (BlockFile);         {erase file}
            CurFile := '';             {no file open, LookGlob}
            ErrorMsg;                  {display any global error,
                                        LookMenu}

          end;
        end;

      end;
  until M.MenuChoice = miEndProgram; {Quit submenu choice made, OpMenu,
                                      LookMenu}
  M.Erase; {erase menu, OpMenu}
  M.Done;  {remove menu from memory, OpMenu}
  if FileWasOpened then
    IndexBits.Done; {remove index buffer object, OpRoot}
  ClrScr;

{remove the braces to find out how much stack space your program uses.
 You can use the result to modify the stack value in the first line of
 Lookup.pas. The stack used value will appear when you exit the
 program.}
{
for Counter := Stacklimit to Sptr do
  if mem[sseg:Counter] <> $AA then begin
    ShowMsg('free stack space ' + Long2Str(counter - stacklimit));
    exit;
  end;
}

  {$I-}
  {return to the directory we were in when we popped up}
  SelectDrive(OldDrive); {change to default drive, OpDos}
  ChDir(OldPath);        {change to default path, TP procedure}
  IoFlag := IoResult;    {problems?}
  if IoFlag <> 0 then begin
    ShowMsg('Can''t switch back to default directory, error: '
           + Long2Str(IoFlag)); {OpString, LookMsg}
    Halt;
  end;
  {$I+}

  if MouseInstalled then begin     {OpMouse}
    {restore mouse to overlaid program}
    DisableEventHandling;          {OpMouse}
    RestoreMouseState(MSP,False);  {OpMouse}
  end;

  {restore the swapped-out application's screen}
  if SaveFlag then
```

```
    RestoreWindow(1,1,ScreenWidth,ScreenHeight,True,BufPtr); {OpCrt}
  RestoreCursorState(SaveXY,SaveSL);                         {OpCrt}

end; {exit and restore swapped-out application to memory}



procedure InstallCheck;
{abort if program already installed}
begin
  if ModuleInstalled(TsrName) then begin {OpSwap1}
    ShowMsg('LookUp already installed'); {LookMsg}
    Halt;
  end;
end;



procedure InitOurPopups;
{define the popup routine, enable popups, and install this module}
begin
  {MainPop in this unit is the procedure that runs when the TSR pops up.
   HotKey was defined at the beginning of this unit}
  if not DefinePop(HotKey, MainPop, Ptr(SSeg,SPtr)) then begin {OpSwap1}
    ShowMsg('Error defining popup procedure');                 {LookMsg}
    Halt;
  end;
  PopUpsOn;                             {enable popups, OpSwap1}
  InstallModule(TsrName,DisablePopUp); {install the module, OpSwap1}
  if MouseInstalled then begin          {OpMouse}
    {allocate the buffer used to save the state of the mouse}
    MSPsize := MouseStateBufferSize;    {OpMouse}

    {if size is 0 or > 1000, assume it is not safe to use the mouse}
    if (MSPsize = 0) or (MSPsize > 1000) then begin
      ShowMsg('This mouse driver does not support TSR functions');
                                                               {LookMsg}
      MouseInstalled := False;          {OpMouse}
    end
    else
      GetMem(MSP,MSPsize);              {reserve heap space for mouse
                                         buffer}
  end;
end;



procedure TryToUnload;
{if LookUp already loaded, try to unload it and report results}
var
```

```
  IfcP : IfcPtr; {OpSwap1}

begin
  IfcP := ModulePtrByName(TsrName); {OpSwap1}
  if IfcP = nil then begin          {OpSwap1}
    ShowMsg('LookUp not loaded, so it cannot be unloaded'); {LookMsg}
    Halt;
  end;

  {restore all vectors taken over by OpSwap's initialization code}
  RestoreAllVectors; {OpSwap1}

  {call the CmdEntryPtr for the resident copy of LookUp}
  IfcP^.CmdEntryPtr;                        {OpSwap1}
  if LongInt(IfcP^.UserData) = 1 then       {LongInt is a typecast}
    ShowMsg('LookUp successfully unloaded') {LookMsg}
  else
    ShowMsg('Unable to unload LookUp');     {LookMsg}
end;



procedure CheckCommandLine;
{check for command line parameters}
var
  S : String;

begin
  if ParamCount > 0 then begin
    S := StUpcase(ParamStr(1));        {OpString}
    if S = '/U' then
      TryToUnload                      {procedure in this unit}
    else
      ShowMsg('Unknown option ' + S); {LookMsg}
      Halt;
  end;
end;



procedure InitializeLookUp;
{initialize the TSR, check for install, init popups, go resident}
begin
  CheckCommandLine; {procedure in this unit}
  InstallCheck;     {procedure in this unit}
  InitOurPopups;    {procedure in this unit}
  ShowMsg('Going resident, <Alt> <~> to popup...'); {LookMsg}
  StayResSwap(ParagraphsToKeep + 4000, {Try to adjust this upwards if you
                                        have memory shortage problems,
                                        determines heap space available,
```

```
                                     will not pop up if too low}
           0,                        {exit code}
           SwapFile1,                {store swapped-out program here
                                      if no EMS available. Defined at
                                      beginning of unit}
           SwapFile2,                {store swapped-out program here
                                      if no EMS available. Defined at
                                      beginning of unit}
           True);                    {if True swaps current program
                                      out of memory. If false leaves
                                      current program in memory and
                                      uses ParasToKeep paragraphs for
                                      itself.}
  ShowMsg('Error going resident');   {LookMsg}
end;

end.
```

The unit is well annotated and further discussion is not required.

LookMenu.pas

```
unit LookMenu;
{menu and error routine for TSR version of lookup}


INTERFACE

uses
  LookGlob,
  LookMsg,
  OpRoot,
  OpCrt,
  OpCmd,
  OpCtrl,
  OpField,
  OpFrame,
  OpWindow,
  OpMenu;


function InitMenu : Word;
{initialize the main menu}

procedure ErrorMsg;
{display any global errors, LookGlob}


IMPLEMENTATION
```

```
function InitMenu : Word;
const
  {Frame constants}
  Frame1 = '╒╘╕╛══││';           {characters to form menu}
  Frame2 = '╤╘╤╛══││';           {characters to form submenu}
  WinOptions = wBordered         {include space for border}
             +wClear             {clear window when first displayed}
             +wUserContents;     {user will restore contents}
                                 {OpWindow}
var
  Result : String;  {store menu choice}

begin
  with M do begin {instance of Menu (OpMenu)}
    if not InitCustom( 2,2,38,2,    {position - X1,Y1,X2,Y2}
                      Colors,       {from colors.inc}
                      WinOptions,   {menu display characteristics
                                     itemized above}
                      Horizontal)   {multiple choices displayed H}
                                    {OpMenu}
                      then begin
      InitMenu := InitStatus; {function return if init failed}
      Exit;
    end;
    mnOptionsOn(mnAlphaMatch          {check for alpha matches}
               +mnSelectOnMatch       {implicit <Enter> on alpha char
                                       match}
               +mnArrowSelect         {select submenus with arrows}
               +mnAllHotSpots);       {exit on any mouse hotspot in menu
                                       system. default is no hotspots}
                                      {OpMenu}

    mnOPtionsOff(mnAllowPending       {if current submenu pulled down,
                                       right arrow will automatically
                                       cause other submenus to appear}
                +mnPopOnSelect        {erase current submenu after
                                       selection}
                +mnUseItemForTopic    {use current item for help topic}
                +mnSelectOnClick);    {accept choice and exit menu}
                                      {OpMenu}

    wFrame.SetFrameType(Frame1);      {menu frame characters, OpFrame}

    AddItem('Choose',         {menu choice}
            2,                {H position from frame edge}
            1,                {char position to use for character select}
            miChoose);        {menu choice identifier}

    AddFramedSubMenu(3,4,17,6, {submenu position - X1,Y1,X2,Y2}
                    Vertical, {submenu item orientation}
```

```
                 Frame2);  {submenu frame characters}

      AddItem('Select file', {submenu choice}
              1,             {first row}
              1,             {char position to use for character select}
              miSelect);     {menu choice identifier}

      AddItem('Create file', {submenu choice}
              2,             {second row}
              1,             {char position to use for character select}
              miCreate);     {menu choice identifier}

      AddItem('Close file',  {submenu choice}
              3,             {third row}
              1,             {char position to use for character select}
              miClose);      {menu choice identifier}

      ItemsDone;  {no more submenu items}

    AddItem('Entry',         {menu choice}
            11,              {H position from frame edge}
            1,               {char position to use for character select}
            miEntry);        {menu choice identifier}

    AddFramedSubMenu(12,4,32,5, {submenu position - X1,Y1,X2,Y2}
                     Vertical,  {submenu item orientation}
                     Frame2);   {submenu frame characters}

      AddItem('Add record', {submenu choice}
              1,            {first row}
              1,            {char position to use for character select}
              miAdd);       {menu choice identifier}

      AddItem('Search for record', {submenu choice}
              2,                   {second row}
              1,                   {char position for character select}
              miSearch);           {menu choice identifier}

      ItemsDone;  {no more submenu items}

    AddItem('Maintenance',       {menu choice}
            19,                  {H position from frame edge}
            1,                   {char position to use for character
                                  select}
            miMaintain);         {menu choice identifier}

    AddFramedSubMenu(20,4,42,6, {submenu position - X1,Y1,X2,Y2}
                     Vertical,  {submenu item orientation}
                     Frame2);   {submenu frame characters}
```

```
      AddItem('Edit record',  {submenu choice}
               1,             {first row}
               1,             {char position to use for character
                               select}
               miEdit);       {menu choice identifier}

      AddItem('Delete record', {submenu choice}
               2,              {second row}
               1,              {char position to use for character
                                select}
               miDelete);      {menu choice identifier}

      AddItem('Remove current file', {submenu choice}
               3,                    {third row}
               1,                    {char position for character
                                      select}
               miRemove);            {menu choice identifier}

      ItemsDone;  {no more submenu items}


    AddItem('Quit',     {menu choice}
             33,        {H position from frame edge}
             1,         {char position to use for character select}
             miQuit);   {menu choice identifier}

    AddFramedSubMenu(34,4,48,4, {submenu position - X1,Y1,X2,Y2}
                     Vertical,  {submenu item orientation}
                     Frame2);   {submenu frame characters}

      AddItem('End program',  {submenu choice}
               1,             {first row}
               1,             {char position to use for character
                               select}
               miEndProgram); {menu choice identifier}

      ItemsDone;  {no more submenu items}
    ItemsDone; {no more menu items}
    InitMenu := GetLastError; {function return value}
  end;
end;



procedure ErrorMsg;
{display any global errors (ListGlob)}
var
 S : String;
begin
  if GlobError <> 0 then begin        {LookGlob}
```

```
      case GlobError of
        NoRoom :                        {LookGlob}
          S := 'Unable to open file';
        FileFull :                      {LookGlob}
          S := 'No room left in file';
        OutofMemory :                   {LookGlob}
          S := 'Out of memory';
        InvalidData :                   {LookGlob}
          S := 'Invalid entry';
        FileExists :                    {LookGlob}
          S := 'File already exists, cannot overwrite';
        NoSeek :                        {LookGlob}
          S := 'Unable to position within file';
        NoRead :                        {LookGlob}
          S := 'Unable to read file';
        NoWrite :                       {LookGlob}
          S := 'Unable to write to file';
        NoFile :                        {LookGlob}
          S := 'No data files available';
      end;
      ShowMsg(S);                       {LookMsg}
      GlobError := 0;                   {reset, LookGlob}
    end;
  end;

  end.
```

These are identical to the function and procedure of the same name in Look.pas, the main program module, in Chapter 5.

Essentially, the InitMenu function initializes the menu. LookMain (MainPop) then loops through the menu, calling procedures in various units and performing operations as required, until the user selects the "End Program" choice. In the annotation, I have tried to remember to note the unit where each called procedure or function resides.

In the line

```
WinOptions = wBordered          {leave room for border}
             +wClear            {clear window when displayed}
             +wUserContents;    {user will refresh contents if required}
```

the complete list of possible options is

wBordered	Make space for window border
wClear	Clear window when it is first displayed
wSaveContents	Save the contents of the window when it is erased.
wUserContents	User will restore window contents
wSoundEffects	Use sound effects during explosions
wAltFrame	Use alternate frame type when not current

wSetMouse	Set mouse window, cursor on entry to window
wFullMouseWindow	Force to full mouse window on entry
wResizable	Can be resized and zoomed
wAllMouseEvents	Any combination of mouse buttons anywhere exits
wStoreContents	Store window contents in streams

The next procedure's last parameter,

```
if not InitCustom( 2,2,43,2,    {position - X1,Y1,X2,Y2}
                   Colors,      {from colors.inc}
                   WinOptions,  {menu display characteristics
                                 itemized above}
                   Horizontal)  {multiple choices displayed H}
                   then begin
```

can be one of the following:

Horizontal	top menu bar choices displayed horizontally
Vertical	top menu bar choices displayed vertically

In the following lines

```
mnOptionsOn(mnAlphaMatch         {check for alpha matches}
            +mnSelectOnMatch     {implicit Enter on alpha match}
            +mnArrowSelect       {select submenus with arrows}
            +mnAllHotSpots);     {exit with ccMouseSel code on any
                                  mouse hotspot. Default is no
                                  hotspots}

mnOptionsOff(mnAllowPending      {submenu stays down after passing
                                  no submenu}
             +mnPopOnSelect      {erase submenu after selection}
             +mnUseItemForTopic  {use menu choices as help topics}
             +mnSelectOnClick);  {implicit Enter on first mouse
                                  click}
```

The list of available options is

mnAllHotSpots	exit on any menu mouse hotspot (default is no hotspots)
mnAllowPending	submenu stays down after passing no submenu
mnAlphaMatch	check for alphabetic matches
mnArrowSelect	select submenus with arrow keys
mnMainHighlight	highlight alpha search characters on high-level menu
mnMainSelect	display top-level menu bar
mnMouseSupport	used by MAKEMENU

mnPopOnSelect	erase current submenu after selection
mnSelectOnClick	implicit Enter on first mouse click
mnSelectOnMatch	implicit Enter on alphabetic character match
mnUseItemForTopic	use current highlighted item for help topic

Compile Order

LookGlob.pas
LookPath.pas
LookMsg.pas
LookIndx.pas
LookSrch.pas
LookData.pas
LookFile.pas
LookDir.pas
LookMain.pas
LookMenu.pas
LookUp.pas

Operation

Load Lookup from the Dos prompt. To popup, press Control-~. You can change this key combination by changing the value of the HotKey variable in LookMain. It would also be possible to add the code to allow the user to change the HotKey value, To unload Lookup type "Lookup /U" from the Dos prompt.

14

Look Application Discussion

Adding Help

See Chapter 8, where adding help to the Loan application is discussed. You can use the same principles here.

Object Instances in LookGlob

The ESName and ESSearch entry screen object instances are designated in the variable list of LookGlob. To possibly save a bit of memory, you might move them to the units where they are initialized: the LookFile and LookSrch units, respectively.

Halts

When object initializations fail, I fall through to the Halt procedure. Perhaps you might wish to decode the error message (probably an out-of-memory error), post a suitable message to the user, and return to the main menu instead.

Flushing

When I add, modify, or delete any record, I flush the new version of the record data file (DAT) to disk by closing and reopening the applicable file. After the application was written and tested, I discovered the FlushDosBuffers function in OpDos. I noted no particular program delay using my original method so did not change the code. You might wish to do so. You will only be able to use the FlushDosBuffers function for the file of records (DAT file); the index bits use the BitSet object's Store method and need not be changed.

Loan.pas

You might wish to make it more difficult to erase a record and index file than I did when the "Remove Current File" menu choice is made. I do put up a verify message, but it could be overlooked. Perhaps you could use a special verify message in red. Or possibly you could verify again after the file to be deleted is selected from the pick list.

Different Record Parameters

As I mentioned in an earlier chapter, all the record data files and index files are the same size and use the same record format and quantity, because BlockSize (LookGlob unit), HeaderSize (LookGlob unit), and the memo editor window width (LookData unit) are constants. It would not be very difficult to change these to global variables and store them in a file—perhaps as an additional stream item in the index file, reserve the first record in the data file, or use a third file. The first scheme would require much less change in the code than the second. Using a third file is not very elegant but would be the simplest solution by far. You would only have to store the three numeric variables. Whenever a Select menu choice is made, the three global variable values would be altered to the stored values. When a new record file is created, you would have to ask the user for these three values, perhaps offering the values I use as the defaults and verifying the value by setting a valid range in the data entry field. Store the three supplied values when you create the record and index files. See the comments in the LookGlob unit for the maximum and minimum values. Remember, these values cannot be altered once the file has been created.

Record Data File Size

After completing the program, I considered changing the file creation to not include all the blank records. You would then let the program append the records to the file as required. The only advantage to doing this is that the file would initially take up less disk space and would perhaps continue to do so throughout its life if all the record space was never used. I think the program would *almost* append records as required as it is written, but I'm not sure. You would definitely have a problem when the program tried to load a nonexistent record, which I believe would occur in several places, probably all in the code that adds a new record and modifies an existing record. For a starter, modify the PutRecord procedure in the LookData unit as required. When you create the DAT file, just save one blank record instead of all of them. Then try adding, modifying, and deleting records and see what happens. When you get an error, you'll find a spot in the code that needs modification. If you delete a record at the end of the file, or modify it when there is room for the edited version of the record between it and the beginning of the file, you would end up with a trailing blank record. I doubt it would be worth truncating (Truncate procedure) the file to get rid of it.

The advantage of creating a file with room for all the records is that if you de-frag your disk before you create the new file, all the records will be adjacent on the disk, making the searches faster.

Search Extensions

In some text databases, when you search for two strings using AND, you can designate that the two strings must be within a given number of words of each other. I suspect this might be rather difficult to implement and might be overkill in this application. Still, the feature might be important for some types of users. I guess it would depend on how many records might fit the search criteria and how large the records were. At any rate, it would be an interesting project.

Another possibility would be to add an XOR operator to the AND and OR operators already available. As you are probably aware, XOR means that one or the other of the strings must be present, but not both. Right off hand, I can't think of a use for such a feature, but perhaps you can.

TSR Changes

You might wish to change the TSR version of the program to include the following:

1. Save the cursor of the overwritten program in case it is not standard and restore it when the TSR exits.
2. Save the screen size of the overwritten program and replace it with an 80 × 25 standard screen, restoring it when the TSR exits.
3. Do not pop up or take precautions if SideKick has been loaded first.

These additions would go at the beginning and end of the MainPop procedure in the LookMain.pas unit. You will see where the screen and mouse have been saved and are restored. The additions would go here. Look at the InitializePopUp procedure in the Deskmain.pas unit and the Smacs program of the OPro-provided examples for additions of this type and more ideas along this line.

15

Useful Utilities

These two little programs have nothing to do with OOP, but I wrote them in the course of putting together this book and found them useful. Maybe you will too.

Since they are so useful, I used several OPro units, as well as LoanMsg from the Loan program. You could substitute writeln() for ShowMsg() if you wished.

Check

This quick-and-dirty little utility is used to be sure that every left bracket, brace, and parenthesis has a mate, and vice versa. I found that the TP compiler ignores a missing right brace, considering the next right brace that comes along the other half of the pair and anything in between a comment, including left braces! This can result in inadvertently making a program line a comment, especially if your editor gives little warning when it cuts off the end of a line.

Here's the code:

```
program Check;

uses
 OpCrt,
 OpString,
 LookMsg;
```

```
const
  LeftBrace    = '{';
  RightBrace   = '}';
  LeftBracket  = '[';
  RightBracket = ']';
  LeftParen    = '(';
  RightParen   = ')';

var
  TextFile : Text;
  Counter,LBC,RBC,LP,RP,LBR,RBR : Integer;
  S : String;

begin
  LBC := 0;  {counter for left brace}
  RBC := 0;  {counter for right brace}
  LBR := 0;  {counter for left bracket}
  RBR := 0;  {counter for right bracket}
  LP  := 0;  {counter for left parenthesis}
  RP  := 0;  {counter for right parenthesis}
  S   := ''; {name of file to check}

  Clrscr;
  S := Paramstr(1); {first parameter in command line}
  if length(S) = 0 then begin
    ShowMsg('Enter full file name to be checked after program name');
    Halt;
  end;
  Assign(TextFile,S);
  {$I-}
  reset(TextFile);
  if IoResult <> 0 then begin
    ShowMsg('File not found');
    Halt;
  end;
  while not EOF(TextFile) do begin
    readln(TextFile,S);
    if IoResult <> 0 then begin
      ShowMsg('File read error');
      Halt;
    end;
    writeln(S);
    S := Trim(S);                              {get rid of leading and
                                                trailing white space}
    if length(S) <> 0 then begin               {skip blank lines}
      for Counter := 1 to length(S) do begin {step through line by
                                                character}
        case S[Counter] of
          LeftBrace    : Inc(LBC);
          RightBrace   : Inc(RBC);
```

```
          LeftBracket  : Inc(LBR);
          RightBracket : Inc(RBR);
          LeftParen    : Inc(LP);
          RightParen   : Inc(RP);
        end;
      end;
    end;
  end;
  {$I+}
  writeln('Left brace: '    + Long2Str(LBC));
  writeln('Right brace: '   + Long2Str(RBC));
  writeln('Left bracket: '  + Long2Str(LBR));
  writeln('Right bracket: ' + Long2Str(RBR));
  writeln('Left parens: '   + Long2Str(LP));
  writeln('Right parens: '  + Long2Str(RP));
  if LBC <> RBC then
    ShowMsg('Braces mismatched');
  if LBR <> RBR then
    ShowMsg('Brackets mismatched');
  if LP <> RP then
    ShowMsg('Parens mismatched');
  close(TextFile);
end.
```

Configur.pas

There are times when you wish to quickly switch from one set of Autoexec.bat Config.sys pairs to another. This little utility will permit as many pairs as you wish. They are stored in an ASCII file you can create and maintain with any editor. The file's name is Configur.dat. Each pair is provided with a unique name, such as "windows," "bare," "network." You choose the name, of course. There is no limit on the name length except Pascal string and command line parameter length. You can optionally reboot after creating a new autoexec.bat and config.sys pair. I prefer to take a quick look at the files to be sure all went well first.

Configure.dat Data File

Here is a sample Configur.dat file. I used a few sets from mine.

First of all, note that each Configure command line begins with a "/".

Each set begins with the command character, followed by the name of the set in uppercase. Thus

```
/ NETWORK
```

for the network set. After the set's lines intended for the autoexec.bat and config.sys files, enter the line

```
/ END NETWORK
```

To indicate the beginning of the lines meant for the Autoexec.bat file, preface the lines with

```
/ AUTOEXEC.BAT
```

End the lines meant for the Autoexec.bat file with

```
/ END
```

To indicate the beginning of the lines meant for the Config.sys file, preface the lines with

```
/ CONFIG.SYS
```

End the lines meant for the Config.sys file with

```
/ END
```

The

```
/ END OF FILE CONFIG.DAT
```

at the end of the Configur.dat file is not required. To automatically reboot the computer after creating the new autoexec.bat and config.sys files, place the line

```
/ BOOT
```

anywhere between "/ CONFIG.SYS" and "/ END" or between "/ AUTOEXEC.BAT" and "/ END" in the desired set.

Here is a sample file with four sets:

```
/ NETWORK
/ AUTOEXEC.BAT
rem NETWORK version
path=c:\qemm;c:\;e:\dos;c:\nc;d:\nu;c:\brief;f:\poly;g:\td;e:\foxmu;
  e:\dbiv;e:\scrm;g:\tp;d:\pckwik
set bpath=;c:\brief\macros;c:\brief\dbrief;c:\brief\qflight
set quiet=c:\brief\qflight
set bhelp=c:\brief\help
set bfile=c:\brief\state.rst
set bbackup=.
set bcbas="qb %%s\;"
set bcasm="masm %%s\;"
set bcpas="tpc /$R+ /UG:\OPRO %%s"
set bpackages=c:t;bas,asm,pas:r
set bflags=-ai60k2Mprt -mKBK -mrestore -mdbrief -Dega -mqfstart
set btmp=\
set INCLUDE=D:\MSC\INCLUDE;%INCLUDE%
set LIB=D:\MSC\LIB;%LIB%
set TMP=%TMP%
set INIT=D:\MSC\SOURCE\ME\INI;%INIT%
set mace=i:\mace
```

```
c:\qemm\loadhi share /F:5000 /L:250
c:\qemm\loadhi mouse
D:\PCKWIK\SUPERPCK /L:5000 /R:1000
D:\PCKWIK\PCKSPL
call c:\maceback
h:
cd \net30
net30
cd \
c:
unyuck
prompt $e[37;44;1m$p$g$e[33;44;1m
c:\qemm\loadhi log
rem "Remember to run format protection programs"
pause
nc
/ END

/ CONFIG.SYS
DEVICE=C:\QEMM\QEMM386.SYS RAM DMA=128
DEVICE=C:\QEMM\LOADHI.SYS DMDRVR.BIN
FCBS=16,8
FILES=100
buffers = 20
STACKS=64,128
break = on
device=c:\qemm\loadhi.sys dasddrvr.sys
device=c:\qemm\loadhi.sys ansi.sys
lastdrive=z
shell = c:\command.com c:\ /p /e:1600
device=h:\net30\n30dev.sys
/ END
/ END NETWORK



/ BARE
/ AUTOEXEC.BAT
rem BARE version
path=c:\;e:\dos;c:\nc;d:\nu;c:\brief;f:\poly;g:\td;e:\foxmu;f:\hs;
  e:\dbiv;e:\scrm;g:\tp;d:\pckwik
UNYUCK
rem "Remember to run format protection programs"
pause
nc
/ END

/ CONFIG.SYS
DEVICE=DMDRVR.BIN
files = 40
```

```
buffers = 40
device=dasddrvr.sys
device=ansi.sys
lastdrive=z
/ END
/ END BARE



/ WINDOWS
/ AUTOEXEC.BAT
rem WINDOWS version
c:\qemm\loadhi c:\qemm\buffers=20
path=c:\;e:\dos;c:\nc;d:\nu;c:\brief;f:\poly;g:\td;e:\foxmu;e:\dbiv;
  i:\windows;e:\scrm;g:\tp;i:\winword;\d:\pckwik
d:\pckwik\superpck /E
unyuck
rem "Remember to run format protection programs"
pause
i:
cd \windows
nc
/ END

/ CONFIG.SYS
DEVICE=C:\QEMM\QEMM386.SYS FRAME=NONE RAM DMA=128
device=c:\qemm\loadhi.sys dmdrvr.bin
lastdrive=z
files = 40
buffers = 1
device=c:\qemm\loadhi.sys dasddrvr.sys
device=d:\pckwik\pckwin.sys
/ END
/ END WINDOWS



/ REGULAR
/ AUTOEXEC.BAT
rem REGULAR version
path=c:\;e:\dos;c:\nc;d:\nu;c:\brief;f:\poly;g:\td;e:\foxmu;e:\dbiv;
  e:\scrm;g:\tp;d:\pckwik
set bpath=;c:\brief\macros;c:\brief\dbrief;c:\brief\qflight
set quiet=c:\brief\qflight
set bhelp=c:\brief\help
set bfile=c:\brief\state.rst
set bbackup=.
set bcbas="qb %%s\;"
set bcasm="masm %%s\;"
set bcpas="tpc /$R+ /UG:\OPRO %%s"
```

```
set bpackages=c:t;bas,asm,pas:r
set bflags=-ai60k2Mprt -mKBK -mrestore -mdbrief -Dega -mqfstart
set btmp=\
set INCLUDE=D:\MSC\INCLUDE;%INCLUDE%
set LIB=D:\MSC\LIB;%LIB%
set TMP=%TMP%
set INIT=D:\MSC\SOURCE\ME\INI;%INIT%
set mace=i:\mace
mouse
unyuck
prompt $e[37;44;1m$p$g$e[33;44;1m
log
rem call d:\pckwik\poweron
rem "Remember to run format protection programs"
pause
nc
/ END

/ CONFIG.SYS
device=dmdrvr.bin
lastdrive=z
buffers = 40
files = 40
break = on
device = ansi.sys
device = dasddrvr.sys
shell = c:\command.com c:\ /p /e:1600
/ END
/ END REGULAR

/ END OF FILE CONFIG.DAT
```

In the file, the "path" commands are shown on two lines. This is just to make them easy to read. In the real file, they must be on a single line.

Congure.pas File

Here is the program code:

```
program configur;

{$V-}
{$R+}

uses
  OpCrt,
  OpString,
  OpInLine,
  LoanMsg;
```

```
var
  IoFlag : Word;
  Found : Boolean;
  AutoexecFlag : Boolean; {creating autoexec if True}
  ConfigFlag : Boolean;   {creating config.sys if True}
  RebootFlag : Boolean;   {reboot if True}
  CDat : Text;            {Configur.dat file variable}
  Name : String;          {name of set}
  NameOnly : String;      {upper case Name}
  S : String;             {line from configur.dat}
  CSys : Text;            {Config.sys file variable}
  ABat : Text;            {autoexec.bat file variable}
  Done : Boolean;


begin
  ClrScr;
  Name := ParamStr(1); {first command line parameter}
  if length(Name) = 0 then begin {no name supplied}
    ShowMsg('Enter name of Configur set to use after program name');
    Halt;
  end;
  NameOnly := StUpCase(TrimSpaces(Name)); {upper case and no spaces}
  Name := '/ ' + NameOnly; {name format in Configur.dat file}
  RebootFlag := False;     {no reboot command yet}
  AutoexecFlag := False;   {not creating autoexec file}
  Found := False;          {set name not found}
  ConfigFlag := False;     {not creating config.sys file}
  {$I-}
  assign(CDat,'CONFIGUR.DAT');
  reset(CDat);
  IoFlag := IoResult;
  if IoFlag <> 0 then begin
    ShowMsg('Reset CDat error. IoResult is: ' + Long2Str(IoFlag));
    Halt;
  end;
  Done := False;
  while not EOF(CDat) and not Done and (length(NameOnly) > 0) do begin
    readln(CDat,S); {get line from configur.dat}
    IoFlag := IoResult;
    if IoFlag <> 0 then begin
      ShowMsg('Readln CDat error. IoResult is: ' + Long2Str(IoFlag));
      Halt;
    end;
    S := TrimSpaces(S); {remove leading and trailing white space}
    if (length(S) > 0) and (S[1] = '/') then begin {not blank and
                                                     potential configure
                                                     command line}
      if StUpCase(S) = Name then begin              {correct set?}
        while not EOF(CDat) and not Done do begin   {yes}
          Found := True;                            {found the set}
```

```
readln(CDat,S);                          {next data line}
IoFlag := IoResult;
if IoFlag <> 0 then begin
  ShowMsg('Readln CDat error. IoResult is: '
          + Long2Str(IoFlag));
  Halt;
end;
if StUpCase(TrimSpaces(S)) = '/ CONFIG.SYS' then begin
  assign(CSys,'CONFIG.SYS');             {start config file}
  rewrite(CSys);
  IoFlag := IoResult;
  if IoFlag <> 0 then begin
    ShowMsg('Rewrite CSys error. IoResult is: '
            + Long2Str(IoFlag));
    Halt;
  end;
  ConfigFlag := True;                    {writing config file}
  writeln('Writing Config.sys');
  while not EOF(CDat) and ConfigFlag do begin {while in
                                           config's lines}
    readln(CDat,S);                      {next data line}
    IoFlag := IoResult;
    if IoFlag <> 0 then begin
      ShowMsg('Readln CDat error. IoResult is: '
              + Long2Str(IoFlag));
      Halt;
    end;
    S := TrimSpaces(S);                  {get rid of white space}
    if StUpCase(S) = '/ BOOT' then       {set reboot flag}
      RebootFlag := True;
    if StUpCase(S) = '/ END' then        {config done}
      ConfigFlag := False;               {set config done flag}
    {not command line, must be config line}
    if (length(S) > 0) and (S[1] <> '/') then begin
      Writeln(CSys,S);                   {send to config file}
      IoFlag := IoResult;
      if IoFlag <> 0 then begin
        ShowMsg('Writeln CSys error. IoResult is: '
                + Long2Str(IoFlag));
        Halt;
      end;
    end;
  end;
  close(CSys);
  ConfigFlag := False; {in case of EOF}
end;
if StUpCase(TrimSpaces(S)) = '/ AUTOEXEC.BAT' then begin
  assign(ABat,'AUTOEXEC.BAT');           {start autoexec file}
  rewrite(ABat);
  IoFlag := IoResult;
```

```
          if IoFlag <> 0 then begin
            ShowMsg('Rewrite ABat error. IoResult is: '
                     + Long2Str(IoFlag));
            Halt;
          end;
          AutoexecFlag := True;                 {writing autoexec file}
          writeln('Writing Autoexec.bat');
          while not EOF(CDat) and AutoexecFlag do begin {while in
                                                          autoexec's
                                                          lines}
            readln(CDat,S);                              {next data
                                                          line}
            IoFlag := IoResult;
            if IoFlag <> 0 then begin
              ShowMsg('Readln CDat error. IoResult is: '
                       + Long2Str(IoFlag));
              Halt;
            end;
            S := TrimSpaces(S);               {get rid of white space}
            if StUpCase(S) = '/ BOOT' then    {set reboot flag}
              RebootFlag := True;
            if StUpCase(S) = '/ END' then
              AutoexecFlag := False;          {autoexec done}
            {not command line, must be autoexec line}
            if (length(S) > 0) and (S[1] <> '/') then begin
              Writeln(ABat,S);
              IoFlag := IoResult;
              if IoFlag <> 0 then begin
                ShowMsg('Writeln ABat error. IoResult is: '
                         + Long2Str(IoFlag));
                Halt;
              end;
            end;
          end;
          close(ABat);
          AutoexecFlag := False; {in case of EOF}
        end;
        if StUpCase(TrimSpaces(S)) = '/ END ' + NameOnly then
          Done := True;  {current set is completed}
      end;
    end;
  end
end;
{autoexec and cinfig files created}
{following are in case '/ END' was not read}
if ConfigFlag then
  close(CSys); {config file}
if AutoexecFlag then
  close(ABat); {autoexec file}
close(CDat);   {data file}
```

```
    if length(NameOnly) > 0 then begin
      if not Found then
        ShowMsg('Name ' + NameOnly + ' not found')
      else begin
        if RebootFlag then
          Reboot;
      end;
    end;
  end.
```

Appendix A

OPro Methods, Functions, and Procedures

Here is a list of all the methods in OPro. This is a modification of the Index file that is supplied with OPro version 1.10. As you can see, the name of the method, the unit, and the object (if applicable) is supplied.

Method	Unit	Object
AbsBCD	OpBCD	———
Activate	OpWindow	VirtScreen
ActivateWrite	OpWindow	StackWindow
ActiveChild	OpWindow	StackWindow
ActiveFramePtr	OpWindow	RawWindow
ActiveItemPtr	OpMenu	Menu
ActiveListPtr	OpMenu	Menu
ActiveSubPtr	OpMenu	Menu
ActiveWinPtr	OpMenu	Menu
Add	OpRoot	StringDict
Add	OpRoot	StringSet
AddAnyHeader	OpFrame	Frame
AddArrayField	OpEntry	EntryScreen
AddBackSlash	OpString	———
AddBCD	OpBCD	———
AddBcdField	OpEntry	EntryScreen
AddBooleanField	OpEntry	EntryScreen
AddBooleanField	OpForm	PrintedForm

AddBox	OpForm	PrintedForm
AddBoxField	OpSelect	AbstractSelector
AddBoxFieldCustom	OpSelect	AbstractSelector
AddByteField	OpEntry	EntryScreen
AddByteField	OpForm	PrintedForm
AddCenteredTextField	OpSelect	AbstractSelector
AddCharField	OpEntry	EntryScreen
AddCharField	OpForm	PrintedForm
AddCheckBox	OpDialog	DialogBox
AddCheckBoxAt	OpDialog	DialogBox
AddCheckBoxes	OpDialog	DialogBox
AddChild	OpWindow	StackWindow
AddChoiceField	OpEntry	EntryScreen
AddCommand	OpCmd	CommandProcessor
AddCompField	OpEntry	EntryScreen
AddCustomHeader	OpFrame	Frame
AddCustomHeader	OpMenu	Menu
AddCustomScrollBar	OpFrame	Frame
AddCustomShadow	OpFrame	Frame
AddDateField	OpEntry	EntryScreen
AddDateField	OpForm	PrintedForm
AddDateStField	OpEntry	EntryScreen
AddDblField	OpEntry	EntryScreen
AddDirective	OpForm	PrintedForm
AddEditControl	OpDialog	DialogBox
AddExtField	OpEntry	EntryScreen
AddField	OpSelect	Selector
AddForm	OpForm	Report
AddFramedSubMenu	OpMenu	Menu
AddHeader	OpFrame	Frame
AddHeader	OpMenu	Menu
AddHeaderColor	OpFrame	Frame
AddHeaderColor	OpMenu	Menu
AddHotBar	OpFrame	Frame
AddHotHeader	OpFrame	Frame
AddHotKey	OpSwap1	———
AddHotKey	OpTsr	———
AddHotRegion	OpFrame	Frame
AddHotSpot	OpFrame	Frame
AddIntField	OpEntry	EntryScreen
AddIntField	OpForm	PrintedForm
AddItem	OpMenu	Menu
AddItemHelp	OpMenu	Menu
AddItemHelpPtr	OpMenu	Menu
AddItemPtr	OpMenu	Menu
AddLine	OpForm	PrintedForm

AddLineField	OpSelect	AbstractSelector
AddLineFieldCustom	OpSelect	AbstractSelector
AddLongField	OpEntry	EntryScreen
AddLongField	OpForm	PrintedForm
AddLongToPtr	OpInline	———
AddMaskHeader	OpDir	DirList
AddMoreHeader	OpPick	PickList
AddMoreHelpHeader	OpHelp	AbstractHelpWindow
AddMultiLineField	OpEntry	EntryScreen
AddNestedField	OpEntry	EntryScreen
AddNestedStringField	OpEntry	EntryScreen
AddNumericBcdField	OpEntry	EntryScreen
AddNumericByteField	OpEntry	EntryScreen
AddNumericCompField	OpEntry	EntryScreen
AddNumericDblField	OpEntry	EntryScreen
AddNumericExtField	OpEntry	EntryScreen
AddNumericIntField	OpEntry	EntryScreen
AddNumericLongField	OpEntry	EntryScreen
AddNumericRealField	OpEntry	EntryScreen
AddNumericSglField	OpEntry	EntryScreen
AddNumericShortField	OpEntry	EntryScreen
AddNumericWordField	OpEntry	EntryScreen
AddPickStringField	OpEntry	EntryScreen
AddPrintMode	OpPrint	Printer
AddPushButton	OpDialog	DialogBox
AddRadioButton	OpDialog	DialogBox
AddRadioButtonAt	OpDialog	DialogBox
AddRadioButtons	OpDialog	DialogBox
AddRealField	OpEntry	EntryScreen
AddRealField	OpForm	PrintedForm
AddRejectString	OpDir	DirList
AddScrollBar	OpFrame	Frame
AddSearchHeader	OpPick	PickList
AddSecondaryCommand	OpCmd	CommandProcessor
AddSeparator	OpMenu	Menu
AddSeparatorColor	OpMenu	Menu
AddSglField	OpEntry	EntryScreen
AddShaded	OpForm	PrintedForm
AddShadow	OpFrame	Frame
AddShadow	OpMenu	Menu
AddShadowColor	OpFrame	Frame
AddShadowColor	OpMenu	Menu
AddShadowedBoxField	OpSelect	AbstractSelector
AddShadowedBoxFieldCustom	OpSelect	AbstractSelector
AddShadows	OpMenu	Menu
AddShortField	OpEntry	EntryScreen

AddShortField	OpForm	PrintedForm
AddSimpleBcdField	OpEntry	EntryScreen
AddSimpleBooleanField	OpEntry	EntryScreen
AddSimpleByteField	OpEntry	EntryScreen
AddSimpleCharField	OpEntry	EntryScreen
AddSimpleCompField	OpEntry	EntryScreen
AddSimpleDblField	OpEntry	EntryScreen
AddSimpleEditControl	OpDialog	DialogBox
AddSimpleExtField	OpEntry	EntryScreen
AddSimpleIntField	OpEntry	EntryScreen
AddSimpleLongField	OpEntry	EntryScreen
AddSimpleRealField	OpEntry	EntryScreen
AddSimpleSglField	OpEntry	EntryScreen
AddSimpleShortField	OpEntry	EntryScreen
AddSimpleStringField	OpEntry	EntryScreen
AddSimpleWordField	OpEntry	EntryScreen
AddSimpleYesNoField	OpEntry	EntryScreen
AddSpanHeader	OpFrame	Frame
AddSpanHeaderColor	OpFrame	Frame
AddString	OpRoot	StringArray
AddStringField	OpEntry	EntryScreen
AddStringField	OpForm	PrintedForm
AddSubMenu	OpMenu	Menu
AddSubMenuCustom	OpMenu	Menu
AddTextField	OpForm	PrintedForm
AddTextField	OpSelect	AbstractSelector
AddTextFieldCustom	OpSelect	AbstractSelector
AddTextFieldDeluxe	OpSelect	AbstractSelector
AddTimeField	OpEntry	EntryScreen
AddTimeField	OpForm	PrintedForm
AddTopicHeader	OpHelp	AbstractHelpWindow
AddUserEditControl	OpDialog	DialogBox
AddUserField	OpEntry	EntryScreen
AddWindowControl	OpDialog	DialogBox
AddWindowField	OpEntry	EntryScreen
AddWordField	OpEntry	EntryScreen
AddWordField	OpForm	PrintedForm
AddWordToPtr	OpInline	———
AddYesNoField	OpEntry	EntryScreen
AddYesNoField	OpForm	PrintedForm
Adjust	OpFrame	ScreenRect
AdjustFrame	OpFrame	Frame
AdjustFrameCoords	OpWindow	RawWindow
AdjustWindow	OpWindow	RawWindow
AdvanceLine	OpPrint	Printer
AdvanceSingleLine	OpPrint	Printer

AllFormat	OpDir	———
Alloc	OpFrame	ScreenRect
Alloc	OpWindow	VirtScreen
AllocateEmsPages	OpEms	———
AllocateMacro	OpMacro	———
AllocateScreen	OpEntry	ScrollingEntryScreen
AllocateScreen	OpSelect	ScrollingSelector
AllocateSelectSet	OpPick	PickList
AllocateStack	OpInt	———
AllocateStack	OpSwap1	———
AltFramePtr	OpWindow	RawWindow
Append	OpRoot	DoubleList
Append	OpRoot	SingleList
ArcTanBCD	OpBCD	———
Array2Str	OpInline	———
ArrayDimensions	OpLarray	AbstractArray
Asc2Str	OpAsciiz	———
AscCenter	OpAsciiz	———
AscCenterCh	OpAsciiz	———
AscCharStr	OpAsciiz	———
AscFromHeap	OpAsciiz	———
AscLeftPad	OpAsciiz	———
AscLeftPadCh	OpAsciiz	———
AscLocase	OpAsciiz	———
AscPad	OpAsciiz	———
AscPadCh	OpAsciiz	———
AscToHeap	OpAsciiz	———
AscTrim	OpAsciiz	———
AscTrimLead	OpAsciiz	———
AscTrimTrail	OpAsciiz	———
AscUpcase	OpAsciiz	———
AssignMacroName	OpMacro	———
AssignNumber	OpWindow	StackWindow
AssignPrnObject	OpPrnLow	———
AttributeSupported	OpEms	———
AvailableEntries	OpRoot	Library
BCDtoReal	OpBCD	———
BinaryB	OpString	———
BinaryL	OpString	———
BinaryW	OpString	———
BiosPrinterStream	OpPrnLow	———
BitIsSet	OpRoot	BitSet
BitSetStream	OpRoot	———
BitsSet	OpRoot	BitSet
BlockCursor	OpCrt	———
BlockMouseCursor	OpMouse	———

BMMakeTable	OpString	———
BMSearch	OpString	———
BMSearchUC	OpString	———
brOptionsAreOn	OpBrowse	Browser
brOptionsOff	OpBrowse	Browser
brOptionsOn	OpBrowse	Browser
BrowserStream	OpBrowse	———
BrowseStatus	OpBrowse	———
BufSize	OpFrame	ScreenRect
ByteFlagIsSet	OpInline	———
CallOldIsr	OpInline	———
CallPrnStatus	OpPrnLow	———
CancelAllPrintFiles	OpDos	———
CancelPrintFile	OpDos	———
Center	OpString	———
CenterCh	OpString	———
ChainInt	OpInt	———
ChangeAllScrollBars	OpWindow	RawWindow
ChangeAttribute	OpCrt	———
ChangeCommandHandler	OpPick	PickList
ChangeConversion	OpDialog	DialogBox
ChangeConversion	OpEntry	EntryScreen
ChangeConversion	OpForm	PrintedForm
ChangeCtrlAttr	OpSelect	AbstractSelector
ChangeDecimalChar	OpAbsFld	———
ChangeDirectory	OpDir	DirList
ChangeDisplayPos	OpMenu	MenuItemNode
ChangeFieldAttr	OpSelect	AbstractSelector
ChangeHeader	OpWindow	RawWindow
ChangeHeaderAttr	OpFrame	Frame
ChangeHeaderString	OpFrame	Frame
ChangeHelp	OpMenu	MenuItemNode
ChangeHidden	OpSelect	AbstractSelector
ChangeHotHeader	OpFrame	Frame
ChangeHotKey	OpSwap1	———
ChangeHotKey	OpTsr	———
ChangeInvisibility	OpSelect	AbstractSelector
ChangeItemWidth	OpPick	PickList
ChangeKey	OpMenu	MenuItemNode
ChangeName	OpMenu	MenuItemNode
ChangeNumItems	OpPick	PickList
ChangeOrientation	OpPick	PickList
ChangePromptAttr	OpSelect	AbstractSelector
ChangeProtectedFieldAttr	OpSelect	AbstractSelector
ChangeProtectedPromptAttr	OpSelect	AbstractSelector
ChangeProtection	OpSelect	AbstractSelector

ChangeRange	OpEntry	EntryScreen
ChangeRequired	OpEntry	EntryScreen
ChangeScrollBar	OpWindow	RawWindow
ChangeSelectedFieldAttr	OpSelect	AbstractSelector
ChangeSelectedPromptAttr	OpSelect	AbstractSelector
ChangeSelectPos	OpMenu	MenuItemNode
ChangeStringProc	OpPick	PickList
ChangeSubPtr	OpMenu	MenuItemNode
ChangeValidation	OpDialog	DialogBox
ChangeValidation	OpEntry	EntryScreen
CharStr	OpString	————
CharToMacro	OpMacro	————
CharToMacro	OpReplay	————
CharXlat	OpPrnLow	BasePrinter
CheckForConflict	OpCmd	CommandProcessor
CheckKbd	OpCrt	————
ChildIndex	OpWindow	StackWindow
ChildListPtr	OpWindow	StackWindow
ChildPtr	OpWindow	StackWindow
CircularListStream	OpRoot	————
ClassifyCursorType	OpCrt	————
ClassifyError	OpWindow	CommandWindow
CleanPathName	OpString	————
Clear	OpFrame	ScreenRect
Clear	OpRoot	PointerStack
Clear	OpRoot	StaticQueue
Clear	OpRoot	StringArray
Clear	OpRoot	StringDict
Clear	OpWindow	RawWindow
Clear	OpWindow	VirtScreen
ClearA	OpLarray	AbstractArray
ClearAll	OpRoot	BitSet
ClearBit	OpRoot	BitSet
ClearByteFlag	OpInline	————
ClearContents	OpWindow	RawWindow
ClearErrors	OpFrame	AbstractFrame
ClearErrors	OpWindow	AbstractWindow
ClearFlag	OpInline	————
ClearLongFlag	OpInline	————
ClearMacros	OpMacro	————
ClearMouseEvents	OpDrag	DragProcessor
ClearPage	OpCrt	————
ClearRejectStrings	OpDir	DirList
ClearSelected	OpPick	PickList
ClearWindow	OpCrt	————
ClearXlatCharTable	OpPrnLow	BasePrinter

Close	OpRoot	DosIdStream
CloseFile	OpBrowse	Browser
CodeVerRegistered	OpRoot	IdStream
ColorMono	OpCrt	———
CommandProcessorStream	OpCmd	———
CommandStringPending	OpCmd	CommandProcessor
CommandWindowStream	OpWindow	———
CompareLetterSets	OpString	———
CompAsc	OpAsciiz	———
CompleteItemString	OpPick	PickList
CompString	OpString	———
CompStruct	OpString	———
CompUCAsc	OpAsciiz	———
CompUCString	OpString	———
ConcatAsc	OpAsciiz	———
ConcatStr	OpAsciiz	———
ConflictsFound	OpCmd	CommandPacker
ControlBit	OpRoot	BitSet
Convert	OpForm	PrintField
Coordinates	OpFrame	Frame
Coordinates	OpFrame	ScreenRect
Coordinates	OpWindow	RawWindow
CopyAsc	OpAsciiz	———
CopyEnv	OpDos	———
CopyFile	OpDos	———
CopyFromScreen	OpFrame	ScreenRect
CopyFromScreen	OpWindow	VirtScreen
CopyFromWindow	OpWindow	VirtScreen
CopyPartToScreen	OpFrame	ScreenRect
CopyToScreen	OpFrame	ScreenRect
CopyToScreen	OpWindow	VirtScreen
CopyToWindow	OpWindow	VirtScreen
CosBCD	OpBCD	———
cpGetHelp	OpCmd	CommandProcessor
cpGetKey	OpCmd	CommandProcessor
cpGetKey	OpDrag	DragProcessor
cpKeyPressed	OpCmd	CommandProcessor
cpKeyPressed	OpDrag	DragProcessor
cpOptionsAreOn	OpCmd	CommandProcessor
cpOptionsOff	OpCmd	CommandProcessor
cpOptionsOn	OpCmd	CommandProcessor
cpUserHook	OpCmd	CommandProcessor
Create	OpRoot	Library
CurrentEntries	OpRoot	Library
CurrentEnv	OpDos	———
CurrentFieldModified	OpEntry	EntryScreen

CurrentFileName	OpBrowse	Browser
CurrentItem	OpMenu	Menu
CurrentTime	OpDate	————
CurrentTimeString	OpDate	————
CurrentTopic	OpHelp	AbstractHelpWindow
CurrentXrefTopic	OpHelp	AbstractHelpWindow
CursorEndLine	OpCrt	————
CursorInWindow	OpWindow	RawWindow
CursorStartLine	OpCrt	————
CursorTypeSL	OpCrt	————
CurUserValue	OpFrame	Frame
DataProductsRegister	OpDevice	————
DateDiff	OpDate	————
DateStringToDate	OpDate	————
DateStringToDMY	OpDate	————
DateTimeDiff	OpDate	————
DateToDateString	OpDate	————
DateToDMY	OpDate	————
DateToSortString	OpDate	————
DayOfWeek	OpDate	————
DayOfWeekDMY	OpDate	————
DaysInMonth	OpDate	————
dcOptionsAreOn	OpCtrl	Control
dcOptionsOff	OpCtrl	Control
dcOptionsOn	OpCtrl	Control
Deactivate	OpWindow	VirtScreen
DeactivateWrite	OpWindow	StackWindow
DeallocateEmsHandle	OpEms	————
DeallocateMacro	OpMacro	————
DcallocatcStack	OpInt	————
DeallocateStack	OpSwap1	————
DecTime	OpDate	————
DefaultDrive	OpDos	————
DefaultErrorProc	OpCmd	————
DefaultExtension	OpString	————
DefaultItem	OpMenu	Menu
DefaultPath	OpMenu	Menu
DefaultTopicMatch	OpHelp	————
DefaultXlatCharTable	OpPrnLow	————
DefineMacro	OpMacro	————
DefinePop	OpSwap1	————
DefinePop	OpTsr	————
DefinePopProc	OpTsr	————
DelayCalibrate	OpCrt	————
Delete	OpRoot	SingleList
DeleteAsc	OpAsciiz	————

DeletedEntries	OpRoot	Library
DeleteEntry	OpRoot	Library
DeletePop	OpTsr	———
DeletePopProc	OpTsr	———
DeltaAdjustFrame	OpWindow	RawWindow
deOptionsAreOn	OpRoot	DirEntry
deOptionsOff	OpRoot	DirEntry
deOptionsOn	OpRoot	DirEntry
Deregister	OpDevice	———
DeselectItem	OpPick	PickList
Detab	OpString	———
dgControlOptionsAreOn	OpDialog	DialogBox
dgControlOptionsOff	OpDialog	DialogBox
dgControlOptionsOn	OpDialog	DialogBox
dgFieldOptionsAreOn	OpDialog	DialogBox
dgFieldOptionsOff	OpDialog	DialogBox
dgFieldOptionsOn	OpDialog	DialogBox
dgOptionsAreOn	OpDialog	DialogBox
dgOptionsOff	OpDialog	DialogBox
dgOptionsOn	OpDialog	DialogBox
dgSecFieldOptionsAreOn	OpDialog	DialogBox
dgSecFieldOptionsOff	OpDialog	DialogBox
dgSecFieldOptionsOn	OpDialog	DialogBox
DiabloRegister	OpDevice	———
diOptionsAreOn	OpDir	DirList
diOptionsOff	OpDir	DirList
diOptionsOn	OpDir	DirList
DirListStream	OpDir	———
DisableEventHandling	OpMouse	———
DisableHeader	OpFrame	Frame
DisablePopup	OpSwap1	———
DisableTSR	OpSwap1	———
DisableTSR	OpTsr	———
Display	OpWindow	PackedWindow
DisplayAt	OpWindow	PackedWindow
DisplayInfo	OpMenu	MenuItemNode
DisplayLErrorProc	OpLarray	———
DisposeAllModes	OpPrint	Printer
DisposeAsc	OpAsciiz	———
DisposeEnv	OpDos	———
DisposeString	OpString	———
DivBCD	OpBCD	———
DMYtoDate	OpDate	———
DMYtoDateString	OpDate	———
Done	OpBrowse	Browser
Done	OpClone	Cloner

Done	OpCmd	CommandProcessor
Done	OpDialog	DialogBox
Done	OpDir	DirList
Done	OpDir	PathList
Done	OpEntry	EntryScreen
Done	OpEntry	ScrollingEntryScreen
Done	OpForm	PrintedForm
Done	OpForm	Report
Done	OpFrame	Frame
Done	OpFrame	ScreenRect
Done	OpHelp	AbstractHelpWindow
Done	OpLarray	AbstractArray
Done	OpMemo	Memo
Done	OpMenu	Menu
Done	OpPick	PickList
Done	OpPrint	Printer
Done	OpPrnLow	BasePrinter
Done	OpRoot	BitSet
Done	OpRoot	BufIdStream
Done	OpRoot	DosIdStream
Done	OpRoot	DoubleList
Done	OpRoot	Library
Done	OpRoot	PointerStack
Done	OpRoot	Root
Done	OpRoot	SingleList
Done	OpRoot	StaticQueue
Done	OpRoot	StringArray
Done	OpRoot	StringDict
Done	OpSelect	AbstractSelector
Done	OpSelect	ScrollingSelector
Done	OpWindow	PackedWindow
Done	OpWindow	RawWindow
Done	OpWindow	StackWindow
Done	OpWindow	VirtScreen
Done	OpWindow	WindowStack
DosBusyFlag	OpSwap1	———
DosBusyFlag	OpTsr	———
DosCriticalFlag	OpTsr	———
DosPrinterStream	OpPrnLow	———
DosVersion	OpDos	———
DoubleListStream	OpRoot	———
Draw	OpFrame	Frame
Draw	OpWindow	RawWindow
Draw	OpWindow	StackWindow
DrawAllSliders	OpWindow	RawWindow
DrawBackground	OpSelect	AbstractSelector

DrawField	OpSelect	AbstractSelector
DrawHeader	OpFrame	Frame
DrawHidden	OpWindow	StackWindow
DrawSlider	OpWindow	RawWindow
DumpEnv	OpDos	———
DupCurrentBlock	OpForm	PrintedForm
DupCurrentPage	OpForm	PrintedForm
EditArray	OpEdit	LineEditor
EditBoolean	OpEdit	LineEditor
EditByte	OpEdit	LineEditor
EditChar	OpEdit	LineEditor
EditChoice	OpEdit	LineEditor
EditDate	OpEdit	LineEditor
EditDateSt	OpEdit	LineEditor
EditInteger	OpEdit	LineEditor
EditKeys	OpMacEd	———
EditLongInt	OpEdit	LineEditor
EditMultiLine	OpEdit	LineEditor
EditNumericByte	OpEdit	LineEditor
EditNumericInteger	OpEdit	LineEditor
EditNumericLongInt	OpEdit	LineEditor
EditNumericReal	OpEdit	LineEditor
EditNumericShortInt	OpEdit	LineEditor
EditNumericWord	OpEdit	LineEditor
EditReal	OpEdit	LineEditor
EditShortInt	OpEdit	LineEditor
EditString	OpEdit	LineEditor
EditTime	OpEdit	LineEditor
EditWord	OpEdit	LineEditor
EditYesNo	OpEdit	LineEditor
efOptionsAreOn	OpField	EntryField
efOptionsOff	OpField	EntryField
efOptionsOn	OpField	EntryField
Elements	OpRoot	StaticQueue
EmmSigFound	OpEms	———
EmsActiveHandles	OpEms	———
EmsErrorMessage	OpEms	———
EmsInstalled	OpEms	———
EmsPageFramePtr	OpEms	———
EmsPagesAvail	OpEms	———
EmsPagesOwned	OpEms	———
EmsStatusOK	OpEms	———
EmsVersion	OpEms	———
EmulateInt	OpInt	———
EmulateInt	OpSwap1	———
EnableAllAlternateOpen	OpMenu	Menu

EnableAllExplosions	OpMenu	Menu
EnableAllNormalOpen	OpMenu	Menu
EnableAlternateOpen	OpWindow	RawWindow
EnableDefaultFont	OpPrint	Printer
EnableEventHandling	OpMouse	———
EnableExplosions	OpMenu	Menu
EnableExplosions	OpWindow	RawWindow
EnableNormalOpen	OpMenu	Menu
EnableNormalOpen	OpWindow	RawWindow
EndPrintStatus	OpDos	———
EnhancedKbdInstalled	OpCrt	———
Entab	OpString	———
EntryScreenStream	OpEntry	———
EnvFree	OpDos	———
EpsonLQRegister	OpDevice	———
EpsonMXRegister	OpDevice	———
Equal	OpRoot	StringDict
EqualBCD	OpBCD	———
Erase	OpMenu	Menu
Erase	OpWindow	RawWindow
Erase	OpWindow	StackWindow
EraseAllSubMenus	OpMenu	Menu
EraseClear	OpMenu	Menu
EraseCurrentSubMenu	OpMenu	Menu
EraseHidden	OpWindow	StackWindow
EraseSlider	OpWindow	RawWindow
Error	OpFrame	Frame
Error	OpRoot	IdStream
Error	OpRoot	LargeBitSet
Error	OpRoot	StaticQueue
Error	OpRoot	StringDict
Error	OpWindow	RawWindow
Error8087	Op8087	———
ErrorA	OpLarray	AbstractArray
ErrorRecovery	OpErrHan	———
esFieldOptionsAreOn	OpEntry	EntryScreen
esFieldOptionsOff	OpEntry	EntryScreen
esFieldOptionsOn	OpEntry	EntryScreen
esOptionsAreOn	OpEntry	EntryScreen
esOptionsOff	OpEntry	EntryScreen
esOptionsOn	OpEntry	EntryScreen
esSecFieldOptionsAreOn	OpEntry	EntryScreen
esSecFieldOptionsOff	OpEntry	EntryScreen
esSecFieldOptionsOn	OpEntry	EntryScreen
EvaluateCommand	OpDialog	DialogBox
EvaluateCommand	OpEntry	EntryScreen

EvaluateMousePos	OpWindow	RawWindow
EvaluatePos	OpWindow	RawWindow
EvaluateStackMousePos	OpWindow	WindowStack
EvaluateStackPos	OpWindow	WindowStack
Exception8087	Op8087	———
ExchangeBytes	OpInline	———
ExchangeLongInts	OpInline	———
ExchangeMemoryRegion	OpEms	———
ExchangeStructs	OpInline	———
ExchangeWords	OpInline	———
ExecDos	OpDos	———
ExecDosSwap	OpExec	———
ExecWithSwap	OpExec	———
ExistFile	OpDos	———
ExistOnPath	OpDos	———
ExpBCD	OpBCD	———
Extent	OpWindow	RawWindow
ExtMemAvail	OpExtMem	———
ExtMemTotal	OpExtMem	———
ExtractWord	OpString	———
FacitRegister	OpDevice	———
FarCall	OpInline	———
FastCenter	OpCrt	———
FastFill	OpCrt	———
FastFillVert	OpCrt	———
FastFlush	OpCrt	———
FastRead	OpCrt	———
FastText	OpCrt	———
FastVert	OpCrt	———
FastWrite	OpCrt	———
FastWriteAttr	OpCrt	———
FatCursor	OpCrt	———
FatMouseCursor	OpMouse	———
fChangeAttribute	OpWindow	RawWindow
fCopy	OpFrame	Frame
fFastCenter	OpWindow	RawWindow
fFastFill	OpWindow	RawWindow
fFastFlush	OpWindow	RawWindow
fFastRead	OpWindow	RawWindow
fFastText	OpWindow	RawWindow
fFastVert	OpWindow	RawWindow
fFastWrite	OpWindow	RawWindow
fFastWriteCtrl	OpWindow	RawWindow
fFlexWrite	OpWindow	RawWindow
fGetLastError	OpForm	PrintedForm
FieldOptionsAreOn	OpForm	PrintedForm

FieldOptionsOff	OpForm	PrintedForm
FieldOptionsOn	OpForm	PrintedForm
FileCapacity	OpDir	DirList
FileHandlesLeft	OpDos	———
FileHandlesOpen	OpDos	———
FileNeedsPacking	OpRoot	Library
FillStruct	OpInline	———
FillWord	OpInline	———
FindAnyDirectoryEntry	OpRoot	Library
FindControl	OpDialog	DialogBox
FindDefaultsEnd	OpClone	Cloner
FindDefaultsStart	OpClone	Cloner
FindDirectoryEntry	OpRoot	Library
FindEntryByIndex	OpRoot	Library
FindField	OpForm	PrintedForm
FindField	OpSelect	AbstractSelector
FindFieldByname	OpSelect	AbstractSelector
FindForm	OpForm	Report
FindItem	OpCtrl	Cluster
FindItem	OpMenu	Menu
FindMacroIndex	OpMacro	———
FindNextField	OpForm	PrintedForm
FindNextTopic	OpHelp	AbstractHelpWindow
FindTextField	OpSelect	AbstractSelector
FindTopic	OpHelp	AbstractHelpWindow
FirstClear	OpRoot	BitSet
FirstSet	OpRoot	BitSet
FlagIsSet	OpInline	———
FlexLen	OpCrt	———
FlexWrite	OpCrt	———
Flush	OpRoot	BufIdStream
FlushA	OpLarray	AbstractArray
FlushDosBuffers	OpDos	———
Font8x8Selected	OpCrt	———
ForceExtension	OpString	———
Form	OpBCD	———
Form	OpString	———
Format	OpDir	DirList
FormatMultiFile	OpDir	DirList
FormFeed	OpPrint	Printer
FormStream	OpForm	———
fPrinterPtr	OpForm	PrintedForm
FracBCD	OpBCD	———
FrameStream	OpFrame	———
FrameWindow	OpCrt	———
fReadAttribute	OpWindow	RawWindow

FreeExtMem	OpExtMem	———
FullMouseWindow	OpMouse	———
FullPathName	OpString	———
fWriteAttribute	OpWindow	RawWindow
GenericEpsonRegister	OpDevice	———
Get	OpRoot	IdStream
GetAddrMappablePages	OpEms	———
GetAllHandleNames	OpEms	———
GetBasePrinter	OpPrint	Printer
GetCmdAssignment	OpCmd	CommandProcessor
GetCodeAndVersion	OpRoot	Library
GetCommand	OpCmd	CommandProcessor
GetCommandProcessor	OpWindow	CommandWindow
GetCommandString	OpCmd	CommandProcessor
GetCrtMode	OpCrt	———
GetCurrentFont	OpPrint	Printer
GetCurrentID	OpSelect	AbstractSelector
GetCurrentItem	OpCtrl	Cluster
GetCursor	OpWindow	RawWindow
GetCursorState	OpCrt	———
GetDefaultChoice	OpPick	PickList
GetDefaultFont	OpPrint	Printer
GetDiskClass	OpDos	———
GetDiskInfo	OpDos	———
GetDisplayPos	OpMenu	MenuItemNode
GetDta	OpDos	———
GetElement	OpSort	———
GetEntry	OpRoot	Library
GetEntry	OpRoot	MemLibrary
GetEntryLength	OpRoot	DirEntry
GetEntryName	OpRoot	DirEntry
GetEntryPtr	OpRoot	Library
GetEntryPtr	OpRoot	MemLibrary
GetEntryStart	OpRoot	DirEntry
GetEnvironmentString	OpDos	———
GetEnvStr	OpDos	———
GetErrorProc	OpLarray	AbstractArray
GetExitCommandPtr	OpWindow	CommandWindow
GetExtMem	OpExtMem	———
GetFieldAttr	OpForm	PrintField
GetFieldCoordinates	OpEntry	EntryScreen
GetFieldPos	OpForm	PrintField
GetFileMode	OpDos	———
GetFileName	OpDir	DirList
GetFooter	OpForm	PrintedForm
GetHandleAttr	OpEms	———

GetHandleName	OpEms	———
GetHardwareConfig	OpEms	———
GetHeader	OpForm	PrintedForm
GetHelpAttr	OpMenu	Menu
GetHelpIndex	OpSelect	AbstractSelector
GetHelpIndex	OpWindow	CommandWindow
GetItemCols	OpPick	PickList
GetItemString	OpPick	PickList
GetKeyAssignment	OpCmd	CommandProcessor
GetKeyPtr	OpCmd	CommandProcessor
GetKeyRecPtr	OpCmd	CommandPacker
GetLastChoice	OpPick	PickList
GetLastChoiceString	OpPick	PickList
GetLastCommand	OpEdit	LineEditor
GetLastCommand	OpSEdit	SimpleLineEditor
GetLastCommand	OpWindow	CommandWindow
GetLastError	OpClone	Cloner
GetLastError	OpCmd	CommandProcessor
GetLastError	OpEdit	LineEditor
GetLastError	OpFrame	Frame
GetLastError	OpWindow	CommandWindow
GetLastError	OpWindow	RawWindow
GetLastField	OpEntry	EntryScreen
GetLastHeaderIndex	OpFrame	Frame
GetLastHotIndex	OpFrame	Frame
GetLastKey	OpEdit	LineEditor
GetLastKey	OpSEdit	SimpleLineEditor
GetLastKey	OpWindow	CommandWindow
GetLPP	OpPrint	Printer
GetLptPort	OpPrnLow	BiosPrinter
GetMatchingFileCount	OpDir	DirList
GetMatchingSize	OpDir	DirList
GetMickeyCount	OpMouse	———
GetMousePage	OpMouse	———
GetMultiDirPtr	OpDir	DirList
GetMultiDirRec	OpDir	DirList
GetMultiFile	OpDir	DirList
GetMultiPath	OpDir	DirList
GetMultiPath	OpDir	PathList
GetNextCommand	OpWindow	CommandWindow
GetNumberOfMappablePages	OpEms	———
GetNumberOfRawPages	OpEms	———
GetNumItems	OpPick	PickList
GetOrientation	OpPick	PickList
GetPagePointer	OpCrt	———
GetPagesByAddress	OpEms	———

GetPagesByNumber	OpEms	———
GetPageSegment	OpCrt	———
GetPagesForAll	OpEms	———
GetPathName	OpDir	PathList
GetPos	OpClone	Cloner
GetPos	OpRoot	IdStream
GetPrintStatus	OpDos	———
GetPrnObject	OpPrnLow	———
GetProgramStr	OpDos	———
GetPSP	OpTsr	———
GetPtr	OpRoot	IdStream
GetRegisteredType	OpPrint	Printer
GetReturnVec	OpStr	———
GetSecondaryKeyPtr	OpCmd	CommandProcessor
GetSelectedCount	OpPick	PickList
GetSelectedDir	OpDir	DirList
GetSelectedDirRec	OpDir	DirList
GetSelectedFile	OpDir	DirList
GetSelectedPath	OpDir	DirList
GetSelectedPath	OpDir	PathList
GetSelectedSize	OpDir	DirList
GetSize	OpRoot	IdStream
GetSizeOfPageMap	OpEms	———
GetSizeOfPartialPageMap	OpEms	———
GetStatus	OpRoot	IdStream
GetStatus	OpRoot	LargeBitSet
GetStatus	OpRoot	PointerStack
GetStatus	OpRoot	StaticQueue
GetStatus	OpRoot	StringDict
GetString	OpRoot	StringArray
GetString	OpRoot	StringDict
GetStringPtr	OpRoot	StringArray
GetTestAndMask	OpPrnLow	BiosPrinter
GetTopicChoice	OpHelp	AbstractHelpWindow
GetUserData	OpForm	PrintedForm
GetUserPointer	OpRoot	DirEntry
GetUserRecord	OpDialog	DialogBox
GetUserRecord	OpEntry	EntryScreen
GetUserRecord	OpForm	PrintedForm
GetUserRecordSize	OpDialog	DialogBox
GetUserRecordSize	OpEntry	EntryScreen
GetUserRecordSize	OpForm	PrintedForm
GetXlatErrorFunc	OpPrnLow	BiosPrinter
GetXRatio	OpPrint	Printer
GetYRatio	OpPrint	Printer
GotError	OpWindow	CommandWindow

GotoLine	OpBrowse	Browser
GotoLineCol	OpEditor	TextEditor
GotoOffset	OpBrowse	Browser
GotoOffset	OpEditor	TextEditor
GotoXYAbs	OpCrt	———
GrabKeyboard	OpSwap1	———
GrabKeyboard	OpTsr	———
GreaterBCD	OpBCD	———
GreaterEqualBCD	OpBCD	———
HandleIsConsole	OpDos	———
HandleMousePress	OpDrag	DragProcessor
HardMouseCursor	OpMouse	———
Hash	OpRoot	StringDict
HaveContents	OpFrame	ScreenRect
HaveSelected	OpPick	PickList
Head	OpRoot	DoubleList
Head	OpRoot	SingleList
Height	OpWindow	AbstractWindow
HelpString	OpMenu	MenuItemNode
HercGraphicsMode	OpCrt	———
HercModeTestWorks	OpCrt	———
HercPresent	OpCrt	———
HexB	OpString	———
HexL	OpString	———
HexPtr	OpString	———
HexW	OpString	———
HiddenCursor	OpCrt	———
HiddenMouseCursor	OpMouse	———
HideBlock	OpHelp	ScrollingHelpWindow
HideMouse	OpMouse	———
HideMousePrim	OpMouse	———
HighestTopic	OpHelp	AbstractHelpWindow
HiWord	OpInline	———
HMStoTime	OpDate	———
HPDeskJetRegister	OpDevice	———
hwOptionsAreOn	OpHelp	AbstractHelpWindow
hwOptionsOff	OpHelp	AbstractHelpWindow
hwOptionsOn	OpHelp	AbstractHelpWindow
IncDate	OpDate	———
IncDateTime	OpDate	———
IncDateTrunc	OpDate	———
IncTime	OpDate	———
InHelpMode	OpHelp	AbstractHelpWindow
Init	OpBrowse	Browser
Init	OpClone	Cloner
Init	OpCmd	CommandPacker

Init	OpCmd	CommandProcessor
Init	OpCtrl	Control
Init	OpDialog	DialogBox
Init	OpDir	DirList
Init	OpDir	PathList
Init	OpDrag	DragProcessor
Init	OpEdit	LineEditor
Init	OpEditor	TextEditor
Init	OpEntry	EntryScreen
Init	OpEntry	ScrollingEntryScreen
Init	OpForm	PrintedForm
Init	OpForm	Report
Init	OpFrame	Frame
Init	OpFrame	ScreenRect
Init	OpHelp	AbstractHelpWindow
Init	OpLarray	AbstractArray
Init	OpLarray	EmsArray
Init	OpLarray	EmsRCArray
Init	OpLarray	OpArray
Init	OpLarray	PrimitiveArray
Init	OpLarray	RamArray
Init	OpLarray	RamRCArray
Init	OpLarray	VirtualArray
Init	OpLarray	VirtualRCArray
Init	OpLarray	XmsArray
Init	OpLarray	XmsRCArray
Init	OpMemo	Memo
Init	OpMemo	MemoFile
Init	OpMenu	Menu
Init	OpPick	PickList
Init	OpPrint	Printer
Init	OpPrnLow	BasePrinter
Init	OpPrnLow	BiosPrinter
Init	OpPrnLow	DosPrinter
Init	OpRoot	BitSet
Init	OpRoot	BufIdStream
Init	OpRoot	DirEntry
Init	OpRoot	DosIdStream
Init	OpRoot	DoubleList
Init	OpRoot	DoubleListNode
Init	OpRoot	LargeBitSet
Init	OpRoot	Library
Init	OpRoot	MemIdStream
Init	OpRoot	MemLibrary
Init	OpRoot	PointerStack
Init	OpRoot	Root

Init	OpRoot	SingleList
Init	OpRoot	SingleListNode
Init	OpRoot	StaticQueue
Init	OpRoot	StringArray
Init	OpRoot	StringDict
Init	OpSEdit	SimpleLineEditor
Init	OpSelect	ScrollingSelector
Init	OpSelect	Selector
Init	OpWindow	CommandWindow
Init	OpWindow	LoadableColorSet
Init	OpWindow	PackedWindow
Init	OpWindow	RawWindow
Init	OpWindow	StackWindow
Init	OpWindow	VirtScreen
Init	OpWindow	WindowStack
InitAbstract	OpPick	PickList
InitAbstractDeluxe	OpPick	PickList
InitAndAlloc	OpMemo	MemoFile
InitAndFind	OpClone	Cloner
InitBuf	OpEditor	TextEditor
InitBufCustom	OpEditor	TextEditor
InitCustom	OpBrowse	Browser
InitCustom	OpClone	Cloner
InitCustom	OpCmd	CommandProcessor
InitCustom	OpDialog	DialogBox
InitCustom	OpDir	DirList
InitCustom	OpDir	PathList
InitCustom	OpEditor	TextEditor
InitCustom	OpEntry	EntryScreen
InitCustom	OpEntry	ScrollingEntryScreen
InitCustom	OpForm	PrintedForm
InitCustom	OpHelp	AbstractHelpWindow
InitCustom	OpMemo	Memo
InitCustom	OpMemo	MemoFile
InitCustom	OpMenu	Menu
InitCustom	OpPick	PickList
InitCustom	OpPrint	Printer
InitCustom	OpPrnLow	BiosPrinter
InitCustom	OpRoot	StringDict
InitCustom	OpSelect	AbstractSelector
InitCustom	OpSelect	ScrollingSelector
InitCustom	OpSelect	Selector
InitCustom	OpWindow	CommandWindow
InitCustom	OpWindow	RawWindow
InitCustom	OpWindow	StackWindow
InitCustomAndAlloc	OpMemo	MemoFile

InitDeluxe	OpHelp	AbstractHelpWindow
InitDeluxe	OpPick	PickList
InitFromMemory	OpWindow	PackedWindow
InitHelpFrame	OpHelp	AbstractHelpWindow
InitializeMouse	OpMouse	————
InitKbdVectors	OpEnhKbd	————
InitMacros	OpMacro	————
InitMem	OpHelp	AbstractHelpWindow
InitMemCustom	OpHelp	AbstractHelpWindow
InitMemDeluxe	OpHelp	AbstractHelpWindow
InitNPP	OpCtrl	Control
InitPops	OpTsr	————
InitScrapMacroPtr	OpReplay	————
InitSequence	OpPick	PickList
InitVector	OpInt	————
InLandscape	OpPrint	Printer
Insert	OpRoot	DoubleList
Insert	OpRoot	SingleList
InsertAsc	OpAsciiz	————
InsertBlockAtCursor	OpEditor	TextEditor
InsertBlockedStringAtCursor	OpEditor	TextEditor
InsertStr	OpAsciiz	————
InsertStringAtCursor	OpEditor	TextEditor
InsertTextAtCursor	OpEditor	TextEditor
Installed8087	Op8087	————
InstallISRs	OpDrag	DragProcessor
InstallModule	OpSwap1	————
InstallModule	OpTsr	————
Int16	OpReplay	————
IntBCD	OpBCD	————
InternationalCurrency	OpAbsFld	————
InternationalDate	OpDate	————
InternationalTime	OpDate	————
InterruptsOff	OpInt	————
InterruptsOff	OpSwap1	————
InterruptsOn	OpInt	————
InterruptsOn	OpSwap1	————
Intersects	OpWindow	RawWindow
IntReturn	OpInt	————
InWindow	OpWindow	RawWindow
IsActive	OpWindow	RawWindow
IsChild	OpWindow	StackWindow
IsCurrent	OpMenu	Menu
IsCurrent	OpWindow	RawWindow
IsCurrent	OpWindow	StackWindow
IsDirectory	OpDos	————

IsFramed	OpFrame	Frame
IsLeapYear	OpDate	———
IsParent	OpWindow	StackWindow
IsProtected	OpMenu	MenuItemNode
IsProtected	OpPick	PickList
IsSemiProtected	OpMenu	MenuItemNode
IsSemiProtected	OpPick	PickList
IsZoomed	OpWindow	RawWindow
ItemIsSelected	OpPick	PickList
ItemKey	OpMenu	MenuItemNode
ItemsDone	OpMenu	Menu
ItemsDoneCustom	OpMenu	Menu
ItemSearch	OpPick	PickList
ItemString	OpHelp	AbstractHelpWindow
ItemString	OpPick	PickList
JumpToOldIsr	OpInline	———
JustExtension	OpString	———
JustFilename	OpString	———
JustName	OpString	———
JustPathname	OpString	———
KbdFlags	OpCrt	———
KeyOrButtonPressed	OpMouse	———
KeyToString	OpMacro	———
KillEntry	OpRoot	Library
KXP1093Register	OpDevice	———
LargeBitSetStream	OpRoot	———
LastClear	OpRoot	BitSet
LastSet	OpRoot	BitSet
leEditOptionsAreOn	OpEdit	LineEditor
leEditOptionsOff	OpEdit	LineEditor
leEditOptionsOn	OpEdit	LineEditor
LeftPad	OpString	———
LenAsc	OpAsciiz	———
leSecEditOptionsAreOn	OpEdit	LineEditor
leSecEditOptionsOff	OpEdit	LineEditor
leSecEditOptionsOn	OpEdit	LineEditor
LessBCD	OpBCD	———
LessEqualBCD	OpBCD	———
LineEditorStream	OpEdit	———
LinkToModes	OpPrint	Printer
LinkToPrinter	OpPrint	Printer
LJCol2Deci	OpDevice	———
LJDeci2Col	OpDevice	———
LJDeci2Row	OpDevice	———
LJDeviceStream	OpDevice	———
LJFontFRegister	OpDevice	———

LJFontGRegister	OpDevice	———
LJIIRegister	OpDevice	———
LJPlusRegister	OpDevice	———
LJRegister	OpDevice	———
LJRow2Deci	OpDevice	———
LnBCD	OpBCD	———
Load	OpBrowse	Browser
Load	OpCmd	CommandProcessor
Load	OpDialog	DialogBox
Load	OpDir	DirList
Load	OpDir	PathList
Load	OpDrag	DragProcessor
Load	OpEdit	LineEditor
Load	OpEdit or	TextEditor
Load	OpEntry	EntryScreen
Load	OpEntry	ScrollingEntryScreen
Load	OpForm	PrintedForm
Load	OpForm	Report
Load	OpFrame	Frame
Load	OpFrame	ScreenRect
Load	OpHelp	AbstractHelpWindow
Load	OpMemo	Memo
Load	OpMemo	MemoFile
Load	OpMenu	Menu
Load	OpPick	PickList
Load	OpPrint	Printer
Load	OpPrnLow	BasePrinter
Load	OpRoot	BitSet
Load	OpRoot	DoubleList
Load	OpRoot	LargeBitSet
Load	OpRoot	PointerStack
Load	OpRoot	SingleList
Load	OpRoot	StaticQueue
Load	OpRoot	StringArray
Load	OpRoot	StringDict
Load	OpRoot	StringSet
Load	OpSelect	ScrollingSelector
Load	OpSelect	Selector
Load	OpWindow	CommandWindow
Load	OpWindow	LoadableColorSet
Load	OpWindow	PackedWindow
Load	OpWindow	RawWindow
Load	OpWindow	StackWindow
Load	OpWindow	VirtScreen
Load	OpWindow	WindowStack
LoadA	OpLarray	AbstractArray

LoadA	OpLarray	EmsArray
LoadA	OpLarray	EmsRCArray
LoadA	OpLarray	OpArray
LoadA	OpLarray	RamArray
LoadA	OpLarray	RamRCArray
LoadA	OpLarray	VirtualArray
LoadA	OpLarray	VirtualRCArray
LoadA	OpLarray	XmsArray
LoadA	OpLarray	XmsRcArray
LoadableColorSetStream	OpWindow	———
LoadDefaults	OpClone	Cloner
LoCase	OpString	———
LoCaseMac	OpString	———
Long2Str	OpString	———
LongFlagIsSet	OpInLine	———
LongIntForm	OpString	———
LongintToBCD	OpBCD	———
LongJump	OpInLine	———
LongToPtr	OpInLine	———
lOptionsAreOn	OpLarray	AbstractArray
lOptionsOff	OpLarray	AbstractArray
lOptionsOn	OpLarray	AbstractArray
LoWord	OpInLine	———
MacroAddress	OpMacro	———
MacroCount	OpMacro	———
MacroRecordingOff	OpMacro	———
MacroRecordingOn	OpMacro	———
MacrosOff	OpMacro	———
MacrosOn	OpMacro	———
MainFramePtr	OpWindow	RawWindow
MakeHiddenAttr	OpCrt	———
MakeInteger	OpInLine	———
MakeLetterSet	OpString	———
MakeLongInt	OpInLine	———
MakeWord	OpInLine	———
MapColor	OpCrt	———
MapColors	OpWindow	PackedWindow
MapEmsPage	OpEms	———
MapMono	OpCrt	———
MarkAllSelected	OpPick	PickList
MarkCurrent	OpWindow	RawWindow
MarkExtMem	OpExtMem	———
MarkNotCurrent	OpWindow	RawWindow
MasterEnv	OpDos	———
MaxBits	OpRoot	BitSet
MaxEntries	OpRoot	Library

MaxLong	OpInLine	———
MaxParagraphsToKeep	OpSwap1	———
MaxParagraphsToKeep	OpTsr	———
MaxWord	OpInLine	———
Member	OpRoot	StringDict
Member	OpRoot	StringSet
MemoError	OpMemo	———
MemoFileStream	OpMemo	———
MemoStatus	OpMemo	———
MemoStream	OpMemo	———
MenuChoice	OpMenu	Menu
MenuStream	OpMenu	———
meOptionsAreOn	OpMemo	Memo
meOptionsOff	OpMemo	Memo
meOptionsOn	OpMemo	Memo
MinLong	OpInLine	———
MinWord	OpInLine	———
mnOptionsAreOn	OpMenu	Menu
mnOptionsOff	OpMenu	Menu
mnOptionsOn	OpMenu	Menu
ModuleInstalled	OpSwap1	———
ModuleInstalled	OpTsr	———
ModulePtrByName	OpSwap1	———
ModulePtrByName	OpTsr	———
MouseButtonPressed	OpMouse	———
MouseButtonReleased	OpMouse	———
MouseEnabled	OpCmd	CommandProcessor
MouseEventsPending	OpDrag	DragProcessor
MouseGotoXY	OpMouse	———
MouseInWindow	OpMouse	———
MouseKeyWord	OpMouse	———
MousePressed	OpMouse	———
MouseStateBufferSize	OpMouse	———
MouseWhereX	OpMouse	———
MouseWhereXabs	OpMouse	———
MouseWhereXY	OpMouse	———
MouseWhereXYabs	OpMouse	———
MouseWhereY	OpMouse	———
MouseWhereYabs	OpMouse	———
MouseWindow	OpMouse	———
MoveExtMem	OpExtMem	———
MoveFast	OpString	———
MoveMemoryRegion	OpEms	———
MoveScreen	OpCrt	———
MoveWindow	OpMenu	Menu
MoveWindow	OpWindow	RawWindow

MultBCD	OpBCD	———
MultipleChoice	OpPick	———
MultipleFile	OpDir	———
MultiplePath	OpDir	———
NameFormat	OpDir	———
NameOfPrn	OpPrnLow	BasePrinter
NameSizeFormat	OpDir	———
NameSizeKFormat	OpDir	———
NameSizeKTimeFormat	OpDir	———
NameSizeTimeFormat	OpDir	———
NameTimeFormat	OpDir	———
NearCall	OpInLine	———
Nec3510Register	OpDevice	———
Nec8800Register	OpDevice	———
NewBlock	OpForm	PrintedForm
NewEnv	OpDos	———
NewPage	OpForm	PrintedForm
NewXlatCharTable	OpPrnLow	BasePrinter
Next	OpRoot	CircularList
Next	OpRoot	DoubleList
Next	OpRoot	SingleList
NextClear	OpRoot	BitSet
NextSelected	OpPick	PickList
NextSet	OpRoot	BitSet
NoCurrItemAction	OpMenu	———
NoCustomization	OpMenu	———
NoExecDosProc	OpDos	———
NoMoveAction	OpPick	———
NoNestedAction	OpHelp	———
NormalCursor	OpCrt	———
Normalized	OpInLine	———
NormalMouseCursor	OpMouse	———
NotEqualBCD	OpBCD	———
Nth	OpLarray	DoubleList
Nth	OpLarray	SingleList
NumberOfDrives	OpDos	———
NumSelectableItems	OpPick	PickList
NumStrings	OpRoot	StringArray
OctalB	OpString	———
OctalL	OpString	———
OctalW	OpString	———
OnStack	OpWindow	StackWindow
Open	OpRoot	DosIdStream
OpenFile	OpBrowse	Browser
OpenStdDev	OpDos	———
OptimizeSize	OpPick	PickList

OptimizeTiled	OpWindow	WStack
OptimizeTiled	OpWindow	WindowStack
Pack	OpRoot	Library
PackedFileSize	OpRoot	Library
PackedWindowStream	OpWindow	———
PackKeys	OpCmd	CommandPacker
Pad	OpString	———
PadCh	OpString	———
PagedHelpWindowStream	OpHelp	———
paOptionsAreOn	OpDir	PathList
paOptionsOff	OpDir	PathList
paOptionsOn	OpDir	PathList
ParagraphsToKeep	OpSwap1	———
ParagraphsToKeep	OpTsr	———
ParentEnv	OpDos	———
ParentPtr	OpWindow	StackWindow
ParsePath	OpDos	———
PathListStream	OpDir	———
Peek	OpRoot	PointerStack
PeekHead	OpRoot	StaticQueue
PeekLastError	OpWindow	CommandWindow
PeekMouseEvent	OpDrag	DragProcessor
PeekStatus	OpRoot	IdStream
PeekTail	OpRoot	StaticQueue
PeekTop	OpRoot	PointerStack
pfOptionsAreOn	OpForm	PrintField
pfOptionsOff	OpForm	PrintField
pfOptionsOn	OpForm	PrintField
pGetLastError	OpPrint	Printer
PickAltStringSearch	OpPick	———
PickAnyCharExit	OpPick	———
PickCharExit	OpPick	———
PickCharSearch	OpPick	———
PickHorizontal	OpPick	———
PickListStream	OpPick	———
PickNoSearch	OpPick	———
PickSnaking	OpPick	———
PickStringSearch	OpPick	———
PickTopics	OpHelp	AbstractHelpWindow
PickVertical	OpPick	———
pkOptionsAreOn	OpPick	PickList
pkOptionsOff	OpPick	PickList
pkOptionsOn	OpPick	PickList
Place	OpRoot	DoubleList
Place	OpRoot	SingleList
PlaceBefore	OpRoot	DoubleList

PlaceBefore	OpRoot	SingleList
PointerRegistered	OpRoot	IdStream
PointerStackStream	OpRoot	———
Poke	OpRoot	PointerStack
Pop	OpRoot	PointerStack
PopHead	OpRoot	StaticQueue
PopTail	OpRoot	StaticQueue
pOptionsAreOn	OpPrint	Printer
pOptionsOff	OpPrint	Printer
pOptionsOn	OpPrint	Printer
PopupsOff	OpSwap1	———
PopupsOff	OpTsr	———
PopupsOn	OpSwap1	———
PopupsOn	OpTsr	———
PosAsc	OpAsciiz	———
Position	OpPrint	Printer
PositionCursorAt	OpSelect	AbstractSelector
PosResults	OpWindow	RawWindow
PosStr	OpAsciiz	———
PreloadDirList	OpDir	DirList
PreloadPathList	OpDir	PathList
PreMove	OpPick	PickList
PrepareExecWithSwap	OpExec	———
Prev	OpRoot	CircularList
Prev	OpRoot	DoubleList
PrevClear	OpRoot	BitSet
PrevSet	OpRoot	BitSet
Print	OpForm	PrintField
PrinterReady	OpPrint	Printer
PrinterStream	OpPrint	———
PrintInstalled	OpDos	———
PrintStr	OpPrint	Printer
PrintStrPos	OpPrint	Printer
PrnError	OpPrnLow	BasePrinter
PrnErrorOp	OpPrnLow	BasePrinter
PrnFlush	OpPrnLow	BasePrinter
PrnLastPut	OpPrnLow	BasePrinter
PrnPutBlock	OpPrnLow	BasePrinter
PrnPutChar	OpPrnLow	BasePrinter
PrnRawError	OpPrnLow	BasePrinter
PrnReset	OpPrnLow	BasePrinter
PrnStatus	OpPrnLow	BasePrinter
PrnXlatErrorCode	OpPrnLow	BasePrinter
PrnXlatErrorCode	OpPrnLow	RigidBiosPrinter
Process	OpForm	PrintedForm
Process	OpForm	Report

Process	OpWindow	CommandWindow
ProcessAutoPilot	OpWindow	CommandWindow
ProcessSelf	OpBrowse	Browser
ProcessSelf	OpDialog	DialogBox
ProcessSelf	OpDir	DirList
ProcessSelf	OpDir	PathList
ProcessSelf	OpEdit or	TextEditor
ProcessSelf	OpEntry	EntryScreen
ProcessSelf	OpHelp	AbstractHelpWindow
ProcessSelf	OpMemo	Memo
ProcessSelf	OpMenu	Menu
ProcessSelf	OpPick	PickList
ProcessSelf	OpSelect	Selector
ProcessSelf	OpWindow	CommandWindow
PromptOptionsAreOn	OpForm	PrintedForm
PromptOptionsOff	OpForm	PrintedForm
PromptOptionsOn	OpForm	PrintedForm
ProPrinterIIRegister	OpDevice	———
Protect	OpMenu	MenuItemNode
ProtectItem	OpMenu	Menu
ProwriterRegister	OpDevice	———
PtrDiff	OpInLine	———
PtrToHuge	OpExtMem	———
PtrToLong	OpInLine	———
Push	OpRoot	PointerStack
PushHead	OpRoot	StaticQueue
PushTail	OpRoot	StaticQueue
Put	OpRoot	IdStream
PutElement	OpSort	———
PutEntry	OpRoot	Library
PutPtr	OpRoot	IdStream
RangeError	OpLarray	AbstractArray
RawError	OpWindow	RawWindow
RawWindowStream	OpWindow	———
Read	OpRoot	BufIdStream
Read	OpRoot	DosIdStream
Read	OpRoot	MemIdStream
Read	OpWindow	PackedWindow
ReadAttrAtCursor	OpCrt	———
ReadAttribute	OpCrt	———
ReadByte	OpEdit	LineEditor
ReadChar	OpEdit	LineEditor
ReadCharAtCursor	OpCrt	———
ReadDiskSectors	OpDos	———
ReadFile	OpMemo	MemoFile
ReadFrom	OpWindow	VirtScreen

ReadInteger	OpEdit	LineEditor
ReadKeyOrButton	OpMouse	———
ReadKeyWord	OpCrt	———
ReadLnAsc	OpAsciiz	———
ReadLongInt	OpEdit	LineEditor
ReadMacroFile	OpMacro	———
ReadMouseEvent	OpDrag	DragProcessor
ReadPointer	OpRoot	IdStream
ReadRange	OpRoot	IdStream
ReadReal	OpEdit	LineEditor
ReadShortInt	OpEdit	LineEditor
ReadSpecial	OpEdit	LineEditor
ReadStr	OpStrDev	———
ReadString	OpEdit	LineEditor
ReadString	OpRoot	IdStream
ReadString	OpSEdit	SimpleLineEditor
ReadText	OpRoot	StringArray
ReadUserPointer	OpRoot	IdStream
ReadWord	OpEdit	LineEditor
Real2Str	OpString	———
ReallocatePages	OpEms	———
RealToBCD	OpBCD	———
Reboot	OpInLine	———
Redraw	OpMenu	Menu
RegisterHier	OpRoot	IdStream
RegisterOldVersion	OpRoot	IdStream
RegisterPointer	OpRoot	IdStream
RegisterType	OpRoot	IdStream
Reinit8087	Op8087	———
ReinitBuffer	OpMemo	Memo
ReInitCrt	OpCrt	———
ReinitEmulator	Op8087	———
Reject	OpDir	DirList
RejectExtensions	OpDir	———
RejectFiles	OpDir	———
RejectNone	OpDir	———
ReleaseExtMem	OpExtMem	———
Remove	OpRoot	DoubleList
Remove	OpRoot	SingleList
Remove	OpRoot	StringDict
RemoveChild	OpWindow	StackWindow
RemoveExecWithSwap	OpExec	———
RemoveISRs	OpDrag	DragProcessor
RemoveMacros	OpMacro	———
RemoveMultiFile	OpDir	DirList
RemovePops	OpTsr	———

RemoveSelectedFile	OpDir	DirList
RemoveSelectedFiles	OpDir	DirList
RemoveString	OpRoot	StringArray
Rename	OpRoot	DirEntry
RenameEntry	OpRoot	Library
ReportStream	OpForm	———
RequestHelp	OpWindow	CommandWindow
ResetBlock	OpHelp	ScrollingHelpWindow
ResetList	OpDir	DirList
ResetList	OpDir	PathList
ResetPage	OpPrint	Printer
ResetScreen	OpSelect	AbstractSelector
Resize	OpRoot	LargeBitSet
Resize	OpRoot	PointerStack
ResizeWindow	OpWindow	RawWindow
Restore8087	Op8087	———
RestoreAllVectors	OpInt	———
RestoreAllVectors	OpSwap1	———
RestoreCursorState	OpCrt	———
RestoreEmsContext	OpEms	———
RestoreKbdVectors	OpEnhKbd	———
RestoreMouseCoordinates	OpMouse	———
RestoreMouseState	OpMouse	———
RestorePageMap	OpEms	———
RestorePartialPageMap	OpEms	———
RestoreVector	OpInt	———
RestoreWindow	OpCrt	———
RestoreWindowCoordinates	OpCrt	———
RetA	OpLarray	AbstractArray
ReturnStr	OpStrDev	———
RevalidateAll	OpEntry	EntryScreen
rGetLastError	OpForm	Report
RingBell	OpCmd	———
RoundBCD	OpBCD	———
RoundToNearestHour	OpDate	———
RoundToNearestMinute	OpDate	———
SafeRetA	OpLarray	AbstractArray
SafeSetA	OpLarray	AbstractArray
SafeToDisable	OpSwap1	———
SafeToDisable	OpTsr	———
SameFile	OpDos	———
Save8087	Op8087	———
SaveContents	OpWindow	RawWindow
SaveEmsContext	OpEms	———
SaveFile	OpMemo	MemoFile
SaveMouseState	OpMouse	———

SavePageMap	OpEms	————
SavePartialPageMap	OpEms	————
SaveWindow	OpCrt	————
ScreenRectStream	OpFrame	————
ScreenWordXY	OpHelp	AbstractHelpWindow
ScrollHoriz	OpWindow	RawWindow
ScrollHoriz	OpWindow	VirtScreen
ScrollingEntryScreenStream	OpEntry	————
ScrollingHelpFile	OpHelp	————
ScrollingHelpWindowStream	OpHelp	————
ScrollingSelectorStream	OpSelect	————
ScrollVert	OpWindow	RawWindow
ScrollVert	OpWindow	VirtScreen
ScrollWindowDown	OpCrt	————
ScrollWindowUp	OpCrt	————
Search	OpString	————
SearchForHandleName	OpEms	————
SearchUC	OpString	————
Seek	OpRoot	IdStream
sefOptionsAreOn	OpField	EntryField
sefOptionsOff	OpField	EntryField
sefOptionsOn	OpField	EntryField
Select	OpWindow	StackWindow
SelectChar	OpMenu	MenuItemNode
SelectDrive	OpDos	————
SelectedFileInCurDir	OpDir	DirList
SelectFont8x8	OpCrt	————
SelectItem	OpCtrl	Cluster
SelectItem	OpDir	DirList
SelectItem	OpMenu	Menu
SelectItem	OpPick	PickList
SelectItemByPos	OpMenu	Menu
SelectorStream	OpSelect	————
SelectSubMenu	OpMenu	Menu
SemiProtect	OpMenu	MenuItemNode
SemiProtectItem	OpMenu	Menu
SendEOI	OpInt	————
seOptionsAreOn	OpSEdit	SimpleLineEditor
seOptionsOff	OpSEdit	SimpleLineEditor
seOptionsOn	OpSEdit	SimpleLineEditor
SetA	OpLarray	AbstractArray
SetActionProc	OpSelect	Selector
SetActiveChild	OpWindow	StackWindow
SetActivePage	OpCrt	————
SetAll	OpRoot	BitSet
SetAllFieldLinks	OpSelect	AbstractSelector

SetAllFormat	OpDir	DirList
SetAllFrameAttr	OpMenu	Menu
SetAllHeaderAttr	OpMenu	Menu
SetAllHighAttr	OpMenu	Menu
SetAllNormAttr	OpMenu	Menu
SetAllProtectAttr	OpMenu	Menu
SetAllSelectAttr	OpMenu	Menu
SetAllSelectMarker	OpMenu	Menu
SetAllShadowAttr	OpMenu	Menu
SetAltItemAttr	OpCrt	ColorSet
SetAltKeySet	OpCmd	CommandProcessor
SetAltSelItemAttr	OpCrt	ColorSet
SetBackChar	OpWindow	RawWindow
SetBeepOnError	OpDialog	DialogBox
SetBeepOnError	OpEntry	EntryScreen
SetBell	OpCmd	————
SetBit	OpRoot	BitSet
SetBlink	OpCrt	————
SetBlock	OpDos	————
SetBlockAttr	OpBrowse	Browser
SetBlockAttr	OpCrt	ColorSet
SetBlockAttr	OpEdit or	TextEditor
SetBlockAttr	OpHelp	ScrollingHelpWindow
SetBlockIndent	OpEdit or	TextEditor
SetButtonAttr	OpCtrl	DialogColorSet
SetButtonAttr	OpDialog	DialogBox
SetButtonShadowAttr	OpCtrl	DialogColorSet
SetButtonShadowAttr	OpDialog	DialogBox
SetByteFlag	OpInLine	————
SetChainedEventHandler	OpDrag	DragProcessor
SetChoice	OpPick	PickList
SetClearFirstFilter	OpEdit	LineEditor
SetClearFirstFilter	OpEntry	EntryScreen
SetClearFirstFilter	OpSEdit	SimpleLineEditor
SetClipLimits	OpFrame	Frame
SetClusterAttr	OpDialog	DialogBox
SetClusterSize	OpDir	PathList
SetCommandList	OpCmd	CommandProcessor
SetCommandProcessor	OpEdit	LineEditor
SetCommandProcessor	OpSEdit	SimpleLineEditor
SetCommandProcessor	OpWindow	CommandWindow
SetConversion	OpForm	PrintField
SetCrtBorder	OpCrt	————
SetCtrlAttr	OpCrt	ColorSet
SetCtrlAttr	OpField	SelectField
SetCtrlAttr	OpMemo	Memo

SetCtrlAttr	OpSEdit	SimpleLineEditor
SetCtrlAttr	OpSelect	AbstractSelector
SetClusterAttr	OpCtrl	DialogColorSet
SetCurrentEnv	OpDos	———
SetCurrentItem	OpCtrl	Cluster
SetCurrentItemProc	OpMenu	Menu
SetCursor	OpWindow	RawWindow
SetCursorSize	OpCrt	———
SetCursorType	OpCrt	———
SetCustomStringProc	OpMenu	Menu
SetDefaultButtonAttr	OpCtrl	DialogColorSet
SetDefaultButtonAttr	OpDialog	DialogBox
SetDefaultChoice	OpPick	PickList
SetDefaultExtension	OpBrowse	Browser
SetDefaultExtension	OpEdit or	TextEditor
SetDefaultFont	OpPrint	Printer
SetDefaultUpcase	OpString	———
SetDefCommand	OpCtrl	Control
SetDelimAttr	OpCrt	ColorSet
SetDelimAttr	OpEntry	EntryScreen
SetDelimiters	OpEntry	EntryScreen
SetDirAttr	OpDir	DirList
SetDirCategory	OpDir	DirList
SetDrawingChars	OpDir	PathList
SetDrive	OpDir	PathList
SetDriveDelim	OpDir	DirList
SetDta	OpDos	———
SetEditProc	OpBrowse	Browser
SetEditProc	OpEdit or	TextEditor
SetEndOfMacroProc	OpMacro	———
SetEndOfMacroProc	OpReplay	———
SetEnvStr	OpDos	———
SetErrorHandler	OpForm	PrintedForm
SetErrorProc	OpEdit	LineEditor
SetErrorProc	OpLarray	AbstractArray
SetErrorProc	OpWindow	CommandWindow
SetExitCommands	OpWindow	CommandWindow
SetFieldAttr	OpCrt	ColorSet
SetFieldAttr	OpField	SelectField
SetFieldAttr	OpSEdit	SimpleLineEditor
SetFieldAttr	OpSelect	AbstractSelector
SetFieldLinks	OpSelect	AbstractSelector
SetFieldPos	OpForm	PrintField
SetFileAttr	OpDir	DirList
SetFlag	OpInLine	———
SetFlexAHelpAttr	OpCrt	ColorSet

SetFlexBHelpAttr	OpCrt	ColorSet
SetFlexCHelpAttr	OpCrt	ColorSet
SetFooter	OpForm	PrintedForm
SetFooterFunc	OpForm	PrintedForm
SetForceMode	OpDialog	DialogBox
SetForceMode	OpEntry	EntryScreen
SetFrameAttr	OpCrt	ColorSet
SetFrameAttr	OpFrame	Frame
SetFrameAttr	OpMenu	Menu
SetFrameLimits	OpWindow	RawWindow
SetFrameType	OpFrame	Frame
SetFullPathMode	OpDir	PathList
SetGetFieldProc	OpSelect	Selector
SetGetFileProc	OpBrowse	Browser
SetGetFileProc	OpEdit or	TextEditor
SetGetKeyProc	OpCmd	CommandProcessor
SetHandleAttr	OpEms	———
SetHandleName	OpEms	———
SetHeader	OpForm	PrintedForm
SetHeaderAttr	OpCrt	ColorSet
SetHeaderAttr	OpFrame	Frame
SetHeaderAttr	OpMenu	Menu
SetHeaderFunc	OpForm	PrintedForm
SetHelpAttr	OpMenu	Menu
SetHelpIndex	OpEdit	LineEditor
SetHelpIndex	OpSEdit	SimpleLineEditor
SetHelpIndex	OpWindow	CommandWindow
SetHelpPadSize	OpHelp	AbstractHelpWindow
SetHelpProc	OpCmd	CommandProcessor
SetHercMode	OpCrt	———
SetHighAttr	OpMenu	Menu
SetHighlightAttr	OpBrowse	Browser
SetHighlightAttr	OpCrt	ColorSet
SetHighlightAttr	OpEdit or	TextEditor
SetHighlightButtonAttr	OpCtrl	DialogColorSet
SetHighlightButtonAttr	OpDialog	DialogBox
SetHighlightClusterAttr	OpCtrl	DialogColorSet
SetHighlightClusterAttr	OpDialog	DialogBox
SetHighlightItemAttr	OpCrt	ColorSet
SetHighlightPromptAttr	OpCtrl	DialogColorSet
SetHighlightPromptAttr	OpDialog	DialogBox
SetHotSpotAttr	OpCrt	ColorSet
SetInitialChoice	OpPick	PickList
SetInternationalUpcase	OpString	———
SetJump	OpInLine	———
SetKeyPressedProc	OpCmd	CommandProcessor

SetKeyPtr	OpCmd	CommandProcessor
SetLastCommand	OpWindow	CommandWindow
SetLeftPad	OpMenu	Menu
SetLineDrawMode	OpDir	PathList
SetLineLimit	OpMemo	Memo
SetLongFlag	OpInLine	———
SetLPP	OpPrint	Printer
SetLptPort	OpPrnLow	BiosPrinter
SetMarkerAttr	OpBrowse	Browser
SetMarkerAttr	OpCrt	ColorSet
SetMarkerAttr	OpEdit or	TextEditor
SetMask	OpDir	DirList
SetMaxLength	OpMemo	Memo
SetMaxScroll	OpHelp	ScrollingHelpWindow
SetMickeyRatio	OpDrag	DragProcessor
SetMickeyToPixelRatio	OpMouse	———
SetMouseAttr	OpCrt	ColorSet
SetMouseCursor	OpDrag	DragProcessor
SetMouseEventHandler	OpMouse	———
SetMousePage	OpMouse	———
SetMoveProc	OpPick	PickList
SetNameFormat	OpDir	DirList
SetNameSizeFormat	OpDir	DirList
SetNameSizeKFormat	OpDir	DirList
SetNameSizeKTimeFormat	OpDir	DirList
SetNameSizeTimeFormat	OpDir	DirList
SetNameTimeFormat	OpDir	DirList
SetNestedFunc	OpHelp	AbstractHelpWindow
SetNextField	OpSelect	AbstractSelector
SetNormAttr	OpMenu	Menu
SetPadChar	OpDialog	DialogBox
SetPadChar	OpEdit	LineEditor
SetPadChar	OpEntry	EntryScreen
SetPadSize	OpPick	PickList
SetPasswordChar	OpEdit	LineEditor
SetPasswordChar	OpEntry	EntryScreen
SetPathAttr	OpDir	PathList
SetPickAttr	OpPick	PickList
SetPickFlex	OpPick	PickList
SetPickPadSize	OpHelp	AbstractHelpWindow
SetPopTicker	OpSwap	———
SetPopTicker	OpTsr	———
SetPositionPrim	OpPrint	Printer
SetPosLimits	OpWindow	RawWindow
SetPostEditProc	OpEntry	EntryScreen
SetPostFocusProc	OpDialog	DialogBox

SetPostSelectProc	OpSelect	Selector
SetPreEditProc	OpEntry	EntryScreen
SetPreFocusProc	OpDialog	DialogBox
SetPrePageFunc	OpForm	PrintedForm
SetPrePostFormFunc	OpForm	PrintedForm
SetPreSelectProc	OpSelect	Selector
SetPrevTopicHotSpot	OpHelp	AbstractHelpWindow
SetPrinter	OpBrowse	Browser
SetPrinter	OpEdit or	TextEditor
SetPrintErrorFunc	OpPrint	Printer
SetProgramStr	OpDos	———
SetPromptAttr	OpCrt	ColorSet
SetPromptAttr	OpField	SelectField
SetPromptAttr	OpSEdit	SimpleLineEditor
SetPromptAttr	OpSelect	AbstractSelector
SetProtectAttr	OpMenu	Menu
SetProtectedButtonAttr	OpCtrl	DialogColorSet
SetProtectedButtonAttr	OpDialog	DialogBox
SetProtectedClusterAttr	OpCtrl	DialogColorSet
SetProtectedClusterAttr	OpDialog	DialogBox
SetProtectedDelimAttr	OpCrt	ColorSet
SetProtectedDelimAttr	OpEntry	EntryScreen
SetProtectedFieldAttr	OpCrt	ColorSet
SetProtectedFieldAttr	OpField	SelectField
SetProtectedFieldAttr	OpSelect	AbstractSelector
SetProtectedItemAttr	OpCrt	ColorSet
SetProtectedPromptAttr	OpCrt	ColorSet
SetProtectedPromptAttr	OpField	SelectField
SetProtectedPromptAttr	OpSelect	AbstractSelector
SetPSP	OpTsr	———
SetQuickFixMode	OpSwap1	———
SetRawMode	OpDos	———
SetRejectFunc	OpDir	DirList
SetRightMargin	OpMemo	Memo
SetRowLimits	OpPick	PickList
SetScreenMask	OpDrag	DragProcessor
SetScreenUpdateProc	OpSelect	AbstractSelector
SetScrollBarAttr	OpCrt	ColorSet
SetSearchMode	OpPick	PickList
SetSearchStart	OpPick	PickList
SetSecondaryKeyPtr	OpCmd	CommandProcessor
SetSelectAttr	OpMenu	Menu
SetSelectDirAttr	OpDir	DirList
SetSelectedButtonAttr	OpCtrl	DialogColorSet
SetSelectedButtonAttr	OpDialog	DialogBox
SetSelectedClusterAttr	OpCtrl	DialogColorSet

SetSelectedClusterAttr	OpDialog	DialogBox
SetSelectedDelimAttr	OpEntry	EntryScreen
SetSelectedFieldAttr	OpCrt	ColorSet
SetSelectedFieldAttr	OpField	SelectField
SetSelectedFieldAttr	OpSelect	AbstractSelector
SetSelectedItemAttr	OpCrt	ColorSet
SetSelectedPromptAttr	OpCrt	ColorSet
SetSelectedPromptAttr	OpField	SelectField
SetSelectedPromptAttr	OpSelect	AbstractSelector
SetSelectFileAttr	OpDir	DirList
SetSelectMarker	OpMenu	Menu
SetSelectMarker	OpPick	PickList
SetSelectPathAttr	OpDir	PathList
SetSelXrefAttr	OpCrt	ColorSet
SetSendFunc	OpHelp	ScrollingHelpWindow
SetShadowAttr	OpCrt	ColorSet
SetShadowAttr	OpFrame	Frame
SetShadowAttr	OpMenu	Menu
SetSingleSwapFile	OpSwap1	———
SetSizeLimits	OpFrame	Frame
SetSizeLimits	OpWindow	RawWindow
SetSliderAttr	OpCrt	ColorSet
SetSliderValue	OpFrame	Frame
SetSortOrder	OpDir	DirList
SetStackProc	OpWindow	StackWindow
SetStatusProc	OpBrowse	Browser
SetStatusProc	OpMemo	Memo
SetSwapFileAttr	OpSwap1	———
SetSwapMsgAttr	OpSwap1	———
SetSwapMsgOn	OpExec	———
SetSwapMsgOn	OpSwap1	———
SetSwapMsgRow	OpSwap1	———
SetTabSize	OpMemo	Memo
SetTestAndMask	OpPrnLow	BiosPrinter
SetTextAttr	OpCrt	ColorSet
SetTextAttr	OpWindow	RawWindow
SetTopic	OpHelp	AbstractHelpWindow
SetUnselXrefAttr	OpCrt	ColorSet
SetUserData	OpForm	PrintedForm
SetUserExitProc	OpSwap1	———
SetUserFormat	OpDir	DirList
SetUserHookProc	OpCmd	CommandProcessor
SetUserPointer	OpRoot	DirEntry
SetUserRecord	OpDialog	DialogBox
SetUserRecord	OpEntry	EntryScreen
SetUserRecord	OpForm	PrintedForm

SetValidateFunc	OpEntry	EntryScreen
SetVecOnReturn	OpTsr	———
SetVisiblePage	OpCrt	———
SetWrapMode	OpSelect	AbstractSelector
SetXlatErrorFunc	OpPrnLow	BiosPrinter
SetXRatio	OpPrint	Printer
SetYesNoProc	OpEdit or	TextEditor
SetYRatio	OpPrint	Printer
sfOptionsAreOn	OpField	SelectField
sfOptionsOff	OpField	SelectField
sfOptionsOn	OpField	SelectField
ShellWithPrompt	OpDos	———
ShowMouse	OpMouse	———
ShowMousePrim	OpMouse	———
Shrink	OpRoot	StringArray
SinBCD	OpBCD	———
SingleChoice	OpPick	———
SingleFile	OpDir	———
SingleListStream	OpRoot	———
SinglePath	OpDir	———
Size	OpRoot	DoubleList
Size	OpRoot	PointerStack
Size	OpRoot	SingleList
Size	OpRoot	StringArray
SizeKeys	OpCmd	CommandPacker
SkipDrives	OpDir	DirList
slFieldOptionsAreOn	OpSelect	Selector
slFieldOptionsOff	OpSelect	Selector
slFieldOptionsOn	OpSelect	Selector
slOptionsAreOn	OpSelect	Selector
slOptionsOff	OpSelect	Selector
slOptionsOn	OpSelect	Selector
SoftMouseCursor	OpMouse	———
Sort	OpSort	———
SortDirName	OpDir	———
SortList	OpDir	DirList
SortName	OpDir	———
SortNone	OpDir	———
SortSize	OpDir	———
SortStringToDate	OpDate	———
SortStringToTime	OpDate	———
SortTime	OpDir	———
Soundex	OpString	———
SP	OpRoot	PointerStack
SqrBCD	OpBCD	———
SqrtBCD	OpBCD	———

srResult	OpFrame	ScreenRect
StackWindowStream	OpWindow	————
StarMicronicsRegister	OpDevice	————
StartMacro	OpMacro	————
StartMacro	OpReplay	————
StartMacroByKey	OpMacro	————
StaticQueueStream	OpRoot	————
StayRes	OpTsr	————
StayResSwap	OpSwap1	————
StLocase	OpString	————
Store	OpBrowse	Browser
Store	OpCmd	CommandProcessor
Store	OpDialog	DialogBox
Store	OpDir	DirList
Store	OpDir	PathList
Store	OpDrag	DragProcessor
Store	OpEdit	LineEditor
Store	OpEdit or	TextEditor
Store	OpEntry	EntryScreen
Store	OpEntry	ScrollingEntryScreen
Store	OpForm	PrintedForm
Store	OpForm	Report
Store	OpFrame	Frame
Store	OpFrame	ScreenRect
Store	OpHelp	AbstractHelpWindow
Store	OpMemo	Memo
Store	OpMemo	MemoFile
Store	OpMenu	Menu
Store	OpPick	PickList
Store	OpPrint	Printer
Store	OpPrnLow	BasePrinter
Store	OpRoot	BitSet
Store	OpRoot	CircularList
Store	OpRoot	DoubleList
Store	OpRoot	LargeBitSet
Store	OpRoot	PointerStack
Store	OpRoot	SingleList
Store	OpRoot	StaticQueue
Store	OpRoot	StringArray
Store	OpRoot	StringDict
Store	OpRoot	StringSet
Store	OpSelect	ScrollingSelector
Store	OpSelect	Selector
Store	OpWindow	CommandWindow
Store	OpWindow	LoadableColorSet
Store	OpWindow	PackedWindow

Store	OpWindow	RawWindow
Store	OpWindow	StackWindow
Store	OpWindow	VirtScreen
Store	OpWindow	WindowStack
StoreA	OpLarray	AbstractArray
StoreContents	OpFrame	ScreenRect
StoreDefaults	OpClone	Cloner
StoreMouseCoordinates	OpMouse	———
StoreMouseEvent	OpDrag	DragProcessor
StoreWindowCoordinates	OpCrt	———
Str2Asc	OpAsciiz	———
Str2Int	OpString	———
Str2Long	OpString	———
Str2Real	OpString	———
Str2Word	OpString	———
StrBCD	OpBCD	———
StrExpBCD	OpBCD	———
StringArrayStream	OpRoot	———
StringDictStream	OpRoot	———
StringFromHeap	OpString	———
StringSetStream	OpRoot	———
StringToHeap	OpString	———
StringToMacro	OpMacro	———
StringToMacro	OpReplay	———
StringToScrapMacro	OpMacro	———
StringToScrapMacro	OpReplay	———
StuffKey	OpCrt	———
StuffString	OpCrt	———
StUpcase	OpString	———
SubBCD	OpBCD	———
SubmitPrintFile	OpDos	———
SubPtr	OpMenu	MenuItemNode
Substitute	OpString	———
SwapNibble	OpInLine	———
SwapSize	OpSwap1	———
SwapStackAndCall	OpInt	———
SwapStackAndCallNear	OpInt	———
SwapWord	OpInLine	———
SwitchInColorCard	OpCrt	———
Tail	OpRoot	DoubleList
Tail	OpRoot	SingleList
teOptionsAreOn	OpEdit or	TextEditor
teOptionsOff	OpEdit or	TextEditor
teOptionsOn	OpEdit or	TextEditor
TestClearBit	OpRoot	BitSet
TestSetBit	OpRoot	BitSet

TextEditorStream	OpEdit or	———
TextFileSize	OpDos	———
TextFlush	OpDos	———
TextPos	OpDos	———
TextSeek	OpDos	———
TimeDiff	OpDate	———
TimeMs	OpDos	———
TimeStringToHMS	OpDate	———
TimeStringToTime	OpDate	———
TimeToAmPmString	OpDate	———
TimeToHMS	OpDate	———
TimeToSortString	OpDate	———
TimeToTimeString	OpDate	———
Today	OpDate	———
TodayString	OpDate	———
ToggleBit	OpRoot	BitSet
ToggleHighBitStripping	OpBrowse	Browser
ToggleModes	OpBrowse	Browser
TopicExists	OpHelp	AbstractHelpWindow
TopicStackPtr	OpHelp	AbstractHelpWindow
TopWindow	OpWindow	WindowStack
ToshibaP321Register	OpDevice	———
Transfer	OpBrowse	Browser
Transfer	OpFrame	ScreenRect
Trim	OpString	———
TrimLead	OpString	———
TrimSpaces	OpString	———
TrimTrail	OpString	———
Truncate	OpRoot	DosIdStream
Truncate	OpRoot	MemIdStream
TruncBCD	OpBCD	———
TurnOffAllActiveModes	OpPrint	Printer
TurnOffByID	OpPrint	Printer
TurnOffByName	OpPrint	Printer
TurnOnByID	OpPrint	Printer
TurnOnByName	OpPrint	Printer
TweakSlider	OpWindow	RawWindow
TypeOfArray	OpLarray	AbstractArray
TypeOfPrn	OpPrnLow	BasePrinter
TypeRegistered	OpRoot	IdStream
TypeVerRegistered	OpRoot	IdStream
UndeleteEntry	OpRoot	Library
UninstallModule	OpSwap1	———
UninstallModule	OpTsr	———
Unprotect	OpMenu	MenuItemNode
UnprotectItem	OpMenu	Menu

UnstackTop	OpWindow	WindowStack
Unzoom	OpWindow	RawWindow
Upcase	OpString	———
UpCaseMac	OpString	———
Update	OpRoot	DirEntry
Update	OpRoot	StringDict
UpdateContents	OpDir	DirList
UpdateContents	OpDir	PathList
UpdateContents	OpHelp	AbstractHelpWindow
UpdateContents	OpPick	PickList
UpdateContents	OpWindow	RawWindow
UpdateContents	OpWindow	StackWindow
UpdateFrame	OpFrame	Frame
UpdateScreenSize	OpMenu	Menu
UpdateScreenSize	OpWindow	RawWindow
UseColor	OpCrt	———
UseEmulator	Op8087	———
ValBCD	OpBCD	———
ValidateNoBlanks	OpField	———
ValidateNotPartial	OpField	———
ValidateSubfields	OpField	———
ValidDate	OpDate	———
ValidDrive	OpDos	———
ValidTime	OpDate	———
vCols	OpWindow	VirtScreen
VirtScreenStream	OpWindow	———
VisitAll	OpRoot	StringDict
VisitAllControls	OpDialog	DialogBox
VisitAllEntryFields	OpEntry	EntryScreen
VisitAllItems	OpMenu	Menu
VisitAllSelectFields	OpSelect	AbstractSelector
VisitAllTextFields	OpSelect	AbstractSelector
VisitAllWindows	OpMenu	Menu
vRows	OpWindow	VirtScreen
VScreenToScreen	OpEntry	ScrollingEntryScreen
VScreenToScreen	OpSelect	ScrollingSelector
WaitForButtonUp	OpDrag	DragProcessor
WasCommandActive	OpSwap1	———
wChangeAttribute	OpWindow	RawWindow
wCopy	OpWindow	RawWindow
wCopy	OpWindow	StackWindow
wFastCenter	OpWindow	RawWindow
wFastFill	OpWindow	RawWindow
wFastFlush	OpWindow	RawWindow
wFastRead	OpWindow	RawWindow
wFastText	OpWindow	RawWindow

wFastVert	OpWindow	RawWindow
wFastWrite	OpWindow	RawWindow
wFastWriteCtrl	OpWindow	RawWindow
wFlexWrite	OpWindow	RawWindow
wGotoXY	OpWindow	RawWindow
WhereSelect	OpPick	PickList
WhereSelectAbs	OpPick	PickList
WhereXAbs	OpCrt	———
WhereXY	OpCrt	———
WhereXYdirect	OpCrt	———
WhereYAbs	OpCrt	———
Width	OpWindow	AbstractWindow
WillSwapUseEms	OpSwap1	———
WillSwapUseXms	OpSwap1	———
WindowNumber	OpWindow	StackWindow
WindowStackStream	OpWindow	———
WithinFrameCoords	OpFrame	Frame
wOptionsAreOn	OpWindow	RawWindow
wOptionsOff	OpWindow	RawWindow
wOptionsOn	OpWindow	RawWindow
WordCount	OpString	———
WordPosition	OpString	———
WordWrap	OpString	———
wReadAttribute	OpWindow	RawWindow
Write	OpRoot	BufIdStream
Write	OpRoot	DosIdStream
Write	OpRoot	MemIdStream
Write	OpWindow	PackedWindow
WriteAsc	OpAsciiz	———
WriteAttribute	OpCrt	———
WriteDiskSectors	OpDos	———
WriteMacroFile	OpMacro	———
WritePointer	OpRoot	IdStream
WriteRange	OpRoot	IdStream
WriteString	OpRoot	IdStream
WriteText	OpRoot	StringArray
WriteTo	OpWindow	VirtScreen
WriteUserPointer	OpRoot	IdStream
wWhereXY	OpWindow	RawWindow
wWhereXYAbs	OpWindow	RawWindow
wWriteAttribute	OpWindow	RawWindow
XlatCharItem	OpPrnLow	BasePrinter
YesOrNo	OpEdit	LineEditor
Zoom	OpWindow	RawWindow

Index

K

L

M

N

O

T

U

V

W

SOLOMON R. BAKER LIBRARY
3 1725 00344 2642

DATE DUE

[redacted]			

DEMCO 38-297

COMPANION DISK FOR
OBJECT-ORIENTED PROGRAMMING WITH TURBO PASCAL AND OBJECT PROFESSIONAL

Save yourself a lot of typing by purchasing this disk set. It contains all the programs listed in the book. You should find the applications or at least some of the modules useful.

You can easily experiment with the applications to see the effects caused by modifications to my code. Or you may wish to change the parameters I used to call the various Object Professional methods. This is a convenient way to learn the results of the many methods and parameters available from Object Professional.

Order Form

Name ______________________________

Shipping Address ______________________________

____

City ______________________________

State/Zip ______________________________

Country ______________________________

Please remit $25.00 per diskette.

Method of Payment:

[ ] Mastercard [ ] Visa [ ] Check [ ] Money order [ ] Cash

Card # ______________________________

Expiration date ______________________________

Signature (for credit card) ______________________________

Disk size: [ ] 3 1/2 in. [ ] 5 1/4 in.

Quantity ______________________________

PLACE
STAMP
HERE

LAWCOM
OOP Disk Order
P.O. Box 10685
Yuma, AZ 85366-8685